The Chaos Frontier

The Chaos Frontier

Creative strategic control for business

Ralph D. Stacey

BUTTERWORTH
HEINEMANN

Butterworth-Heinemann Limited
Linacre House, Jordan Hill, Oxford OX2 8DP

 PART OF REED INTERNATIONAL BOOKS

OXFORD   LONDON   GUILDFORD   BOSTON
MUNICH   NEW DELHI   SINGAPORE   SYDNEY
TOKYO   TORONTO   WELLINGTON

First published 1991
First published as a paperback edition 1993

British Library Cataloguing in Publication Data
Stacey, Ralph D.
  The chaos frontier: creative strategic control for business
  I. Title
  658.001

ISBN 0 7506 0950 8

Printed and bound in Great Britain by
Redwood Press Limited, Melksham, Wiltshire

Contents

Preface

The purpose of this book is to introduce senior business executives to a new scientific way of explaining the creative behaviour of dynamic systems, one of which is the successful business organization. It is a way of thinking and understanding which makes more sense of a highly uncertain business world than those explanations to which managers currently pay explicit attention. It points to more effective ways of managing and controlling innovative organizations in turbulent times. It provides a framework within which we can more easily understand what managers actually do as opposed to what they say they do.

This new way of understanding dynamic behaviour is to be found in the theories of chaos and self-organization developed by mathematicians, physicists, chemists and biologists. In its scientific sense, chaos does not mean utter confusion or a complete lack of any form. It means that systems driven by certain types of perfectly orderly laws are capable of behaving in a manner which is random and therefore inherently unpredictable over the long term, at a specific level. But that behaviour also has a 'hidden' pattern at an overall level. We do not know what the weather will be like next month, in specific terms; but we do know that there will be familiar patterns of sunshine or rain. We do not know how the stock market will perform next month, but we do know that it will display characteristic patterns of rise and fall. Scientific chaos explains why we observe recognizable patterns of overall behaviour, or categories, within which no two individuals or events are ever exactly the same. No two fern leaves are exactly the same, but they are all nevertheless fern leaves. No two business organizations in the electronics market are ever exactly the same, but they are clearly electronics businesses. Chaos is creative individual variety within an overall pattern of similarity. Chaos explains feedback behaviour, the self-reinforcing virtuous and vicious circles which are so familiar in business life. Scientific chaos explains turbulence as the chaotic state which systems experience as they change from one form to another. Water passes through a turbulent state to become steam, and business organizations too pass through turbulence as they develop new strategic direction. Self organization theory explains the process by means of which dynamic systems create innovation and new order out of chaos.

The widespread applicability of chaos and self-organization explanations has been demonstrated in nature's systems. And the central
message of this new way of understanding how the world works is
revolutionary because it tells us that creativity, innovation, significant
change, new strategic direction, all depend fundamentally upon conditions of disorder, ambiguity, chance and difference. Successful
systems, creative systems, do not function like machines or gradually
adapting organisms. Instead, they develop and control over the long term
through an unpredictable, creative, spontaneous self-organizing process
which depends inherently upon chance. This book argues that chaotic
dynamics apply as much to successful business organizations as they do
to nature's systems.

The predominant belief, today, amongst managers and those who
would advise them, is that success flows from clear future direction to
which those in the organization are harnessed in some way. Success
depends upon order. It follows that top management should know in
advance what their organizations are to do; that commitment and consensus should be the norm; that cultures should be strongly shared; that
organizational capabilities should be matched to future change in the
environments. The buzz words are 'visions', 'plans', 'pulling together',
'matching competitive capability to market requirements'. Scientific
chaos is a revolution because it demonstrates why future direction is
unknowable – visions and plans are then either aspirations based on what
we know now, or dangerous illusions. Since self-organization theory
shows that innovation arises in conditions of instability, it means that
business success is dependent upon a lack of consensus: different cultural
values and perspectives. And because innovation arises out of chaos
through a process of self-organization, success depends upon spontaneity and individual initiative in an organization. Successful businesses
do not simply match capability to market requirements, they play their
part in creating and shaping such requirements and it is in chaotic,
unstable conditions that such creativity is possible.

And perhaps the key conclusion of all, the real reason chaos is a
revolution for managers, is that no one can control the outcomes of a
creative system. Such outcomes are unpredictable. Top managers cannot
control the strategic direction of the business in the sense of a captain
steering the ship. What they can do is create the conditions in which
unpredictable creativity may occur. Creative strategic directions are the
result of a complex intertwining of determined initiative on the part of
managers, and chance. Scientific chaos focuses attention on the strategic
direction of a business as a creative journey of exploration into the
unknown, which is accomplished by spontaneous learning and political
activities. Such activities are conducted within constraints provided by
different cultures and different levels of power. Chaos focuses attention

on the importance, for strategic direction, of intuitive thinking, insight, judgement, common sense, reasoning by analogy and experience.

Why should busy managers invest their time in exploring chaos? The reason is simple. All managers spend every day dealing with change and that change is becoming more and more rapid, more and more volatile. Such change is being written about using the terms 'chaos' and 'turbulence'. Study after study on the work patterns of managers show them to be of a disorderly nature. All managers experience and deal with what feels like chaos every day of their lives. Now we have a scientific approach to understanding such chaos.

On a more subtle level, the predominant approaches to thinking about business in the Western world have all been imported from the natural sciences. The world of business cannot therefore afford to ignore developments in the natural sciences which are generating a fundamentally new view of the world. No sensible business continues to use obsolete imported components in its products. Sensible managers should not continue to build their thinking on outdated, imported conceptual frameworks. And it is entire conceptual frameworks, an overall view of how the world works, which has been imported; not simply a few relevant approaches and techniques. Those explanations to which practising managers pay attention and use all fall within a frame of reference which sees the world as a machine. In the world of business, that machine is the electronic computer. The literature on management and organization does contain ideas which fall outside that frame of reference, but such ideas have had little impact on the thinking of business practitioners.

Scientific chaos, by focusing our attention on the irregular, the disorderly, the uncertain, the constraints provided by difference, encourages us to reject a simplistic machine view of the business world. Scientific chaos provides us with a framework quite independent of any political ideology within which to understand the highly uncertain and the operation of chance. Improved ability to cope with something has in the past usually followed from a greater understanding of it.

Managers must surely benefit from understanding chaos because they are the ones who have to deal with it; they operate in the borders of chaos.

I am grateful to Richard Turton of the Hatfield Polytechnic Business School, Martha Birtles of Doctus Management Consultancy, Sheila Cane of the Strategic Planning Society, Professor Robert Ryan of the Management Centre at the University of Southampton and Dr Ronnie Lessem of City University Business School, for their very helpful comments on earlier drafts of this book. I am also grateful to the Hatfield Polytechnic Business School MBA students of 1989/90 – our classroom discussions helped me to understand and clarify much of what is written here. Thanks are also due to colleagues at Doctus Management Consultancy Limited – working with them helped me to see the practical relevance of chaos theory. Finally, thanks to John Mant for his assistance and support.

1 Introduction

Today senior managers in business organizations are focusing more and more explicitly on how to handle change. There is widespread recognition of the accelerating rate of change in customer requirements, competitive pressures, regulatory frameworks, political and economic conditions. We all know that this acceleration is generating higher levels of uncertainty. We are confronted with more and more ambiguous and confusing issues which have to be dealt with if a business is to survive and prosper. It is now commonplace to describe current business conditions as turbulent or chaotic, and such conditions give rise to the same key concern which senior managers in just about every company express over and over again. That concern is with what needs to be done to cope with turbulent change, to promote continuing innovation, to ensure that managers throughout the business think and act strategically. This book is addressed to that intertwined concern with innovating, thinking strategically and managing change in turbulent times.

Who this book is addressed to

This book is addressed to those managers in the business community who seek more dynamic explanations of, and prescriptions for dealing with, the confusing, ambiguous, conflicting and disorderly conditions in which they now have to operate. The intention is to present such managers with new insights which have been developed by natural scientists concerned with complex system dynamics – the theories of chaos and self-organization. Such insights provide managers with the opportunity of exploring and testing their own personal views on how to control in conditions of turbulence, how to manage change, how to promote innovation and develop new strategic directions.

The aim of this book is to use new scientific insights to widen perspectives on what the control of an organization means in turbulent and highly uncertain environments. It focuses on what managers actually do in such circumstances, rather than on what they and their advisors say they should do. It points to highly relevant explanations of managing and organizing to which managers currently pay little explicit attention. Because this new way of thinking contradicts many of our deeply held views, it is not immediately easy to grasp. It requires a rather different language and vocabulary which may seem at first to be jargon.

But it is worth mastering the concepts and the vocabulary, because revolutionary new scientific explanations of the dynamics of nature's systems have direct relevance to managers. These explanations:

- are all about turbulence, the central concern of management today;
- generate new perspectives on the control of a business in conditions of turbulence;
- direct attention to ideas in the management literature which have had little impact on practising managers;
- provide a framework within which to incorporate those ideas into a more comprehensive explanation of management and control in conditions of great uncertainty;
- generate some key questions which no thinking manager can today afford to ignore.

This introductory chapter outlines why we need a more dynamic explanation of management. It sets out why practical, task oriented managers need to be so concerned with explanations. It will explore in outline some aspects of the explanations managers use today and the problems this leads them to. It will then describe the structure of the rest of the book.

Mixed success in coping with turbulent change

Change is today's central business concern. Generating a continuing flow of innovative activity to build and sustain competitive advantage is consequently the most important general task facing managers. The challenge is creatively to develop and control the complex behaviour of that highly interconnected system which is the modern business organization. The problem is that we are by no means clear on how to do all this. It is true that some managers carry out the task and meet the challenge with spectacular success. Entirely new ranges of products have been brought to the market in unprecedentedly short time periods to transform our lives – information technology products are perhaps the most obvious examples but not the only ones. Old products and services have been repackaged and transformed beyond recognition – food, travel, leisure and financial services all provide examples of this. Enterprises have grown at phenomenal rates to cover the globe. But other managers fail to meet the challenge, with equally spectacular results. Large established companies collapse and whole industries in the UK and USA have succumbed to more innovative competitors.

When we come to explaining the difference between what the successful do to meet the challenge and what the rest do to fail the test, we run into real difficulties. We produce diametrically opposed explanations, some of which see success as the result of careful long term planning and others of which see success as the consequence of hectic entrepreneurial action.[1] Some explanations identify international success with the maintenance of national origins and others tie it firmly to abandoning those origins in favour of world citizenship.[2] Consequently, we have great difficulty in prescribing how to organize and manage a complex interactive business system so that it can cope with high levels of uncertainty to produce continuing streams of successful innovations. Some prescribe simple hierarchies and clear job definitions as the route to success,[3] while others call for complex matrix structures and intersecting job assignments.[4] Some advise managers to distribute power, so empowering many people to become involved in decision making and innovative activity;[5] yet others suggest unequal power distribution by emphasizing the importance of hierarchy and authority.[6] One consultant tells a group of managers who cannot agree on a new organizational structure that they must develop a vision before they do anything else. The next consultant they turn to tells them that they need team-building exercises because conflict is the obstacle they must remove before they can progress. Despite the techniques and prescriptions in a vast management literature applied by a rapidly growing consultancy industry, managers experience fresh confusion each time they face a new strategic issue.

Unintended and contradictory outcomes

Our difficulty in explaining and prescribing how to manage in turbulent times is illustrated by the frequency with which we produce unintended outcomes. In the course of my consulting work I see this over and over again and it cannot be dismissed as bad management or incompetence. Highly intelligent and competent managers who behave innovatively in extremely difficult circumstances also keep doing that which they had no intention of doing. A common example is the conduct of the board or top executive team of most of the companies I have worked with. Both as individuals and when they discuss the matter as a team, board and executive members keep saying that their prime role is one of strategic management. They are quite explicit that they should devote the major part of their time together to the handling of strategic issues. But each time they meet they spend 80 to 90 per cent of their time performing symbolic and legitimating functions, attending to administrative procedures, and reviewing the past. Consequently they keep shelving strategic issues to be tacked on to the agenda for a later meeting or to be progressed informally.

There are many examples of contradicting actions and circular games in business too. Managers devote resources to preparing five-year financial projections which they consider at board meetings despite the fact that no one believes those projections past the first or second year. They may all agree that it is impossible to forecast long-term outcomes in today's rapidly changing environment, but then they say that they must forecast long term outcomes before they can make an investment decision. For a lengthy period I watched managers who had agreed to diversify their business by acquisition. First they discussed the general criteria for acquisition. Then they said it made no sense to take the discussion further in the absence of specific proposals. They were presented with specific proposals but concluded that they could not make a decision in the absence of general criteria. So, they returned to the general criteria only to reach the conclusion that they should consider specific proposals. Those managers went around this loop for over a year. We also find groups of managers who all agree that they should be a cohesive team. They spend a weekend on team-building exercises, and for a week after they return they do cooperate more than before; but then they continue to conflict.

The point is that undoubtedly intelligent, successful and very busy groups of people such as those described above could not have intended to move around loops which go nowhere. As intelligent people they can hardly be designing these outcomes intentionally. In all the illustrations given above, managers were not only producing unintended outcomes, they were also perfectly aware that they were doing so. Indeed their puzzlement was usually the reason for the consultancy assignment through which I know about them. And furthermore, as a consultant I was often (privately!) as puzzled as they were.

The most important task facing managers today is making choices in conditions of great uncertainty. But what we find is not just conflicting explanations of business success leading to conflicting prescriptions, we also find intelligent managers in successful companies behaving in ways which produce conflicting and unintended consequences. And those conflicting explanations to which managers and consultants pay the most prominent attention have little to say about why managers produce unintended consequences, or why existing techniques do not lead clearly and rapidly to the resolution of each new strategic issue. We have a real problem with the most prominent explanations of managing and organizing that we use today. We therefore continually encounter problems in acting coherently.

And these problems are not confined to managers and consultants in the world of business. Politicians design actions to help the less affluent sections of society. They set up grant systems to subsidize housing repairs for them. But the middle classes make the most use of the grants, buying up and restoring properties in run down areas. In so doing they raise house prices and drive the less affluent out of the area. Here a well intentioned political action worsens the plight of the less affluent. International bodies and economic development experts design irrigation schemes to increase water supplies and put a halt to the encroaching desert in the Sahara. But the inhabitants increase livestock, overgrazing accelerates, ground cover declines and the desert encroaches even faster. The production of unintended consequences which follow self-reinforcing virtuous and vicious circles seems to be a common feature of human systems which continues to surprise us. Why do we continue to experience difficulties in explaining how such systems work and designing actions to deal with them?

Defective understanding of business dynamics

The root of the difficulty we experience in explaining business behaviour so that we may choose and act more effectively is encapsulated for me by the following incident. A new chief executive was appointed to a UK energy company. This chief executive's planning department had prepared a review of the market as a background to the development of a strategy for the business. The principal conclusion of the review was that growth in demand was likely to average 1.4 per cent per annum for the next 10 years compared with the 1.2 per cent previously thought likely. Other conclusions related to the bands within which competitors' prices were thought likely to move and an estimate of when surplus manufacturing capacity was likely to be fully utilized. The chief executive's comments on this substantial and thorough piece of work ran along these lines:

> It's taken six weeks to tell me that demand growth will rise by an insignificant amount and that competitors' prices will fluctuate within bands. All this makes absolutely no difference to any decisions we have to make. What's missing is the dynamics of the market. We need some view on the moves which players in the market might make and how each of us might respond to the moves of the others. We need some feel for how the interactions might develop.

I believe that this chief executive has put his finger on the key problem we are having today in explaining management and prescribing what we need to do to make sensible choices in highly uncertain conditions.

That key problem has to do with the understanding we have of the dynamics of human systems, including that system which is a business organization. The explanations of managing and organizing to which we pay the most attention, do not capture enough about the continuing interactions between individuals and groups within the business itself, or between them and those people outside the business. Today's most prominent explanations are not built upon the feedback nature of those interactions. The essence of choosing and acting within and between organizations lies in the manner in which one choice or action feeds into another, leading to self-reinforcing virtuous and vicious circles. One firm cuts its price, another follows and the first responds in a vicious down-

ward spiral. Or, one firm attracts slightly more market support for the
VCR video player than its rival does for Betamax. This sets off the former
on a virtuous circle which leads to market domination. And it sets off the
latter on a vicious circle resulting in the disappearance of the product.
This book argues that we are surprised at the unintended consequences
of our actions because we are interpreting them using models which do
not capture enough of the feedback nature of business dynamics.

However, over the past two to three decades there have been significant developments in mathematics and the natural sciences which throw
considerable light on just this kind of dynamic interaction. The understanding of complex dynamic feedback systems in nature has been ad-
vanced by two scientific developments. The first is called chaos theory
and the second self organization theory. It is the purpose of this book to
expose managers to these new ways of thinking about dynamics. If we are
puzzled and disappointed because the explanations of business success
to which we pay most attention are failing us, new scientific understandings of system dynamics have great potential in directing us to more
useful explanations. Once we have more useful explanations then we can
devise more effective actions.

The importance of explanatory models for action

The key to coping with today's accelerating change in business conditions
lies in our ability to explain how a successful business works. Or, to put it
another way, the key lies in the models managers use to make business
choices and design their actions. The more useful a manager's model in
any given circumstances, the more successful that manager's choices and
actions will be. We must therefore begin a search for the source of
sustained competitive capability in the mental models managers use to
design their actions.

The importance of a model as the basis of any action lies in the nature of
our brains. In order to make a choice to perform even the simplest action
we have to process information obtained through the senses of sight,
touch, hearing and smell, or retrieved from our long-term memories. The
working part of our brain, its short-term memory and its processing
capacity, is severely limited. We can only hold five to seven bits of
information in the short term memory at any one time, and the speed
with which we can process new information is rather slow. It also takes
seconds to transfer processed information for storage in the long term
memory. We overcome these rather severe limitations in two important
ways.[7]

Building models

First, we select and simplify the information to be processed for the
making of a choice and the action consequent upon that choice. We

circumvent the fundamental limitations of our brains by ignoring most of the reality around us, focusing on what we believe to be the most important aspects and causal relationships. This is nothing other than constructing a model. And the model we construct in any new situation, the bits of information and the limited number of causal connections we focus on in that situation, is determined by the models we have already acquired in previous situations and stored in our long term memories. Thinking, choosing and acting all depend fundamentally on models derived from what we have learned in the past, the models we have previously constructed and stored through experience and education. These constitute the frame of reference within which we approach any problem or opportunity. What we look for, how we explain and therefore what we do, all depend upon this frame of reference.

Explicit and implicit models

The second mechanism we use to overcome the physical limitations of our brains is one closely akin to automation. It would greatly slow us down if we had consciously to retrieve and examine large numbers of previously acquired models in order to construct a new one to meet each new situation. Many of these previously acquired models are therefore pushed below the level of awareness into the unconscious mind. We seem to use some form of recognizable pattern in a new situation to trigger automatically the use of past models developed in analogous previous situations. Experts do not examine the whole body of their expertise when they confront a new situation. Instead they detect recognizable similarity in the qualitative patterns of what they observe, and automatically produce models which they modify to meet the new circumstances:

> For example, a chess Master perceives patterns and relationships between the pieces on a chess board which are missed by the novice, and it is from these perceptions that his superiority derives. The Master is no better than the novice in deciding what to do when the pieces have been set out randomly. Knowledge of the patterns and the moves appropriate to each one is in some way stored in the Master's memory and drawn on as required.[8]

Once we have recognized some pattern we proceed to develop a new model by analogy:

> Analogy pervades thought . . . To make the novel seem familiar by relating it to prior knowledge, to make the familiar seem strange by viewing it from a new perspective – these are fundamental aspects of human intelligence that depend on the ability to reason by analogy. This ability is used to construct

new scientific models, to design experiments, to solve new problems in terms of old ones, to make predictions, to control experiments, to construct arguments, and to interpret literary metaphors.[9]

We overcome our very limited physical brain working capacity to produce unlimited mental capacity by simplifying and selecting, building models, and then automating those models by pushing them below the level of awareness. We use qualitative similarities between one situation and another to develop more appropriate models in new situations. Managers design their business actions through this process just as physicians and physicists do. It therefore follows that if we are to understand the behaviour of managers, or of any other expert, we must distinguish between the two kinds of model they use. First there are the explicit models. These are the models they are aware of and articulate. These are what we hear when managers say what they do or should do. Ask managers what they do and most will say that they organize and plan. Second, there are the implicit models. These are below the level of awareness and are consequently very difficult to articulate. Both models drive behaviour, but highly learned expert actions, such as those performed by competent managers, are driven more by the implicit models than anything else. Observe what managers actually do and we see them dashing from one task to another in a manner which is not all that planned or organized.

Furthermore, these all important implicit models are triggered and affected by emotions as well as by more objective factors. Since there are two models, since emotion plays an important part in triggering one category of model, it is quite possible that different explicit and implicit models will be applied to the same situation. This means that in any situation there could be differences between what we say we do and what we actually do. It is therefore quite possible that we will find ourselves acting in ways which produce unintended consequences. We may claim that we are designing actions according to some specified explicit model, but when we act we may switch, perhaps perfectly appropriately, to a different model. We will then find ourselves saying one thing and doing another, perhaps in the process producing actions we did not explicitly intend.

Sharing models

Managers do not choose and act as isolated individuals. They interact with each other, choosing and acting in groups. Simply by being part of a group, individuals learn to share the models they use to explain, choose and act. In this way they cut down on the communication and information flows which are required before they can act together. The more they share their implicit models, the less they need to communicate in order to secure cohesive action. This sharing of implicit models or values is what we mean by the culture of the group or the organization. Groups and organizations develop cultures, company and industry recipes or retained memories, in order to speed up their actions. However, that sharing is rarely complete, so that to varying degrees individuals also have different perspectives. Interaction between managers may then generate conflicting and unintended consequences because they do not completely share the models they use to design their actions.

Altering models

And there is another important consequence of the distinction between explicit and implicit mental models, some of which are shared by others and some of which are not. It is extremely easy in times of rapid change for models to become inappropriate. This applies with particular force to the implicit models which managers in a group share – to their culture. Since these models are below the level of awareness, they are difficult to bring to the surface and examine. Since some are strongly shared, group pressures for conformity block the questioning of them. Those models can then all the more easily become inappropriate. The more turbulent the times, the more vital it becomes to examine and question continuously the implicit models which drive our behaviour. It is vital to be aware of the basic assumptions we are making and to question the industry and company recipes we are using. It becomes vital consciously to explore the impact our individual implicit mental models and our culture are having on our effectiveness.

If we are to make useful prescriptions for innovative management behaviour, they must be derived from explanations of management which are sensitive to the fundamental nature of how managers think, choose and act in groups. The prime concern of this book is with the explicit models to which managers pay attention; what we might be able to say about their implicit models; and what modern scientific understandings of system dynamics might have to say about their appropriateness. This book is written from a conviction that the most important source of competitive advantage lies in the models in managers' minds and the manner in which they continually develop those models to cope with highly uncertain situations through analogous reasoning. It is concerned with how managers interact through a process in which ideas, choices and actions feed back into each other. This process lies at the heart of dynamic management.

It is this dynamic process which is inadequately dealt with in the most prominent explanations of business success to which managers pay attention. It is argued here that the reason we have problems with today's explanations has to do with the frame of reference within which these explanations have been developed. The problem lies in the implicit models we use when we come to explain, choose and act in turbulent times.

So, what can we say about today's explicit and implicit management models, and about the frame of reference within which they have been derived?

What managers say about strategic choice

Over the past few years I have been conducting an informal survey in a number of companies where I have worked on consultancy assignments. I have been asking teams of top executives what they believe they should be doing to manage strategically. The same question has been put to groups of middle managers on the MBA programmes I teach. Without exception, the answers given by both top executives and middle managers run along the following lines.

First, to manage strategically the leaders of companies should set objectives, make statements on missions, articulate visions, dreams or intents. These should all establish where the company is going, and what it is to be at some point in the long term future. These missions and visions are described as relatively permanent statements, usually of a general qualitative nature, outlining some future state which is to be achieved. They are the overarching goals which should drive and guide the actions of all in the company. For example, the mission may be to beat the competition and become the leading player in particular market segments – Komatsu's mission is 'Encircling Caterpillar'. An often quoted example of a vision is Fred Smith's. He envisioned a future in which low-cost overnight deliveries of documents and parcels would be made using air transport, a national sorting hub and a number of collection and delivery depots. The realization of that vision was Federal Express.[10] But despite the general acceptance of the importance of missions and visions, few people seem to be clear on how these are to be developed. The prescription is to analyse the business, and this should somehow prompt some kind of creative leap of the mind.

Second, managers assert that to manage strategically the leaders must inspire all members of the company to believe in the vision. Strongly shared cultural norms (implicit mental models) must be fostered to sustain continuing states of consensus and commitment around that vision. Managing change is seen in terms of moving cultures to those which are appropriate for achieving the goals. This is recognised to be very difficult but there is more advice available on how to do this than there is on how to formulate visions. There are many organizational behaviour techniques available to accomplish culture change.

And third, managing strategically requires action. Most see it as necessary to embody this action in a long term plan. This sets out the route to the goal. It is the action steps which are to be taken at future points in time which will achieve the goal or realize the vision. That plan has to be general and flexible; it is accepted that it will be necessary to change it frequently. At this stage we find that there are numerous techniques available to analyse strategic positions and select general strategic options. A few managers in my informal survey saw action less in terms of plans and more in terms of trial and error steps which lead to the vision.

Finally, most managers in the informal survey saw the purpose of this whole strategic management process in the same terms. The purpose is to match the company's capabilities to the requirements of its customers in a more effective manner than the competition. There are many analytical techniques available to determine the key success factors which will lead to this match.

We have then a widely accepted view of what companies need to do to succeed in turbulent times, and an acceptance of the techniques prescribed for managing strategically. From what I can remember of management attitudes 20 years ago, I doubt that we would have found such widespread acceptance of an explicit model setting out how to manage successfully. This acceptance is perhaps a measure of the impact which business schools and the management literature have had on the way managers think today.

The problem with visions and plans

The question to ask now is whether this widely accepted approach actually works as a method of developing and controlling the long term future of a business. Does it describe what managers actually do when they are confronted with great uncertainty? Or, do they switch to different implicit models? There are, I believe, a number of reasons for stating that the explicit model described above does not work. Managers switch to implicit models which are different when they make and enact strategic choices. Consider first some of the problems around missions, visions and shared values.

Visions and shared values

Where companies prepare missions, these statements show a remarkable similarity to one another. They almost always set out intentions to become the leader in some market segment; to become bigger and more profitable; to meet customer requirements; and to promote good employee relations. Most of us would agree that business success comes from innovating and being different from the competition. It therefore has to be questioned whether mission statements, which are much the same from one competitor to another, are making any contribution to innovative action.

When I have asked managers to describe the vision of their company's future, the reply has also frequently been a general statement about being bigger or beating the competition. Those replies contained very little that could be described as a picture of a future state. It was hard to see how those general statements were having an impact on specific actions being taken now. Other replies to the question took the form of a list of current aspirations which were at the time commanding the attention of top management. For example 'a presence in the USA housing market', or 'diversification into the building products industry'. On asking the same question some time later the list had frequently changed. It might then be a vision of 'establishing real partnerships with customers', or 'building a pan-European presence'. Such lists are not the relatively constant pictures of some future state which qualifies them as a vision. They are not overarching goals which provide the guiding principle for long periods. They are simply statements on important issues which are attracting the attention of top executives at the time.

When we look back and interpret how a particular company developed, we tend to forget the many issues on the agenda at some past point in time. We select that issue which was successfully implemented. This is then given as the 'vision' which drove the company to its success. And that often quoted example of Fred Smith and Federal Express illustrates this kind of selective interpretation. It is true that Fred Smith did develop and enact a whole set of issues around the question of cost-effective overnight delivery of parcels and documents. But later he had another 'vision'. This time it was Zapmail in which an expensive telecommunications system was established to deliver documents electronically. Competition from cheap fax machines plugged into the public telephone network turned this venture into a major financial loss because it provided a much cheaper solution.[11] Vision can lead to disaster as well as to success. It can turn out to be a disadvantage that everyone strongly believed the vision and did not argue against it. When we ascribe successful strategic management to a particular vision and the strong support it was accorded, we selectively ignore the 'visions' that were simply abandoned or never succeeded. We seem to be using a frame of reference which directs us to look only for orderly patterns in what happened in the past. This frame of reference seems to encourage us to ignore the messy, disorderly and unintended aspects of what happened.

The paragraphs above suggest that in fact it is not one relatively stable view of a future state that is the precondition for success, but a number of issues (opportunities, problems, challenges, aspirations) that are continually explored. As we go through time, some of these issues are dropped, some are acted upon and lead to failure, and some are successfully enacted. What comes to be described as the vision was at the time one aspiration, ambition or issue among a number of others that were being simultaneously dealt with. What happened is more contentious, interactive and dynamic than an explanation based on one vision suggests.

Where significant innovations are made, they do not usually emerge from the kind of strongly shared values so widely prescribed for success. Innovations emerge from differences of viewpoint and the conflict which accompanies this. Innovative strategic moves change the way we do things and this threat to existing frameworks is bound to lead to conflict. Innovation and different values are clearly closely connected. Despite the techniques available for promoting consensus, we observe continuing differences of view, and conflict in companies which are actively doing new things, because without difference and conflict new things are impossible.

Plans

So, observation of strategic management and innovation in practice raises important questions as to the role that visions and shared values actually play. It is even less clear that the long term plans produced by so many companies actually impact on their future direction. I have found that few managers challenge the following assertions:

- Strategic plan documents are almost always long lists of strengths, weaknesses, opportunities and threats. It is normally rather hard to draw any conclusions from these lists. Or the plans are a collection of vague statements backed by pages of financial projections for the next five years which no one actually believes past the first year.
- Long term plans are supposed to constitute an overall framework within which strategic issues are dealt with as they occur. To qualify as a plan it should actually anticipate the most important strategic issues. But when you observe a group of top managers dealing with a specific strategic issue, they hardly ever refer to that long term plan which frequently does not even mention the issue under consideration. After the plans have been ceremoniously approved by the board they are filed, only to be looked at again when the next revision cycle comes around.
- If strategic control is actually being practised in the manner described by the widely accepted view, then it would be reasonable to expect managers to monitor the progress of their company against the long-term plan or some measure of the extent to which the vision is being realized. This is hardly ever done because it is so difficult to establish meaningful measures of performance in a long-term sense. In a messy, uncertain world, a very recent dip in market share could be a temporary setback or it could reflect long-term performance

problems. If we cannot predict the future we cannot know which of these it is. In this sense monitoring presents a problem. I have never witnessed managers monitoring long-term plans or vision realizations according to results. The monitoring relates to the short term plans and budgets.

- The long-term plans are usually out of date after six months. After any five-year period the company is most likely to have gone in substantially different directions from those set out in the original plan. Many actions set out in plans are simply never carried out and many others turn out to be different from the plan expectation.
- Despite the by now well-known techniques and prescriptions on strategic management, despite the strategic analysis that managers perform and the plans they prepare, they continue to experience difficulty in identifying strategic issues and making choices where there are conflicting views. Each new conjunction of events seems to require thinking afresh and applying old models often does not help.
- This whole planning approach encourages a focus on matching existing resources to customer requirements and meeting existing competition. It leads to strategies of imitation rather than creative innovation. And that exposes companies to more imaginative rivals.[12]

Managers do something else

The conclusion to be drawn, I believe, is that managers in successful companies do not actually use the framework of missions, visions and plans in the real strategic development and control of their business. They do not use these explicit models because such models do not work in turbulent times. These observations suggest that managers use implicit models which differ from the explicit. They suggest that interaction between managers leads to outcomes which are not captured by the explicit explanations. They suggest that we do not understand at all well the implicit models managers are using. All this gives rise to three questions. Why are the vision and plan models not applicable in turbulent times? Why do managers continue to espouse those models when they do not actually use them? If managers do not see visions and use plans for the long term, what then do they do to control and develop the business?

Why visions and plans are inappropriate

The models of visions and plans are inapplicable in times of turbulence because those models are based upon assumptions which are not valid. One assumption is that it is possible to foresee enough of the long-term future to enable the formulation of visions and goals which are specific enough to guide actions taken now. This book will argue that experience shows that this is not possible, that the future is unknowable. It will also be argued that a business is a dynamic system and that new scientific explanations of dynamic systems give a deeper insight into why their futures are unknowable. Furthermore, the visionary and planning models are not practical because they in effect assume that the formation of visions and long-term goals is not the major problem. Those models of strategic choice start to explain what happens once there are visions and goals. This book will argue that the real difficulty, when the future is unknowable, is the making of choices about aspirations and goals. Improving strategic management is primarily a matter of improving the process by which such choices are made, and here today's explicit models contribute relatively little. We need a more dynamic approach which explains how aspirations and goal are discovered and developed.

Why managers continue to espouse visions and plans

There are a number of reasons why managers who accept the failings of the vision and plan models nevertheless justify their continued use:

- Although the plan itself is of little use, the analysis and discussion process through which it is put together encourages strategic thinking by managers. It is a means of raising strategic issues and gaining attention for them.
- Even if real strategic control is not accomplished through encouraging belief in visions and through plans, their abandonment would be a signal to managers that is is acceptable to forget about strategic thinking. It would amount to encouragement simply to react and pay attention only to short term tactics.
- Even if abandoning the vision and plan models did not kill strategic thinking, it would remove essential constraints on the strategic choices and actions of managers in large complex organizations. There would be nothing to ensure consistent strategic action throughout the organization. We would find everybody doing everything and shooting all over the place.
- Without visions and plans, the role of the top management team of a large corporation would be reduced to that of passive observer, irrelevant to the operating activities of those below.
- Visions and plans are a means of protecting most people from exposure to great uncertainty. Visions and plans raise comfort levels and provide a motivational tool.

This book will argue that these are questionable reasons for continuing to espouse a framework which does not achieve the main purpose for which it is intended. The reasons given at best seek to use the framework as an indirect method of encouraging strategic thinking, when more explicit attention to strategic thinking itself would yield better results. Formal long-term planning too quickly becomes a ritual which blocks rather than encourages innovation. Visions too easily become restrictions on new ideas, and run the risk of encouraging blind allegiance to an idea which could be going wrong. Such blind allegiance is the last thing we want in times of turbulence. At worst the above reasons for continuing with visions and plans amount to the promotion of an illusion of certainty and a traditional understanding of control. They therefore provide dangerous false comfort. This book will also argue that there is a need to question how appropriate it is to require continuing consistency in turbulent times. Here too modern scientific understanding of the behaviour of dynamic systems has insights to offer.

Building strategic issue agendas

If we abandon the models of visions and long-term plans then what do we put in their place? This brings us to what successful managers actually do when they confront high levels of uncertainty. They build dynamic agendas of strategic issues. The issues are the current problems, opportunities, aspirations, challenges, preferences and potential goals that managers are identifying. Such issues are strategic because they have widespread and long-term consequences. They are often small changes or anomalies which are difficult to detect and harder to understand. Those strategic issues reach the organizational agenda because sufficiently powerful managers pay attention to them. That agenda is dynamic and alive because it is always changing – as managers deal with them, some issues drop off the agenda, and as managers create and detect changes new issues appear. At the heart of innovation and strategic management lies this dynamic strategic issue agenda. That agenda is not a relatively constant picture of some future state, but the changing set of strategic issues commanding attention in the here and now.

This book argues that instead of trying to build pictures of some future state, we should be concerned with how issues reach the strategic agenda, how choices are made to deal with those issues, and how unpredictable outcomes of those choices in turn provoke further choices. Instead of promoting visions and preparing plans, we should be creating the conditions within which a dynamic strategic issue agenda can thrive and be acted upon in the here and now. What matters is not an intention to do something tomorrow, but action now to deal with issues having long-term consequences. Creating the conditions for effective choice requires explicit analysis of, and attention to, the political and learning processes through which issues are identified, given organizational attention and acted upon. It requires surfacing and questioning the implicit models managers are actually using. These dynamic processes have far more impact on the strategic directions which actually emerge, than analytical techniques and specific lists of prescriptions supposed to apply in a general sense.

Focusing on the dynamic issue agenda means direct rather than indirect attention to strategic thinking, because such thinking is about strategic issues. The manner in which the strategic issue agenda is managed and shaped provides the degree of consistency which is appropriate to the circumstances. Creating the conditions, shaping the agenda, is the role of the top management and this is far from being a passive role. This book argues that we should transfer the concern with what the outcome might be to a concern for how issues with unknowable long-term consequences are to be handled at the present time. And here recent scientific conclusions about the behaviour of dynamic systems suggest a rather different perspective to that which most of us are used to. This book is concerned with a different, more dynamic way of thinking about the process of strategic choice itself, one provoked by new scientific views on the nature of dynamic systems. To put this new way of thinking into perspective, consider how we go about explaining what is going on in the world of business. Such consideration may indicate why we continue to adhere to models which have important drawbacks.

Thinking about the strategy process

The models we put forward to explain how to make strategic choices are derived from analyses of how organizations have made decisions in the past and from interpretations of what led to business success. Whenever we analyse, interpret and explain we always start from a subjective selection of what we judge to be important – we use our existing implicit models. So, one interpretation of Honda's success sees it as consequent upon a strategic intent to build a core competence in engines. On this view Honda chose to compete in the 50 cc motor cycle segment in the US market because that was an undefended territory at the time. Early success in this relatively easy segment then gave Honda time to build its competence in other geographic areas before it mounted an assault on automobiles in the US.[13] This interpretation is one of an orderly set of steps to realise a prior intent. Another interpretation, based on interviews with the executive involved in the diversification of Honda into the US market, describes the entry into the 50 cc motor cycle market in a completely different way.[14] A few Honda executives simply arrived in the USA to see if they could sell their larger motor cycle range in that market. They had carried out no market research and they had no plans. They failed to sell the larger cycles and were on the point of pulling out when they noticed the interest aroused by the smaller 50 cc cycles they were personally using as low-cost transport. So they abandoned their original intention and sold small cycles instead. This interpretation is one in which the strategy emerged in a manner partly determined by management initiative and partly by chance.

It is all too easy to look back on what happened and select an orderly pattern to the events we observe. Having done that, we then prescribe that orderly pattern for the future. Because we are conditioned to look for order, we build an orderly explanation. How we select events and build up explanations depends very heavily on our frame of reference, on what we are conditioned to look for in the first place, on very basic assumptions submerged below the level of awareness and therefore rarely questioned. Humans do this in every area they try to explain from mathematics and physics to management and organization. It is therefore a matter of great importance for us to try to surface which frame of reference lies behind the models we currently develop and attend to when it comes to prescribing what to do to control a business in turbulent times.

The reader is therefore requested to suspend the requirement for specific prescriptions and to consider instead some practical points about the frame of reference we have been using to explain managing and organizing and why it can now be seen to be inappropriate. How we frame problems and opportunities determines the strategic choices we make and the actions we take. The more turbulent the times, the more important it is to surface and examine those frames of reference we use to structure the problems and opportunities facing us. Later discussion will return to the question of strategic agenda building and how the process can be improved.

Frames of reference

During the past few years, I have had contact with more than 30 companies covering many different sectors of business in the UK, USA and Southern Africa. That contact has led me to believe that almost all managers address the concern over extreme uncertainty within the same frame of reference; within the same rarely questioned set of beliefs around how the world of business works. Managers and consultants look for general lists of prescriptions which they can apply to many specific situations, so enabling them to avoid or overcome the turbulence and the chaos they now so frequently encounter. They believe that it is possible to retain conventional control in a turbulent world. We believe that those at the top of the organization can control the direction of the business; that they can 'own' and drive the strategy. We look up to the next rung in the management chain in the belief that they know what to do in turbulent conditions.

We avidly read the studies which claim to identify those characteristics of excellent companies which account for the results they achieve in today's chaotic environment. And we then try to install those characteristics in the belief that they will lead to success. Or we read other books and attend conferences and seminars where we are exhorted and inspired to love change and devote particular attention to some selected key source of success such as customer care, total quality management or participative decision making. When the stock market falls we look for the cause; when the performance indicators of our businesses change direction we look for the causes. This behaviour suggests that we all have a fundamental belief that the world of business is governed by laws which it is possible to identify and that the application of those laws leads to outcomes which are to some useful extent predictable. We share a common, largely unspoken belief that we are trying to explain and secure order in the world of business – we are trying to be as objective and scientific as possible.

On the basis of such a belief we widely subscribe to the view that business success follows from:

- developing a clear vision of where and what we are to be as a business in the long-term future;
- analysing information on how and why the business environment is changing and will change in the future;
- continuously matching our competitive capability to the change, maintaining a dynamic equilibrium so that we continue along our predetermined path into the future;
- inspiring and enthusing everyone in the organization to commit to the vision and work together as a closely knit team with strongly shared cultural norms.

At a very fundamental level we think of a business organization as some combination of an information processing machine and an organism which continuously adapts to its environment. With this as our frame of reference, the almost universal response to the turbulence and chaos of the business world is to try to impose some form of consistency and harmony. We believe that success follows when chaos, which comes predominantly from outside the business in its environment, is removed and overcome. We must therefore be implicitly believing that the turbulence and chaos we observe around us is really a reflection of our own ignorance – somewhere there is a recipe which will tell us how to deal with it in specific terms.

The sources of today's frame of reference

Consider the source of this frame of reference. Our way of thinking about the most basic of business problems, those of control and development over the future, is heavily conditioned by the scientific traditions within which we have been educated. Those same traditions have conditioned all the explanations of management and organization to which practitioners pay attention. Traditional science is concerned with an objective world, where time and space is fixed, which can be accurately measured and which follows fixed laws having predictable outcomes. Traditional science looks for balance between one thing and another, for the forces leading to equilibrium, the mechanisms leading to adaptation to the environment. It seeks to identify and explain patterns of order and pre-ordained paths of development into the future. Turbulence in nature, evident disorder, always presented a problem within this frame of reference. Because it could not be explained, turbulence was regarded as the consequence of complex laws which scientists had not yet discovered – it was a reflection of our own ignorance. The belief was that by studying the world in finer and finer detail man could identify those complex laws and intervene, through decidable step by step procedures, in ways which yield predictable results. Within this framework of thinking, it was believed to be possible for man to control more and more of the outcomes of nature's processes. Those outcomes emerge from machine-like processes and as soon as we understand the machine we can alter the outcome.

Because this scientific way of thinking had such evident success in our control over some aspects of the natural world, we have imported it lock, stock and barrel into the social sciences, and into understanding the managing and organizing of businesses. We have done this in the belief that it will yield similar benefits of control in human systems. And so we believe that we can identify the cause of success in advance of acting; we can set long-term objectives and control the movement of a business organization along some future path to achieve these.

A new frame of reference for dynamic systems

Scientists have developed a new frame of reference. The natural scientists have moved on and now see the traditional scientific approach as applicable only to limited special cases. In this new science, time and space are not fixed, and the motion of a person observing them partly determines how that person perceives reality – what you observe depends upon where you are (Einstein on relativity). In the new science it is impossible to measure both the speed and the position of a particle beyond a certain limit of accuracy – the act of measuring disturbs that which is being measured (Heisenberg on uncertainty). In the new science, some propositions cannot be decided upon using step-by-step procedures – strictly rational thinking breaks down (Gödel on undecidability). In the new science, simple fixed laws can generate inherently random outcomes which nevertheless have a 'hidden' order (Lorenz, Mandlebrot, Feigenbaum and others on chaos). In the new science, dynamic systems use instability to shatter existing order and make unpredictable choices at critical points which may lead to new complex forms of order (Prigogine and self-organization). These propositions, probably unfamiliar to most in business, will be explored and related to business later on.

The natural scientists, particularly over the past three decades, have developed a new frame of reference within which they explain the workings of the world. It is a frame of reference which stresses uncertainty, unpredictability, irregularity, discontinuity and self-organization, in direct opposition to the traditional view. It is a frame of reference which provides the tools for understanding turbulence and chaos – they are real phenomena generated by simple laws, not reflections of our ignorance. Chaos and turbulence are the essence of reality and there is often no cause when events change direction. And this has led to the realization that the development of most of nature's systems is a continuing process of creation which depends significantly on chance, so making it impossible for man ever to control all the outcomes. The focus has shifted from the machine view of order and pre-ordained paths of development, to the creative nature of disorder, irregularity and chance. The weather system, for example, is now seen to be a chaotic system, the long-term development of which is inherently unpredictable and which therefore can never be controlled by man.

We in management have yet to consider what this whole new way of thinking means for organizing and controlling a business. We are still using the conceptual tools imported from a source where they are now regarded as outdated and applicable only to special cases. We all know what happens to a business which continues to offer outdated products to a shrinking niche market. Much the same is likely to happen to managers who continue to act upon understandings and explanations of their world within a frame of reference which is outdated. What if a business is not the information processing machine or the adapting organism of traditional science? What if it is really a chaotic system, like the weather, in which strategic direction depends partly upon chance? What if the chaotic behaviour is a consequence of the structure of the business system itself, not simply a consequence of changes occurring in its environment? What if there are no recipes available for use in many specific situations? What if most of our current views on strategic control are simply illusions?

Outline of the following chapters

This introductory chapter has argued that the most pressing task facing managers today is that of acting in a continuously innovative manner in a business world where the future is very far indeed from certainty. Since we can only act coherently if we develop appropriate models to design our actions, that pressing task is really one of effectively understanding and explaining the process of managing and organizing in conditions of extreme uncertainty. But here we are seriously hampered by a frame of reference which drives us to formulate the problem of managing and organizing in the relatively static terms of information processing machines and gradually adapting organisms. We consequently ignore the messy, disorderly and conflicting aspects of the business reality we face when we come to explicitly explain what is going on. We have difficulty then in accounting for the unintended consequences of what we do, for self-reinforcing virtuous and vicious circles which we provoke and into which we are sucked. We have a great need for a more dynamic model of choosing and acting in a business. And here the recent development of a science of complex dynamic systems has very exciting insights to offer us:

> Dynamics freed at last from the shackles of order and predictability . . .
> Systems liberated to randomly explore their every dynamical possibility . . .
> Exciting variety, richness of choice, a cornucopia of opportunity.[15]

The rest of this book is in a sense an exploration of this description of modern dynamics. The chapters in Part One establish what is required of a dynamic explanation of business activity. Those chapters explore the change situations which a business faces and the control forms which are appropriate to those situations. They are particularly concerned with the open-ended change having unknown consequences, which is so much a feature of modern business life. Such situations give rise to ambiguity and provoke anxiety, conflict and equivocal responses. A dynamic explanation of how we discover goals and objectives, how we continually build and explore agendas of strategic issues is then required. And these processes of discovery, exploration and learning all involve feedback from one choice and action into others. A dynamic explanation of how such feedback loops lead to self-reinforcing virtuous and vicious circles is then required. We need to explain how a business develops endless, innovative variety.

Having established the principal requirements of dynamic models of management, the chapters in Part Two then examine how today's most prominent models of managerial choice and action all fall short of the criteria necessary for a useful dynamic model. They have all been developed within the machine frame of reference of traditional science.

The chapters in Part Three then turn to the recent scientific theories of chaos and self-organization. One chapter briefly outlines how those theories explain the behaviour of complex dynamic systems. The first three Appendices give a more detailed treatment. These theories lead us to explain strategic choice and action in a business in terms of a continual process of organizational learning and political choice. These process are examined in the last three chapters of Part Three. Part Four explores the implications dynamic models have for management roles and management actions. The penultimate chapter compares a chaos approach to management with today's most prominent models. The final chapter outlines what all this means for the strategic role of managers. The final Appendix gives a glossary of terms used in the science of chaos and self-organization.

References

1 Writers such as P. Drucker and A. Ansoff stress the rational approach and those such as T. Peters and B. Waterman put forward an entrepreneurial approach. References to their works are given in later chapters.
2 See the arguments presented by Ohmae, K. *The Borderless World*, (1990), Harper Business; and Porter, M. *The Competitive Advantage of Nations*, (1990), Free Press.
3 Drucker, P. (1967), *The Practice of Management*, Heineman.
4 Moss Kanter, R. (1985), *The Change Masters*, Simon & Schuster.
5 Moss Kanter, R., op. cit.
6 Drucker, P., op. cit.
7 Marquand, J. (1989), *Anatomy and Change*, Harvester Wheatsheaf.
8 Marquand, J., op. cit., p. 67.
9 Gick, M. L., Holyoak, K. J., 'Schema introduction and analogical transfer', *Cognitive Psychology*, Vol. 15, pp. 1–38.
10 Rowe, A. J., Mason, R. O., Dicken, K. E., Snyder, N. H. (1989), *Strategic Management, A Methodological Approach*, Addison-Wesley.
11 Quin, J. (1988), Federal Express, in Quin, J., Mintzberg, H., James, R., eds., *The Strategy Process*, Prentice-Hall.
12 Hamel, G., Prahalad, C. K. (May–June 1989), Strategic Intent, *Harvard Business Review*.
13 Hamel, G., Prahalad, C. K., op. cit.
14 Pascale, R., The Honda Effect, in Quinn, J., Mintzberg, H., James, R., eds., op. cit.
15 Gleick, J., (1988), *Chaos*, Heinemann, p. 306, reprinted by permission of William Heinemann Ltd.

Part One
The Concerns of
Dynamic Management

The chapters in Part One seek to establish the key elements which managers need to incorporate into a dynamic model of managing if they are to design effective actions in today's turbulent business world. A useful dynamic guide to managerial action needs to be built upon:

- Our experience that there are different kinds of change situation. Managers face change which ranges from predictable closed change in the short term to that open-ended change which eventually dominates at some point in the long term. Dynamic management has to be simultaneously concerned with controlling the reasonably certain short-term consequences of existing business activities and with handling the highly uncertain long-term consequences of new business developments. Appropriate actions have to be designed taking account of our experience that close to certainty we find it easy to set objectives before we act. But high levels of uncertainty and ambiguity provoke anxiety, confusion and conflict, making it difficult to discover and develop aspirations and goals before we act.
- A recognition that the form of control and development we actually apply alters as we move from one general type of change situation to another. When we are near to the certainty of closed changed it is possible and highly desirable to make choices and to act in a rational planned manner. Observation of the behaviour of managers, however, shows that they make choices in a political manner when the future is open-ended. Here managers learn in groups in order to clarify issues and discover their aspirations and goals, so guiding their actions. A dynamic model of management has to be concerned with both the rational planning and the political learning forms of control and development. To be a useful guide to managerial action in open-ended situations, dynamic models should explain how personality and group behavioural dynamics affect the political learning which leads to strategic choice and action.
- The feedback nature of organizational choice and action. A useful dynamic model of management should explain the self-reinforcing virtuous and vicious circles we observe in business life. It should explain how small

changes can escalate into large consequences. And in real life we know that luck or chance plays some part in business success alongside initiative and determination. A useful dynamic model of management should incorporate the intertwining of chance and the manner in which managers create their own futures.

The chapters in Part One explore what these requirements of a dynamic model of managing and organizing entail.

2 Goals, behaviour and change

The immediate concern of any dynamic approach to managing and organizing is with change. More specifically, the concern is with the impact which change has on the behaviour of those individuals and groups of people in the organization who are affected by that change and have to make choices to deal with it. If they are to act effectively in the face of change, managers must design their actions using mental models which incorporate key features of change and the kinds of behaviour it provokes.

As managers face the future from the here and now, they are confronted by different change situations. Some of these change situations have predictable consequences and some do not. This chapter develops a framework within which to think about change and peoples' behaviour, goals and aspirations as they are affected by change.

The future is a combination of change situations

In describing a general change situation facing the managers of a business, we need to specify:

- the timing of change, that is, when the change occurs and how long it takes for the consequences of that change to be felt;
- the magnitude of the consequences of the change;
- the degree of predictability of the change and its consequences.

The present

Consider first all those events occurring to the business, and all those actions taken by people in the business, now in the present. This is depicted in Figure 2.1. The vertical axis measures the magnitude of the consequences (without distinguishing between the positive and the negative) of all events occurring and actions being taken in the present. The horizontal axis measures the time in which those consequences have their impact.

Closed change

The consequences of some of the present events and actions are entirely predictable for a short time into the future. These are depicted as the shaded area in Figure 2.1. Such events and actions are predictable because they relate to the normal conduct of the existing business. So, a major existing customer substantially increases orders for an existing line of products and the company increases its output. Or an existing supplier increases the price of an existing component and the company replaces it with a close substitute. All the cash flow consequences of these events and actions taken now are predictable to a high degree of accuracy. We can know what is causing the change, why it is causing the change and what the consequences will be for the short-term future. We are simply repeating, almost exactly, what we have done frequently in the past. In the short-term, small changes occurring now which might upset this repetition do not have sufficient time to build up into significant differences. The situation is one of closed change.

Contained change

There will be other events occurring and actions being taken now which are less exact repetitions of the past. A new customer may place orders for some variation of an existing product line and require shorter delivery times. Another supplier may increase component prices and substitutes may require some change in the production process. The consequences will still be predictable, but with much less accuracy. There may also be large numbers of the same events and actions, where the consequences of any single event or action are not accurately predictable. But their combined outcome may well be because of the large number of repetitions involved. The company may be producing and selling large numbers of, say, video recorders. It is not possible to predict which specific recorder in a batch will be rejected by quality control, or which will be returned as defective by a customer. But reasonably accurate predictions that, say, only 2 per cent will be rejected and only 1 per cent returned can be made. Here we can say what is probably causing the change, why it is probably causing the change and what the probable consequences are. This is made possible by large numbers of the same events or by approximate repetition of what has occurred in the past. It is then possible to apply probability concepts and statistical techniques. Here we have the con-

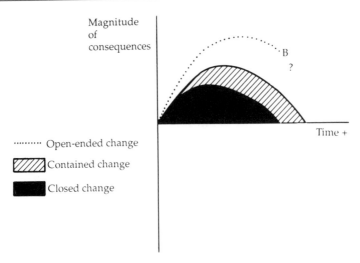

Figure 2.1 *Consequences of present actions and events*

tained change depicted in Figure 2.1 as the cross-hatched area. The possibility of making forecasts extends some way further into the future than is the case with closed change – less accuracy is traded for more time. Again the time period has to be short enough to allow us to ignore any build up of small unnoticeable changes which may have major consequences.

Open-ended change

And yet other events will be occurring and actions being taken now which are one-off and unique. They are new to the business; they have never occurred in that form before; they may well be small and apparently insignificant. A foreign competitor may be setting up a business in a related area which will eventually prove to be a platform for expansion into the market of an unsuspecting domestic company. The research and development department may be developing a glue for which no one can see any application, one which eventually turns into a highly profitable yellow 'Post It Note' product line. In another boardroom some company may may be planning a take-over. In a foreign market the army, or a religious group, may be embarking on a coup which will lead to cancellation of contracts and non-payment of monies owed. Cows may develop an unheard of disease, eggs may be discovered to be infected with salmonella, studies may show margarine to be less healthy than was once thought, CFCs are found to harm the ozone layer, and so one could go on.

The point is that many of these changes start off as small and usually unnoticed, but over a period of time they escalate with major consequences for many companies. Because the events are unique and often small, because the consequences for a particular company depend upon how that company and its competitors act, such consequences are unpredictable. This is open-ended change where at first we do not know what is causing the change, why it is causing it and what the consequences will be. It is depicted in Figure 2.1 as the blank area under the dotted line which ends in a question mark. And open ended change is the predominant feature of the long-term future. As we look further forward in time, more and more consequences are open-ended. We eventually get to a point where we do not know what the total consequences will be.

The basis for this distinction between three change situations is our past experience. We all know that tomorrow's business outcomes are largely predictable, but those in 10 or 20 years time are not. We may have different views on the level of predictability between those time spans.

The past and the future

So far, we have considered change in terms of consequences of events occurring and actions taken in the present. Figure 2.2 adds the consequences of events and actions in the past and the future to those of the present. Movement away from 0 in either direction along the vertical axis represents increasing magnitude of the consequences of events and actions (without distinguishing positive from negative). The horizontal axis is extended to the left to include what has happened in the past. The curve B and its components are the same as that given in Figure 2.1 – it represents the consequences of events and actions of the present.

But now we add curve A which shows the magnitude of events and actions which have already occurred at some time in the past. Many of the

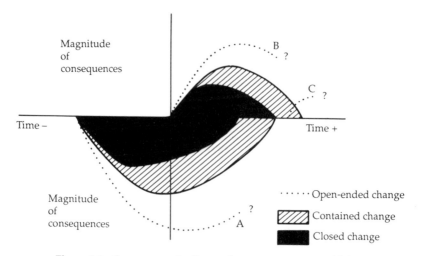

Figure 2.2   *Consequences of actions and events past, present and future*

consequences of these events and actions have already occurred and will be known and understood. This is depicted by the dark area under curve A to the left of 0. We know what happened and why it happened. But some of those past consequences may not be all that clear, and we will find ourselves resorting to words such as 'most likely' or 'probably' as we describe what has happened and why it happened. This is presented by the cross-hatched area under curve A to the left of 0, the probabilistic or contained change which occurred in the past as seen from the present. And there will also be some events and their consequences which have already occurred where we are not at all clear what happened and even less clear why it did. This is represented by the blank space under curve A to the left of 0.

On one consultancy assignment I listened to members of the top management team discussing why there had been a dramatic decline in the profits of one of their subsidiaries. That subsidiary carried out road repair contracts, largely for local governments. One view was that the profit decline had been caused by pricing policy, another that it had to do with particularly bad weather, and yet another that the cause lay primarily in a local government expenditure cut. No definitive cause was agreed upon. In another company I listened to a review of an over-hasty acquisition which had led to a large loss. One director explained how painstaking the preparation for the acquisition had been – he seemed to have forgotten how rapidly it had all been done. Instead of ascribing failure to careless preparation, he saw it as an unforeseeable consequence of market decline and culture differences between the two companies. On many occasions managers resort to interpretations, rumours, myths, rationalizations after the event, self-justification, to provide an explanation of what happened. Sometimes the past is open-ended.

Furthermore, all these events from the past will continue to impact into the future. Going into the future, some of the consequences of the past may be quite clear, some statistically predictable and some may be unknowable so that eventually we cannot predict the total magnitude – the question mark at the end of line A.

To complete the picture we have to add curve C to represent events and actions which may well occur in the future. These may have closed, contained and open-ended aspects as viewed from time 0.

Figure 2.2 therefore represents the total change situation facing an organization. The total change situation is a consequence of actions, events and interactions past, present and future. As the organization stands at the present, time 0, it faces a past, some aspects of which are difficult to interpret and understand. At time 0 it also faces a total change situation at each point into the future, which consists of a mixture of closed, contained and open-ended change. But the balance of these components alters as it considers longer and longer periods into the future. The very short term is predominantly closed change; a little further out it is predominantly closed and contained; even further out it is predominantly open-ended. Viewed from the present, all time frames, both past and future, are similar in that they all have the same change components. But they are not exactly the same, the component balance alters.

A key feature of today's business environment is, I suggest, that closed change increasingly applies to shorter and shorter periods into the future. In most businesses we can probably only apply the term to a period some months ahead. Open-ended change is also moving closer to us in time terms. For most businesses time periods two to three years ahead are probably predominantly open-ended.

Open-ended change affects all time periods

The next point to make is that although the change situations in any time frame have been described and depicted as separate components, they are in fact highly interrelated. So we cannot say that because closed and contained change predominate in say the short-term, it is possible then to ignore the open-ended. In the longer term too, the fact that it will be possible to forecast some change may not help all that much in practical terms.

Take even the past. We may know a great deal about the history of the organization, but there may be some very important events, especially in the recent past, which are totally unclear. People have difficulty in deciding what to do next if they do not understand what has just happened; what has just happened may continue to affect what happens next. Coherent action depends upon explanation. The activity of interpreting the past, trying to understand what went wrong and why, is therefore an activity of major importance in dealing with the future. It accounts for much of what managers do at meetings.

Next consider the short-term future. It is usually possible in business reliably to predict the short-term consequences of many events and actions which have occurred and are occurring. The inevitable lags in adjustment see to that. So the revenues a business will earn over, say, the next three months may be fairly accurately predicted because orders have already been placed and the consequences of sales efforts now being made are relatively clear. We are talking about lags in adjustment, regularity and repetition. But even in the short term there is an element of the unpredictable open-ended change – a major customer may suddenly be acquired by a competitor or go into liquidation, so completely nullifying even short-term projections.

And turning to the long term, some change which will impact on the organization will simply be reflections of changes which have already occurred at some time in the past. For example, because of changes in the birth rate since the end of the First World War, events which have already occurred, we can confidently forecast changes in most age cohorts of the population in the UK over at least the next 10 to 15 years. We know by how much and when the 25- to 35-year-old age group will decline; when and by how much the 45- to 55-year-old age group will increase; by how much and when the 70-plus age group will increase.

We can then make forecasts with some degree of confidence of what will happen to the demand for certain basic, non-fashion goods and services such as perhaps housing. Demands for these goods are likely to be a repetition of that which has occurred in the past, dependent primarily on the size of the group normally buying them. So given that we can say something about the demand for housing, forecasts can then be derived with some degree of confidence, of say roof tiles and plastic drainpipes.

So some events which will occur in the future are either the unwinding of past events with long time lags or they are highly likely repetitions of that which we have already experienced. But the problem is that open-ended change could easily overcome and nullify the probabilistic. You may use demographic forecasts and repetitive patterns of consumer expenditure to conclude that it is worth investing in a new factory to produce roof tiles. But unknown to you, as your factory is completed, a competitor may be doing just the same thing. The resulting over-capacity will destroy profitability, the accurate forecast of demand providing cold comfort.

At any one time, therefore, business organizations face three very different interconnected change situations in which they must now exercise control; three situations in which they must accommodate change in some way by action taken now; three change situations only partially related to different time periods into the future. And one of these change situations is fundamentally different from the other two. In the case of closed and contained change you can forecast, but in the open-ended you cannot. It is the unknown which dominates long-term consequences and contaminates even the past and the short-term future.

Open-ended change, ambiguous goals, confusion and anxiety

Open-ended change is qualitatively different from closed and contained change. It is unique change, while both the others involve some repetition or large numbers of events. Information is always inadequate in open-ended change situations and it is conditioned by how people interpret it. Interpretations are conditioned by the received wisdom and by what people are trying to achieve personally and in group terms. We seem to have an inherent tendency to avoid the open-ended because it

challenges existing positions. Open-ended change is ambiguous and our
response to it is equivocal. Because its consequences are unpredictable it
is impossible for those involved to form immediately clear preferences on
what they would like to see happen or what actions they should take. It is
impossible to set objectives immediately. Where long-term consequences
are unknown it is also, by definition, impossible to formulate visions or
missions of a future state.

And the impact of open-ended change on the behaviour of people is
significant. Because it is the unknown its prospect provokes distinctive
behaviours. People typically feel confused and insecure; they may conflict; they may avoid the issues; they may become excessively dependent
on their leaders. They will turn to those amongst them who are able to
provide plausible interpretations of what is going on. Thus, those who
possess this ability come to exercise considerable influence.

This can be seen quite clearly in the dealing rooms of organizations
which trade securities. Typical practice is a meeting each morning of all
brokers, at which the analysts and economists present their message.
Since open-ended change is just about the only change such organizations face, even on a day-to-day basis, the economists in fact achieve
very little in the way of forecasting success. Any forecasts are very general
and hedged with escape clauses. But those with a coherent interpretation
of what has happened the day before in New York and Tokyo, what some
of the possibilities are for that day, are held in very high regard and paid
large sums of money. The influence such analysts exert in financial
markets has much to do with their interpretive skill and its benefits in
reducing perceived uncertainty, and little to do with actual forecasting
success.

Open-ended change is different

There are six differences of immense importance between the three
change situations:

- It is possible for the preferences and objectives of organizational
  actors to be reasonably clear cut in closed and contained change. This
  makes it possible to choose between goals and proposed actions,
  either by bargaining where the objectives conflict, or by rational
  decision making where they are agreed. In open-ended change preferences and objectives cannot initially be either clear cut or agreed,
  simply because the level of uncertainty is so high. Choices can therefore only be made by means of complex forms of learning and political
  activity in which preferences and objectives are discovered.
- Causes are easily understandable and consequences predictable in
  closed situations. Sensible statements about likelihood can be made in
  contained change situations. There are clearly identifiable links be-

tween cause and effect. In closed and contained situations visions and missions can have meaning as some picture of a future state. In both, rational decision-making processes utilizing some form of forecasting are possible and they make the major contribution in dealing with the change. Effective thinking and learning in these situations is essentially a step-by-step procedure. We can use general models of the organization as an evolving, adaptive organism or as an information processing machine to deal with large numbers of specific situations. But open-ended change situations are difficult to understand in their past form and unpredictable in their future form. It follows that missions and visions as pictures of the future are impossible. We have to talk instead about aspirations, ambitions, or lists of issues we are attending to. Cause and effect links are difficult to identify. Where open-ended change is predominant, or even of only significant importance, control methods based on forecasts or visions of future states, will be ineffective. Thinking and learning in this kind of situation is intuitive and based on qualitative analogies with similar situations. Traditional models of the organization as an evolving organism, or an information processing machine, will be seriously misleading.

- Insignificant events or actions undertaken now have insignificant consequences in closed change situations and are highly likely to have insignificant consequences in contained situations. We can safely ignore small changes and concentrate on the larger ones. In open-ended situations, however, we know that tiny changes can escalate through the system and have major implications. They can totally change the behaviour of the system within relatively short time periods. For example, a careless statement by a member of the government on the presence of salmonella bacteria in eggs, escalated into a major decline in egg consumption in the UK in 1988. A television programme attacking the construction methods used by a major UK house builder led to the virtual demise of timber-frame house construction in the UK in the early 1980s. Small changes cannot therefore be safely ignored and detecting small changes becomes a matter of vital importance.

- In closed and contained situations, change impacts on an organization from outside that organization, and it adapts. The organization can be changed in anticipation of likely external change, using relatively fixed rules and procedures of control. The system used to control the change remains constant as the change is dealt with. In open-ended situations, organizations have to develop new approaches to control and development as they handle the change. This is because that change is unique and has never been confronted in that form before. The organization's rules and relationships themselves have to be altered as it handles change from external sources.

The instrument being used to manage change, is not a constant and therefore generates change itself.

- In closed situations learning is achieved in advance of change and there is nothing new left to learn as it occurs. In contained situations much is learned in advance and the rest by purposeful adaptation through trial and error search as the change occurs. But that learning is minimal because most of the change has been foreseen. But in open-ended situations, learning as discovery is of major significance. It becomes part and parcel of dealing with the change. It proceeds with the handling of the change in real time. It is in fact the way we deal with such change. It becomes difficult to describe such learning as adaptive, since it is not at all clear what one is adapting to. Action taken and that which is learnt from it, have a significant bearing on what happens next.

- In closed and contained situations, people feel secure and behave in relatively understandable and predictable ways. When they are confronted with open-ended change, those same people may well behave in ways which are difficult to understand and may even be quite bizarre.

Open-ended change is the situation in which we do not know what we are doing, and when we face that situation we find out; we explore; we learn; we do all this in conflict or cooperation with other people; we engage in complex political learning processes; and in so doing we develop new meanings. The other change situations describe that where we know what we are doing and when this is the case we practise rational decision making and simple forms of political bargaining.

Open-ended change is therefore fundamentally different from other change situations. And it is present in all time frames, although to different degrees. It has to be handled simultaneously with those other change situations. And because open-ended change is fundamentally different from other change, it has to be handled in a fundamentally different way, a matter to be explored in the next chapter.

Unpredictability and recognizable patterns

Although the consequences of open-ended change are unknown in specific terms, we also know from experience that history has a habit or repeating itself in general terms. We also know that when we confront totally new situations which we have been unable to predict, we can usually detect some similarity with events that have occurred before or are occurring elsewhere. We recognize qualitatively similar patterns which we use to develop new mental models to cope with the new situations. We use analogies based on similarity to cope with the unexpected when we are confronted by it.

Take for example a company I worked with for a number of years. In the mid-1960s that company had diversified its activities, but a major investment had turned out to be unsuccessful during the market recession at the end of the decade. The company's profits then declined dramatically and it experienced a substantial cash outflow. Its response was to centralize its structures, tighten its control systems, rationalize its activities and curb its investments. By the early 1970s it was back in profit and had accumulated a large cash surplus. The next few years were ones of expansion and diversification through first a market boom, then the major recession of the mid 1970s and the small recovery of the late 1970s. The control systems were not applied as rigorously and business units were encouraged to identify investments, diversify and expand. Although the structure had not changed significantly the balance of power had shifted to divisional management. But in the late 1970s a number of markets weakened or even dried up. A number of investments and diversifications turned out to be unsuccessful. Once again profits declined and cash poured out of the business. The early 1980s were then years of tightening controls and rationalizing activities, this time accompanied by decentralisation. This led to a rapid restoration of profitability and a complete turn-round in the cash position. Even before the mid-1980s the business was once more seeking diversification opportunities and making major investments. And the mid to late 1980s was a period of high profitability.

At each point through more than two decades, the specific outcomes were completely different. There was nothing predetermined about them – one acquisition may have failed, but if it had been some other acquisition it may well not have done so. One diversification succeeded, but if it had been another instead, it may well not have. However, in more than two decades, the pattern of events in general was similar. There were periods of expansion and periods of contraction; periods of tightening controls and periods of loosening them; moves from decentralization to centralisation and back again. History repeats itself, but never in the same way. As we stand in the here and now we know that specific long-term outcomes are unpredictable. But we also know from past experience that we will recognize qualitative similarities in events as they unfold.

General patterns of this kind are used by managers when they make choices. Such patterns constitute experience. In specific uncertain circumstances managers call upon analogous experience. But such general, qualitative similarity is not specific or quantitative enough unequivocally to determine actions taken now. We know that profits will fluctuate; we know that some new ventures will succeed and some will not. But we do not know when or which ones. We cannot decide far in advance what specific action to take, but when something happens we know from experience what might work, because we have seen similar things before. The self-similarity of unfolding unexpected events builds up general, recognizable patterns of perception which constitute experience. And that general experience is applied to specific situations never encountered in that specific form before. Open-ended change is unpredictability in specific outcomes combined with a general pattern of similarity. And where they cannot predict, managers use their previous experience of those general patterns to build new mental models with which to design their actions.

Conclusion: what a dynamic model should explain about change

Open-ended change is present in all time frames and dominates the long-term. It is unique uncertainty which makes it extremely difficult, if not impossible, to forecast outcomes. Open-ended changes throw up ambiguous and ill-structured issues on which we have inadequate information. It is difficult to identify the problem or opportunity to be dealt with. The difficulty is to know what questions to ask in the first place, never mind how to answer them. Open-ended change provokes equivocal responses and leads to unclear preferences and objectives for people within an organization. And it causes insecurity, conflict and confusion. But it is also characterized by the repetition of similar qualitative patterns at a general level – history repeats itself. Because of these general patterns we are able to cope with specific unpredictability by means of analogous reasoning. But the result is irregularity in the time path which the organization follows. Peters and Waterman identified IBM as an excellent company in their 1982 book. In his 1988 book Peters concluded that there are no excellent companies. He described how everyone described IBM as an excellent company in one time period and then pronounced it dead in another, only to call it excellent later on. Open-ended change makes it impossible to secure predetermined, perfectly stable patterns of performance. All these features can be directly confirmed by observing managers when they are confronted with open-ended change, and by examining the pattern of their organization's performance. The difficulty comes when we try to explain the source of the uncertainty and the consequent irregularity in the time path of performance. And it is important to do this because it affects how we design our actions.

Consider how we usually explain the performance of an organization, or an economy, as it moves through an uncertain future. We approach the problem within a traditional scientific frame of reference. We seek to decompose the observed erratic patterns of performance in some way. We seek to extract underlying patterns of uniformity from the observed data – trends or cycles of one kind or another. This uniformity is then held to be generated by the underlying laws governing the behaviour of that system – that economy or that organization. We look for the basic causes and their effects as shown in the trends and cycles. We usually cannot specify the underlying laws of cause and effect in an exact manner. Consequently we cannot explain the trends and cycles exactly. Reality will deviate from our explanations and we call this 'noise' or experimental error. But if the causal model is good enough, this 'noise' will be relatively unimportant and we can ignore it. The causal model is then taken as the explanation of the orderly underlying part of the system's behaviour that we observe.

However that system operates in an environment which may be changing. Much of this change can be explained using models of environmental behaviour. We can then determine the impact on the behaviour of the system we are concerned with – our business. The system can take environmental change into account in its plans. We still have uniformity. If we cannot explain those environmental changes, then we think of them as random shocks which impact on the system, moving it from the nearly uniform path it would otherwise follow. The major part of the erratic behaviour we observe is then due to those random shocks coming from the environment.

The traditional explanation of the dynamic behaviour of a system therefore splits into two parts – the underlying laws governing the system generate uniformity or regularity (disturbed in a minor way by noise), and random shocks from outside the system account for any significant deviations from this uniformity. Open-ended change is then the result of unpredictable random shocks hitting the organization, or the economy, from outside in its environment. The high level of uncertainty is due to our inability to explain and forecast all the changes in government policy, consumer fashions, technologies and so on. We see open-ended change because we are ignorant of the full range of causes and effects, as well as the way in which they are related. Because of this uncertainty arising in the environment, the performance of the organization or economy will display erratic movements around an otherwise regular path. Success then flows from adhering to the underlying laws, from creating a system which operates in an orderly and harmonious manner. To the extent that a business is affected by chance, that is due to random shocks coming from the environment. To these we have to adapt as rapidly as possible.

Such an explanation leads to the conclusion that we should deal with open-ended change by overcoming our ignorance as much as possible. We should gather more information and do more research. Such an explanation leads to the conclusion that the qualitatively similar patterns we observe can be identified in more specific terms. We do not see these general similar patterns in more precise terms because we do not know enough. And this ignorance relates to what is happening in the environment, so our information gathering, research and analysis problems are mainly those to do with the environment.

This, as will be shown in the chapters of Part Two below, is the explanation of open-ended change which underlies today's most prominent models of managing and organizing. It leads us to design actions on the basis that success flows from an orderly organization which conducts an orderly search to identify the random shocks and anticipate them as much as possible. We then conduct our affairs on the basis that we can know, to a reasonably useful extent, what the future holds, if we pay enough attention to the matter. We can use the underlying orderly part of the change to set up a number of different likely scenarios or to formulate visions. Open-ended change is here seen as the presently unknown, not the totally unknowable.

The problem with this explanation is that it does not accommodate a number of the features of open-ended change which it is so easy to observe. We observe that small changes can escalate into major consequences. We observe that changes feed into each other in virtuous and vicious circles. There is nothing in the idea of random shocks coming from the environment which explains these observations. As we will see in the chapters in Part Three, new scientific understandings of the behaviour of complex dynamic systems have much to say about escalating small changes, as well as virtuous and vicious circles. The insight provided by modern dynamic models is that the long-term future for some systems is absolutely unknowable because of their very natures. Some systems have a feedback structure which escalates small changes and generates vicious and virtuous circles. No amount of information gathering and research can alter this internal structure which leads to an unknowable future. Open-ended change is then not the presently unknown, but the inherently unknowable. If we accept such an explanation then we will arrange our affairs on a very different basis from that to which the traditional explanation leads us.

A useful model of business behaviour must take account of the nature of open-ended change. It must answer questions such as the following. Is open-ended change the consequence of unpredictable random shocks which keep knocking an otherwise orderly business system off course? Is it ignorance to be cured by research and gathering more information? Or is open-ended change, at least in part, a direct consequence of the structure of the business organization itself? A useful dynamic model of business should explain why open-ended change is unpredictable in specific terms and yet involves the recurrence of events which are similar in general terms. It should incorporate how managers learn and build up experience with which to deal with unpredictable specific outcomes using analogous reasoning in relation to similar patterns elsewhere.

But open-ended change is not the only form of change. Organisations also simultaneously face closed and contained change. Here we observe that managers can and do set objectives and predict the consequences of the actions they take. A dynamic model should also incorporate this aspect of change and explain why business systems face both the predictable and the unpredictable.

A business must simultaneously accommodate two very different types of change. One kind of change has short-term, largely but not totally predictable consequences. The other kind has long-term, predominantly unpredictable consequences giving rise to ambiguity and equivocal responses. Both must be accommodated by action taken now against a background in which some historical changes are not clearly understood or agreed upon. The next chapter examines how successful organizations handle diametrically opposed change situations and what requirements this places on dynamic models to design managerial action.

3 Relationship between control form and change situation

The last chapter described how business organizations face a spectrum of change situations in every time frame. At one end of that spectrum there is the closed change which generally predominates in the very short term – an existing customer increases orders for existing products and services. All the cashflow consequences can be predicted. At the other end of that spectrum there is the unpredictable open-ended change which predominates in the longer term – changes in the markets of Eastern Europe in 1990 which make it difficult to identify the problems and the opportunities in the first place. To such change we cannot usefully attach probabilities simply because it is unique. In between there are change situations in which it is practically meaningful to describe consequences in statistical terms, based on similar experiences in the past. These consequences may stretch well into the long term because they represent the unwinding of change that has already occurred (the composition of the population) or some regular repetition of specific past events (seasonal demand for a product). Although different kinds of change predominate in different time perspectives, as seen from the here and now, all kinds of change are present in all of these perspectives. And this statement applies to the past as well as the future, with the consequence that some aspects of the past need to be interpreted and understood as part of acting in the present.

The immediate focus of a dynamic explanation of business success is therefore on the nature of the changes facing the organization and all its parts, at all levels in the management hierarchy, in all time frames. The fundamental organizational problem is one of anticipating, reacting to, creating, accommodating and managing very different types of change at the same time. If the organization faces complex time paths which cover a spectrum of situations, then effective control will have different meanings, in detail, according to the change situation in which it is practised. To succeed, an organization must apply a form of control appropriate to the change situations it faces.

Control is coherent, rather than haphazard, ways of dealing with change. Organisational control is practised by groups of people. People form groups, organizations develop, because we know that groups and organizations enable greater coherence in dealing with change in a complex world. Large numbers of individuals facing a complex world, in the absence of interaction with each other, are compelled by complexity to behave haphazardly. We organize ourselves into groups even when we have no clear, specific purpose because this puts us in a better position to behave coherently when we come face to face with the totally unexpected. We may well organize into groups even before we have a clear common purpose because other people in the group may have contributions to make when it comes to dealing with the unexpected. Before groups have a purpose they form because of reciprocal expected contributions, because of the means not the ends.[1] The point is that we do not have to start a discussion on control by requiring that there be a clear purpose. All we need is for behaviour to be coherent in some sense.

For the behaviour of a group of people to be coherent, three elements are required. The first is discovery. The group must utilize some process to discover what is changing. The second element is choosing. The group must deploy some process to select some way of dealing with the changes which have been discovered. Since this process of choosing is a group process, members of the group must be persuaded, or forced, to adhere to the choice made. The third element is action. The choice made must be carried out or implemented. Behaviour cannot be controlled unless it incorporates all three elements of discovery, choice and action. Haphazard behaviour is action without any realistic attempt to discover and choose what to do. And control is a feedback loop because the action taken itself represents a change which must be discovered. The process of control itself therefore has dynamic properties which need to be explained.

Control means the same thing in general terms, no matter what the change situation. But the meaning of each element, the detailed meaning of effective control, alters dramatically from one change situation to another.

Short interval control for closed change

The key features of closed change are unambiguous problems, opportunities and issues, clear connections between cause and effect, and the possibility of accurately forecasting the consequences of change. Faced with such change, people tend to behave in easily understandable ways. Given the nature of such change, it is possible for control to take on a very precise meaning.

Discovery

Discovery means the formalized analytical scanning of changes occurring within the organization and its environments. It is possible to identify, analyse and quantify key changes in the markets (through market research) and in the competitive capability of a company. It is possible to construct reliable quantitative models which explain and predict the functioning of markets and business organizations in a large number of different specific circumstances. We can build general models for all situations which can be described as closed. Since we know what we are looking for in closed change, we can formalize the process of discovery – rules and procedures can be established in advance on what is to be discovered, where, how, by whom and when. In other words, carefully organized market research, environmental monitoring and quantitative forecasting can be carried out by clearly specified job holders.

Choice

Choice also takes on a precise meaning. It is the setting of time definite, tightly constrained objectives. Quantitative objectives can be set for fixed points in the future and no excuse accepted for failure to achieve them. Since discovery yields adequate information and the relative certainty of outcomes prompts fairly reliable behaviour in people, objective setting is not a major problem. People can immediately form clear objectives. When their objectives conflict, trade offs can easily be identified, allowing the playing of predictable bargaining games to establish compromise objectives. Having set the objectives, choice is then a step-by-step analytical procedure for deriving a sequence of actions over the future which will achieve the objective. These action steps can be embodied in a plan which sets out their financial consequences. We can decide what to do well in advance of doing it.

Action

The third element of control is action. In closed change, action is largely the pre-programmed implementation of the plan. It is primarily proaction, accompanied by reaction when unforeseeable consequences are

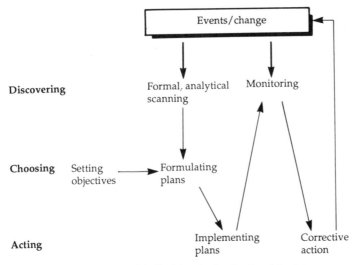

Figure 3.1 *The control feedback loop in closed and contained change*

encountered. To complete the control loop, the consequences of action have to be discovered. This takes the precise form of monitoring the quantitative outcomes of actions against plan forecast, the identification of variances and corrective action to bring outcomes back into line with the planned path. As the organization proceeds through time, it simply moves around the single, well defined loop shown in Figure 3.1.

What this loop describes is of course the well-known principles of short interval financial control. It incorporates the whole process of sales plans, production scheduling, budgeting and annual planning. It requires on-going investment in management information and control systems, information technology, training and development. The practice of such control is an absolute prerequisite for success in a corporation of any size and its benefits are so predictable that consultants are able to guarantee the financial savings of its installation.

The key features of short interval control

The key features of this short interval form of control are as follows:

- It employs rational decision-making techniques. The processes of control are formal, analytical and quantitative. They are most effectively applied within simple hierarchies of managers where job definitions are clear and unambiguous. This form of control utilizes step-by-step thinking. It does not involve learning in real time since the learning is done in advance of the action and is embodied in a plan.
- It deals with change which is regular and seeks to automate responses

to that regularity. It does not succeed completely because even in the short term, events are not completely predictable. Action taken in the first period is fed back into the system over a number of periods later on and it may be some time before the impact can be accurately assessed. This creates a problem in how to react in the second period. It will not yet be clear whether the period one action has had the desired effect or not, unless these events too are predictable. So, profits are coming in below budget and the response is to raise prices. When reviews are next conducted, profits are still below budget because volumes have fallen. But is this only a temporary reaction? Some more informal judgemental process will be required to answer the question. Even in the short term we have to rely, to a limited extent at least, on some other form of control.

- It is a damping form of control aimed at rapidly correcting any deviation from the planned route. It seeks to sustain the planned adaptive equilibrium between the organization and its environments. So, monitoring shows that customers are returning 2 per cent of the product when the standard calls for less than 1 per cent. Quality control procedures are immediately tightened up. The short interval control system is neither meant for, nor capable of, coping with innovative, amplifying interactions with the environments. Here too we have to look for another form of control.

- It is driven by clear purpose and clear preferences where alternative ways of achieving the purpose are known. Techniques for choosing between the alternatives are available. It is an algorithmic, step-by-step, thinking and decision-making activity. We know that the goal is less than 1 per cent rejects and we can set out all the steps to achieve it. But when preferences and goals are not clear at all, we need another form of control.

- At some points, different individual purposes, different individual preferences, have to be dealt with. Here political processes of a bargaining type take over. The marketing director proposes increasing the advertising budget to stimulate demand and get back onto profit targets. The production director proposes cutting advertising expenditure to reduce costs. The chief executive with his greater power decides between them. Here preferences and objectives are still clear and what we are dealing with is simply difference. Political bargaining then occurs, the outcome of which is determined by stable power patterns and procedures which are laid down in advance to govern bargaining. Power here is derived from status and position more than anything else.

- The arenas (meetings, document circulation lists) in which communication takes place are predetermined. They have already been set up in advance of the change. They are serially arranged with information flowing along prearranged channels from one arena to another. Those who are to participate in the arenas are well defined and stable in the sense that the same individuals always participates. Procedures lay out in advance what kind of matter is to be referred to particular arenas. The communication arenas for short interval control are the institutionalized management and board meetings and the flows of reports and budgets to which they attend.

- The functions that each communication arena is to perform are quite clear. There are restricted membership meetings right at the top of the hierarchy which perform mainly symbolic functions (for example, approving budgets and plans, thus giving them legitimacy). Other meetings may perform administrative functions. Many one-to-one meetings perform choice or decision functions from which action flows. Many of the meetings and documents perform rationalization functions of explaining what has already happened (for example, reviewing performance against budget). These functions of communication arenas will be set out in greater detail in Chapter 10, but the point to note here is the importance of symbolic, legitimating, administrative, reviewing the past and decision making functions in the arenas relevant to short interval control. Dealing with issues, especially those of an open-ended nature, is not a prominent feature of institutionalized communication arenas for reasons which are to be explored in Chapter 10.

- Installing a short interval control system in the first place, or changing it in any significant way, directly affects the work patterns of everyone in the organization and therefore has important behavioural implications. The system can only function if those people operating it are committed. Short interval control requires strongly shared cultural norms relating to the performance of existing tasks. Installing or changing such a control system therefore requires political processes of persuasion and negotiation. But once established, once commitment is secured, the system tends to operate predominantly through instruction on a one-to-one basis.

The short interval form of control is a significant source of stability for a business. It utilizes the possibility of short-term forecasting.

Long-term planning for contained change

Contained change situations are those in which it is possible to make probabilistic forecasts. It is possible to forecast the most likely consequences of events occurring and actions taken now, as well those of past and future events and actions. This is possible because such consequences are to a significant extent repetitions of what has happened in the past. Or they are unwindings of events that have already occurred. Or they relate to large numbers of essentially the same event. As a manager looks further into the future, accurately predictable closed change declines in relative importance, while less reliably predictable contained change increases in relative importance. The control feedback loop shown in Figure 3.1 still applies. The decline in forecasting reliability does not require any significant rethink of what we mean by control. We can continue to apply the same conceptual framework, simply extending the time horizon covered.

But, the choice element of control necessarily becomes less precise. Objectives become missions and broad qualitative goals, which cannot be as time definite as is the case in closed change. Routes to objectives also become vaguer, taking the form of broad grand designs, based on forecasts of most likely outcomes or forecasts of a number of scenarios. This is long-range or corporate planning which seeks to anticipate change. The discovery element of control also becomes less precise. It becomes a more qualitative form of environmental and organizational scanning and analysis. This provides the information upon which the long-term plans are based. Discovering the consequence of the planned actions taken can be no more than a judgemental check on whether outcomes seem to be in accordance with the plan. Because the time span of the plan is long term, one cannot wait for that long-term outcome in order to take corrective action – it will be too late. Any corrective action is based therefore not on an actual deviation from plan, as in closed situations, but on a qualitative judgement. Ensuing action is more likely to take the form of a change in goals and routes, than is the case in closed change.

The emphasis is firmly on the choice element, clearly defined as planning. In contained situations, control is still driven by specific purpose. Effectiveness is measured in terms of goal achievement. But adaptation to change is no longer nearly automatic and the learning element is somewhat more important – it is adaptive learning about the means by which goals can be achieved. Control is still largely a rational decision-making process and it is still directly applied to the change which is to be managed – it is about securing foreseeable outcomes. Control does not mean something fundamentally different to what it means in closed change situations.

And that is what makes it completely inappropriate as a method of controlling a successful business over the long term where open-ended change is important. In open-ended change, outcomes are unpredictable and the planning/monitoring loop requires predictability. Simply stretching out the short interval control form over time will not do.[2] When it comes to open-ended change, we require a different understanding of strategic control. Strategic control based on long-term plans does not take account of the unpredictable nature of open-ended change. Nor does it take account of the behaviour which great uncertainty and ill structured problems provoke in people. They then find it hard to identify the objectives they require before they can start to plan.

Both the short interval control appropriate to closed situations and the long-term planning form which can only work in contained situations, rely on quantification, the use of probability concepts, forecasting and simulating. Both short interval control and long-term planning rely on the ability to measure and to construct general models of how an organization and its markets work in a large number of specific circumstances. These models must be general in the sense that the same model applies to many specific circumstances – we do not have to keep changing the model with each new set of circumstances. If we did it would be impossible to plan. The purpose of such models is to yield reasonably specific information about the future to guide present actions. When such techniques and models fail in practice, we are advised to rely on visions of the future. But that too assumes that we can say something usefully specific about the future. Since open-ended situations are unique, specific changes with unknown long-term consequences, this too will not be possible. As soon as we leave closed and contained change, the models and techniques we use in these situations become suspect.

What form for open-ended change?

Control in open-ended situations in practice means something completely different, at a detailed operational level, from what it means in closed and contained situations.

In open-ended situations, the past is ambiguous – it requires acts of interpretation, understanding and agreement amongst those concerned with the change. When an acquisition fails to yield adequate profits, that may be due to having paid too much for it in the first place. Or it may have been due to failure to understand the culture difference between the two companies. It may have been due to inadequate appraisal of the quality of the new management. Or it may have been the consequence of unforeseen market changes. Managers will differ in their interpretations and those interpretations will affect the approach to the next acquisition, if there is one.

In open-ended situations, the future consequences are unknown and forecasting is totally impossible. For example, the outcome of setting up some joint venture in Poland in 1990 is unknown. Furthermore, the specific purpose to be achieved in relation to a particular set of changes is ambiguous and the preferences of the actors involved may be equivocal. When an express delivery company detects the competitive threat of fax machines to its letter delivery business, some managers may see it as simply another form of letter delivery into which they should diversify. Others may see it as a completely different business, primarily an electronic equipment business, which they should avoid. What the change means for the express delivery business is at first not clear and different managers have different preferences as to what should be done.

The whole situation being confronted is ill structured and accompanied by inadequate information; subjective information conditioned by values, beliefs and personal ambitions. Because we have problems in interpreting data and in applying statistical techniques in uniquely uncertain conditions, forecasting and simulation become problematic. Rational forms of decision making are inadequate. In open-ended change situations we do not know the consequences of what we are doing until we do it.

How do successful organizations in fact control when they do not know what they are doing? How do they control when they do not know where they are going? They do what mankind has always done. They go on voyages of exploration. They conduct experiments. They do something. They act. But they also reflect on what they have done and are doing and try to attach meaning to such actions. And they do this to increase their knowledge, to learn. The situation is such that a specific purpose, and the route to it, cannot be decided in advance. We simply do not know enough to do so. Instead there is a general purpose, that of learning through reflection and experimentation about specific purpose and the means of achieving it. The route to the general purpose is the creation of those conditions which make it possible for the organization to learn. In open-ended change the choosing element of control is at first an indirect, general one. It has to do with designing the right conditions for discussion, reflection, learning and experimentation. In this manner, behaviour at an organizational level can be described as controlled, even though at the group or individual level it may be somewhat haphazard in the early stages of dealing with open-ended change.

Control in open-ended change situations, then, is nothing more or less than a process of organizational learning which takes place in groups of people. It is therefore also a political process because power is used by some to persuade or force others to accept particular points of view; and as such, control in open-ended situations is fundamentally different to control in closed or contained situations.

Figure 3.2 depicts the elements of control in open-ended situations. It shows the connecting loops between elements of organizational learning and politics.

How do managers discover, choose and act when they are confronted with open-ended change? Consider first the phase of detecting and selecting issues shown in Figure 3.2.

Discovering: detecting and selecting issues

What managers are trying to discover in open-ended situations is always ambiguous, unclear and often the small beginnings of some change

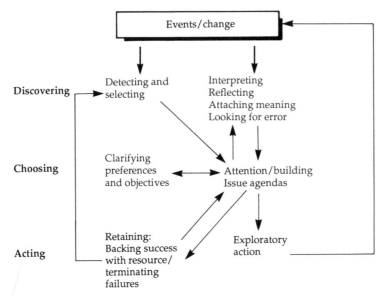

Figure 3.2 *The control feedback loop in open-ended change*

which could eventually have substantial consequences. They cannot therefore use pre-arranged techniques or procedures. They cannot include the discovery of open-ended change in anyone's job description because it is too nebulous. It is dangerous to confine the discovery of open-ended change to the top levels of the management hierarchy because small beginnings are more likely to be noticed first by those lower down in the hierarchy at the front line of the business. The detection of open-ended changes and the initial selection of those to be pursued therefore have to rely upon the spontaneous initiative and intuition of individuals anywhere and everywhere in the organization. People detect open-ended changes when they are sensitive to anomalies and different interpretations of what is going on. People in a company will be more prone to detect open-ended change when they are different from each other; when they have different cultural values; when they reason from different basic assumptions; when they use different mental models to interpret what is happening; when they have the time to do all this. The beginning of strategic control, the creative response to open-ended change, therefore lies in spontaneity and difference. This will only happen if the context within which people work encourages such behaviour. Small changes in the context provided by attitudes and time pressures can easily affect what people notice. Right at the start, control in open-ended situations, real strategic control, is influenced by chance.

These points are illustrated by the beginnings of the float glass process which Pilkington developed in the late 1950s, a development which transformed the glass industry world-wide. Around mid-1952 Sir Alistair Pilkington was able to do some thinking because, according to his own account, he was bored. He had been very busy in production operations but had then been transferred to work under the technical director where he had much less to occupy him. He became aware that it would be desirable to make plate glass directly from the molten state, rather than polishing and grinding cold glass. An idea of how this might be done came to him while he was helping his wife wash the dishes:

> ... the idea ... had nothing to do with the act of washing up. It was just one of those moments when your mind is able to think and then it was sort of 'bang' – like that. Indeed the final solution was very similar to the original idea, though it was an awfully long journey from concept to making saleable glass.[3]

Individuals notice some discrepancy between what is happening and what is desirable, or what they previously expected, and begin to pay attention to it. They intuitively put together bits and pieces of information, perhaps from a number of different sources, to form an outline of some issue. This usually does not take the form of a clearly defined issue or some vision of a future state. It is more likely to take the form of a rather vague perception of some problem or opportunity, some ambiguous challenge or half-formed aspiration. The process of communicating and discussing with others will begin to shape the vague perception so that it begins to take the form of a potential issue, aspiration or intention. Sir Alistair Pilkington saw the conceptual outline of a possible new process. Although it turned out to be the right concept, it need not have been. And he did not know how it would be done, how long it would take, whether it would be a success, how much it would cost, or what impact it would have on the glass industry. But in this case clarity on the issues did emerge early on. If we examine how, in the early 1960s, IBM developed a fully compatible new range of products to replace completely its old disparate range, the issue took longer to clarify. It seems to have emerged from a number of unsuccessful product developments, together with observations by top executive Learson that customers were looking for compatibility and that IBM was wasting resources on separate software developments for incompatible products.[4]

Gaining attention and building issue agendas

To move from discovery to choice, individuals who have detected and selected the outline of an open-ended issue must then attract organizational attention for it. And this is a political process. The person with an issue must use influence or authority to build political support for it and ensure that it enters the communication arenas of those who have the power to back its progress with resources. Sir Alistair Pilkington was able to obtain the rapid approval of the Pilkington board to pursue his idea. It rapidly became an issue on the strategic agenda of those at the top of the organization. The choice element of strategic control therefore centres on the organization's strategic issue agenda. (We move from detecting and selecting to agenda building in Figure 3.2 above.) That agenda consists of all those issues, aspirations, intentions and challenges which are under active consideration by those who have the power to progress them. The issue agenda is dynamic – it changes continually as executives switch effective attention from one set of issues to another. At Pilkington the float glass issue remained on the agenda for 12 years, but there were many others which came and went – public flotation, management succession, strikes, other product developments, acquisitions and so on.

The continuing process of building strategic issue agendas is spontaneous and it depends upon people having different perceptions and values. At some critical point in the life of an issue, sufficient consensus and commitment to it emerges and a choice is made to progress it. What happens to a particular issue on the agenda depends upon the context within which it is being considered. It depends upon the time pressures on executives, on the range of other functions and issues they have to attend to, on the personalities of those involved, on the dynamics of their interaction with each other. Small changes in these contextual factors can lead to one issue being dropped or deferred while another is progressed. The initial choice element in strategic control is therefore also affected by chance.

Exploratory action

Because the long-term outcome of an identified open-ended issue cannot be predicted, the action element of strategic control takes the form of exploration. The initial action is one of carrying out an exploratory experiment using a task force or multi-discipline project team. (We move from building agendas to carrying out exploratory actions as shown in Figure 3.2 above.) So, the issue may be one of geographic expansion and the exploratory action may be that of stationing two executives in a foreign market to carry out business ventures on a small scale. In the case of Pilkington's development of float glass, a task force was put together and the experiments lasted for 12 years. The task force was learning to control the quality of the glass through a series of trials and errors. On one occasion, an important discovery was made because a piece of equipment was broken. This and other discoveries were described by Sir Alistair as pure, fantastic strokes of luck.

The exploratory action will itself cause changes and provoke new issues. Through this action the company begins to discover what the potential consequences might be. The information is fed back into the choice stage through the issue agenda as top executives discuss whether to proceed with the experiments or not. The company is learning in real time about the consequences of what it is doing. Executives reflect upon what is happening, they question and discuss it, they search for errors in what is being done (see Figure 3.2 above). In this manner they clarify their preferences, aspirations, intentions and objectives. When they come to look back at what happened, they may well describe the form the issue has taken at this point as a vision. It is at this point too that more rational planning processes may well become practically possible.

Backing success

Where exploratory actions show promise of success and aspirations take on a clear form, the corporation may choose to back the exploration with further resource. We can then talk about the emergence of a new strategic direction. In the Pilkington case Sir Alistair recalled:

> . . . it is difficult to locate an exact moment when the decision was made. It was sometime during the discussions about whether to put down a production scale plant. There were no detailed calculations of such things as the ultimate capital implications of the process or its effects on our overall capital structure. Nevertheless, over a period of time a consensus crystallized with great clarity. This evolved from a series of formal and informal discussions . . . [5].

The production scale plant eventually worked and the glass industry was transformed. In doing all this, Pilkington created its own new market environment. Because the new process reduced capital intensity and because Pilkington decided to license the process rather than hold on to it, the structure of the glass industry changed. It changed from an industry in which there were few competitors to an industry in which competition was heightened. The new process led to new and more widespread ways of using plate glass. It affected the sheet glass market as well. And if Pilkington had decided not to license the process, as it well might have done, the outcome would have been different. If Pilkington had aborted the experiments after a few years, the outcome would have been different. There was nothing pre-ordained about what happened.

Retaining the memory

As the managers of a company move continually around this strategic control loop, they in effect build an organizational memory (see Figure 3.2 above). This history of which methods and kinds of project worked and which did not becomes embodied in the company's recipe. It becomes the culture, the basic assumptions which then heavily affect what new open-ended issues will be detected and selected. It provides one of the most important principles governing the selection of open-ended changes for attention. The organization's retained memory is therefore a principal source of stability in the strategic control loop. But that retained memory is also the principal blockage to the detection of the new. Consequently, the organizational learning process is a highly complex one. It has to involve the continual questioning of the recipe, the basic assumptions, the culture. It is these things which govern how the organization learns. The organization therefore has to learn in real time about the consequences of what it is doing. And it has to keep learning in real time how to learn – that is, it has continually to question its culture, or shared implicit models. There is no general model to apply to all specific cases – each new specific case requires the development of a new model. Learning is changing old models and developing new ones.

A political learning process

Strategic control, then, is a political learning process which depends in its crucial initial stages on spontaneity, informality and difference. The context of time pressures, power, personality and group dynamics within which it occurs is of major importance. Small changes in context could have a major impact on what happens to an issue. Strategic direction is then significantly dependent upon chance. But it also depends upon the intuition, initiative and determined endeavours of managers to create their own environments. The outcome depends upon the intertwining of chance and intention. Top managers create the context within which the spontaneous process occurs, through the manner in which they exercise power. Top managers create the context, identify and explore issues, shape the organization's strategic issue agenda and back success with resource.

Control in open-ended situations is as much about coherent behaviour as it is in closed situations. But the detailed meaning of coherent behaviour changes. In closed situations, it is orderly movement towards a fixed objective applying the same general model, the same list of specific prescriptions, to many specific situations. In open-ended situations it is more complex. At an overall level there is a pattern to control in the sense that it follows a clear sequence through detection to agenda building, to exploratory action, to the emergence of new strategic direction. But at the specific level it is disorderly in the sense that it depends upon different perspectives and individual spontaneity. At a specific level it depends partly upon chance and the specific outcome is therefore unpredictable. There is no general model for many specific situations. Each specific situation is new and requires a new model. Developing new models is organizational learning.

The whole process of control in open-ended situations is one of organizational learning to cope with ambiguity and uncertainty. But it is not wild haphazard action. It is not just any action, the bigger the better. It is the combined action and reflection, conditioned by retained memory of what did or did not work in the past, which is organizational learning. Overall stability is sustained by retained memory, and by interpretation and reflection. And since that retained memory can block new perception, it is part of the learning process continually to question it. Non-algorithmic processes of judgement, intuition and reflection conditioned by retained memory, enable the organization to create adequate responses to a turbulent environment. Stability is also sustained by unequal political power. The organization cannot do just anything because the support of those at the top is required to pay attention and back experiments and success with resource. The whole control process is one of interactive, creative learning and political action.

But while there is some stability due to reflection, retained memory and power, the activity of control by creative, interactive learning is not orderly in any clear cut, traditionally accepted sense. It is in many respects disorderly and confusing; it is certainly felt to be so by the individuals involved. While there are elements of stability at the macro level of the organization, there is considerable disorder at the micro level of innovative individuals and groups.

Creative, not proactive or reactive

A common response to this description of the nature of strategic control is to say that it is reactive. Underlying this response is the assumption that the important changes are those occurring out there in the environment. The environment is seen as a distinct and separate reality outside the business organization itself. There is furthermore the assumption that the organization secures success most effectively by anticipating the environmental change, by forecasting it and then doing something to adapt before the change actually occurs. The most effective and desirable approach is then the proactive one. Failing that, the organization has to fall back on reaction to the change once it occurs and that may be too late. The role of the organization is to adapt to given environmental change by being proactive or failing that reactive. The next chapter questions this assumption. It suggests that the environment is not simply given. How an organization's environment unfolds is significantly affected by what that organization itself does. Pilkington did not adapt to an environment that would have been there no matter what it did. It created an environment. How the environment unfolds depends on many actions, both large and small, which the people in an organization take. Because of this we cannot anticipate the long-term changes because we cannot know what they will be. Neither can we simply react to a given change because what we do affects what happens. What we are really doing is interacting with others in the environment and this can be either creative or destructive. The process of organizational learning just described as the form of control we adopt when we deal with open-ended issues is therefore creative, not reactive or proactive. Through this process we are actually partially changing our environment and learning what that change means. We are taking part in creating our own future which will also depend upon chance.

Key features of control in open-ended situations

The points to note about the meaning of control in open-ended change situations are:

- Control is indirect rather than direct. The change is too ambiguous to allow the setting of even vague objectives, let alone the forecasting of outcomes. The control elements of discovery, choice and action have to be put in place not by clear predetermined procedures, but by establishing the conditions in which open-ended change can be explored and learned about.
- Control becomes an organizational learning experience in the fullest possible sense. It is learning about purpose, aspirations, values, beliefs and meanings as well as about the means of achieving anything. In open-ended situations we create meaning and discover new things. We alter old mental models and develop new ones.
- Control is political activity. Learning in the sense of discovering preferences and agreeing objectives is accomplished by political interaction between people in groups.
- Control as coherent behaviour emerges at an organizational level from what can be haphazard, experimental behaviour at an individual level. Confusion and ambiguity at the individual level is handled spontaneously by individuals to produce periodic consensus and commitment. Control is therefore a 'split' phenomenon; it may be apparent at one level but absent at another, apparent at one time but not another.
- Control in open-ended situations is creative interaction. It cannot be anticipation and it is not reaction. It relies on intuition, reasoning by analogy, judgement and experience, rather than analytical techniques and models, or step-by-step thinking.

Simultaneous application of different control forms

To survive, a business must sustain competitive advantage. Today that requires continuing innovation which is creative interaction with environments. To do this, all businesses have to accommodate the impact of change on their basic flows of orders and requisitions, inputs and outputs, and money. And all businesses face disturbances to those flows caused by change which is simultaneously arising in different change situations.

Different change situations require different forms of control. All companies therefore have to apply different forms of control to the same business simultaneously if they are to succeed. Change arising in closed situations has consequences which nowadays extend over the next few months and the control form which works is short interval control – a control form which is capable of being applied as a fixed system of control. Change in contained situations can be accommodated by extending the principles of short interval control – a fixed control system which also uses forecasting and analysis to produce plans, albeit with less precision. Nowadays such contained change has consequences which do not extend all that far into the future for most businesses.

In addition to, and at the same time as, closed and contained change, all businesses face disturbance generated by change in open-ended situations. And change in these circumstances has consequences which primarily impact a year or two hence, but can also impact on the very short term. It is here that we find the cutting edge of strategic control. The really difficult control problem lies in accommodating change in open-ended situations. Parts of the control system itself have to be adjusted and even created as control actually proceeds. Control is in fact largely permissive in the sense that it enables creative learning.

An even more difficult problem which almost all businesses will increasingly face is this: it is necessary simultaneously to control in both closed and open-ended situations. This requires combining fixed, directing short interval control operated largely in institutionalized communication arenas, with a flexible, opportunistic, political system which permits creative learning and operates largely through spontaneous communication arenas.[6]

First, consider the different demands made by the two forms of control. They are summarized in Figure 3.3.

Requirements for control in closed situations

Control in closed situations, taken in isolation from the need to practise any other form of control, requires:

CLOSED CHANGE			OPEN ENDED CHANGE
Analytical/formal	Control process	Intuitive	
Planning	Control element focus	Discovery	
Tight/fixed	Objectives constraints	Loose/tentative	
Short term	Objectives time frame	Discovering long term	
Tight	Resources	Slack	
Restricted/status/duty	Participation factors	Open/trust/contribution	
Few institutionalized	Communication arenas	Many spontaneous	
Authority/responsibility	Role attributes	Initiative/collaboration	
Position/resources	Role constraints	Power/personality	
Parochial	Role perceptions	Holistic	
Directing	Role relationships	Facilitating	
Specific skills/knowledge	Matching people to roles	Wide competencies	
Personal performance	Rewards	Team related	
Conservative	Culture	Radical	
Clear hierarchy	Organization structure	Clear hierarchy	
Unequal	Power distribution	Unequal	

Figure 3.3 *Tensions created by simultaneously applying different forms of control*

- The application of formal, analytical, instructing processes to the elements of control with the prime emphasis on the planning element.
- Monitoring and corrective action within comprehensive planning.
- Objectives which are short term and fixed. They have to be tightly constrained in that they are precise and taken literally.
- Tight resource constraints to achieve efficiency.
- Participation in communication arenas which is related to status and duty, restricted to the selected few with immediately relevant contributions.
- Relatively few communication arenas which are institutionalised.
- Roles of people carrying out control tasks primarily defined in terms of authority and responsibility, being constrained by formal position in the hierarchy as well as by resource availability.
- Role perceptions which are parochial in that people see their roles in terms of the part of the organization in which they are operating.
- Relationships between one role and another which are primarily of the directing kind. People are given objectives and instructed to take corrective action.

- Selection and development of people, using criteria of specific expertise, specific bodies of knowledge and a limited number of personal skills.
- Rewards which are closely related to individual short term performance.
- Cultures which are conservative with relatively unquestioning acceptance of objectives and instructions.
- Organizational structures in which hierarchical levels and managerial jobs are clearly defined.
- Power which is unequally distributed.

These are the requirements of the ideal short interval control system being applied in a very orderly environment and in isolation from the need to practise any other form of control. The practice will never be that mechanistic, partly because of the human behaviour factor, partly because some events will still be unforeseen and partly because other forms of control have to be used at the same time.

Requirements for control in open-ended situations

Control in open-ended situations, taken in isolation from the need to practise any other form of control, imposes requirements which are diametrically opposed to those of control in closed change situations. Requirements are:

- Individual initiative based on intuition and judgement, the use of informal rules, procedures and modes of communication, the use of persuasion and negotiation.
- Discovering small changes occurring now and having important long-term consequences. And discovering preferences and objectives in relation to such changes. Planning, in its comprehensive, grand design sense, is no longer possible. Action is opportunistic and exploring.
- Long-term objectives have to be discovered and cannot be tightly defined in advance of action. Experimentation demands tentative, changeable, loosely defined objectives.
- Sufficient resource slack to allow the formation of spontaneous communication arenas and the exploration of issues.
- Participation in communication arenas on the basis of trust, mutual contribution and gain.
- Many communication arenas which emerge spontaneously.
- Roles with attributes of collaboration and initiative, constrained by power, personality and organizational culture.
- Perceptions of roles which are holistic in the sense that people are more concerned with the good of the whole organization than with

the good of a part of it alone. They have to be concerned with integration and synergy, with the effectiveness of the parts functioning together.

- Relationships between roles which are facilitating in order to allow the surfacing of whatever inadequate information is available, to allow the experimentation and innovation which is central to control in open-ended situations.
- Selecting and developing people where the criteria are difficult, to identify personal competences rather than specific skills and knowledge. It means management development which seeks to develop intuitive, team-working competences above specific analytical and instructional skills.
- Rewards related not to short-term individual performance but to team performance and willingness to experiment.
- Radical, pluralistic cultures to foster the questioning of objectives, perceptions and actions. Shared conservative cultures block the kind of control required in open-ended situations.
- Organizational structures based on clear hierarchies and job descriptions. Spontaneous communication cannot be built into structures, but has to rely on political processes. Clear structures provide necessary constraints on the spontaneity.
- Power which is unequally distributed since this also provides boundaries around spontaneity.

In most respects therefore, short interval control in isolation and control in open-ended situations, taken in isolation, demand the diametric opposite of organization and behaviour. Only with regard to organizational structure and power distribution do the requirements of the two control forms coincide.

Successful organizations apply both forms of control

Of course these different forms of control cannot be taken in isolation; both have to be applied simultaneously. Control in its total sense therefore imposes severe tension on a business and its management, especially since both forms compete for scarce management time. Control is not just about accommodating the impact of change on the basic business flows; in practical terms it is even more about resolving control tension. And this is why we observe in practice that the handling of strategic issues is always accompanied by even more attention to what needs to be done within the business than to what is likely to happen in the future out in the marketplace. Strategic issues, those generated by open-ended change situations, tend to disrupt any balance which management has struck between the extremes of the control tensions. New balances have to be struck.

Control in the modern business world is a continuous balancing act; an ongoing search for an appropriate way of relieving control tension. And that control tension is itself an open-ended situation which can only be resolved by learning and political processes. This juxtaposition of very different change situations puts into context the polarity between the two predominant models of management and organization, that between mechanistic and organic business systems. The former is appropriate to short interval control in closed change and the latter is an interpretation of political learning in open-ended situations. There is no question of choosing between them; both must be applied to achieve success. The choice is not between one or the other; the choices relate to how they are to be combined to secure effective total control.

This conclusion is supported by an impressive study of differences between Japanese and US companies by Kagono and others.[7] They conducted an in-depth study of 19 Japanese companies (including NEC, Hitachi, Toyota, Sumitomo, Suntory and Matsushita) and a similar number of US companies (including General Motors, Sears, 3M, Texas Instruments and IBM). These in-depth studies were then followed by questionnaires completed by 227 US and 291 Japanese companies, all in the late 1970s. The samples were representative in terms of company size and industrial distribution.

The study identified significant differences between Japanese and US companies in terms of organizational form and strategic orientation. The former more frequently adopt the organic model of organization with flexible structures based on group dynamics and they tend to pursue operations-led strategies. The latter more frequently adopt the mechanistic form of organization, based on what the authors call bureaucratic dynamics, and product-led strategies. The authors ascribed this difference to the different environments in which the US and Japanese companies operated. Most interestingly of all, however, they then compared groups of high performers in the US with high performers in Japan and they also compared groups of low performers in both countries with each other. They summarized their results as follows:

> These findings suggest that the combination of group dynamics and product orientation, typified by entrepreneurial, creative companies in variable environments, outperforms other combinations in both the United States and Japan...
>
> The findings also suggest that a symbiotic combination which includes some elements of bureaucratic dynamics and the operations orientation as well as those of group dynamics and product orientation, can be more appropriate than the pure combination of group dynamics and product orientation. This is especially so in variable environments.[8]

So, while the 'typical' approach in Japan differs from that in the USA, the most successful companies in both countries adopt similar styles which combine mechanistic and organic approaches.

Can we expect the same managers to control in both of these ways? Can we expect them to operate in both formalised hierarchies and loose networks? It means that the same person must function effectively in the morning as a member of a formal hierarchy participating at an institutionalized meeting and then function just as effectively in an informal network of colleagues, from different hierarchical levels, over lunch. In the morning we obey the rules of the hierarchy and over lunch we ignore them. The possibility of this occurring depends quite simply on people's attitudes and it is in fact quite common to find this switch in behaviour. We are, most of us, used to participating in different groups where different rules apply. Control tension is not resolved by choosing one form of control as opposed to another, but by alternating between one and the other and also by simultaneously applying different forms of control in different parts of the organization.[9]

Conclusion: what a dynamic model should explain about control

We know from observation that successful companies apply different forms of control in different circumstances. We see managers utilize short interval feedback control loops in which they prepare plans, monitor performance and take corrective action. Many successful companies also prepare long-term corporate plans. This chapter has argued that these rational short interval and long-term planning approaches are appropriate in the reasonably predictable circumstances of closed and contained change. But we also know from observation that managers frequently do not use long-term plans they may have prepared. Instead they handle the strategic issues arising in open-ended change on a one-by-one basis. The manner in which they handle them is highly political and is accompanied by confusion and conflict. Personality and group dynamics clearly influence the process and the outcome of that activity. Strategic choices are to some extent dependent upon the context of personality, group dynamic, time pressures and other factors. Managers can be observed to explore the future in trial-and-error ways through which they innovate and learn about that future. And we know that the outcome of the strategic choice we make and enact depends to some extent on chance or luck. What happens to us as individuals and as organizations is the result of our own intentions and efforts, intertwined with chance events.

A useful dynamic model of how business organizations function would have to incorporate all the key features outlined in the above paragraph. It would have to say something about how organizations learn and about the nature and role of politics in choosing and acting. It should explain how instability arises and what part it plays in choosing and acting, what part spontaneity and difference play in control and what part creative intention and chance play in outcomes. A useful dynamic model would be one which includes stability and instability, uniformity and variety. It would be an explanation of how choices are made and enacted in a continuing loop through time. It would establish the conditions which are necessary for the effective practise of totally different forms of control at the same time.

Part Two will examine how far today's most prominent models of managing and organizing meet these requirements. It will argue that those models fall far short of what is required. Part Three will then present some insights into complex dynamic systems from the natural sciences which it will be argued provide a far more useful explanation. But before that we need to consider what a useful dynamic model would need to explain about the relationship between a business organization and its environments.

References

1   Weick, K., (1979), *Organizational Psychology*, Addison-Wesley.
2   Stacey, R. D., (1990), *Dynamic Strategic Management for the 1990s*, Kogan Page.
3   Quinn, J., (1988), Pilkington Brothers PLC, in Quinn, J., Mintzberg, H., James, R., *The Strategy Process*, Prentice-Hall p. 782.
4   Quinn, J., The IBM Case A: The 360 Decision, in Quinn, J., Mintzberg, H., James, R., op. cit.
5   Quinn, J., Pilkington Brothers PLC, in Quinn, J., Mintzberg, H., James, R., op. cit., p. 785.
6   These points are discussed in more detail in Stacey, R. D., op. cit.
7   Kagono, T., Nonaka, I., Sakakibura, K., Okumura, A., (1985), *Strategic vs Evolutionary Management: A US – Japan Comparison of Strategy and Organisation*, North Holland Elsevier.
8   Kagono, T., et al., op. cit., p. 213.
9   Weick, K., op. cit.

4 The mechanisms driving business development

The last two chapters have been concerned with the nature of change and the forms of control which it is possible for managers to practise in what are fundamentally different change situations. As they stand in the present and look out into the future, managers face a spectrum of change situations. At one extreme of that spectrum, the consequences of what is happening to them and of what they are doing are close to certainty – predictable closed change. At the other extreme of that spectrum, consequences are very far from certain – open-ended change.

The manner in which managers make choices and act, the form of organizational control and development they practise, is dictated by this spectrum of change situations. Close to certainty it is possible to make choices using the rational, analytical decision-making mode. The development of the organization over time is then controlled by a feedback loop in which deviations from plan are fed into subsequent actions, the outcomes of which are then compared with plan. Further deviations again feed into later actions. The development of the organization over time is driven by a planning and monitoring control loop. And it is quite clearly a damping loop in that it keeps pulling the organization back to a planned path.

Far from certainty, the development of an organization is driven by more complex feedback loops in which changes are discovered, pressed upon the attention of the powerful, discussed, shaped, and explored through experimental action. That experimental action feeds back into further discoveries which feed into later actions. Here the development of the organization is driven by political and learning feedback control loops. And these are quite clearly amplifying loops. They are the means of amplifying small changes so that the organization can do something about them.

Since almost all organizations face a wide spectrum of change situations, managers have to control and develop utilizing both feedback control loops at the same time, if they are to be successful. To design their actions, managers therefore need dynamic mental models which explain how these amplifying and damping feedback control loops operate and what consequences they generate.

But the feedback nature of organizations is far more widespread and basic than has so far been described. Feedback is not confined to control loops. This chapter will explore the proposition that business organizations are fundamentally sets of amplifying and damping, that is non-linear, feedback mechanisms. Useful models of business dynamics will be those which are built upon an understanding of the properties and consequences of non-linear feedback. And the key point here is whether those feedback mechanisms operate to produce stable equilibrium behaviour or whether success requires some form of non-equilibrium behaviour. Today's most prominent models of managing and organizing, to be discussed in Chapter 5, are firmly based on the assumption that business success is a stable state of equilibrium in which the organization adapts to its environment. The prescription is to design structures, systems and incentives to move the organization towards that orderly state of regular performance in which dynamic equilibrium with the environment is maintained. That prescription recognizes that even the most successful will not always achieve perfectly regular performance because all businesses will be affected by some unforeseeable events occurring in their environments. The conclusion to be drawn from this is that success is a state of regularity, unfortunately disturbed by irregularity due either to random shocks hitting a dynamically stable successful business or to management incompetence.

This chapter will argue that the whole view set out above is not consistent with the feedback nature of a business system. It will be argued that a useful dynamic model will explain success in business in terms of operating away from stable equilibrium states. Here organizations do not simply adapt to their environments. Instead, they creatively interact with those environments. A useful dynamic model of managing would then have to find some reason other than random shocks hitting a stable equilibrium business, to explain the irregular performance which even the most successful display. And this, as we shall see in the chapters in Part Three, has very important consequences for the manner in which managers should design their actions if they are to innovate successfully. The prescription will be to avoid stable equilibrium states. The key to this argument lies in the feedback nature of all business organizations.

Business organizations are feedback mechanisms

A business organization is a system in which performance achieved in one time period feeds into that of a subsequent period in a manner determined by the firm's decision-making processes and its relationships with the environment. Feedback means that a system now plays a continuing part in determining its own future in the sense that what it does now affects what happens to it in later periods. Decisions about investing in capital assets, either replacements or additions, boil down to allocating part of last period's profit to capital expenditure. That capital expenditure has an impact on this, or some subsequent, period's profit. The same applies to research and development expenditure, promotion and advertising, expanding the size of the sales force and so on. Since the results of one period heavily affect the results in subsequent periods, a business is clearly a set of feedback mechanisms.

Furthermore in a business the feedback mechanisms relate behaviour over time in a non-proportional or non-linear way. That is, performance now is sometimes an amplified and sometimes a damped version of that in previous periods. Performance can then be self-reinforcing and generate vicious and virtuous circles. For example, a backlog of orders undelivered could lead to flat out production with inadequate maintenance of plant. Plant breakdowns could then lead to even lower output and bigger backlogs.

The great importance and widespread presence, in business organizations, of non-linear feedback loops of one kind or another is quite apparent as soon as one considers examples of almost any organizational action, even the simplest. Consider a few such examples which should make it clear that non-linear feedback applies not only to control, but also to performance and to business behaviour generally.

Some examples of feedback in business

Senior managers of an insurance administration company meet to review budgets. Since profits are below budget, the managing director insists that costs be cut. The director of customer service decides that the easiest way to meet that demand is to stop using all temporary staff in his division. Consequently the number of unanswered telephone calls rises dramatically and the managing director gives a pert instruction to keep to the 5 per cent calls lost target. Managers in the the customer service departments comply by switching staff from replying to letters to answering calls. The letter backlog rises and the number of telephone calls also rises as irate customers telephone to ask where the reply to their letter is. Lost call targets are not achieved and letter backlogs continue to rise. A major client, dissatisfied with the administration of his insurance scheme, takes his business elsewhere. This is quite clearly a feedback sequence. It is non-linear and amplifying, since one action is leading to more than proportional reactions and consequences.

A new chief executive arrives at an old established company operating in a secure market niche. His style is highly aggressive and competitive. He launches repackaged products at lower prices, backed by an advertising campaign. The other companies in the market have no option but to change their cosy cooperative behaviour and they too start aggressive advertising campaigns, product launches and price cuts. The new chief executive becomes even more aggressive. Another non-linear feedback loop in which the chief executive is actually creating his own environment.

A new manager is appointed to a sales department. He concludes that it has in the past been run in far too lax a fashion and as a result the salesmen are lazy and sloppy. They spend too long with unimportant customers; they have too many pleasant chats with people in the design and production departments. So, he installs volume sales targets, daily reporting back to the office, and he aggressively tackles non-achievers. Volumes rise, but morale deteriorates, new sales leads decline, cross-fertilization of ideas to design and production staff ceases, customer satisfaction declines and sales volumes fall. Once again we have non-linear feedback loops between series of actions. Once again they are amplifying and once again the organizational actor is creating the environment.

We can conceive of other aspects of the organization in much the same way. Prices now are more often than not fixed by applying some inflation factor to the previous price, subject to the constraint provided by a judgement on what the market will bear. Or they are fixed by a constant mark-up on last period's inflation adjusted costs. Output level decision rules are frequently simple ones which relate this period's output to that achieved in the last period, subject to capacity constraints and market judgements. Or they are based on forecasts of sales which are in fact simple adjustments to last period's sales and therefore last period's output. Investment decisions for this period are frequently made on the basis of last period's profitability, subject to constraints of borrowing and cashflow. The structure of the organization in this period clearly depends on that of the previous period. Changes from one period to another run into diminishing returns and the more you change the structure in one period the more constrained you are, by human reactions, from changing it in the next. The relationships between people in a group, and between different groups in the organization, depend on the state of the relationships in the last period. Changes to improve effectiveness are built slowly from one period to another and they run into diminishing returns. We could go on to make similar points about most aspects of the organization, its culture, its reward systems, its management development programmes, the interactions between people and groups of people, and so on.

Self-reinforcing behaviour

It is extremely easy, then, to find a great many examples of self-reinforcing behaviour in which managers are playing a part in creating both the organization's future and its environments. Vicious and virtuous circles abound in business. The conclusion is that at a perfectly obvious level, an organization is a set of non-linear feedback mechanisms relating past performance to present performance in a continuing loop over time. The above examples also indicate that the behaviours and choices determining performance are themselves non-linear feedback loops.

This aspect of the nature of a business system has such important consequences, to be discussed in the chapters in Part Three, that it is worth examining it more carefully.

The nature of feedback

To see what feedback means, in more precise terms, consider a system very far indeed from the business world – a population of insects. The present size of an insect population depends upon, or feeds back into, its size in a previous period. The factor, or parameter, relating the present population to its past size, is a combination of the natural birth rate and the natural death rate. If the natural birth rate exceeds the natural death rate, then the parameter is positive and the population grows. Population growth is driven, or controlled by, increasing or decreasing the parameter. But that insect population exists within certain boundaries provided by its environment. The important boundary condition in this case is the limited supply of food. This eventually provides a constraint to the growth of the population. Sooner or later, starvation will cause the population to fall, even though the parameter fixed by the natural birth and death rates remains positive and constant. At some point the population will be small enough to survive on the limited food supply and it will start to grow again. This amplifying and damping effect is what we mean when we say that the feedback mechanism has a non-linear structure. And that non-linear structure occurs because there are boundary conditions; there are constraints upon the operation of the system. This kind of system means that the insect population is playing a continuing part in its own future and its behaviour is self-reinforcing. It displays virtuous circles of growth and vicious circles of decline.

If the natural birth rate only slightly exceeds the natural death rate, the parameter in the feedback mechanisms will be low and the population will grow only slowly. It will take some time for the level of the population to bump gently against the food constraint. At low values of the parameter in the feedback mechanism, the pattern of the behaviour of the population over time will be characterized by stability. But if the natural birth rate far exceeds the natural death rate, the parameter will be high. Population will grow explosively, crash into the food constraint, decline dramatically for some time and then grow again rapidly. At high parameter values the behaviour of the population over time will be characterized by explosive instability. The parameter in the feedback mechanisms determines the kind of behaviour the system displays.

Now consider the feedback mechanisms of a business to see how essentially the same points apply to the pattern of business performance over time.

Feedback in performance

At the most obvious level, any business organization is what it does. It is an inflow of orders translated into a outflow of requisitions for materials and labour; an inflow of those materials and labour to which value is added to produce outputs of product sales; all accompanied by flows of money. And one of those flows is profit. All those flows can be measured as performance indicators. And every element of all those flows, every performance indicator, is driven by a feedback mechanism as we will now go on to show.

The result of any business activity in a given time period is some inflow of cash. That cash inflow provides the funding for the expenditure in a subsequent period, necessary to generate a further cash inflow. So, what the business did during a previous period ($t - 1$), results in a cash inflow which it then uses to fund an inflow of material and labour in this period (t). Expenditure on materials and labour in this period then enables production and sales which lead to the inflow of cash for this period. And that will fund the expenditure of the next period. This is of course a feedback loop and it is depicted in Figure 4.1.

Conducting a business is moving around this loop. The same kind of feedback loop applies to profit. The profit which is earned in the last period plays an important part in the decision to spend money in this period, on all the elements of working capital, on advertising, on the sales force, on research and development and so on. Expenditure is related to previous profits through decision rules. And that expenditure generates

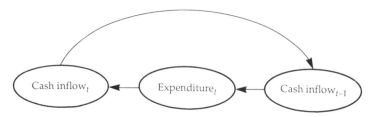

Figure 4.1   *The cash flow feedback*

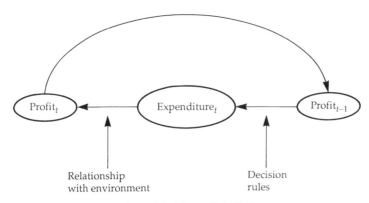

Figure 4.2 *The profit feedback*

subsequent profit because customers buy the product. Subsequent profits are thus linked to current expenditure through relationships with people and organizations in the environment. And profit in this period is fed back into expenditure in the next. Profit too is driven by a feedback mechanism and the link between profit in one period and another is provided by the decision rules managers use and the relationships between the organization and its environments. That link is what we mean by the parameter in the feedback mechanism. This mechanism is depicted in Figure 4.2.

Decision rules

To see what kinds of profit performance pattern this feedback mechanism will generate, we need to look more carefully at the decision rules and environmental relationships which determine the value of the parameter. It is this which will determine whether profit performance is stable or unstable. In general, the decision rules we observe managers using in practice are such that as profit increases, more is spent on working capital, capital investments, advertising and so on. This is in order to expand a profitable business. The decision rules may be simple proportional, or straight line, rules. Some constant percentage of profit may be ploughed back into each expenditure category. But, more typically, we find that as profits rise, expenditure on working capital and other expenditure categories first rises more than proportionally and then levels off – a reflection of the product life cycle. The relationship takes some non-linear form rather than a linear or straight line form. This relationship is depicted in Figure 4.3.

Two decision curves are shown in Figure 4.3 to illustrate different degrees of responsiveness in the decision rule. The rule may be such that as profits rise, expenditure is increased only gradually. This is the curve labelled B. Here managers do not rapidly expand their business when

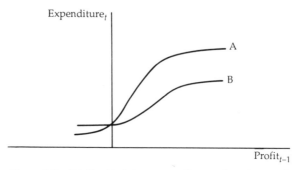

Figure 4.3 *Relationship between expenditure and previous profit*

profits are increasing. They adopt a more cautious approach, waiting to see whether the increase is likely to be sustained. But other managers will respond rapidly to enlarge the size of the business as profits rise. This is the decision curve A which slopes upwards more steeply. And in this case the feedback link between profit in one period and another will be more sensitive than it will be for the managers using the less responsive decision rule. A profit increase now will feed more rapidly into subsequent profits, because the expenditure decisions are more responsive. That is, the parameter in the profit feedback mechanism will rise as the decision rules are made more responsive. As the decision rules are changed, as the proportions ploughed back change, so will the parameter in the profit feedback mechanism.

All this says nothing about how the decisions are made. Managers may plan to plough back some proportion of profit into working capital, based on their forecast of future demand and their analyses of different options open to them. Or they may do it by entrepreneurial trial and error. Or they may use a simple rule of thumb. They may decide to plough back more than the total profit utilizing their borrowing capacity which will depend on past profit history. However they do it, and whatever the proportion, there is always the plough back of profit which links previous profit to current expenditure and the proportion ploughed back is the result of the decisions made.

Relationships with the environment

While the link between previous profit and current expenditure is provided by the decision rules, that between current expenditure and subsequent profit is through relationships with the environment. These relationships must then also play a part in determining the parameter of the profit feedback mechanism. In general the relationship between what we spend on, say, working capital in this period and subsequent profit, is such that profits first increase as we spread fixed costs. But sooner or later

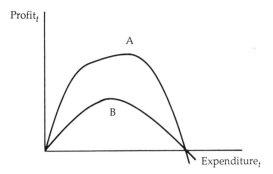

Figure 4.4 *Relationship between profit and expenditure*

profits will decline as we increase expenditure, because we will have to reduce prices to sell more and eventually we will saturate the market. This means that the relationship between expenditure and profit in this period is not a straight line. It too is non-linear. This general relationship is depicted in Figure 4.4.

Once again two curves depicting the relationship with the environment are shown in the figure. These illustrate different degrees of responsiveness to the product offering which results from expenditure on working capital, advertising and so on. So, curve B describes the situation where the customers respond slowly to the increased offering. Curve A describes the situation where the customers are far more responsive, allowing the business to increase its prices faster and sell more, with consequent larger profits. Because its customers are more responsive to what it is being offered, company A will find that a profit increase now feeds more rapidly through to profit levels in the next period. The feedback loop is more sensitive. The parameter linking profit over time is higher. So, as the environment becomes more responsive the parameter value in the profit feedback mechanism increases. As customers change what they want more rapidly and as they become more demanding, the parameter fluctuates more.

The profit feedback mechanism becomes more sensitive in the sense that profit now feeds more rapidly into profit later on, as the decision rules and the environment become more responsive. That is to say, the parameter in the feedback mechanism rises as the decision rules and the environment become more responsive. The more volatile the decision-making process and the relationships with the environment, the more the parameter will fluctuate. Furthermore, because the decision rules and the relationships with the environment take a non-linear form, it follows that the feedback link between profit in one period and the next is also non-linear.

Output feedback

We can explain the link between output in one period and the next in much the same way. Part of the output of last period will have been siphoned off to satisfy orders placed in that period. The rest feeds into the inventories available for this period. Or, if orders are very high output feeds into order backlogs, a negative inventory. Changes in inventories and backlogs in this period are thus linked to output in the last period through relationships with people and organizations in the environment and the orders they place. They are linked by customer behaviour and patterns of demand. And those changes in the levels of inventories and backlogs play an important part in deciding what the level of output is to be in this period. Output now is then linked to changes in inventories and backlogs through decision rules. And of course the output of this period feeds into changes in the inventories or backlogs of the next period. Once again we have a feedback mechanism, this time driving output over time in which the parameter is determined by environmental relationships and the decision-making process. This is depicted in Figure 4.5.

The first link in the output feedback is that between previous output and changes in inventories or backlogs. As demand rises, as the markets become more responsive to the product offering, changes in inventories or backlogs will be bigger. For any given decision rules, bigger backlogs or bigger inventory reductions will lead to bigger output adjustments in this period, subject to capacity constraints. The parameter connecting output last time to output this time will therefore rise; the feedback mechanism will become more sensitive. The next link, that between inventories / backlogs and current output is through the decision rules. The more responsive the decision rules, the more rapidly current output levels are affected by previous output levels through their impact on inventories and backlogs. The output feedback mechanism becomes more sensitive, its parameter rises. And this mechanism is also non-linear because of

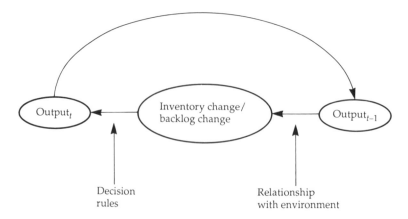

Figure 4.5 *The output feedback*

capacity constraints and because as customers take more of the product they want smaller and smaller additional amounts of it.

So output, profit and cashflow are all driven by non-linear feedback mechanisms. Actions and events in the last period feed into actions and events in this period. And actions and events in this period will feed into the next in amplifying and damping ways because the feedback is non-linear. The parameters in all these mechanisms will rise as the environment becomes more responsive and as the decision rules become more responsive. Higher parameter values means that the feedback is more sensitive; it all happens faster.

Similar reasoning to that applied to cashflow, profit and output can be applied to every other performance indicator of a business and the results are always the same. Every performance indicator is always a feedback mechanism. This follows from two simple facts. First, a business is an interconnected system in which every input and output element is ultimately connected to every other. Second, there are time lags in the adjustment of any one to another. Consequently every element in the input and output flows has to be related to its own past value in a manner interconnected with some other element. And all these feedbacks have two important features in common. First, the feedbacks are all non-linear because business systems are constrained. Second, the parameters always depend upon the same broad categories – relationships with people and organizations in the markets, and on the decision rules.

The constraints

We saw in the example on insect population above that non-linearity follows from constraining the operation of the feedback loop in some way, by placing boundary conditions around it. Returning to the output example used above, the most obvious constraints are those created by limited capacity to produce the product. That constraint can be overcome in the short run by holding inventories and in the long run by capital investment. Both run into the constraints of financing – the internal financial resources and the ability to raise external capital are both ultimately limited. Scarcity then is a fundamental constraint – limited availability of skill and expertise, of physical capacity, time and finance all constrain the operation of the feedback mechanisms. Further constraints are provided by basic economic laws. The more a customer consumes a product, the less that customer wants additional product. The more the customer is exposed to advertising, the less effective additional advertising becomes. The more is spent on research and development, the less effective each additional unit of expenditure becomes. The more capital expenditure, the less effective each addition becomes. So fundamental economic laws of diminishing returns constrain the operation of the feedback mechanisms of a business. Then, general psychological reactions also provide constraints – for example, there are limits to people's patience, cooperation and willingness to follow instructions.

The operation of all the feedback mechanisms governing the performance of a business is bounded by all manner of constraints. Those mechanisms therefore have to be non-linear.

The parameters in the performance feedback mechanisms

From the above examples we can see that the parameter relating each of the performance indicators, output, cashflow and profits to its own past value from one period to another, is determined by two broad sets of factors.

The first broad set of factors is relationships with people and organizations in the business's environment. For example, any given level of expenditure will generate larger profits, the more responsive the markets are to the product offerings we make.

The second broad set of factors determining the parameters in the feedback mechanisms is the whole decision-making, or control process. In the above examples, these processes lead to the rules which people within the organization employ to fix expenditure levels in the profit feedback. As the rules are altered to make expenditure more responsive to profit, the parameter linking profit now to profit next time increases. So, the more responsive the decision rules, the higher the parameter in the feedback mechanism and the more sensitive the feedback becomes.

The decision-making rules follow from the processes used to control the organization. The organization's decision rules may be simple in form. The rule may be as simple as increasing expenditure this period by some percentage of profit last period. But deriving the actual percentage is a highly complex matter. The actual percentage in the decision rule will depend on the processes by which people make decisions. And this will depend upon the systems, structures, rewards, training and development, and many other aspects of the organization. Most important of all, the precise form of the decision rule will depend upon people, their motivation, their interrelationships, their personal desires and ambitions. As relationships, structures and procedures within the organization are improved to make decision making processes more responsive, the decision rules will become more responsive. The effect is to increase the parameters in the feedback mechanisms making them more sensitive.

The parameters in the non-linear feedback loops which are a business will move up and down as relationships with the environment change and as decision rules and the processes leading to them are altered. The performance of the organization over time will be driven by what happens to those parameters. A dynamic model of managing and organizing would need to explain what happens as those parameters are moved up and down.

Stability and instability

One possibility is that the feedback system will generate stable equilibrium behaviour. This will occur when the parameter values in the feedbacks are low; when the feedbacks are insensitive because environments are relatively unresponsive and so is the decision making process. As we saw in Chapter 3, feedback of a damping kind may be used to correct deviations from a planned path; indeed that is the purpose of the short interval and long-term planning forms of control. So, when we are able to forecast the changes in the environment we can adapt the business slowly in advance of the changes happening and so keep it on the stable, adaptive equilibrium path of success. But, we only have to compare listings of the top 100 companies in the USA or the UK at different points in time to see that even the most successful are not in a continuing state of stable equilibrium. Names drop off the list, names are added and rankings change dramatically even within a five-year period. Even successful companies demonstrate considerable irregularity in performance, strategic choices and managerial behaviour. Peters and Waterman[1] studied excellent companies to identify what led to their excellence. Soon after the study was published, a significant number of those companies, such as IBM, could no longer be described as excellent. Stable, adaptive equilibrium behaviour does not therefore seem to be a realistic description of the behaviour of that non-linear feedback system which is a business organization.

The other well-known possibility for the behaviour of a feedback mechanism is explosive instability. This occurs when the parameter values in the feedbacks are very high; when the feedbacks are highly sensitive due to very responsive environments and decision-making processes. Here the system would grow very rapidly until some external factor prevented it. It might then collapse. This is an even more unsatisfactory description of the successful behaviour of business feedback mechanisms, than that which runs in terms of simple stability. We do not observe explosive growth followed by collapses as the business norm. We do observe some degree of regularity in the form of similar looking trends and cycles, combined with irregularity in the form of deviations from those trends and cycles.

Irregularity as management failure or random shocks

We currently explain that mixture of regularity and irregularity in one or both of two ways. The first explanation ascribes the irregularity in performance to preventable management failure. When performance is largely regular we say that the company is one of the band of excellent companies and when that performance displays greater degrees of irregularity we say that it is no longer excellent. Now irregular performance may well be due to poor performance, but it cannot be the whole reason. Using this reasoning, we say that IBM is excellent at one point, then we say that IBM is dead and then we say that it is excellent again. This is simply a description made with the benefit of hindsight, not an explanation of irregular performance.

A more acceptable explanation runs in these terms. Success is basically a state of stable equilibrium in which the organization is adapted to its environment, but it is continually disturbed by unforeseeable changes coming from that environment. Observed irregularity in successful business performance is then due to random shocks from the environment impacting on a stable equilibrium organization. The successful organization maintains the basic orderly equilibrium through its planning systems. It foresees as much of the environmental change as possible and adapts in advance. It is then reducing the parameters in the feedback mechanisms, slowing them down through foresight and making them less sensitive. This generates more stable performance. But random shocks cannot be foreseen, by definition. The successful organization then adapts as rapidly as it can to those random shocks. It maintains, as closely as possible, a dynamic equilibrium with the environment. According to this explanation, IBM is not judged to have been an excellent company in every time period, either because its planning is defective, or because in some time periods it is hit by random shocks to which it has not been able to adapt quickly enough. If it could adapt more quickly to random shocks then it would display less irregularity.

This view leads to prescriptions for flexible, fast-acting organizations. If the organization has a large number of responses available, if it can move very quickly, it can cope with the random shocks to maintain dynamic adaptive equilibrium. And this amounts to making the whole decision-making process more responsive so that it can cope with a volatile and responsive environment. But if you think in feedback terms, what you are doing by following this prescription is making the feedbacks very sensitive. Both environmental and decision-making responsiveness are then pushing the parameter values up towards values which generate highly unstable performance, the very thing you are trying to avoid.

Now this undesirable result would not occur if the responsive decision-making process could always produce from its many available responses, that one which offset the random shock. This means that you have to get the timing right. But by definition this is impossible – the shock is random. It could be argued that it is not necessary to get the timing of every shock right in order to maintain stability. Since there are large numbers of random shocks and the flexible organization is applying large numbers of trial-and-error responses, then by the laws of large numbers, the mismatches between random shocks and trial and error actions would cancel out. The result would be an approximately stable adaptive equilibrium and approximately regular performance.[2] So, even in a highly volatile environment we should be able to sustain something close to stability if we are flexible and active enough. Irregular performance should therefore be insignificant in successful organizations and if it is not then they are being incompetent.

The problem with this explanation is as follows. For the laws of large numbers (probability) to apply, we have to be talking about large numbers of repetitive events. The random shocks and the offsetting trial and error actions would all have to be repetitions of the same kinds of shock and action. But it is the very nature of open-ended change that the shocks are unique; they are not repetitions of the same events. This point was established in Chapter 2. Furthermore, the shocks and actions would have to be large numbers of small ones, independent of each other, which did not escalate into bigger ones. If there is feedback, if small shocks and actions feed into each other and escalate, then we would have to be sure that we had the right response ready for a specific shock, otherwise we could get escalation. It is the very nature of open-ended change that small shocks and events can escalate. This point was also established in Chapter 2. This brings us back to the problem of timing. Since the shocks are random we cannot have the right response ready at the right time. So, the random shocks will be unique and they will have escalating consequences because they arise in open-ended situations. A very responsive decision-making process cannot alter this. In open-ended situations, designing a very responsive decision-making process will simply raise the parameters in the feedbacks, making performance even more unstable than it would otherwise have been. We will return to the implications of this in Chapter 6.

We are left then with an explanation of the irregularity we observe in the performance of even the most successful company, which ascribes that irregularity to random shocks. Explanations which try to reduce observed irregularity to management incompetence alone have serious flaws. Even when managers are as competent as they can be their businesses will still be affected by random shocks. Those random shocks hit stable equilibrium organizations, knocking them off course. But, this amounts to saying that we do not know why successful companies experience irregular performance. And once we take account of the feedback nature of a business we have to recognize these shocks as irreducible sources of instability, which current prescriptions for planning or hectic trial-and-error action cannot remove.

There seems to be something fundamental about irregularity which we are not explaining. Could it be that the notion of success as a stable-equilibrium state of dynamic adaptation to the environment is the source of our problems in explaining irregularity? This may sound like a highly abstract question, but the answer is of great practical importance. The answer determines whether success is simply a matter of order and stability or whether it also has something to do with disorder and instability. It determines whether we should try to design orderly equilibrium organizations to adapt to their environments, or those which operate in some other way.

The dynamic of business feedback mechanisms

To explore the question about the source of observed irregularity further, consider a simple model of the feedback mechanisms described earlier on in this chapter. This model is depicted in Figure 4.6. At the centre of that diagram there is a set of requirements presented by customers, in a particular time period, for some combination of product volumes, features, quality, delivery times and prices. The customer requirements which exist now will change from one period to the next due to changing economic, technological, demographic, fashion and perception factors. Such change is depicted as feeding into the customer requirements of a particular period from the change box at the bottom of the diagram. Information on these changes feeds into the decision-making processes of organization A and its competitors – the dotted lines running from the change box. That information will include predicted changes in requirements which will be incorporated into plans for product offerings, thus securing a match between offering and customer requirement. Perfect predictability would lead to regular performance by the business. But some changes will not have been predicted and these will constitute random shocks to the business. Because of periodic mismatch between offering and requirement, the performance of even the most successful business will demonstrate irregular patterns. On this view instability comes from continuing random shocks.

To the right of the customer requirement circle there is a loop representing the feedback mechanism which is a particular business, organization A. The feedback loop is made up of a decision leading to some product offering in a given time period: some combination of product volume, features, service levels, price, delivery time and image. The product offering leads to a response from the customers and the sensitivity of that response depends upon how close the offering is to customer requirements. The connection between customer response to Organisation A's offering and customer requirements, is labelled (*a*). This measures the relationships of A to people and organizations in its environment. That (*a*) is the parameter which measures just how sensitive the customer response is. Note that the relationship runs in one direction

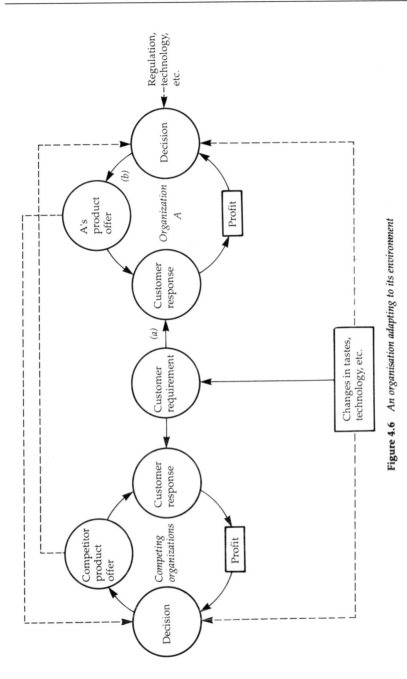

Figure 4.6 *An organisation adapting to its environment*

only – the customer presents a requirement and that ultimately determines what the business offers. On this view the creativity of managers is restricted to adapting to what the customer wants.

The customer response to organization A's offering leads to some level of profit, which in turn affects the decisions to be taken on product offering for the next period. Also affecting that decision is information flowing in about changes to customer requirements, competing product offerings, technology and regulatory frameworks shown by the dotted lines. The connection between the decision and the subsequent offering is labelled (*b*). It is a measure of how responsive the decision-making process is to what was achieved in the last period and to the information flowing in about change, including forecasts of that change. This then is a feedback loop where what happened in the last period feeds into what happens in this period. As time passes, organization A moves around this loop. The speed with which it moves around the loop depends upon the parameters. That speed depends upon just how responsive the decision-making processes and the relationships with actors in the environment are.

To the left of the customer requirement circle, there is another feedback loop representing all those competing with organization A to meet the customer requirements. It is essentially the same loop as that which organization A follows. Both are non-linear because as more of a particular offering is made, customers will require less of it according to the basic economic laws of diminishing returns.

Consider an example of how organization A might behave as it follows its feedback loop. The following example is based on a rather simplified account of some developments in the market for paint containers in the UK. In the early 1980s emulsion paint manufacturers in the UK were presenting a set of requirements for tin can containers, covering a range of sizes with fixed dimensions, quality and delivery time specifications. The demand for paint and therefore paint cans had declined in line with the general economic recession, but it was a mature and fairly predictable market. The changes feeding through from one period to the next had mainly to do with fluctuations in volume. From one period to the next therefore organization A, in this example a company called Francis Packaging, and its competitors, Metal Box and Nacanco, had to make decisions mainly about the volume and price components of product offering, primarily based on what had happened in the previous period. The customers, the major ones being ICI and Crown Paints, were not very responsive to any change in product offering and the decision-making process was not all that responsive to any change in customer requirement. The parameters were low, the feedback loop rather insensitive and consequently the whole market was characterised by stability.

Then, one of the paint manufacturers, ICI, decided that its customers were reacting adversely to the rust which developed around the rim of the tin cans, when half used cans were stored. The rust interfered with subsequent use of the emulsion paint. After a period of relative stability then, a new customer requirement was presented to the tin can manufacturers – a rust-free container. We can think of this as a random shock coming from the environment, disrupting the stable equilibrium into which organization A and its competitors had settled.

Market research, in this case simply listening to the customer, fed this information into the decision-making processes of Francis Packaging and its competitors. Francis Packaging decided that the need for rust-free cans was not a real one; that this paint manufacturer was demanding over-engineered products as it usually did; that the fuss about rust would soon die down. As a precaution, however, some minimal effort was put into developing a can with multiple layers of lacquer on the inside to overcome the rust problem. One of the competitors, Metal Box, took the matter more seriously and started to develop a plastic container, but to its own specifications rather than those of the customer. The situation was thus one where the decision-making process of Francis Packaging and its competitors was rather unresponsive. The parameter (*b*) was low. The relationship with the environment, (*a*), stayed the same for some time because the customers had no alternative. Stability was maintained.

Frustrated by the lack of interest shown by the suppliers, ICI encouraged two plastics manufacturers, Mardon Illingworth and Superfos, to develop a plastic emulsion paint container to the required specifications. After two or so years, two additional competitors entered the market with their plastic containers. The customer response to Francis Packaging's offering declined and before too long it had lost most of its emulsion can business and eventually collapsed.

Adapting to customer requirements

Now the dynamic in this example can usefully be described in terms of adaptive equilibrium. Before rust was identified as a problem, the market was in a state of equilibrium, with three main competitors having roughly constant market shares and customer requirements staying roughly the same. Business was simply a matter of going around the same loop. Then came the change, a random shock which had not been adequately foreseen, requiring a new equilibrium position. Francis Packaging did not respond or adapt its capability to the change in requirement and therefore did not survive. The plastic packaging manufacturers did adapt so that their capability matched the new requirements and they prospered. Where the response matched the change there was success; where it did not, the organization collapsed. Success comes from adaptation to reach a new equilibrium. The dynamic is driven by the search for the order of a new equilibrium made necessary by a random shock from the environment. As an organization moves from one equilibrium to another in response to a random shock (an unforeseen change); its performance displays irregularity. Once it reaches equilibrium its performance is stable. Instability is not a continuing state unless there are continual random shocks.

It would have been possible for packaging manufacturers, in the above example, to move from one equilibrium state to another by predicting the change and then adapting to it in a planned way. They could have done this because the paint manufacturer told them what was required. That some did not, is a simple case of management failure. But this purely rational approach will not always be possible. Most companies today face much more volatile changes in customer requirements than those described in the above example, and predicting the changes is extremely difficult. An organization confronted by an inability to predict how customer requirements will change then has to act entrepreneurially. It has to make a decision about a product offering and then judge from the response whether to continue with that offering or not. This in effect means that the dotted lines representing the information flows in Figure 4.6 become far less useful as input to the decision process. The organization then makes its decisions by trial-and-error, by acting and then looking at the consequences, by going around the loop and seeing what happens. We are still talking about the same loops, but trial-and-error search has replaced rational planning as the means by which the organization moves from one equilibrium to another. So, an entrepreneur develops an electric automobile prototype and then tries to sell it. It does not meet customer requirements and fails. He, or some other entrepreneur then develops an alternative and tries that. Rational planning does not work here because customer responses are too uncertain. But trial-and-error will eventually yield the appropriate match between product offering and customer requirement. In this entrepreneurial approach decision-making has to be flexible, responsive and sensitive to change.

This explanation of managing and organizing sees success as flowing from the underlying order of equilibrium in which the capability of the organization is matched to customer requirements. When some significant change occurs the organization must then change its capability to restore equilibrium. The dynamic of success is the drive to adaptive equilibrium.

Creating and shaping customer requirements

However, the feedback loops shown in Figure 4.6 omit interconnections which are of great importance in reality. These interconnections are those which have to do with creativity and the manner in which changes in product offering spread through the customer population. The additional loops required are shown in Figure 4.7. Because of these interconnections, the relationship between organization A and its customers is now itself a feedback loop. We have replaced a straight line connection between a cause (the customer requirement) and an effect (A's product offering) with feedback loops.

The first additional loop to consider is that which runs from organization A's product offering to the customer requirements and thence into the competitors' decision-making processes. This loop states that A's offering directly affects the customer requirements, quite apart from the changes in incomes, fashion and whatever else it is that we normally think of as determining customer requirements. This loop is stating that the offering itself creates, or at least shapes, the customer requirement. And this loop states that competitors are aware of this possibility and try to counter it in their product offerings. In the same way, competitors' offerings create or shape the customer requirement. This is taken into account in A's decision-making process. Organization A is then directly creating its own environment, at least partially, in terms of competitor and customer responses. In Figure 4.6, the sensitivity of the customer response had an impact on the sensitivity required of the decision process, but that decision process did not affect the sensitivity of the customer response. Now it does, and the whole loop consequently becomes much more interconnected and sensitive.

So, in the tin can case, it was open to Francis Packaging to respond rapidly to the requirement for a rust-proof container by putting forward prototypes of tin cans with additional layers of internal lacquer. That might well have satisfied ICI who might not then have encouraged the development of a plastic container. In this way the customer requirement could have been shaped and the outcome could have been different. This is hypothetical and did not happen. But the general rule is that it normally can happen and in successful companies it does. When a client approaches a management consultant, that client rarely has a clearly specified set of requirements. The consultant normally plays a significant part in shaping what may emerge as an assignment. The same point applies to any company supplying integrated information and communication systems. Such companies help the customer to identify what information that client actually needs and what the communication flows and mechanisms need to achieve. In doing so the supplier is shaping the requirement through the product offerings it makes.

There are a great many examples of companies shaping and creating customer requirements. Today it is the norm rather than the exception. The product offering of a Sony Walkman created a customer requirement to walk around the streets of cities throughout the world wearing ear plugs and emitting tinny sounds. Compact discs, video recorders, televisions, fax machines, photocopiers and portable telephones have all created customer requirements which cannot realistically be said to have

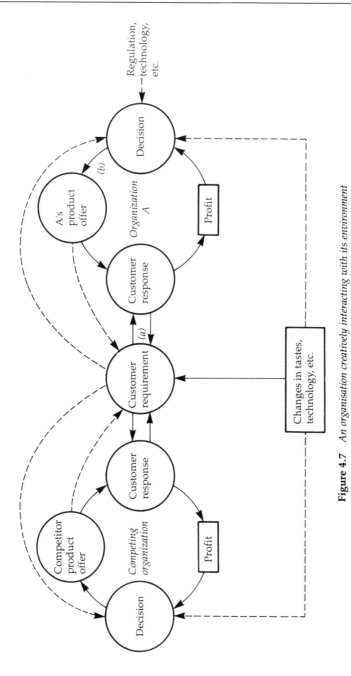

Figure 4.7 An organisation creatively interacting with its environment

existed before the product offering was made. Because telephones are now offered in a variety of colours and shapes, with many different add-on features, customers have discovered a requirement to have more than one or two in their homes. In a real sense the product offering has created, or at least shaped, the requirement. The same point applies to home computers. The kinds of holiday people now take have been shaped by the offerings of the package tour industry. And the point applies just as much to industrial and commercial customers. Requirements for automation, just-in-time delivery and car telephone communication have been shaped by product offerings which enable these things to be done. The creativity of managers is more than simple adaptation.

Spreading of customer requirements

The other additional loop shown in Figure 4.7 is that which runs from the customer response to organization A's offering back to the customer requirement. The same loop applies to the competitors. This states that the response customers make to any offering in one period feeds back into the requirement of the next period. It means that as customers accumulate the offering over time, the level accumulated affects subsequent requirements. Where the connection runs simply from requirement to response and not back again, it means that if organization A offers 200 washing machines now, the response will be the same as offering 200 washing machines in the previous period. But the fact that the buying public already has 200 additional machines may itself have an impact on how many it will take in this period. Typically, when a new or repackaged product is introduced, a relatively small number of people buy it. Others see them with it and decide that they want it too. The effect spreads through simple copying. The effect may also spread because of coordination benefits – it may pay to be part of a network.

An example of coordination benefits is the demand for IBM compatible computers. The more people have them, the more there is the possibility of network connections. There are also advantages of wider access to software. Eventually, due to the effect of spreading, penetration rises to some saturation point and demand drops to replacement requirement. So, each period does not start afresh; the history of what went before is important. There is not a given set of requirements which exists in some sense independent of the response customers make. Spreading and copying effects link the two. The links are provided by the well known concepts of product life cycles, experience or learning curves, and market penetration rates. The consequence of taking into account the spreading and copying effects is that the feedback loop which is organization A becomes even more sensitive.

And the creative or shaping impact of A's product offering, taken with the spreading or penetration property of that offering, together have important implications for the way in which we think about the dynamic. We can no longer think in terms of a given set of changes occurring outside the feedback mechanisms of organization A or those of its competitors, which establishes some equilibrium position to which those organizations have to adapt if they are to be successful. We can no longer think entirely in terms of random shocks which establish a new equilibrium position to which the successful organization adapts. The environment is not given at all – it develops continuously, partly as a result of factors such as incomes and demography, but partly also due to the creative response which organizations themselves make and the manner in which their product offerings spread through customer populations. It is not at all clear who is adapting to whom. The whole concept of organization A matching its capability to some set of equilibrium requirements, of organization A dynamically adapting to its changing environment, ceases to have much meaning because organization A is partially creating and shaping its own environment. And organization A does not have to be large to shape customer requirements. A two-man band of management consultants does this just as much as a major corporation. The only difference is the number of customers concerned. Successful organizations are not just adapting to random shocks generated by their environments. They are themselves creating change and playing a part in their own futures. They are related to their environments through self reinforcing virtuous and vicious circles.

The effect of taking these additional factors into account is to make the feedback loops of organization A and its competitors much more sensitive, at least if they are acting creatively in relation to their customers. And in highly sensitive amplifying and damping feedback loops, small changes can escalate to have major consequences.

Small changes escalate

At equilibrium it takes a significant change in customer requirements to lead to a significant change in product offering. And it takes a significantly different product offering to provoke a noticeably different customer response. Some rather small change in requirements will lead to only small changes in the offering, and some small change in the offering can have only a small impact on a customer. When feedback loops are operating in equilibrium states it is not possible for small changes to escalate up into major alterations in the performance of an organization. If we observe that this does in fact happen with some frequency, then that is strong evidence that the organizations involved are operating away from equilibrium.

In fact there are numerous examples of small changes in product offering which escalate up into major customer or competitor responses and thus major changes in business performance. In a company for which I carried out a consultancy assignment, one of the main products was automobile batteries. That company decided to reduce the size of the battery and package it in a bright, easy-to-carry plastic container. The result of this small change was a substantial increase in its market share. In the 1970s Barratt Developments in the UK offered new houses already furnished, and backed this with intense advertising campaigns. It grew from one of the smallest to the biggest house builder in the UK within a few years. In the 1980s, Amstrad built up a major presence in the home computer market by assembling low cost computers in the Far East and presenting them as a package complete with software. It became a large corporation within a few years, not through a major technological development, but through relatively small changes to do with assembly and add-on features. A new plastic container for one litre engine oil completely displaced the tin container because it had a screw-on cap. Small changes to telephone designs, colour and shape, led to an explosion in the demand for telephone instruments. The market for coffee was revitalized by packaging differently ground coffee for espresso, filter and percolator coffee. By adding a soil testing service to its sales of fertilizer, one company I worked with secured a dominant position in the sugar beet farming market. A building block producer significantly increased market share by shrink wrapping the blocks and reconfiguring the package to make the use of pallets unnecessary. Coca Cola made minor changes to the formula and lost market share. Small changes to product offerings are going on all the time and they often have major consequences, both positive and negative.

And we are always observing small actions in the market place which escalate to produce major consequences. One subsidiary of a company I worked with recently sold a small number of modems at a low price as an entry route to a particular customer's integrated information systems business. That successful sale was made in competition with a competitor who had offered the same modem product. Both competitors had bought modems from the same source, which happened to be a sister subsidiary of the successful competitor. The competitor of the first subsidiary was a major customer of the second subsidiary and as a result of losing the modem sale it withdrew its business from the latter. Consequently, conflict between the two subsidiaries increased, adding pressure to demands for reorganization. A small sale of modems was escalating with major consequences. The manner in which microchips were introduced in one place and then escalated up into major changes in almost every industry is another striking example of how relatively small changes can escalate.

For example – video recorders

Another instructive example is provided by the battle between VHS and Betamax video recorders:

> The video technology of Sony's Betamax exhibits market self-reinforcement in the sense that increased prevalence on the market encourages video outlets to stock more film titles in Betamax; there are coordination benefits to new purchasers of Betamax that increase with its market share. If Betamax and its rival VHS compete, a small lead in market share gained by one of the technologies may enhance its competitive position and help it further increase its lead. There is positive feedback. If both systems start out at the same time, market shares may fluctuate at the outset, as external circumstances and 'luck' change, and as backers manoeuvre for advantage. And if the self-reinforcing mechanism is strong enough, eventually one of the two technologies may accumulate enough advantage to take 100 per cent of the market. Notice however we cannot say in advance which one this will be . . . If one technology is inherently 'better' than the other . . . but has 'bad luck' in gaining early adherents, the eventual outcome may not be of maximum possible benefit. (In fact, industry specialists claim that the actual loser in the video contest, Betamax, is technically superior to VHS.) . . . Once a 'solution' is reached, it is difficult to exit from. In the video case, the dominant system's accrued advantage makes it difficult for the loser to break into the market again.[3]

Successful companies are those who continually innovate. They have creative relationships with customers and suppliers, playing an important part in shaping and developing their requirements. Such organizations have highly sensitive decision-making processes which, through creative product offerings, promote sensitive response from customers. The result will be escalating small changes – vicious and virtuous circles. In other words, such companies are not operating in equilibrium states. When we observe how relatively small changes in product offering can have substantial effects on their performance, how such changes spread or escalate through the system, then the evidence that successful organizations must be operating away from equilibrium is strong. This provides a much more useful and meaningful explanation than the idea that success is simply adapting to a given, equilibrium set of customer requirements. Management creativity is far more than this.

From all these examples we conclude that the relationship between a company and its environments takes the form of non-linear feedback mechanisms. Such mechanisms may operate in a highly stable state. By definition such a state will be one in which the organization is doing nothing new in relation to its environments. Until plastic cans burst into its markets, Francis Packaging was in a stable equilibrium state. But its stable equilibrium state was one of isolation. It was in effect expecting the environment to adapt to it. The other possibility is that the organization can be in an unstable state in relation to its environment. This will occur when the company is adapting to its environment's every requirement. It may be segmenting offerings and its markets into smaller and smaller segments to meet more and more detailed requirements. Or it may be supplying precisely to customer specifications. An example here is the food manufacturer supplying a supermarket chain for that chain's own brand products. At the extreme therefore, adaptation is an unstable equilibrium in which the company is continually changing to meet its customers' every requirement. And there are strong tendencies pulling companies either to isolation or to adaptation – these are the easiest states to be in. Isolation can, of course, never be success. The costs of continual adaptation will mean that this too is not success. Success then lies away from equilibrium, between stability and instability. Here the organization interacts with its customers, negotiating with them and shaping their requirements.

A useful dynamic model of managing and organizing will need to explain business behaviour in states of non-equilibrium between the equilibrium states of isolation and adaptation. It will need to incorporate the possibility of small changes escalating into large consequences, which seems to have something to do with the sensitivity of the feedback nature of the organization itself. A useful model will need to explain virtuous and vicious circles. Ascribing the irregularity we observe in business performance to a series of random shocks coming from the environment is too simple.

The dynamic of the decision-making process

The case for the view that successful organizations operate in non-equilibrium states is strengthened if we consider some of the basic characteristics of an organization's decision-making framework. It is this framework which has a powerful impact on just how responsive the decision-making process is and therefore how sensitive the whole feedback system is. The basic decision-making framework will determine whether an organization is in an equilibrium or a non-equilibrium state.

In designing the structures and systems for a decision-making process, every business organization has to make choices between a number of fundamental, conflicting extremes. These choices set parameter values in the feedback mechanisms which drive its behaviour. The fundamental conflicts are: task division versus integration; market segment and production process separation versus synergy; individual aspirations versus group goals; the individual's motivational factors which fulfil a desire for order versus those motivational factors which fulfil the emotional and creative desires, a form of disorder; equally distributed and highly concentrated power; groups cohering under unquestioning conservative cultures and groups fragmenting under radical, multiple perspective cultures. Every business organization, no matter what industry it operates in, no matter what its size, faces choices between these basic extremes, and every part of any organization faces them too.

The equilibrium of integration

Consider what happens when an organization puts the major emphasis on integration, synergy, motivational order, organizational goals, strongly shared cultures and highly concentrated power. It then adopts management styles and designs organizational structures, control systems, rules and procedures, to bring information and key decision-making to the centre. It establishes procedures and structures to manage the overlaps between its units and specify their decision-making powers. Such an organization may operate in one market where it seeks to achieve economies of scale, in which case it will probably design simple functional structures. Or it may operate across a number of differentiated markets, in which case it will use systems and procedures to manage the overlaps and preserve the synergies. It may design complex matrix structures to do this. Or it may decentralize and apply tight financial controls and detailed policies on which unit is to operate where.

A situation very close to this was outlined to a team of consultants of which I was a member. The company is a major multinational chemical concern. Management described an organization which consists of:

- major business units in the UK organized along matrix lines by product and functional discipline, reporting to a director responsible for the UK;
- production sites in the UK each manufacturing product for a number of business units, with site managers reporting sometimes to a head office production function director and sometimes to a business unit or product manager;
- overseas subsidiaries in many countries, predominantly sales and marketing organizations, each selling a wide range of product and reporting to an overseas director;
- production sites in a number of those countries, each producing product for a number of different national marketing companies and usually reporting to an overseas production function director, but sometimes to the manager of a national marketing company;
- overlapping boards of directors, regional coordinating bodies, liaison committees and departments, regulations on formal communication at the same levels in the management hierarchies of different units and companies.

These complex structures and procedures had been adopted to meet the needs of the market and facilitate control, while benefiting from interconnections and synergies. Each site is multiproduct to achieve economies of production and transport costs. Sales organizations are national multiproduct ones to achieve synergies across customer groupings, but also to benefit from differentiation arising from national differences. To keep it all together there are complex matrix structures, formal coordination bodies and formal hierarchical communication rules. It is an old established company with a very strong culture. Only two years had passed since the last major reorganization had been initiated, parts of which were still being put into place. And this reorganization had followed a reorganization two years before that. Now management were talking to consultants about further reorganization. They were doing so because communication had become laborious and cumbersome. It was breaking down in many areas. Conflict was growing as it took longer and longer to make necessary changes. And these were much the same problems which the previous reorganization was supposed to have addressed.

These problems were very similar to those of another company with which I worked. There the structure was certainly simpler. It was a large product fuel processing company with a clear, functional structure: finance, sales, production, engineering and research directors reported to the managing director. But the management style, the rules and procedures, showed the same concern with integration as those of the company mentioned above, this time to secure the benefits of scale and operational safety. Communication channels were heavily formalized and decision-making concentrated at the top. What could and could not be done was carefully laid down in the rules. The company was experiencing the same difficulties of slow decision-making and inability to change.

Both of these companies had established internal relationships and decision rules which:

- integrate tasks to secure the benefits of interconnection between them;
- serve market segments where any differentiation is accompanied by strong interconnections in segment and production process terms, or where low cost and large scale are the most important sources of competitive advantage;
- attach the greatest importance to the goals of the whole organization and those individual personal aspirations which are related to group participation;
- motivate everyone by an appeal to the formal and orderly motivational factors;
- concentrate power at the top;
- foster group cohesion through strong, shared, conservative, unquestioning cultures.

Management in both cases was seeking to alter structures and systems because it recognized that continuing to apply these rules and relationships would take the organization to a state of ossification. The integrative rules, procedures and structures were stifling initiative, and control was becoming more and more cumbersome. Ignoring purely personal aspirations and circumscribing creativity with heavy formality was producing frustration; people were resigned to doing the same thing. It was becoming harder and harder to respond to change. And the experience of these two companies is typical of all others I have seen adopting a highly integrative approach.

These highly integrative choices for organizational relationships and decision-making processes in effect fix parameter values in the performance feedback mechanisms. They are equivalent to fixing low parameter values, making a change now relatively unresponsive to a previous change, because of the rules and procedures required to be followed before a decision can be made. The result is short-term stability. Both the example organizations mentioned above were profitable and internally stable. In the absence of severe environmental change, the rules and the structures could cope. Change was the reason for the concern which top management was expressing. The organizations were clearly ossifying and becoming increasingly incapable of coping with rapid change.

All organizations are faced with the need to integrate in some way and as they increasingly try to do so, they are pulled or attracted to ossification. And this is a stable equilibrium position in the sense that it is very difficult to shift an organization from it. If managers in either of the example companies did nothing, things would simply go on as they were until the organization was overcome by rapid change. And they were finding it very difficult to move the organization from its present state. Once a company embarks on an integrative approach there seems to be a natural tendency for those integrative controls to proliferate, drawing the organization increasingly to ossification.

The equilibrium of division

Suppose that the multinational chemical company cited above were to make a dramatic move to simpler concepts of stand-alone, profit responsible, national business units, each with its own marketing and production functions, having production sites dedicated to only a few product lines. The focus then would be on task division, market and process separation and more room for individual aspirations. The cost would be lost benefits from economies of scale, common research and development and synergies of all kinds. But it would be impossible to remove all the overlaps between one business unit and another. So, there would still be communication and control problems, they would simply take a different form.

Another company I have worked with, this time in the agricultural sector, provides an example of what happens in this kind of situation. That company was structured into a number of separate but overlapping business units. Each unit was fiercely independent and any commitment of their managers was to the unit rather than the organization as a whole. Any cultural sharing took place at the unit level. The managers of the units were mostly concerned with their own personal goals for their unit. For various reasons there was little effective intervention from the top management; power was distributed to the units. The consequence was poor communication between units, very little cooperation between them, and the company as a whole was making losses.

Here internal relationships and decision rules are characterized by:

- emphasis on task division rather than integration;
- focus on differentiation rather than synergy;
- satisfying personal aspirations of individuals above the goals of the organization as a whole;
- satisfying the creative motivational needs of people rather than their more orderly needs;
- widespread distribution of power;
- loose, radical, questioning, pluralistic cultures rather than strong, commonly held, conservative ones.

Such organizations move to a state of disintegration. They tend to serve smaller and smaller differentiated market segments; to sacrifice group needs to individual ones; create more and more specialized tasks without giving enough attention to integrating these; to allow individuals extreme freedom for creative endeavour with groups fragmenting into smaller and smaller factions; to generate great numbers of different, conflicting perspectives. In this system, integrative processes have been specifically designed out. There are few structures or procedures to keep the increasingly atomizing organization together.

Relationships and rules of this kind also fix particular parameter values for the non-linear feedback mechanisms of the organization's performance indicators. And these are analogous to high values; changes now could be a large amplification of change in a previous period because there is virtually no restriction on what the head of a business unit can do. The decision-making process is far from cumbersome – it depends largely on one person in a small unit. The result is a high level of instability. At these parameter values the organization is pushed to disintegration. But it is still an equilibrium state in the sense that it is extremely difficult to change an organization once it has moved to this position. If the top managers do nothing it will simply continue as it is, disintegrating until it is overcome by bankruptcy. And once an organization embarks upon these divisive paths, the natural tendency is for it to be sucked closer and closer to disintegration.

Far-from-equilibrium

Both of the equilibrium states, disintegration and ossification, are incapable of dealing with rapid change. Organizations at or near to these equilibrium states can effectively do little that is new – the one because it is hidebound by complex structures and formal rules, the other because there is no cooperation across units. In the extreme, both are states of organizational death. As the organization approaches disintegration it finds it harder and harder to control its disparate parts and reap some of the benefits of synergy. It eventually splits up through take-over or bankruptcy. Ossification is ultimately the death of the organization too, because its lack of flexibility means that it cannot deal with change.

Reality requires both division and integration; both separation and synergy; satisfying both individual aspirations and group goals; appealing to both orderly and disorderly motivational factors; balancing conservative and radical cultures; distributing power unequally. Success is avoiding attraction to either disintegration or ossification. Success therefore lies between equilibrium states for a set of non-linear feedback mechanisms. A useful model of the dynamics of business control and development must take account of this. Success is far-from-equilibrium.

Far-from-equilibrium, the organization is unstable because it is in practice so difficult to design a system which will continually balance diametrically opposed extremes of integration and division, especially when confronted with change from outside the system. In dynamical mathematical terms it takes the form of a 'saddle' from which the organization keeps slipping. It is continually changing its structures and systems to avoid the pull to either disintegration or ossification. It is far-from-equilibrium and it takes a great deal of effort to keep it there. So in practice we find that organizational structures are continually changed, sometimes towards centralisation and sometimes towards decentralisation, all in an attempt to stay far-from-equilibrium and not be sucked towards either the stable or the unstable equilibrium states.

Conclusion: what a dynamic model should explain about business development

In this chapter we have been looking for the criteria of a useful explanation of the dynamic of a successful business organization. That is, an explanation of the fundamental forces driving the patterns of performance, choice and behaviour we observe in those successful businesses.

And what we always observe is some combination of regularity or uniformity and irregularity or variety. No successful business goes from strength to strength in a stable manner. They all have ups and downs. A useful explanation is one which adequately accounts for this combination of order and disorder, stability and instability.

This chapter has taken five simple and well-known understandings of the nature of organizations. The first is that organizations are sets of feedback loops between performance indicators, between people within the organization, between people within and outside the organization. This idea is to be found in the literature on organizational behaviour and group dynamics. It is to be found in the literature and prescriptions of control theory and the management decision sciences. The second idea is that of constraints on a system – psychological, physical and financial. This idea is found in the standard economic theories of diminishing returns and returns to scale. The third idea is that business organizations create and shape customer requirements through the product offerings they make and that these offerings follow life cycles and penetration rates. This idea is to be found in the marketing, management and economics literatures. The fourth idea is that product offerings spread through customer populations in self-reinforcing ways.

Taken together, these four ideas mean that business organizations are sets of non-linear feedback mechanisms. Practising managers are perfectly aware of the amplifying and damping characteristics of the behaviour and control loops in their organizations. There is nothing at all surprising in the idea that these behavioural and control loops can generate instability. But it is not normally recognised that the operation of non-linear feedback loops makes it very difficult to talk about a successful organization as one which adapts to its environment. Since it is partially creating its own environment, there is an important sense in which the environment is adapting to it. Furthermore, escalating small changes and the appearance of virtuous and vicious circles make it very difficult to think of a successful organization as being in some kind of dynamic equilibrium with its environments. It is more useful to think of organizations being powerfully attracted to equilibrium states of isolation on the one hand and adaptation on the other. Success, creative interaction, then lies in the border between them.

The fifth simple understanding is that, at the most basic level, organizations have to resolve a number of tensions. On the one hand, there is the need for division of labour, tasks, processes and market segments. On the other hand, there is the need for integration. All organizations have to find a balance between the forces of division and those of integration, between decentralisation and centralisation. This is a simple basic idea found in economic theory and in the literature on organization and management. And practising managers are also perfectly aware of this tension. There is nothing surprising in the idea that every organization is powerfully pulled, at the most basic level, in two diametrically opposed directions.

But this balance is usually thought of as a position of dynamic equilibrium with its connotation of something predictable and orderly. This chapter has put forward the proposition that the balance between division and integration is a state far-from-equilibrium. Complete division and complete integration are equilibrium states which are very difficult to escape from. Neither of these states constitute success because in neither of them is the organization able to handle open-ended change. Success then lies in the border between equilibrium states of a set of non-linear feedback mechanisms and that state of success is very difficult to sustain. Companies keep slipping from it, pulled to ossification and isolation or disintegration and adaptation. A useful dynamic model would explain the behaviour of an organization which is far-from-equilibrium, in a difficult-to-maintain position in the borders between equilibrium states. The next chapter demonstrates that all today's most prominent models of managing and organizing are cast in equilibrium terms. But as will be shown in the chapters in Part Three, the latest developments in complex system dynamics have much to say about border areas between equilibrium states.

It may sound highly abstract to be concerned about whether a successful business is in some equilibrium or some far-from-equilibrium state. But as we shall see in Part Three, this conclusion has highly important implications for how it is possible to control and develop a business. It has great significance for how managers design their actions.

This chapter has been concerned to show that the performance of an organization is driven by non-linear feedback mechanisms. It is the parameters in these mechanisms which will determine whether performance displays stable or unstable patterns over time. At low parameter values the performance is stable. At high parameter values the performance is unstable. Both are equilibrium states. The parameters are determined by relationships with the environment. These are feedbacks. The more responsive the environment the higher the parameter values. Those values are also determined by the whole decision-making process of the organization. These too are feedbacks. The more responsive that decision-making process, the higher the parameter values. The received wisdom is that success lies in a state of stable equilibrium. The received wisdom is that organizations adapt. The conclusion put forward here is that success lies far-from-equilibrium.

The chapters in Part Two now go on to show how all today's most prominent models of management see success adaptive as equilibrium. Part Three then examines the far-from-equilibrium state and what it means for managerial action.

References

1   Peters, T., Waterman, R. (1982), *In Search of Excellence*, Harper & Row.
2   This is the cybernetic principle of requisite variety.
3   Arthur, W. B. (1988), Self-Reinforcing Mechanisms in Economics, in Anderson, P. W., Arrow, K. J., Pines, D., eds., *The Economy as a Complex Evolving System*, Addison-Wesley p. 10.

Part Two
Today's Most
Prominent
Management Models

The chapters in Part One have suggested a number of key features which should be central to a useful model of dynamic business behaviour. If managers design their actions using mental models which omit and cannot explain the essential dynamics of business behaviour then they are unlikely to cope with an increasingly turbulent business world. It has been argued that dynamic models of business success will be built on the following features:

- A spectrum of change situations ranging from those which generate outcomes close to certainty (closed change) to those generating outcomes far from certainty (open-ended change).
- Typical human behaviour and interactions in change situations close to certainty which are very different to those in situations far from certainty. In the former case people in organizations can know what to expect, they can choose objectives immediately and plan their actions in advance of doing anything. They can use rational decision-making methods, settle conflicts through simple bargaining games and easily share the same values and perspectives. There is a general model which can be used to design action in all specific situations. But far from certainty, people in organizations face ambiguous and ill-structured opportunities and problems. They consequently adopt equivocal positions, find it difficult to frame the problem, become anxious and conflict with each other. They approach such change with different perspectives and therefore have to develop consensus and commitment as a group on each new issue they face. They have to discover their aspirations, preferences and objectives as they act. There is no general model which can be applied to design actions in a wide range of specific situations. A useful model of dynamic business behaviour must be able to explain what managers do in such situations.
- Since an organization faces different change situations which have different

characteristics and provoke different behaviours, the form of control and development has to be different. Close to certainty managers control and develop the business through objective setting, planning, monitoring and action feedback loops. At the same time they also have to control and develop by deploying political and learning feedback loops through which they create and discover what to do. A useful dynamic model of business behaviour should incorporate both of these feedback loops.

- Every aspect of performance, behaviour, choice action, control and development in a business organization has the characteristics of amplifying and damping feedback mechanisms. They are all interconnected and one choice and action feeds into another in ways which amplify and spread or are damped and contained. Because of this, small changes can escalate into large outcomes. Because of this, the development of a business over time is characterised by self-reinforcing virtuous and vicious circles. Because of this, organizations play a part in creating their own futures. But chance also plays some part. A useful dynamic explanation of business must take account of these well-observed phenomena.

- The set of feedback mechanisms which is an organization cannot operate in a stable equilibrium state if that organization is to be successful. Sensitive feedback between an organization and its environments means that concepts of dynamic equilibrium in which an organization continually adapts to a given environment is not a useful understanding of what actually goes on. Successful organizations create their own environments in part, making it unclear who is adapting to whom. Internally too, states of equilibrium make it impossible for an organization to cope with rapid change. Success lies in some state between stability and instability. A useful dynamic model of business should explain what happens in non-equilibrium states, between stability and instability.

The contention is that managers will not be able to design effective actions unless they employ mental models which take account of the above features of the world they operate in. Many managers do operate effectively and successfully. The chapters in Part Two argue that they do so despite rather than because of today's most prominent explicit models of managing and organizing. It will be argued that managers today articulate explicit models which may be labelled 'rational' and 'entrepreneurial'. Neither of these models incorporates the key elements required of a useful dynamic model as outlined above. They fail to do so because they have been developed within a frame of reference which sees the business world as an information processing machine or a gradually adapting organism. Because these models are inadequate from a dynamic point of view, managers in practice design their actions using implicit models. These models are below the level of awareness and are consequently not well understood. Using different models – the explicit 'to say what to do', and the imperfectly understood implicit models 'to do' – leads to anomalies and unintended outcomes. Because successful managers, like all other experts, are relatively unaware of their own implicit models, it is difficult to prescribe what others should do to become successful. Part Three will go on to argue that new scientific understandings of complex system dynamics give us a different perspective. From this perspective we may be better able to identify the implicit models successful managers use. A better understanding should lead us to more effective performance.

5 Rational planning, entrepreneurial enthusiasm and political power

There are two comprehensive explanations of how successful organizations function to which managers today pay the most explicit attention – the rational and the entrepreneurial. The rational approach prescribes decision-making and control which is based on clear, well defined organizational structures, analytical techniques and the orderly motivation of people. The entrepreneurial approach prescribes decision-making and control which is much looser. It is based on far less clear cut organizational structures and job definitions, experimentation and inspirational motivation.

That both the rational and the entrepreneurial models, and particularly the rational, are having a profound impact on the practice of management in the Western industrialised world can hardly be in any doubt. Most modern managers are aware of and talk in terms of these models. The rational models, with closely associated views on team building and motivation from the organizational behaviour tradition, provide the basic bag of tools of management consultants. The millions of copies of management books sold each year testify to the impact of the entrepreneurial models. Most companies apply the rational model in their financial control and long-term planning systems. Major companies such as General Electric and British Petroleum are currently following the entrepreneurial prescriptions. They are stripping out layers of management and trying to create network structures in which people will behave more innovatively. There are of course variations in the presentation of both the rational and entrepreneurial schools. There are some important conceptual and practical differences within each model. But such variations do not affect the most important assumptions, general principles and prescriptions which variants on each model share in common. And such variations do not affect the arguments of this chapter. For the purpose of this chapter it will therefore aid clarity to think in terms of only two different schools of thought – the rational (mechanistic) and the entrepreneurial (organic).

There is, of course, much more to the literature on management and organization than is encompassed in these two terms. But although much of the literature which falls outside these two approaches was written 20 years or more ago, it has had little noticeable impact on practising managers. For this reason it is the rational and entrepreneurial approaches which are referred to throughout as today's most prominent models of managing and organizing, or the received wisdom. It is the received wisdom that managers articulate when they say what they do. Literature outside this received wisdom often has much to contribute to understanding what managers actually do and this will be referred to in the next chapter.

This chapter, then, is concerned with what managers say they do. It describes those concepts and approaches in models of management and organization to which practising managers pay attention. It tries to separate out the underlying core explanation of how a successful business works from the descriptive material around it. The proposition put forward here is that today's most prominent models have all imported their methodology from traditional science. And with that methodology they have imported the machine frame of reference within which traditional science explains how the world works. Today's prominent models of managing and organizing are consequently as inappropriate to the understanding and explanation of turbulence and disorder in the business world as the traditional sciences are in the natural world. All today's most prominent models see the successful organization as one which continuously adapts to its environments, maintaining a dynamic equilibrium in much the same way as natural phenomena are postulated to do in traditional science.

Each of the management models described below is illustrated using the example of metal packaging manufacturers already encountered in Chapter 4. That example related to the market for tin paint cans around the mid-1980s in the UK. Three main competitors, Metal Box, Nacanco and Francis Packaging, supplied the paint manufacturers with tin cans. ICI and Crown Paints dominated the paint market. One of the paint manufacturers, ICI, decided to switch the packaging of its emulsion products from tin to plastic containers to increase customer satisfaction. The tin can manufacturers did not act all that quickly to meet the new requirements. This led to the entrance of of two plastic packaging companies into the market. They were Mardon Illingworth and Superfos. As a result, a substantial part of the tin can market disappeared. During this period Francis Packaging was acquired by the conglomerate Suter plc, who removed the managing director and installed a new chief executive. It proved difficult to turn Francis Packaging around and eventually it was sold to Metal Box. But the market difficulties continued and not all that long afterwards, Metal Box sold its packaging interests to a French company. The experience of Francis Packaging is used to illustrate how the rational and entrepreneurial models would explain what Francis should have been doing.

Rational explanations of management and organization: the mechanistic approach

Rational models include all the management sciences,[1] operations research, decision sciences,[2] quantitative business methods, information technology applied to business, applied systems theory, organization development and most of that which is to be found in standard textbooks on management,[3] organization theory and organizational behaviour.[4] Among the writers most visible to practising managers in this area today are Drucker,[5] Ansoff,[6] and Porter.[7]

As far as the rational theories are concerned, organizations are groups of people with a common purpose. There is a clear boundary line which separates the organization from the environment within which it operates – the markets, the society, the national and international political systems, as well as the physical environment. The environment is changing. But it is one of the basic assumptions upon which the whole edifice of the rational model is built, that such change is largely predictable, at least in a statistical or probabilistic sense when enough sophisticated attention is devoted to the matter. Rational models are predominantly concerned with closed and contained change as defined in Chapter 2. In these circumstances, the common purpose of the organization can be expressed in terms of precise, quantitative objectives for the short-term future and rather more qualitative future missions for the longer term.

To be successful, the organization has to adapt to its changing environment. That is, it has to secure fit between its resources and its environment. It has to match its competitive capability with the sources of competitive advantage. It seeks congruence with a complex but predictably changing environment. It establishes equilibrium with that environment. So, when paint manufacturers decide to package their emulsion products in plastic rather than tin cans, the tin can manufacturers have to change their technology, their raw materials and their labour skills if the organization is to survive.

And to do this the organization utilizes predictive, and failing that, reactive, adaptation mechanisms. The predictive mechanisms are, of course, the short- and long-term plans – the routes to be followed to achieve the objectives and the missions. So, successful tin can manufacturers will predict the switch from tin to plastic cans, set plastic can market share objectives, draw up development, manufacturing and marketing plans to achieve their objectives and then proceed to implement these. Where the predictive mechanisms fail there is reactive adaptation through clear procedures of monitoring plans and taking corrective action to offset deviations or variances. The organization is a proactive and reactive sensor of, and adaptor to, its environment. If the aimed-for plastic can market share is not being achieved on schedule, corrective action is taken, perhaps in the form of an advertising campaign or a price cut.

Modes of decision-making

These sensing and adapting activities are in fact the processes of decision-making. And there are four clear modes of decision-making:

- *The rational mode* Where comprehensive scanning of the environment and accurate forecasting of all outcomes are possible, where time and cost are not constraints, where the objectives are time definite and clear cut, where the objectives are agreed by all the organizational actors, where these actors share the same preferences in terms of what they value, what they want and how they believe it is acceptable to achieve these things, then decision-making follows the clear rules and procedures of the purely rational mode to achieve the optimum outcome. These rules and procedures generate all possible action options and utilize clear criteria to choose the options which yield the maximum benefit. Powerful quantitative decision-making tools are available to do the job in even the most complex of situations characterized by vast amounts of data. This is where you get all the facts, predict and analyse all the options, and choose the best. What we are describing is clearly algorithmic – a logical, predetermined step-by-step procedure which leads to a maximized goal. This mode of decision-making requires only algorithmic forms of thinking and learning and computers will do it better than we can. So, the paint can manufacturers would continually conduct market research, analyse market statistics and forecast all possible outcomes of what is happening and what they are doing. They should set clear objectives. They would then select those actions which secure the maximum possible profit.
- *Bounded rationality* Where there are time and cost constraints, where the environment is such that the possibility of scanning and forecasting the environment falls some way short of the fully comprehensive, but where all the other conditions established above hold, then decision-making still follows clear rules and procedures. But now these rules and procedures do not generate all possible action options

or outcomes, only those selected as the most important. A searching procedure, following clearly predetermined criteria on what constitutes success or failure in moving towards a goal, is used to reject or retain options in a predetermined step-by-step sequential manner. In this way large arrays of options do not have to be considered at the same time. This searching procedure involves no random elements. It is a logically predetermined sequence of steps. It uses standard operating rules to reduce uncertainty.[8] Here you are selective: you decide in advance what the most important facts are, you classify the requirements into needs and wants, you consider only the most important options and then you make a choice which leads to a satisfactory, if not the best, outcome. The outcome depends upon the sequence in which options are discovered, and hence the decision makers' perceptions. Here the paint can manufacturers would conduct occasional market research in response to important questions that managers have identified. They would set out a limited number of options, for example to improve their product by adding layers of lacquer or to develop a plastic can. In selecting the options to consider they would be guided by their mission statement with which they would all agree. They would analyse the outcomes of selected options and follow that which yields a satisfactory profit. This is known as bounded rational decision-making and the price paid for greater speed and simplicity, as well as lower cost of decision-making, is that of achieving a satisfactory rather than an optimal outcome. Since we have not considered every possible option or outcome, we cannot be sure that we have chosen the best one. All we can know is that we have chosen a reasonably satisfactory one. This is still an algorithmic process and requires only algorithmic forms of thinking and learning.

- *Unprogrammed decision-making* Where there are time and cost constraints; where anything approaching comprehensive scanning of the environment and forecasting is not possible because of high levels of uncertainty but where all the other conditions are met, then the decision-making mode switches to what is called unprogrammed decision-making. Now this may be called 'unprogrammed' decision-making, but in a very real sense there is a programme and that programme is one of trial-and-error search. It is heuristic search in which small incremental steps are taken and tested before proceeding. Objectives, or criteria, are set to determine whether each step constitutes a success or a failure, and that fixes the next step to be taken. Failure to meet the criteria terminates search down a particular avenue, while successfully meeting the criteria means that further steps down that avenue are taken. But here the search procedure does involve some random elements – at least the initial options considered may have to be random within certain limits. But before long, the criteria for success and failure take over and guide the search towards a satisfactory goal. These are unique decision-making situations requiring innovation. Innovation, in the rational theory approach, is quite consistently rational. It is work. It is not about taking huge, wild risks.[9] And it is an heuristic search, dependent upon algorithmic thinking and learning. Here you cannot decide in advance what the most important factors and options are; you find out by trial and error thinking and acting. It is a form of adaptive learning. Following this mode, the paint can manufacturers would not conduct market research and analyse options because the customer requirement is too uncertain. They would make a few new can prototypes and try them out on the customer.

• *The bargaining mode* But how does adaptation to the environment, decision-making, proceed when some of the other conditions for the three decision-making modes described above are not present? What happens when there are conflicting objectives? Here the bargaining mode of decision-making is deployed by the actors involved. Provided that basic behavioural values are still shared, and provided that reasonably comprehensive environmental scanning and forecasting is possible so that participants have a reasonable idea of the probability of different outcomes occurring and therefore can have clear preferences and objectives, then rules and procedures can be deployed to trade off costs and benefits and so reach a reasonably stable outcome. And this outcome will be quite predictable from the stable relative distribution of power between people. This bargaining mode of decision-making is also algorithmic. It also utilizes rules and procedures which can be specified in advance to reach a decision. It is based on stable power structures and procedures in circumstances where outcomes are reasonably predictable. It is a bargaining game which can be played on a computer. So, some executives in the paint can manufacturing company may want to improve the existing tin product, while others may want to develop a new plastic product. Yet others may dismiss the whole thing as unimportant. Those with the most power will determine what happens.

The rational organization is a computer

It is important to note three points at this stage. The first is that rational models do not contemplate situations where environmental scanning and forecasting are totally impossible, such that even a predetermined step-by-step, trial-and-error search is out of the question as an immediate response.

The second point is that rational models do not envisage a situation in which all the conditions for deploying all of the above decision-making modes are absent – an unknowable environment, wildly conflicting objectives and completely different preferences on the part of organizational actors.

The third important point, one already stressed, is that all four decision-making modes – rational, bounded rational, unprogrammed and bargaining – can be reduced to predetermined rules and procedures, or algorithms. In a very real sense, rational models envisage a process covering inputs of data gathered about the environment now and in the future. Software programmes with their operating rules and procedures and their selection criteria then process the inputs to, and outputs of, decisions. The organization is a computer! The sensing of the environment, the analysing, the thinking, the forecasting, the decision-making are all clearly algorithmic. Those algorithms may be highly complex. They may be heuristic. They may be bargaining games. But they are all algorithms nonetheless. Hence in principle they are capable of being preformed by suitably high-powered computers. It would be reasonable to conclude that within 20 to 30 years computers will take over from managers and do a much better job, at least when it comes to making decisions.

But how are wildly conflicting objectives and completely different preferences on the part of organizational actors to be avoided so as to maintain equilibrium with the environment? The answer is provided by hierarchical structures and team building.

Hierarchical structure

All the decision-making mechanisms are deployed within an hierarchical structure. Organisational equilibrium with highly complex environments is maintained by the use of hierarchy. All the primary tasks which the organization is required to perform, including the control tasks, are divided into clear components. This is to accommodate the limited ability of any one individual to gather, store and process the information which is necessary to carry out tasks and make decisions efficiently and effectively.

Thus each individual has a clearly defined role. That individual has a job description which sets out the tasks to be performed and a set of precise task related objectives which are to be achieved. In this way each individual has to deal with only a limited amount of complexity. Integration is accomplished by grouping individuals under a supervisor, supervisors under middle managers, middle managers under senior managers and senior managers under corporate managers responsible to a chief executive, responsible in turn to a board of directors. We have a hierarchy of people, of objectives, of plans to achieve objectives, of decision-making rules and procedures. We have in fact hierarchies of algorithms, programmes with subroutines, which in turn have subroutines and so on. The analogy with a network of computers is striking.

In rational models this hierarchy is a vital part of the adaptation mechanism required to keep the organization in equilibrium with its environment. The hierarchical structure must therefore fit the environment and it must be appropriate to the size of the organization itself. The manner in which the successful organization is decentralized and centralized is contingent upon its size and upon the nature of the environment. The features which determine the degree of centralization are the levels of uncertainty and complexity, the sources of competitive advantage, the disparate markets the organization operates in, and the integration or otherwise required for its production processes. So where the source of competitive advantage is low cost and the production process are integrated, large size is required. Where the firm operates in one market which is stable, then this large size should be accompanied by a high degree of centralization to secure the best fit with the environment. Where the source of competitive advantage is differentiation and production processes are not highly interconnected, and the firm operates in many markets which are rapidly changing, then a high degree of decentralization is called for.

Any tension that there may be between task division and integration, market synergy and differentiation, production process separation and integration, centralization and decentralization, are all matters to be resolved in such a way as to secure equilibrium. It is important to note this point – tensions created by a number of opposing forces, such as task division and integration, are resolved, according to rational models in an equilibrium manner, by the structures, rules and procedures established by the successful organization. The previous chapter has argued that these tensions cannot be resolved in an equilibrium manner. Equilibrium occurs when the organization in a sense gives in and moves either to the extreme of ossification or to that of disintegration. The equilibrium states are ossification or disintegration. Success lies in the border between these equilibrium states. It cannot be an equilibrium state itself because it is so difficult to maintain. The organization has a natural tendency to move away from balance between ossification and disintegration. Dynamic models need to explain how organizations behave away from equilibrium.

Team building

Now so far the rational model has been outlined with little reference to people. The model is built squarely on the assumption that people seek order, security and certainty, at least in the work situation. They are motivated by clear tasks and goals, by reviews of performance against

goals and by rewards tied to goal achievement. In the successful organization people are bound together by hierarchy and goal clarity.

It is usually recognized that people are complex,[10] and that interpersonal and intergroup differences are important as far as the organization
adapting to its environment is concerned. Personal goals can and do
conflict with each other and people have aspirations outside the work
situation, as well as aspirations within it which have little to do with the
work itself. But all these things are obstacles to the organization achieving
fit with its environment. The obstacles are to be removed by rules and
procedures which motivate, build teams, inspire loyalty, select, train,
develop and reward people, promote common beliefs and missions, and
in general bring about harmony.

Organisational behaviour incorporated into rational models is all about
securing that internal organizational equilibrium which is harmony, so as
to remove obstacles to external equilibrium. Just as people learn to perform tasks, achieve goals and make decisions, so they learn interpersonal
skills and group loyalty. Just as analysing and thinking are algorithmic, so
is learning – learning proceeds according to complex rules and procedures which involve memorizing, processing, questioning and trial-
and-error search routines. The human mind operates, just as a computer
does, in a serial, one step at a time, algorithmic manner in acquiring the
necessary group harmonizing skills.

Rational models and traditional physics

By now it is clear how close rational models of business are to traditional
physics and to a lesser extent Darwinian evolution theory. All have
a common paradigm. That paradigm is one in which the world is a
machine, and in the case of rational models that machine is the computer.
Algorithmic methods are used throughout the piece to:

- sustain the adaptive equilibrium of the organization with its environment, so allowing it to achieve its goals;
- secure the internal equilibrium of harmony between people, without
  which adaptation to the external environment could not, according to
  the model, occur.

Rational models are in many respects as deterministic as traditional
physics. There are rules and procedures which determine equilibrium,
just as there are Newtonian laws which establish equilibrium between
natural bodies. Where such determinism breaks down, rational models
fall back on the laws of probability, similar to those found in Darwinian
evolutionary theory. Just as organisms in nature use genetic mutation in a
step-by-step fashion, so organizations use step-by-step trial and error to
deal with very high levels of uncertainty.

Rational models are reductionist in much the same way as classical physics. In both cases, greater understanding, greater control, is secured through breaking the whole into smaller and smaller parts for detailed study.

And all rational models share, in common with traditional science, a concern with order and harmony. The only form of disorder recognized is that due to ignorance; either disorder which is repetitive and to which the laws of large numbers apply, or disorder due to random shocks coming from the environment to which the organization adapts. Disorder is banished by increased understanding and control; it is in no way useful. Rational models of management and organization do differ from traditional physics and Darwinian evolution in that organizations are driven by purpose while physical bodies and organisms are not. Traditional physics and Darwinian evolution are about mindless obedience to laws, while human organizations are about the purposeful obedience to laws in order to achieve goals. But it turns out, from the manner in which purpose is handled, that it is not really of the essence; natural bodies, organisms and human organizations all function like machines according to the theories.

The rational model of management and organization is an impressive, coherent, aesthetically pleasing body of theory, in much the same way as the traditional physics to which it bears so strong a resemblance. Rational models of management do not of course achieve anything like the same predictive accuracy as classical physics, but they have had an enormous impact on business organizations, at least in the Western industrialized world. They have in many respects been responsible for the ability of such organizations to handle the increasing complexities of scale. But just as classical physics, it turns out, cannot deal with all natural phenomena, so too rational models of management fail to deal with all business phenomena.

And this applies with particular force to a key question – how do you manage when you do not know what you are doing? In other word, how do you manage open-ended change? This question does not even arise in the rational model – the problem itself is defined away. Indeed it is an inadmissible question. If you assume that events in the world are substantially predictable, as rational models do, then you have no excuse for asking the question in the first place. What you have to do is gather the data and perform the algorithmic procedures and you will have the answer. In the end the rational models are applicable only in conditions of closed and contained change as outlined in Chapter 2. Consequently they only deal with the first feedback control loop shown in Figure 3.1 in Chapter 3 – objective setting, planning, monitoring and corrective action. This is a damping feedback loop and amplifying loops of the kind which are appropriate for open-ended change (Figure 3.2, Chapter 3) are in fact to be removed according to this model. Rational models are special case ones, applicable primarily to the short interval control of the organization.

Entrepreneurial explanations of management and organization: the organic approach

The entrepreneurial models only joined the ranks of the received wisdom during the 1980s as a result of the writings of, most prominently, Peters,[11] Waterman[12] and Moss Kanter.[13] However much of the content of these models can be found in earlier publications. For example, those by Burns and Stalker in 1961[14] and by Chester Barnard[15] and Mary Parker Follett[16] even before the last war. It was perhaps the increasingly turbulent change in the business world and the disillusionment with the excessive trend to analysis and rigid hierarchies, which provided an atmosphere open to receiving such models in the 1980s. Certainly, the entrepreneurial models present in the main a frontal attack on the rational, rejecting them almost lock stock and barrel. Entrepreneurial models today are a reaction against the machine paradigm which holds the rational model so clearly in its sway. But to what extent have the entrepreneurial models escaped the clutches of the machine? What follows is an interpretation of the core explanation which the entrepreneurial view presents. It identifies key causal links, trying to strip away the descriptive material which surrounds them.

Entrepreneurial models also see the organization as a group of people having a common purpose. They think in terms of clean, clear boundaries separating the organization from its external environment. That is, they do not take account, in an essential way, of those feedback loops between an organization and its environment outlined in Chapter 4. And at the centre is the same drive to adapt the organization to its environment in order to achieve its purpose. The organization is still a proactive or reactive sensing device seeking equilibrium with its environment. In this model the organization seeks a fit between its customer's requirements and its own capabilities. The manner in which the organization creates its own environment is not taken into account in an essential way.

Turbulent environments

At the outset, entrepreneurial models prominently proclaim the turbulent, highly uncertain, unknowable, highly competitive characteristics of change in the business environment of the present time. Those models deal with aspects of open-ended change; they see it primarily as random shocks coming from the environment. This is not substantially different from the rational view; it is just that there are more of them. There is a much higher level of unpredictable uncertainty. Consequently entrepreneurial models do not postulate detailed objectives and long-term future mission as the driving force of the organization. Where change is so uncertain that it cannot be forecast then these things are impossible. Entrepreneurial models express purpose, instead, as a less precise vision. The leader of the organization articulates a vision of what the organization is to be in the future. The leader is a heroic figure, inspiring others in the organization to believe in and share the vision and a number of core values. This model is therefore firmly based on the assumption that it is possible to say something useful about the long-term future. But that something useful is always general and qualitative. So, the chief executive of the paint can manufacturer would inspire his team with the vision of being the biggest, highest quality and most responsive can manufacturer in the market. He would see a future in developing plastic cans to meet changing customer requirements. This would provide the driving force for the firm.

Because of the high level of uncertainty, the organization cannot use predictive adaptation as the mechanism for securing fit with the environment. It cannot use the rational approach of methodically scanning the environment, forecasting and then applying the pure, or bounded, forms of rational decision-making. Instead, it senses the environment by listening to its customers. It forms links with suppliers. It may also form alliances with competitors. It uses all manner of strongly personal links between people inside and outside the organization. Personal contact and active listening replace formal scanning and analysis. So here, the paint can manufacturer would maintain constant links with its customers and its designers. Through listening it would be acutely aware of changing customer requirements.

Trial-and-error action

And the processing applied to the inputs of information is not the straightforward algorithm of bounded rationality. It is, instead, that of heuristic search. The organization adopts the step-by-step procedure of trial and error, recognized by the rational model but accorded little attention by it. In this way the organization explores its highly uncertain environment in specific terms by experimental actions. Those experiments which succeed are pursued and those which fail are discontinued. This heuristic search is driven by the purpose of achieving the vision, and criteria are provided in advance for deciding whether an experiment is to be embarked on and then continued, or not. The criteria are that the experiments are only admissible if the have a logical connection with the existing business (the 'stick to your knitting principle'[17]) and if they accord with the shared values of the organization and its vision. The paint can manufacturer would try out prototype cans to meet the specifications of their customers. They would decide that developing a new plastic can was close to their core business, that such a development was required by core value of providing the highest quality to their customers and the vision of being the biggest and best.

The overwhelming emphasis placed on this heuristic search method of making decisions, requires the great stress placed by the models on action. It is only by doing something and then examining the consequences of the action, that the organization can find out what is going on in specific terms. Specific meaning then becomes retrospective rather than prospective as it was in the rational model – interpreting what has just happened becomes all important. It is this which leads quite logically to the exhortations of entrepreneurial theorists that organizations should do something, do anything;[18] that wild action is better than orderly idleness.[19] Organizations in this scheme of things learn from their mistakes. The mechanism which secures equilibrium with the environment is one of adaptive action learning about specific outcomes, driven by a vision and broad criteria. So, a tin can manufacturing behaving entrepreneurially will listen to paint manufacturer customers to understand their needs for new forms of packaging, form a joint venture with package designers and produce prototype plastic cans. The customer may reject the first attempts but the tin can manufacturer will try again. A new strategic direction in plastic packaging will be driven by the vision of a new plastics business.

The emphasis on action sometimes leads enthusiasts to exhort organizations to make mistakes, to make big mistakes, in order to learn.[20] But quieter reflection shows that actions must be small, incremental, and logical in some sense.[21] This must be so, because if the specific outcomes of actions are unknown, dramatic failure of one action could be a terminal matter for the organization. Equilibrium in the face of high levels of uncertainty requires gradual adaptation. Small incremental steps, some of which fail and others of which succeed, are built up, and according to the laws of probability, will take some organizations to equilibrium adaptation, just as is the case in Darwinian theories of evolution.

The entrepreneurial models differ from the rational so starkly because they place all the emphasis on this form of decision-making; this gradual adaptation through heuristically driven action. They differ also in that they describe this form of decision-making as an exciting, emotional process; one utilizing those motivating factors which are to some extent disorderly – passion, aggression, the desire to win, the need to be part of a family-like group. Rational models, on the other hand, describe the process, when they pay attention to it, in the colder terms of work, rational risk taking, formal search. But both are about equilibrium adaptation to the environment and both assume that it is possible to say something useful about the long-term future. The entrepreneurial model sees this something useful in broader more qualitative terms than the rational model does.

Network structures and politics

Because of the major emphasis on uncertainty, on action packed trial-and-error search, the entrepreneurial models take a rather different view of the nature of hierarchy. Since turbulent change is taking place at all levels in an organization, since scanning the environment cannot be specialized, all people in the organization are required to be in touch with the environment and to respond to it. All are required to act in the face of change. Clear roles and task definitions are then quite inappropriate. All people in the organization have to be involved in everything and clear goals cannot be set for each individual. Widespread participation and the empowering of people is called for. Rigid hierarchies make no sense in this kind of situation and instead we need loose networks between people, champions who push issues, task forces with fluctuating memberships. The activities of champions and task forces are seen as political in nature. Stable distributions of power determine which ideas are implemented. It is the role of the most powerful to support and encourage the development of innovation, the trial-and-error search. There is a typical pattern of coalition formation in which support is built up for any proposed innovation.[22] Most practising managers however do not in my experience seek to explain what they are doing in political terms. Their behaviour is of course highly political, but such behaviour is not generally seen as central to strategic management. We will return to political models of strategic choice later in this chapter.

There are still levels of management. The organization is still stratified into layers: the leader, his immediate team, senior managers, middle managers and supervisors (although Peters[23] would apparently abolish the last named). These levels are still necessary in order to secure financial control. The resources of the organization still have to be allocated and controlled. But the important point is that these stratified levels are not rigid. People can and do work across and around them. There is still a structural form. But it is one of strong decentralization. Or in another view it should be one of complex matrices. These are the structures required for equilibrium with a highly uncertain environment, and markets which are fragmented, with differentiation as the prime source of competitive advantage. Note how the structure and the mode of decision-making are both predominantly determined by the nature of a given environment, just as they are with rational models.

Shared values and financial controls

This entrepreneurial organization is far from being anarchic. The loose, overlapping, ill-defined task division, the overlapping separation of

markets and production processes, are all integrated through two important mechanisms. The first is shared values. Groups within the organization, and the organization itself, are all held together by strong cultures.
These powerful values to do with quality, service levels and belonging all
bind people together. There is a commitment to and a love of change. And
the leader's vision is part of the binding force. The vision and the values
are jealously and fanatically guarded by the leadership. The second
integration mechanism is strong financial control. Hierarchy makes its
contribution to the adaptive mechanism here, by tightly holding the
financial reigns and by zealously protecting core values. And here we find
a logical weakness in the entrepreneurial model. It prescribes strong
financial control together with loose organizational structures, widespread participation, dispersed power and vague job definitions. These
must however make strong financial control extremely difficult. Strong
financial control requires clear hierarchies and job definitions. Without
these we cannot have clear objectives against which to monitor performance. And unequal power is required to ensure that planned paths are
adhered to. The model does not indicate how this logical incompatibility
is to be resolved.

People are creative

The model of an organization as an organic mechanism adapting to its
environment is erected on the assumption that people are responsible
and creative; that they respond to the challenges of collaborating and
winning; that they are mobilized by enthusiasm, excitement and passion.
The model is also firmly built on the assumption that any disorder associated with such emotions can be harnessed and made orderly by shared
values, beliefs and vision.

Entrepreneurial models, like rational ones, derive their assumptions on
human behaviour from organizational behaviour theory. They do
however focus on very different aspects. The rational model focuses on
the orderly motivational factors influencing behaviour, and the entrepreneurial models focus on the disorderly factors of passion and emotion.
But in the end they reach, by different routes, the same harmony of
internal equilibrium so as to enable the organization to adapt to its
external environment. The whole approach of entrepreneurial models is
about team building, harnessing creative tendencies, creating harmony.
The underlying view is also that human beings learn. But instead of doing
so in advance, they learn through acting and then questioning the experience which such action generates. That learning then conditions subsequent action.

Note how this model deals with the admitted conflicting forces of task division and integration, market and process separation and synergy, personal and organizational goal conflicts, radical and conservative cultures. As with the rational models the recognized tensions which these cause are to be removed, to be harmonized and brought into equilibrium. As we saw in Chapter 4 a useful dynamic model would take a very different view. It would be concerned with how resolving these tensions sustains the organization far-from-equilibrium.

The result is a model which is certainly more exciting than the rational one. In conditions of very rapid, highly uncertain change, it is arguably more appropriate than the rational model. It does address open-ended change more fully. It provides an interpretation of the political learning feedback control loop (see Figure 2 in Chapter 3) required for control in open-ended situations. But it does so within an equilibrium framework and in effect assumes that the long-term future is not completely unknown or unknowable – visions are still possible. It does not explain small changes which escalate or vicious and virtuous circles. And the entrepreneurial models are not as comprehensive as the rational – they lack the detailed explanation of how to install what is proposed. Rational models explain in detail how, where and when to set objectives, how to define tasks, maximize performance measures, and so on. But how do you empower people? How do you create shared values? How do you formulate a vision? How do you identify issues and conduct trial-and-error experiments? How do you secure tight financial control when all its requirements have been abolished? The answers to all these questions are by no means well defined.

Entrepreneurial theory and Darwinian evolution

Now it certainly sounds as if the entrepreneurial models have escaped from the machine paradigm. But before reaching this conclusion, consider why this approach is called organic.

It is so called because it has the essential features of flexible adaptation which we associate with living organisms. Living organisms adapt to their environment using a mechanism consisting of a generator and a test.[24] The generator is random mutation, in which the genes spontaneously rearrange, triggered by some selected change in the environment. That rearrangement, or experiment, is passed on to the next generation through reproduction. The test is natural selection, the survival of the fittest. If the random mutation, within the confines of the environmental changes selected for response, results in a better fit of the organism to its environment than its rivals, then the mutation survives and is built upon by further experiment in the next generation. If the mutation does not survive the test, then the organism is destroyed by its rivals and the mutation with it.

Surviving organisms in nature build up layers of competitive advantage and, as a result of each incremental step, they maintain equilibrium with the environment, so increasing their chances of continuing survival. The more rapidly the environment changes, the more rapidly the organism must produce random mutations if it is to survive. The safest strategy is to produce large numbers of small mutations; one large mutation could spell its end.

Now this is exactly the same process as that proposed by the entrepreneurial models of human organizations. The generator, the equivalent of random mutation, is trial-and-error action within certain criteria. And such action is in a real sense random, within the criteria, because we have no means of specifying in advance actions with a particular outcome. The test in the mechanism is market selection. If the random action is successful, if it taps a source of competitive advantage, our organization builds on it. If the random action is a failure, it drops it. To survive in a rapidly changing environment, the organization must generate relatively large numbers of successful action experiments, and hence a much larger absolute number to offset failures, than its rivals. And the safest strategy is to keep the action experiments small.

Large numbers of random actions and the laws of probability will secure success for the business organization, just as large numbers of random mutations and the laws of probability will secure success for the organisms in nature. Equilibrium demands that the rate of random experimentation within the organization must match the rate of change outside in the environment. Organizations which do not move fast enough will not maintain success.[25] A high rate of experimentation can only occur in an organization if everyone is involved in everything, if structures are flexible.

The consequences of importing Darwinian evolutionary theory

Quite clearly, organic, entrepreneurial models of human organizations have imported the entire theoretical structure of Darwinian evolution. And a number of important points follow from this.

First, the adaptation mechanism is purely algorithmic. The generator, the random mutations/actions, are simply a set of rules and procedures which pick out mutations/actions at random, provided that they meet criteria to do with visions, values and existing businesses (equivalent to the environmental changes to which the organism selects to respond). A computer can do this using a random numbers table and the relevant criteria. The test is natural/market selection, the survival of the fittest in competition. The computer can play this game too, provided we set criteria for fitness and survival, say profit. So, we could in principle achieve the same results as entrepreneurial models if we used people to feed in thousands of titbits of information from customers, competitors and suppliers, used computers to generate a high enough level of random actions within the value, vision and 'stick to the knitting' criteria, got people to carry out those experimental actions and input the results, and then got people to perform the consequent feedback commands of the computer.

The entrepreneurial model is a software programme

In principle, and given the rate of information technology progress in the practice of the not too distant future, organizations could be run by computers and obedient human beings, purely along entrepreneurial lines. Developing the vision in the first place might cause the computer some problems. But strong believers in artificial intelligence will believe that in principle there is no reason why computers should not also develop visions and shared values together with team-building and belief-generating exercises. Managers would hardly be required in this arrangement. Entrepreneurial models have imported the machine paradigm together with that software programme which is the theory of Darwinian evolution.

The second point to be made is that the entrepreneurial models are in some sense as deterministic as traditional physics and in all respects as deterministic as Darwinian evolution theory. The entrepreneurial models posit that flexible organizational structures, which empower people and operate through networks bound together with shared visions and values, will produce experimental actions through which they will survive in rapidly changing market places, provided that they produce the actions fast enough. Darwinian theory makes just such a prediction for natural organisms. Neither theory can predict which specific organism or organization will survive, because we cannot know until after the event which mutated / acted fast enough. But some certainly will. There is also nothing in either theory which allows us to predict that more complex, higher levels of order and organization will emerge from the process.

The third point to make is that the entrepreneurial models are all about securing equilibrium with the environment, just as the rational models, traditional physics and natural evolutionary theories are. They are all about order and harmony. They are about the abolition of disorder, even where disorder is recognized. Entrepreneurial models use chance, they use disorderly motivational factors of people, as mechanisms where the outcome is determined. That outcome is success – there may be some disorder at an individual level, but the overall effect on the organization is one of order and harmony. Disorder is ignorance which we can handle by means of heuristic search.

In the end, the entrepreneurial models also do not provide us with any satisfactory answers to a key question – how do you manage a business when you do not know what you are doing? In other words, how do you handle open-ended change? Entrepreneurial models have also defined the question away. You may not know what you are doing in detail, but you have the vision and the shared values. The model does not consider what happens when preferences are not agreed – that is values not shared – when visions conflict, when visions are ambiguous. It does not consider the possibility that the future is so open ended that visions of some future state cannot be seen.

Political explanations of management and organization: the power approach

It has already been pointed out that managers generally do not explain their strategic management activities in terms of the exercise of power. In the literature too, political activity receives relatively little emphasis. But there have been a number of studies on political activities in organizations. These depict a process of choice by means of which those organizations cope with high levels of uncertainty and internal conflict. It is a process through which they innovate and develop new strategic direction. This choice process follows a rhythm or broad series of steps, which is held to apply in all organizations, although there are differences in detail from one organization to another and from one occasion to another.

Galvanizing events

The first step identified in studies of the political process of innovation is some departure from tradition. Some crisis or galvanizing event is required. Particular individuals with vision are prime movers in bringing this about. Some upset to existing perceptions is required through non-routine ways of doing things.[26] Real change requires crisis conditions to break inertia.[27] Some ideological shift occurs, resulting from external crisis, shifts in leadership or from the properties of the ideology itself. Such shifts increase uncertainty, so that it is difficult for people to make commitments. This shift has to be completed before action can occur.[28] The period we are talking about is one of generating different perceptions and points of view.[29] Those studying and explaining political activity in organizations talk about divergent goals and consequently conflict in conditions of uncertainty. These conclusions are based on detailed studies of individual companies over time,[30] and cross-sectional studies of a sample of highly innovative and much less innovative companies in the USA.[31]

So, in the case of the paint can manufacturers referred to earlier on, the galvanizing events at Francis Packaging were the take-over of the company by Suter, the dismissal of the chief executive and the arrival of a new one. All this occurred as ICI was switching to plastic cans, a move that Francis Packaging had avoided becoming involved in. The effect of these changes was great uncertainty on the part of the remaining managers. They had to develop new perspectives on what their business was all about and how they should change it. They had to deal with the often suppressed conflict which ensued.

Support building

The second phase, commonly described in the literature on political activities in organizations, is that of developing special interests, making demands and generating support. Here individuals or, more particularly, organizational subunits, identify uncertain changes which will affect them in some way and they make demands for particular choices in their own interests. To further these demands they obtain support from other individuals and units.[32] Or, from the observations of other writers, individuals and groups acquire information on what is going on, they define the problems emerging from the questioning of old ways, and build coalitions to gain attention for the problem and their solution to it.[33] All this support building and coalition forming is focused not just on the problems and opportunities generated by change, but also on individual careers and subunit positions and aspirations. Support building and coalition forming are of course political activities.

This could be detected at Francis Packaging. Coalitions formed around the closing of some of the plant to respond to the decline in demand, and this inevitably affected the career prospects of some of the managers. Others formed coalitions around the issue of updating some of the plant to improve the quality of the remaining business. The new chief executive had to build political support for proposals to develop the business. Political activity is the use of power to affect outcomes, to make and implement choices.

Power

Power is seen by the majority of those writing on the subject as the ability of one individual or group to get others to do something against their will. Power involves overcoming resistance.[34] Power is usually distinguished from authority. The latter derives from the structures, rules and procedures of the organization, and the former does not. Power in this sense is seen by some as illegitimate in organizational terms.[35] It is seen by those espousing rational views on deciding and controlling as dysfunctional activity arising from the pursuit of individual self-interest as opposed to organizational goals. But most writers define power as both authority and influence. They see the utilization of power as an inevitable and necessary process for making organizational choices in conditions of uncertainty and ambiguity. They see it as inevitable because it arises from the very structure of the organization itself. The division of tasks, the design of separate functions and business units, immediately leads to differing subunit goals, which in turn generates conflict which can only be resolved by the application of power.[36] Yet others take an even more favourable view of power as the ability of one individual or group to enable others to do what they could not otherwise have done.[37] Here the focus is on cooperation, consensus seeking and organizational transformation. Power seen as influence is also the ability to enable others to do what they would not otherwise have done because they lacked the information or the perception.[38] Here the emphasis is on cooperative discussion to develop ideas. And power can take an unobtrusive form in which the decision situation or the cultural norms around decision-making are manipulated to prevent different perceptions, and thus conflict, from emerging.[39]

Power, then, is a relationship between individuals and groups which determines how one affects or responds to the other in making an organizational choice. The relationships existing now are strongly affected by those which existed and were built up in the past.[40] The choice that an organization makes is determined by relative power built up over a number of periods. Once one has identified the power source of the actors involved and determined their relative power positions, the choice itself is predictable.

The sources of power lie in:

- sanctions: power increases with the ability of one person or group to reward or punish another in terms of prestige, status, money or career progression;
- interdependence: one individual or group is relatively more powerful than another if it controls more resources, has greater access to information, performs critical activities upon which the others depend for their performance, has greater access to communication channels or to more powerful channels, has control over communication agendas or the decision-making situations;
- contribution: relative power increases with the personal skills and expertise of particular individuals and their ability to interpret ambiguous situations and so reduce uncertainty for others.

Choice

The next phase in the political process is described as mobilization and completion; it is acquiring legitimacy from higher authorities;[41] choice itself;[42] planning and action. The outcome is the overcoming of conflict, the avoidance of conflict, cooperation, innovation, new strategic direction. For some, this choice is part of an incremental process.[43] For others it can be a revolution.[44] So, at Francis Packaging, the power of the Suter board and the individual power of the Francis chief executive resolved important conflicts to do with the closure of some plant, rationalization and selective investment.

Planned implementation or trial-and-error action

Having made the strategic choice, implementation may be realized by following an agreed plan setting out the action steps required to achieve the chosen goal. Or where the environment is characterized by great uncertainty that goal may be reached by trial-and-error action. Here the success of each trial step is judged against criteria for success. Such criteria usually relate to the core values of the business and to some logical connection with its existing activities. Francis Packaging decided to invest in some new facilities to produce tin products for segments it had not operated in before. Some of them turned out to be reasonably successful. It also started negotiations with Metal Box to buy those Metal Box subsidiaries which competed with it. This particular trial-and-error action ended with Metal Box buying the business of Francis Packaging instead. Not long afterwards, Metal Box sold its packaging interests to a French company.

That the political process is the means through which organizations learn in conditions of uncertainty is clear from the above framework. The organization can only learn from doing something and to get to this point it has to employ support building political activities. Despite the fact that this is what they are actually observed to do, managers very rarely reply in these terms when asked to describe how they make strategic decisions. The political system of a business rarely receives the explicit attention of its managers.

Politics as order from order

So, over the past 20 years or so, research into political activity in business organizations has produced explanations of how organizations make choices in conditions of uncertainty, ambiguity and conflict. The messiness, the difficulties, the tendency to regress from cooperative activity observed in practice, are all recognized descriptively. But they do not form essential parts of the core explanation of how political activity produces organizational choice. We also know that luck or chance often influences political outcomes. Although disorder and chance may be mentioned in passing, in most explanations of political activity they are in a shadowy background, not at the centre of the stage. Any disorder starts the process off, but is not used to explain how it unfolds. The impact of group dynamics, the possibility of dysfunctional group dynamics and neurotic forms of leadership, are not part of the explanation. Such matters are dealt with separately in the psychoanalytic tradition on organizational matters.[45] The interactive impact of personality differences on what choices are made is not incorporated. These matters are treated separately as well.[46] Thus the dysfunctional politicking, which in practice always accompanies functional political learning, is separated out as 'raw politics'[47] and its impact on what happens is not built into the explanation in an essential way.

What is presented by current models of political decision-making is therefore an orderly sequential process. It occurs to overcome an initial disorderly state of ambiguity and conflict. The outcome is predictable once the sources of power have been identified and measured, once the relative power positions have been determined. Deterministic laws on power relativity yield predetermined outcomes. The normal state of the successful organization is one of commitment, consensus and cooperation.

The mechanisms and the outcomes are deterministic in another sense. Certain conditions can be established in which the kind of political behaviour required to secure innovation will occur. This will happen when:[48]

- people are free and empowered – the required conditions are the wide dispersal of power, local autonomy, and decentralised resources;
- people participate and collaborate with each other, and there is a willingness to share – team building and the fostering of strongly shared cultures is thus essential;
- there is a culture of commitment and pride in the organization and its accomplishments – it must also be a culture which values and loves change;
- the cultures, structures systems and relationships between people are integrative rather than segmentalist;
- there is open communication and networks which operate both informally and are built into the structures;
- job assignments are ambiguous and non-routine – job definitions are loose and job territories intersecting;
- leadership is persuasive and visionary, but also sets tough standards;
- there is an orientation to action.

Establish these conditions and people will participate to discover, choose and act, so producing innovations.

We have then a political explanation of organizational choice which is presented within a machine frame of reference. Political interaction occurs in a step-by-step fashion, with outcomes predictable from the distribution of power. Those outcomes will be innovation if power is widely enough dispersed, people participate and show continuing commitment and consensus under persuasive, visionary leadership which stresses action. Disorder at an individual level does not contribute to the outcome in any essential way other than to start the whole process off. Such disorder does not render the sequence of choices unpredictable. Different values, different goals and the ensuing conflict in effect cause a problem which is to be overcome by the process of political activity so as to secure a state of continuing commitment and consensus.

Conclusion: today's models all focus on machine-like order

This chapter has argued that all the explicit models of managing and organizing which managers and consultants try to use to design their actions show clear signs of the frame of reference within which they have been developed. That frame of reference is the machine paradigm of traditional science. Rational, entrepreneurial and the most conspicuous power models all interpret effective business behaviour in terms of orderly step-by-step procedures which lead to an orderly outcome. None of these models sees the observed messiness of actual business life, lack of consensus and different cultural norms as central to the explanation of business success. All these models treat the dynamic as a drive towards equilibrium – the equilibrium of internal harmony and adapting to the external environment.

It is true that writers using the entrepreneurial and power models do describe the disorder and messiness of business life. They discuss and prescribe creativity. They emphasise the importance of different perspectives and turbulent environments. It might therefore be argued that the presentation of these models in this chapter and the conclusions drawn about them are something of a wooden caricature of what they present. However what this chapter has sought to do is to strip away the descriptive material and get at the underlying explanatory models which are being used. And in those models, the disorderly aspects of business life do not play an essential part in explaining how success is achieved. The chapters in Part Three will go on to indicate another model where these elements do play an essential part.

The conclusion is that none of today's prominent models of managing and organizing are built firmly on the feedback nature of the organization.

They do not account for escalating small changes and vicious and virtuous circles. They all maintain that it is possible to say something useful about the long-term future. They all fall within the machine frame of reference. Because of this underlying frame of reference, these models lead us to ignore, or downplay important aspects of the dynamic of business life. Set against the criteria put forward in the chapters in Part One, today's most prominent models of business do not provide an adequate understanding of the dynamic. The following chapter explores what thinking in terms of today's most prominent models leads us to ignore.

References

1   For example, Taylor, F. (1947), *Scientific Management*, Harper & Row.
2   For example, Simon, H. A. (1981), *The Sciences of the Artificial*, MIT.
3   For example, Koontz, H., O'Donell, C. (1968), *Principles of Management*, McGraw-Hill, Robbins, S. P. (1988), *Management Concepts and Applications*, Prentice-Hall.
4   For example, Robbins, S. P. (1986), *Essentials of Organizational Behaviour*, Prentice-Hall.
5   Drucker, P. (1964), *Managing for Results*, Harper & Row; Drucker, P. (1967), *The Practice of Management*, Heinemann; Drucker, P. (1979), *Management: Tasks, Responsibilities and Practice*, Heinemann; Drucker, P. (1980), *Management in Turbulent Times*, Heinemann; Drucker, P. (1985), *Innovation and Entrepreneurship*, Heinemann.
6   Ansoff, I. (1964), *Corporate Strategy*, McGraw-Hill; Ansoff, I. (1984), *Implementing Corporate Strategy*, Prentice-Hall.
7   Porter, M. (1983), *Competitive Strategy*, Macmillan; Porter, M. (1985), *Competitive Advantage*, Macmillan.
8   Simon, H. A. (1970), *The New Science of Management Decision*, Harper & Row; Simon, H. A. (1979), 'Rational Decision Making in Business Organizations', *American Economic Review*, 69.
9   Drucker, P. (1985), *Entrepreneurship and Innovation*, Heinemann; Quinn, J. B. (Fall 1978), Strategic change: Logical Incrementalism, *Sloan Management Review*, 1, 20.
10 H. A. Simon, however says they are not.
11 Peters, T., Waterman, R. H. (1982), *In Search of Excellence*, Harper & Row; Peters, T., Austin, N. (1985), *A Passion for Excellence*, Collins; Peters, T. (1988), *Thriving on Chaos*, Macmillan.
12 Waterman, R. H. (1988), *The Renewal Factor*, Bantam Books.
13 Moss Kanter, R. (1985), *The Change Masters: Innovation and Entrepreneurship in the American Corporation*, Simon & Schuster; Moss Kanter,

R. (1989), *When Giants Learn to Dance, Mastering the Challenge of Strategy, Management and Careers in the 1990s,* Simon & Schuster.

14 Burns, T., Stalker, G. M. (1961), *The Management of Innovation,* Tavistock Publications.

15 Barnard, C. (1938), *The Functions of the Executive,* Harvard University Press.

16 Parker Follet, M. (1929), *The New State,* Peter Smith.

17 Peters, T., Waterman, R., op. cit.

18 Peters, T., *Thriving on Chaos,* op. cit.

19 Weick, K. (1979), *The Social Psychology of Organising,* Addison Wesley.

20 Peters, T., op. cit.

21 Quinn, J. B., op. cit.

22 Moss Kanter, R. (1985), op. cit. This pattern is summarized later in this chapter.

23 Peters, T., op. cit.

24 Simon, H. A., *The Sciences of the Artificial,* op. cit.

25 Peters, T., op. cit; Weick, K., op. cit.

26 Moss Kanter, R. (1985), op. cit.

27 Pettigrew, A. M. (1973), *The Politics of Organizational Decision Making,* Tavistock Publications; Pettigrew, A. M. (1986), Some Limits of Executive Power in Creating Strategic Change, in Srivasta, S. & Associates, *Executive Power,* Jossey-Bass.

28 Pettigrew, A. M. (1986), op. cit.

29 Srivasta, S., Barrett, F. J., Conclusion: Functions of Executive Power: Exploring New Approaches in Srivasta, S. & Associates, op. cit.

30 Pettigrew, A. M. (1985), *The Awakening Giant: Continuity and Change in Imperial Chemical Industries,* Blackwell.

31 Moss Kanter, R. (1985), op. cit.

32 Pettigrew, A. M. (1973), op. cit.

33 Moss Kanter, R. (1985), op. cit; Quinn, J. B. (1980), *Strategies for Change: Logical Incrementalism,* Irwin; Pfeffer, J. (1981), *Power on Organizations,* Bakkinger; Bacharach, S. B., Lawler, E. J. (1980), *Power and Politics in Organizations,* Jossey-Bass.

34 Pettigrew, A. M. (1973), op. cit; Pfeffer, J., op. cit.

35 Mayes, B. T., Allen, W. R. (1977), Towards a Definition of Organizational Politics, *Academy of Management Review,* 2.

36 Pettigrew, A. M. (1973), op. cit; Pfeffer, J., op. cit.

37 Srivasta, S. Barrett, F. J., op. cit.

38 Moss Kanter, R. (1985), op. cit.

39 Pettigrew, A. M. (1986), op. cit.

40 Pettigrew, A. M., op. cit; Pfeffer, J., op. cit.

41 Moss Kanter, R. (1985), op. cit.

42 Pettigrew, A. M., op. cit; Pfeffer, J., op. cit.

43 Quinn, J. B., op. cit.

44 Mintzberg, H. (1978), Patterns in Strategy Formation, *Management Science*, 24.

45 Zaleznik, A., Kets de Vries, M. F. R. (1985), *Power and the Corporate Mind*, Bonus Books.

46 Meredith Belbin, R. (1981), *Management Teams*, Heinemann; Kiersey, D., Bates, M. (1984), *Please Understand Me*, Gnosology Books.

47 Moss Kanter, R. (1985), op. cit.

48 Moss Kanter, R. (1985), op. cit; Srivasta, S. Barrett, F. J., op. cit.

6 Today's models: a limited understanding of management dynamics

While entrepreneurial models of management do differ from the rational in many important respects, they share a number of important features. Both focus on success as the establishment of an equilibrium adaptation to the environment. That environment is seen as quite distinctive from the organization itself. It is a separate reality out there to be scanned or discovered and adapted to. Both models see the only source of open-ended uncertainty confronting a successful competently run business as random shocks coming from the environment. Both are built upon the assumption that it is possible to say something operationally useful about the long-term future, at least in general qualitative terms. If we cannot have a precise quantitative objective, we can at least have a vision of some future state. Both models are goal driven and action oriented. Both are concerned with order and harmony. They deal with what managers do once the ambiguity of issues and equivocal responses to them have been removed. Chance, in so far as it features at all, does so as a mechanism in a trial-and-error search. Both are deterministic in the traditional sense of some cause in the environment leading to an effect in the organization, in the sense of a given input into a causal relationship having a fixed outcome. They are both built squarely within the computing machine paradigm. Political power models of management choice, incorporated as an element of the decision-making process in entrepreneurial models, are about predictable choices flowing from stable patterns of power distribution. They too fall within the machine paradigm.

Today's models are dominated by considerations of environmental complexity and by adaptation mechanisms. Irregularity and disorder are seen either as the result of management incompetence or as a consequence of random shocks arising in the environment. Those shocks have to be accommodated by an orderly organization. Orderly organizations quickly overcome the disorder created by random shocks and the internal conflict they provoke. Organizational behaviour which is conflicting and contradictory, which often has little clear purpose or cause and is quite frequently even bizarre, plays no essential part in explaining how successful organizations deal with open-ended change. Today's models mention interpersonal conflict. They describe tension between personal and organizational goals. But they then skate on in order to put forward, sometimes with little indication of how they are to be achieved, harmony generating devices such as shared values.

Because of the predominance of the electronic machine paradigm, there are a number of essential aspects of the dynamics of managing and organizing which the received wisdom largely ignores.

Feedback, small changes, virtuous and vicious circles

The rational models of managing and organizing focus almost entirely on the first of the feedback control loops which were discussed in Chapter 3 (Figure 3.1). This control loop runs from objective setting through planning to monitoring and corrective action. That control loop is only applicable in closed and contained situations – those in which the consequences of change can be forecast to some useful degree. The feedback in this loop operates to dampen any deviations from plan, so restoring the organization to its pre-ordained path over time. All other aspects of the explanation run in terms of straightforward cause and effect. Performance, behaviour, choice and action are not seen in terms of feedback mechanisms. Consequently, little attention is paid to small changes and there is no accounting for how they might escalate into major differences in behaviour. The possibility of virtuous and vicious circles simply does not arise. Rational models are consequently special case ones applicable to the short-term control of an organization. They have little to contribute to an understanding of control and development in open-ended situations when the future is an unknown. But as a set of prescriptions for short interval control they are vital to success. They provide managers with a useful model of the short interval control loop.

The entrepreneurial models of managing and organizing focus almost entirely on the second feedback control loop described in Chapter 3

(Figure 3.2). They provide an interpretation of the behaviour involved in that feedback loop and the conditions required for it to operate. This is the control loop appropriate to open-ended change, in which managers discover changes and respond through political support-building processes and trial-and-error action. However the operation of this loop is explained in damping terms. Visions and fanatically shared core values damp out the disorderly effects of widespread participation and the empowering of people. The model operates to overcome conflict and differences in perspectives. It does not use confusion and conflict in an essential way, as part of the process through which organizations innovate and develop new strategic direction. Furthermore the effects of the widespread presence of feedback mechanisms driving performance and behaviour throughout the organizational process is not recognized. These models too cannot explain how small changes come to substantially alter the direction the organization takes. There is no explanation of how virtuous and vicious circles develop and what part they play. The entrepreneurial model uses the idea that large numbers of random shocks and large numbers of trial-and-error actions will offset each other to produce stable states close to equilibrium. We saw in Chapter 4 that this is not possible for feedback systems operating in open-ended change situations.

The power models of organizational choice also do not take account of the amplifying effect of feedback between one political choice, or action, and another. They do not explain how small changes in, say, the group dynamic can escalate to produce totally different political outcomes. Once again we are left without an explanation of the virtuous and vicious circles we observe in political behaviour. The unintended outcomes of political action are left unexplained.

The wider management literature, primarily that which approaches management from a social psychology perspective, does explicitly take account of amplifying and damping feedback loops. It explains management behaviour in terms of feedback between individuals and between groups.[1] Those models do explain how such interaction generates virtuous and vicious circles, often from small changes. But they do not provide general models indicating what part such loops play in the control and development of the business organization as a whole. And these feedback models of interpersonal and group behaviour have had little discernible impact on the thinking of most practising managers.

We have then a situation in which feedback loops and their amplifying and damping consequences are of fundamental importance in the functioning of business organizations. This was demonstrated in Chapter 4. But the explicit explanations managers use to guide their actions substantially ignore this fact. The feedback concept is widely used in the decision sciences, but there the concern is almost entirely with feedback as a damping, stabilizing form of control. Because of the limited and partial manner in which feedback mechanisms are incorporated into our models of business behaviour, we lack explicit models to design actions which take account of essential aspects of business dynamics.

Operation in non-equilibrium states

One of the principal conclusions reached in Chapter 4 was this: when we take a fuller account of the amplifying and damping nature of the feedback mechanisms which drive a business organization, we see that the concept of organizations continually adapting to their environments is far from useful in understanding business dynamics. Managers create their own environments to a considerable extent, through the creative shaping of customer requirements by the product offerings they make. Such product offerings spread through the customer population making the feedback between customers and the organization highly sensitive. It then becomes unclear who is adapting to whom. This idea appears in the management literature as approached from a social psychology perspective[2] and in the literature on marketing. But once again, these ideas are not central building blocks in general models of organizational control and development. And they are accorded little explicit attention by most practising managers.

All today's prominent models in effect assume that there is a clean, clear line separating the organization from its environment. The organization then acts across the boundary to bring itself into balance with the changes occurring in the environment. The environment is a real, given thing 'out there' to be scanned or listened to actively. It is required that the organization should adapt either by means of action in accordance with a plan, or by means of exploratory trial-and-error action to fulfil a vision. Change in the environment prompts managerial action to respond to that environment.

But in fact we know that this is not so. The reality is interaction. There is a feedback loop in which the actions of the organization can change its environment, and the organization must then handle the change it has itself created. In a real sense the organization creates a part of its environment. Indeed that is the explicit intention of, for example, advertising. Furthermore, action is undertaken in response to perceptions of the environment and sometimes those perceptions may not accord with what is really there. You may perceive that customers are no longer buying your tin cans because they rust. In fact they may have stopped buying them because of your poor service levels. You will then undertake action directed at an illusory environment, one you have invented.

When we take account of the fact that parts of the environment are created and invented by the organization, then the boundary line between it and its environment is no longer clean and clear cut, but blurred.

And as the organization grows in size, that line becomes even more blurred because larger organizations have more impact on their environments. The processes by which the organization interacts with its environment must consequently become more complex than those envisaged by either of today's prominent models. A greater understanding of the border between the organization and its environment is then required. And insights into this complexity are available in the literature, but remain unabsorbed by today's prominent models.[3] Chapter 4 concluded that successful organizations do not adapt in an equilibrium manner but operate in non-equilibrium borders between equilibrium states. Appendix B speculates on the nature of this border.

Chapter 4 also argued that successful organizations are those whose internal systems and structures are in a non-equilibrium state. All today's most prominent models see the dynamic of success as movement towards that internal equilibrium which is harmony. We have no reasonably clear understanding of what operation in a non-equilibrium state entails. What we need, if we are to understand business dynamics more fully, is a model which explains business success in terms of avoiding equilibrium states and operating in non-equilibrium ones. The rational model prescribes structures and processes which taken on their own, lead to the equilibrium state of ossification described in Chapter 4. The entrepreneurial models prescribe structures and processes which could well lead to the equilibrium of disintegration described in Chapter 4. Success lies in a border between these states. A useful dynamic model should have something to say about this border area.

The more enthusiastic proponents of the entrepreneurial model uncompromisingly reject the rational. More cautious writers see the mechanistic and organic approaches as polar extremes in a continuum where organizations in reality adopt a position somewhere between the extremes.[4] But how do you combine coldly rational planning with wildly enthusiastic trial-and-error? What kinds of tension would attempts to find a compromise between the two create? Each model refers to some tension between, for example, personal and organizational objectives; long-term and short-term objectives; task division and integration and so on. However such tensions are not the basic building blocks of the theory. When tensions of this kind are resolved, managers may well not use algorithmic procedures, heuristic or otherwise. If this is so, then models conditioned by the electronic machine paradigm will find it hard to explain the consequences of such tensions.

What organizations do when they do not know what they are doing

As we have seen, today's prominent models do not admit this as a serious possibility. In the rational models the first prescription is for organizations to set hierarchies of objectives and then draw up plans to achieve these. In the entrepreneurial models they are to create visions and then act within the constraints of shared values and logical connection with the existing business. Thereafter, in both cases, organizations know what they are doing. Both models assume that it is possible to say something useful about the long-term future. They are both in effect saying that the long-term future is not essentially unknowable; it is rather, to different degrees, presently unknown. Neither constructs an adequate explanation of the effects of confusion and anxiety in searching for new goals. And this is a central feature of open-ended change.

What do managers do when they recognize that the long-term future is unknowable? What happens if the preferences of individuals are not clear? What happens if objectives and visions are not clear? We are not talking about a situation in which there are conflicting preferences and objectives, where bargaining can be used to resolve the issue. We are talking about a situation in which the actors involved actually do not know what they prefer, or what they want in any operational sense. They really do not know, in a given situation, what will happen or what is best for them. This is not a situation that the power models of managerial choice envisage either.

When it comes to appointing a deputy manager to report to you, you may not be all that clear as to whether you should appoint a particular man who is hard working and loyal, but somewhat pedestrian; or a woman who is sharp and imaginative, but highly ambitious and aggressive. Will he prompt ideas which will bring you 'kudos' at the board meeting? Will she shine so much as to threaten your position? When two projects, equally attractive, are competing for scarce resources, you may not be at all clear as to whether to throw your weight behind the project backed by an old colleague who is your friend; or behind the one backed by a new director who is on the fast track to the chief executive office. In a new reorganization, will it be better for you to press for clear definitions of the roles and responsibilities of your colleagues and yourself, or to try to keep the options open and fluid? Where should the balance be struck? At the start of every strategic management assignment I have ever been on, the directors involved have not known what their preferences, objectives or visions are. But neither received model deals with these situations and nor do the power models.

There are many situations, as we all know only too well, where the preferences and objectives of a number of powerful individuals in the organization are both unclear and conflicting. There are many situations where what is happening is ambiguous and responses are equivocal. Simple procedures of rational decision-making, bounded or otherwise, do not adequately explain what happens in such situations. Nor do trial-and-error searches or bargaining procedures.

Now the literature does put forward some interesting insights to explain what happens in the kinds of business situation just described.[5] Concepts of organizational anarchy, 'garbage can' models of decision-making, the science of muddling through in conditions of ignorance, can all be brought to bear.[6] So too can the literature on complex organizational learning processes as well as those of organizational culture as underlying basic assumptions on how to manage.[7] Ideas along these lines were put forward some 20 to 30 years ago and probably even earlier. All these ideas are highly relevant to managing in conditions of extreme uncertainty, but they receive little explicit attention from most practising managers. Then there is the literature which comes from the direction of psychotherapy and social psychology.[8] This explores intra- and intergroup behaviour and looks at the consequences of not knowing what one is doing. The confusion and hostility provoked by such situations have implications for the kinds of decisions which get made. This too has not found its way into explanations managers pay much attention to.

The starting point for all of today's prominent models is that organizations are groups of people with a common purpose. We have to admit that any operational purpose may not always be all that clear, but to suggest that there might not be even the slightest glimmering of common purpose at all, certainly does jar with the received wisdom. How can the computing machine take even the first step if it is given no goal, no criteria whatsoever?

On reflection, however, we see that loose groupings of people may and do form without any common purpose at all. For example, three or four executives may well lunch together with reasonable frequency, not because they have some particular common objective in mind; not even because they like each other all that much. They form a loose group, but a group nevertheless, because of the means that each has at his or her disposal.[9] Each may have some expertise or powerful connection which the others believe may one day be useful. They may each have different objectives. Or the objectives and the shared values may come later. Until then, it is the means which binds them together, not the ends. Such networks have, as we all know, considerable impact on what happens in organizations. But today's prominent models with their focus on common objectives and shared values do not adequately incorporate this kind of behaviour.

Managers in the business world are not permitted to admit that they do not know what they are doing.[10] In private, a chairperson or chief executive may jocularly make such an admission. But the financial markets and powerful investors would reward such public honesty with an immediate and sharp markdown in the company's share price. And colleagues and employees would quickly conclude that the leader was incompetent. Much energy is therefore invested in creating the myth of rationality, in providing comforting rationalisations of what has happened to the organization. Much of what happens in business organizations does not readily make sense, unless one recognizes first that this kind of rationalizing is going on and second why it is going on. And why it is going on, I suggest, has much to do with that machine paradigm which so powerfully governs the way we think.

The dynamic of organizational politics

Rational models largely ignore political activity. Where this is addressed, it is seen either as a bargaining process for the resolution of clear but conflicting objectives, or, it is seen as an obstacle to achieving the behavioural harmony necessary for the dynamic equilibrium adaptation of the organization to its environment. Political activity is seen largely as 'politicking'; a process utilized by individuals for personal gain largely at the expense of the organization. The political system in a business organization is described as an obstacle to the adaptation process. The behavioural principles of rational theory are all about suppressing and controlling political activity in the interests of harmony.

Entrepreneurial models do explicitly incorporate political activity. They describe a sequence in which innovators and champions develop new ideas, collaborate with others and generate support through building coalitions. Stable distributions of power, combined with clear preferences on the part of the organization's members, determines the choice. And this productive form of politics is distinguished from dysfunctional individual politicking to secure career progression.[11] Here functional politics is seen as that which occurs within a framework of continuing commitment and consensus. These explanations of political activity do not pay much attention to the possibility that sometimes organizations, and the managers within them, do not know what they are doing. Nor do they give much prominence to the role that conflict and different cultural norms must play in developing new perspectives. If we recognize the continuing lack of clarity in preferences, and the importance of conflict and difference in values, then we would see political activity as the process which clarifies preferences and objectives and makes choices about them. It is then seen as a complex, vital group activity which must often precede the kind of trial-and-error action routine on which the entrepreneurial models place so much emphasis, or the objective setting and planning procedures which the rational models stress.

Political activity is often muddling through,[12] it can be garbage decision-making.[13] It is the process where power, influenced by ideological values, actually determines opportunities and constraints as well as strategic choice.[14] It is about decision-making in conditions of ignorance where the key is the search for error.[15] It is through political activity that ambiguity and equivocality are preserved and utilized by the organization to deal with highly uncertain change, the unknowable. But these ideas are not part of the explanations to which managers pay much attention.

Power models of political activity

Consider the explanation of the political process put forward in power and entrepreneurial models. At some points, organizational choice is not driven by any overarching goal, mission or vision. Instead there are conflicting individual and subunit goals or visions which have to be resolved by the application of power. The application of political power will produce an orderly sequence of choices between conflicting goals when the following conditions are present:

- Each of the conflicting individuals and subunits have clear, predefined preferences for particular outcomes throughout the process. They all know what their goals are. Such goals are clear to each individual and group. The problem is only that they conflict and this leads to the early messy stage of challenge to the underlying ideology. Outcomes will therefore be the result of intention, or purpose, on the part of some individual or group. We will be able to look back and say that the outcome happened because that individual or that group intended it. The problem is, which individual or group intended it. And that problem can be resolved by finding out what the distribution of relative power is.
- The distribution of power is determined in a stable manner by sanctions, interdependence and contribution which make some individuals and groups more powerful than others. It is the choices of the more powerful which will prevail. Relative power is altered when the source of power is changed. These sources are relatively constant so the distribution of power is stable.
- The distribution of power over time is stable. The individuals or groups who possessed and exerted power in previous time periods will do so in this time period. Those who consented and were willing to accept the exercise of that power in previous time periods, will continue to do so in this.
- The distribution of power over different issues is stable. Those who exerted and consented to the use of power to make a choice in relation to one issue will do so in relation to all issues. Or, relative power will at least determine which issues certain groups and individuals will always attend to, given that there are very large numbers of issues but scarce resources, including time, to deal with them.
- A choice is always made and acted upon. The outcome of the political process is resolution taking the form of accepting and implementing a choice or rejecting it for well considered reasons.

Widespread participation and dispersed power

The conclusion reached in the entrepreneurial and power models is that this process will contribute most effectively to making choices in highly turbulent environments when the following conditions are present.

- Power is widely dispersed through the organization and applied predominantly in the form of influence.
- People are empowered and organizational structures installed to encourage widespread participation.

Complex matrix and network type structures will encourage this widespread participation. Defining jobs loosely with ambiguous and overlapping content will encourage people to become involved in everything. This will mean that the organization will detect more of what is going on in its rapidly changing environment and more knowledge will be brought to bear on decision-making. Decision making will therefore be more effective. When participation of this kind is accompanied by strongly shared values, it will generate consensus seeking behaviour. All this will lead to creative and innovative political behaviour which will overcome any periodic conflict touched off by different perceptions and hence different goals.

In these conditions harmony is the norm and conflict the exception. On these assumptions we build an explanation of the political process in a business organization which has the rhythm of that described in the previous chapter – there will be phases in which some crisis generates different perceptions and conflicting goals; champions will build political support for a particular choice; a particular choice will be made depending on which champion has or builds up, the greater power. There will be no essentially chance or random outcomes. A stable flow of choices will emerge over time which will not be significantly affected by the specific context within which a choice is made at a particular time. When we look back we will be able to say that a particular choice was made because a particular individual or group intended it and secured it through greater power. We will be able to say in advance which of a range of choices will be made, once we know enough about the power distribution.

There are a number of problems with this kind of explanation. It underestimates the importance of continuing difference and conflict in generating a stream of new perceptions. It does not take account of the fact that subordinates are likely to experience the same learning difficulties as superiors. It excludes the possibility that subordinates repeat the same kinds of learning error. Simply widening participation is then unlikely in itself to alter the learning process or improve decision-making.[16] For this reason, power and entrepreneurial models are inadequate explanations of the dynamics we observe in actual political processes in a business.

Furthermore, different sources of power, and hence different forms of power, may apply at different times in relation to different issues, despite a stable overall power distribution. These possibilities arise because the context within which power is applied and consented to is of importance. For example, there may be dysfunctional, bizarre group dynamics. Some remark or behaviour by one person may touch off some unconscious response from another. This could affect the willingness to exert, or consent to the application of yesterday's relative power balance in today's choice. Neurotic leadership behaviour might result in the application of unacceptable forms of power today, or an unwillingness to apply power today. Leaders may judge it unwise to apply their power at all in certain circumstances. The importance of issues could be misunderstood. Time pressures could lead to issues being avoided or overlooked by the relatively more powerful. Certain types of issue might alter the willingness to exert or consent to the use of power. For example open-ended issues may be avoided. Workload and issue type may well affect the application of power. So, entrepreneurial and power models ignore the importance of context.

Then, there may not always be a well-thought-out choice. Decisions might be made by oversight or they may not be implemented. Chance might well play a part in the decision which is made. And widely dispersed power and widespread participation can produce anarchic decision-making, a point to be developed in the next section.

The only way that the entrepreneurial and power models account for observed political behaviour which is messy, related to personal career progression and personal goals, is to say that it is all dysfunctional. Those models see such dysfunctional political activity as separable from functional political activity. Dysfunctional political activity can and should be removed because it plays no part in the successful operation of the political system. But in adopting this approach we are left with much to explain.

Chance explanations of political activity

There are other studies of political choice making which give a very different perspective from the power models. A very different political process has been found to apply in universities and some state bodies.[17] These explanations of political activity account for many of the behaviours and outcomes which were listed above as being excluded by the entrepreneurial and power models. Universities and some state bodies are characterized by widely distributed power and by complex, unclear hierarchical structures. The hierarchical structure is such that just about any issue can be taken to just about any forum by just about anyone. This is a bit of an exaggeration of course, but not much. These institutions are noted for widespread participation in decision-making and for ambiguous and intersecting job definitions. They are however not characterized by strongly shared cultural values across the whole organization. This is the kind of situation prescribed by the entrepreneurial and power models, with one major difference. Those models also prescribe strongly shared organizational values. What is found in the conditions prevailing at universities and some state bodies is the following:

- individuals and subunits do not have clear goals;
- no individual has much power, and the distribution of power is not stably determined by sanctions, interdependence and contribution; it fluctuates with the context within which decisions are being made and consequently;
- the distribution of power over time is not constant;
- the distribution of power over issue is not constant;
- choices are often avoided, deferred, made by oversight or never implemented.

These conditions are the opposite of those assumed in the power and entrepreneurial models and they lead to very different outcomes. Here outcomes occur largely by chance in what are called organized anarchies. The flow of choices over time is erratic and haphazard. The power approach described earlier produces explanations of organizational choice in terms of global rhythm flowing from new perception, through building support based on power which determines the stable flow of choices made over time. The focus is on global order and on specific choice stability. The chance approach,[18] however exhibits little global rhythm to the process. Here there is a continuing flow of problems, opportunities, solutions and choices coming together in a largely haphazard manner. This happens because there is no simple and clear hierarchy and because the distribution of power is close to equality.

Where power is widely dispersed so that there are no powerful actors who can enforce their wills, where power is therefore unstable over time and issue, where there is little sharing of values, where there are heavy workloads on individuals and meetings, where participation in decision-making is open and fluid, where access to choice situations and participation structures are open and unclear, then choice will be determined largely by chance. The choice will depend entirely upon the context in which it is attended to. It will depend upon the level of attention paid to it in the light of all the other issues; upon who was present and participated; upon how they participated and how others interpreted that participation. Looking back it will not be possible to say that the choice occurred because some individual or group intended it. In this sense intention or purpose is lacking in the choice process. There is no overall rhythm to the process and the specific sequence of choices is random and without any pattern. The sequence of specific choices can shoot anywhere because important constraints provided by unequal power, clear hierarchies and job descriptions have been removed. Action is then the result of habit, custom or the unpredictable influence of others. It is impossible to predict the choice without knowing all the small details of the context. Intention is lost in the flow of events and goals are the product of sense making activities after the event.

These studies have shown that where participation is widespread and power equally distributed, where job assignments are unclear and hierarchies complex, where values are not strongly shared, then we get sequences of choices which depend largely on chance. Now the entrepreneurial and power models prescribe most of these conditions. They differ only in stressing the importance of leaders with visions (that is some power inequality) and the strong sharing of values. Avoiding organized anarchy with its chance decisions therefore depends entirely on visions and strong sharing of values. These may well be difficult conditions to meet in practice. And it will be argued in Chapter 9 that if they are met, they will obstruct the handling of open-ended change.

So power models are essentially about order from order and chance models are essentially about disorder from disorder. Neither provides an adequate explanation of the political dynamic of a successful business organization because what we observe in such organizations is a mixture of order and disorder. We observe some stability in the flow of choices that such successful business organizations make. But we also observe unintended actions, choices which sometimes depend upon chance, escalating consequences, self-reinforcing virtuous and vicious circles. We need some combination of the power and chance models if we are to explain adequately the dynamic of business behaviour.

Organizations learn about the process of learning

In both the rational and the entrepreneurial explanations of organizational behaviour, the process by which the organization is to be controlled and developed is set out in advance of any action. Learning on the rational view is then largely confined to finding out how the environment is changing and incorporating appropriate responses in plans. As the plans are implemented, variances to plan are identified by monitoring. This is a limited learning process in which the organization discovers how appropriate its plans are. In the entrepreneurial approach the organization learns about its environment through trial-and-error action. In both cases the learning is about what to do and why to do it.

But in highly uncertain environments, which are rapidly changing, organizations need to learn about how to do what they do. They need to be monitoring, or applying trial-and-error search to the processes they are using to control and develop the business. It is not enough to be concerned with the 'what' and the 'why', that is the outcomes of open-ended change. Since open-ended change is a stream of unique events, it requires the continual development of new mental models to deal with it. Managers then have to be concerned with the 'how' as well. They have to be aware of and improve the processes by means of which they together develop new mental models. And this requires delving into and reflecting upon basic cultural assumptions which govern how things are done.[19] This learning about the process by which open-ended change is handled is not incorporated into today's most prominent models in any essential way.

Conclusion: what managers actually do

It is important to draw a distinction between explanatory models which are exposed to and have an impact on practitioners, and other ideas which are to be found in the management literature. Models can only be useful if managers are paying attention to them. All today's most prominent models have imported their methodology from the traditional natural sciences. All have been developed within a frame of reference in which the world is seen as an orderly, well-regulated machine at or near to equilibrium. That economics has imported this concept lock, stock and barrel is not difficult to see. It is built upon assumptions of rational man who makes step-by-step rational decisions. While models of management and organization have adapted the concepts more significantly to take account of real human purpose and behaviour, they have nevertheless done so substantially within a frame of reference which sees the relevant aspects of human behaviour as driven by algorithmic modes of thinking and learning. They see the world of business behaviour in terms of software packages for electronic machines. And most managers pay attention to these models because they too are affected by the machine frame of reference.

The rational and entrepreneurial models start from two very different sets of assumptions. The former assumes that the environment is substantially orderly and predictable, that people at work are motivated by that which is orderly and regular. The latter models assume that the environment is substantially disorderly, that people at work are motivated by that which is disorderly, exciting and emotional. The task which both models address however is exactly the same: to secure internal harmony among people in the organization as a precondition to securing the adaptive equilibrium with the environment which ensures survival, success and consistent streams of profit.

Because of the different assumptions the two theories make about the conditions within which the task is carried out, they produce dramatically different rules and procedures for carrying out the task. But both produce rules and procedures which are essentially algorithmic. Both produce software packages which are to be run on the same machine to the same end; it is simply that the software packages differ. The rational package is an algorithm which does not normally rely on any random procedures – it is straightforward logic. Objectives / missions are formulated and implemented in a logical, serial manner. The entrepreneurial package incorporates an heuristic search routine, utilizing random search within specified criteria. Visions, shared values and the existing business define the area within which the random, experimental action is used to adapt to the environment. The two software packages are usually presented as alternatives – the machine cannot run both at the same time.

But neither received model envisages a continuing situation in which objectives / missions and visions / shared values are absent. Neither seriously deals with the situation which exists before these things become clear and agreed or after they cease to be agreed. Neither model allows the question – how do you manage when you do not know what you are doing? This must be because both assume that you can only ask this question if you are ignorant; that the random and the disorderly are in fact ignorance or dysfunctional behaviour. And ignorance can be conquered by gathering data and analysing the facts, or by developing a vision and shared values. Dysfunctional behaviour can be cured by team building and culture change programmes. Both models ignore operation in non-equilibrium states and take little account of feedback mechanism and the virtuous and vicious circles they are capable of generating.

And the entrepreneurial model has serious flaws as an interpretation of the learning political control loop appropriate to open-ended change (Figure 3.2, Chapter 3.) It prescribes widely dispersed power which runs the risk of creating organized anarchy. It prescribes widespread participation which does not necessarily improve learning ability and therefore decision-making. It prescribes strongly shared values which block new perceptions. And it prescribes visions of the future when the future is at least unknown, if not unknowable, and when strong belief in one vision could be dangerously restrictive. It interprets the political learning control loop in equilibrium terms, where equilibrium is maintained by large numbers of trial-and-error actions offsetting random shocks. This is impossible in open-ended situations. Furthermore, the entrepreneurial model excludes simultaneous application of the planning control loop. It prescribes unclear structures and loose job definitions which make tight short interval financial control impossible.

When we observe what managers actually do, we find that they frequently behave in ways not envisaged by the received wisdom. We find they sometimes behave in direct contradiction to those models. Managers frequently form groups which have no immediately clear purpose. They use political processes to discover preferences and objectives; they sometimes use power to make choices and decisions and at other times they avoid using it. They do not simply respond to environmental change, they sometimes create or invent it. They do not behave in accordance with any one explicit model, but shift from one to another, or apply both simultaneously. Successful organizations learn in ways which are not as simple as step-by-step procedures of either the logically predetermined or the trial-and-error search types. The behaviour of managers is full of anomalies. They go to great trouble to prepare long-term plans and appraise investments and then make the choice on some other basis. They make substantial changes in organizational structures in the absence of major change in their environments. It is often hard to detect any relationship between periodic swings from centralization to decentralization and what is happening in the markets or elsewhere in the environment. And we have difficulty in explaining all this with the most prominent models at our disposal, other than to preach against it as dysfunctional.

Clearly, explicit models which see disorder simply as ignorance, which explain only in terms of order and equilibrium are not adequate. When it comes to the disorderly aspects, the behaviour of managers is probably driven partly by the explicit models we have been discussing, but even more by their own personal implicit models of management and organization. These implicit understandings and explanations are rarely examined or questioned. They have largely slipped below the level of awareness. Nevertheless such understandings and explanations exert a powerful influence on how managers behave, what they do and why, particularly when they are faced with high levels of uncertainty. So what does it matter? By one means or another, managers do deal with the reality of extreme uncertainty and disorder.

It matters because this split between what managers say they do (the explicit models they pay attention to) and what they actually do (driven by implicit models below the level of awareness) can and does have highly dysfunctional consequences. The implicit theories of managers may be:

- Out of touch with reality. Understandings which exist below the level of awareness are built up through previous experience of what has worked and what has not worked in the past. But the world changes and what worked in the past may well not work now. Because implicit explanations are so rarely examined, managers can quite easily be unaware of the fact that those explanations no longer work. Because such models so frequently take the form of strongly held beliefs, company and industry recipes, they are very hard to change. The difficult processes of reflection, introspection, discussion and testing are required to change them at all. So, important explanations which are rarely examined, difficult to change and quite possibly out of touch with reality, can and do drive managers and their organizations to disaster.

- Regarded as pathological. Inconsistency between what we say we do and what we actually do is widely regarded as irrational, even hypocritical. The pressure to do what we say we do can therefore lead to attempts to remove the implicit models and the behaviours they give rise to. The rational response is to get back to behaving according to the explicit models. The sensible response is to change the culture so that people behave according to explicit models of how the organization should work. In conditions of great uncertainty this may well be a completely misguided response. And until we know more about the implicit models managers use, we cannot say whether this response is misguided or not.

Today's most prominent explicit models of managing and organizing do not meet the criteria we would expect for useful dynamic models. As guides to managerial action they are of questionable value. We need to look for more useful explicit explanations, ones which get us nearer to the implicit models managers so often use. In search of such explanations Part Three turns to new scientific understanding of complex dynamic systems.

References

1 Weick, K. (1979), *The Social Psychology of Organising*, Addison-Wesley.
2 Weick, K., op. cit.
3 Weick, K., op. cit.
4 Burns, T., Stalker, G. M. (1961), *The Management of Innovation*, Tavistock Publications.
5 Thompson, J. B., Tuden, A. (1959), Strategies, Structures and Processes of Organizational Decisions, in *Comparative Administration*, 1, University of Pittsburgh; Child, J. (1972), Organizational Structure, Environment and Performance: The Role of Strategic Choice, *Sociology* 6; Pfeffer, J. (1981), *Power in Organizations*, Pitman; Vredenburgh, D. J., Maurer, J. G. (1984), A Process Framework of Organizational Politics, *Human Relations*, vol. 37, no. 1,
6 March, J. G., Ohlsen, J. P. (1976), *Ambiguity and Choice in Organizations*, Bergen, Norway: Universitesforlaget; Weick, K., op. cit.
7 Argyris, J. (1982), *Reasoning, Learning and Action*, Jossey-Bass; Schein, E. (1985), *Organizational Culture and Leadership*, Jossey-Bass.
8 Miller, E. J., Rice, A. K. (1967), *Systems of Organization*, Tavistock Publications; Lindblom, L. (1959), The Science of Muddling Through, *Public Administration Review*, 19, pp. 79-88; Bion, W. R.

(1961), *Experiences in Groups and other Papers*, Tavistock Publications; de Board, R. (1978), *The Psychoanalysis of Organizations*, Tavistock Publications; Weick, K., op. cit.

9   Weick, K., op. cit.
10 Weick, K., op. cit.
11 Burns, J. Stalker, G. M., op. cit; Moss Kanter, R. (1985), *The Change Masters*, Simon & Schuster.
12 Lindblom, L., op. cit.
13 March, J. G., Ohlsen, J. P., op. cit.
14 Thompson, J. D., Tuden, A., op. cit; Child, J., op. cit; Pfeffer, J., op. cit.
15 Collingridge, D. (1980), *The Social Control of Technology*, F. Pinter.
16 Argyris, C., op. cit.
17 March, J. G., Ohlsen, J. P., op. cit.
18 Cohen, M. D. March, J. G., Ohlsen, J. P., A Garbage Can Model of Organizational Choice, in March, J. G. (1988), *Decisions and Organizations*, Blackwell.
19 Schein, E., op. cit; Argyris, C., op. cit.

Part Three
Scientific Chaos and
Dynamic Management

The main points made in previous chapters are as follows. The nature of the human brain makes it impossible to act coherently in the absence of some mental model, that is some selective simplification of how the world works. The actions managers design are determined by the models in their minds. Organizational effectiveness, the ability to sustain competitive capability, depends fundamentally on these models. All humans design their actions using both explicit models which they can fairly easily articulate and implicit models which have been pushed below the level of awareness. The more expert the action, the more it is designed using implicit models because this is a faster way of designing actions. These implicit models are difficult to surface, examine, question and change precisely because they are below the level of awareness. But when times are turbulent it becomes vital to question both the explicit and the implicit models driving behaviour in order to keep them appropriate to changing circumstances. Superior performance flows from superior understanding and explaining. Sustaining that superior performance comes from changing the models in appropriate ways and this is the same thing as continual learning.

In turbulent times, one model is superior to another to the extent that it incorporates the dynamic of the world we are acting in – the patterns of change we have to cope with and what drives those patterns of change. It was argued that from what we commonly observe in the business world, a useful dynamic model would be constructed squarely on:

- A spectrum of change situations ranging from those close to certainty to those far from certainty where consequences are unknowable.
- Control and development feedback loops which are appropriate to the degree of predictability possible in, and the kinds of human behaviour provoked by, different change situations.
- The feedback nature of behaviour, choice, action and performance so common within business organizations and in their relationships with those in their environments. Such feedback is associated with small changes escalating into large outcomes, chance and virtuous and vicious circles.
- The non-equilibrium states within which successful organizations operate,

associated with the creative manner in which they interact with and partially create their environments.

The world of business is characterized by order and disorder, stability and instability, uniformity and variety. A useful dynamic model of business behaviour would be one which accounts for these features. It would provide reasons for irregular business performance and behaviour which are more coherent than simply ascribing such irregularity to ignorance or incompetence.

When we review today's most prominent models of managing and organizing, those which are the explicit models managers use, we find that they are seriously defective. They do not meet the above criteria for a useful dynamic model with which to design effective managerial actions. They have all been developed within a frame of reference which sees the business world as one operating like a computing machine. They focus on the order, stability and uniformity of the business world and therefore fail adequately to explain the disorder, instability and variety we also see. They have difficulty in accommodating and explaining the creative management behaviour we actually observe.

But managers deal with the real dynamic, sometimes with highly successful results and sometimes not. It seems that they do not always use the explicit models they articulate, but turn automatically to implicit models instead. Managers then say one thing and do another. As a result we find anomalies and conflicting behaviour which we find hard to explain. Managers do cope when they do not know what the outcome of their actions will be. But we find some difficulty in explaining how they do this. We therefore find it difficult to produce helpful prescriptions for success. Unless managers keep surfacing and questioning the implicit models they use, unless they make them explicit, they could well be designing actions which are inappropriate and lead to failure.

Part Three turns to a new understanding of complex system dynamics. This understanding, I believe, will provoke managers to question the models they are using to design their actions. This could well lead to more useful models and therefore more effective action.

7 What scientific chaos means for managers

This chapter provides a brief summary of what the scientific theories of chaos and self-organization are all about.[1] It explores the principal implications for controlling and organizing a business. The first three appendices provide further information on the nature of these theories and where they have been found to apply in physics, chemistry, biology and economics. The fourth appendix gives a glossary of terms because much of the terminology used will be new to those in business. The four chapters following this one explore the implications of complex system dynamics for the control and development of a business in open-ended change.

Nature of scientific chaos

Scientific chaos is an explanation of why most of the phenomena we observe in nature and in human behaviour have characteristics of order and stability on the one hand, accompanied by disorder and irregularity on the other. It is about the source and nature of combined patterns of uniformity and variety in the behaviour of systems as far apart as the human heart and the market for oil. All oak trees have uniform characteristics which make them clearly recognizable as oak trees, but within that category there is great variety with no oak tree being exactly the same as any other. Business organizations have certain characteristics which allow us to classify them as such, but within the category there is a great variety of different companies, even in the same market. The same point applies to the behaviour of individual human beings, to any grouping of human beings, in fact to just about anything one can think of. The weather system has orderly patterns in which one season follows another, in which some weather conditions are found in some areas but not in others. But the weather system is also disorderly and irregular, with storms and hurricanes rapidly following heatwaves. The output of the economy sometimes appears to follow orderly cycles and at other times it jumps about in an irregular manner. Share prices sometimes follow clear trends and at other times they fluctuate in a random way. The chapters in Part One demonstrated that these points apply to business organizations as well.

Scientific chaos is particularly concerned with explanations of how categories and their components change over time. It is concerned with turbulent phenomena in systems – abrupt changes in the weather, phase transitions as liquids freeze or turn to gases, complex chemical reactions, irregular movements in share prices and exchange rates.

We can appreciate how scientific chaos explains such phenomena by considering a much simplified example from the world of business. Around the corner from my home there is a street vendor who sells flowers every Saturday from a stall outside the supermarket. I have no idea what he does for the rest of the week. Early each Saturday morning he purchases a quantity of flowers from the wholesale market. For the sake of simplicity suppose that the unit cost of these flowers is always constant. This vendor uses a simple rule of thumb to decide on the quantity of flowers to purchase, that is on the working capital to invest in the business for that day. He always ploughs back a fixed proportion of last Saturday's profits into this Saturday's working capital. He has an absolutely fixed decision rule. So if his profit last week was £100 and his decision rule is to plough back 75 per cent of his profit, then his working capital this week will be £75.

As he increases the quantity of flowers purchased, the working capital, his profits first rise because he spreads the fixed costs of transport and the vendor's licence over a larger volume sold. Eventually however, profits fall as he increases the level of working capital because he has to cut prices to sell more and he has to dispose of unsold inventories at the end of the day. This relationship between investment in working capital and consequent profit is primarily a function of the market conditions and it is a non-proportional or non-linear relationship. So, as working capital is increased from £75 to £100, his profit may increase from £120 to £160 because fixed costs are being spread. But, as his working capital rises from £100 to £120, profits may decline from £160 to £130 because he has to reduce prices to sell more. The relationship can be depicted in Figure 7.1 – it is a curve not a straight line, that is, it is non-linear.

The relationship between working capital and profit is a curve rather than a straight line because limited demand and competition provide a constraint which prevents the relationship from being proportional or linear. Suppose for the sake of simplicity that the relationship of the vendor to his customers is always the same so that profit always varies with working capital in the same way. It first rises at a given rate as the investment in working capital is increased and then it falls at a given rate. The curve in Figure 1 remains constant. We are then excluding all changes

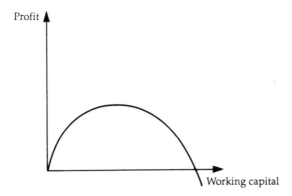

Figure 7.1 *Relationship between working capital and profit*

in the environment, and all changes in the vendor's relationships with his customers, in order to keep the argument at the simplest level.

In the simple circumstances just described, profit on this Saturday is related in a fixed manner to working capital (primarily because of the vendor's relationship with his customers and competitors) and that working capital is related in turn in a fixed manner (through the fixed decision rule) to the profit of last Saturday. The decision rule and the market relationship have established a fixed loop between profit now and profit last week. And profit now will be fed back into that loop to determine the profit for next week. This feedback loop is depicted in Figure 7.2.

The dynamic of the flower vendor's business, the pattern of his profit over time, is driven by this fixed feedback mechanism connecting profit in one time period to profit in another. And that feedback mechanism has to be non-linear because the relationship with the market is non-linear. Consequently, profit now does not have to be a constant proportion of profit last time; it may sometimes be larger than last week's profit (an amplification) and sometimes smaller (a dampening). What the flower

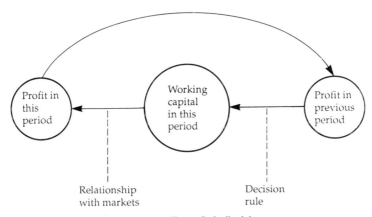

Figure 7.2 *The profit feedback loop*

vendor does this Saturday and what happens to his business this Saturday, all contribute to what will happen next Saturday. The flower vendor is playing some part, through his decision rule, in determining what happens to his business in the future. We have here the kind of feedback mechanism which is the subject matter of scientific chaos. And despite its extreme simplicity that feedback loop captures the essence of any business system, as was explained in Chapter 4 above. The difference between this simple example and any reasonably complicated business is simply one of degree – a more complicated business is a large set of feedback loops in all performance indicators, behaviour choice and action.

Principal features of scientific chaos

Now consider what this non-linear feedback mechanism means for the simple business of the street vendor. This vendor has a vision. He wishes to become the largest and best purveyor of flowers on that particular high road. He also has a long-term objective, that of securing sustained, stable growth in profits. His strategy is to achieve this by ploughing back a constant proportion of profit into working capital. His market research has revealed the general shape and constant nature of the relationship between profit and working capital. Unfortunately that research has been unable to establish the precise relationship – he does not know just how responsive his customers are to the increased volumes he may offer or to the price cuts he may undertake. He now decides to prepare his budget and long-term financial projections. To do this he must answer this question: what pattern of growth in profit will result from different proportions of profit ploughed back, combined with different degrees of customer responsiveness and competitor reaction?

Fortunately, the vendor's son has just completed an MBA, which followed a degree in mathematics. The son explains that the problem is one of exploring the behaviour of a very simple non-linear feedback mechanism connecting profit in one period to profit in the previous one. The control parameter in that mechanism is determined by the actual proportion of profit ploughed back (the decision rule) and the actual responsiveness of profit to working capital levels (dependent upon the market relationship). It is a simple matter to run this model on his personal computer and answer the 'what if' questions for different values of the parameter as posed by his father, the vendor. Note at this point that the model, the feedback rule, is extremely simple. Note also that everything in the environment remains exactly the same and that the decision rule is absolutely fixed. All the vendor's son is doing is exploring the consequences of different proportions in the fixed decision rule and different potential degrees of responsiveness in the fixed market relationship. This exploration will illustrate eight important features of the dynamic behaviour of this system.

1 Complex patterns of behaviour

The first feature of scientific chaos is that simple feedback control loops produce amazingly complex patterns of behaviour, some of which are inherently random. (See Appendix B for a simple mathematical demonstration of this feature.)

The vendor watches as his son plugs different parameter values into the feedback rule and the computer graphs the time pattern of the implied profits into the future. The son starts with a low parameter in answer to the question, 'what if the proportion of profit ploughed back is low and the responsiveness of customers is weak in the sense that profit rises and falls only gradually as working capital is increased?' (The curve in Figure 7.1 is rather flat.) At that low parameter value, the computer displays a profit time series in which profit fluctuates unevenly for a few weeks and then settles down into a perfectly constant path over time. If the vendor sticks to that proportion of plough back and the degree of market responsiveness stays at that level and nothing else changes, then he can count on achieving an objective of a stable but constant profit path for evermore. The computer printout of this outcome is given in Figure 7.3 below.

But the vendor wants growth as well as stability. So, what if the proportion of profit ploughed back is increased. The vendor wants to continue assuming a pretty unresponsive market and explore the conse-

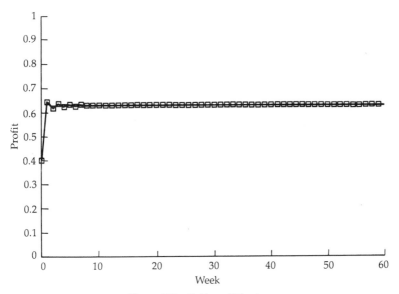

Figure 7.3 *Stable profit levels*

quences of changing simply the proportion in his own decision rule. To show the effect of this, the son increases the parameter value somewhat. The result of tuning the parameter up in this way, of making the feedback more sensitive, is a higher constant level of profit, once the initial fluctuations are out of the way. This will also persist for evermore in the absence of any change in the decision rule or the market conditions. And as they tune the parameter up further, they discover higher and higher levels of constant profit. The son explains that at all of these parameter values, this business system is attracted to a final state of profit behaviour which is a stable, constant level of profit. In mathematical terms, the attractor is a stable equilibrium in which there is a constant path over time.

The vendor is just reaching the conclusion that he can achieve his vision and his objective by simply increasing the proportion of profit ploughed back, when his son tunes the parameter up further. This time the profit level fluctuates unevenly for some time but never settles down to a constant path. Instead it eventually follows a regular, stable cycle, moving from a fixed peak to a fixed trough and back again. And at that parameter value profit will follow this cycle for evermore. The attractor at this parameter value is a cycle of period two (one peak and one trough) and it is also a stable equilibrium. This printout is shown in Figure 7.4 below.

The objective of the vendor must be to avoid this attractor because he is looking for stability. But the problem is that he does not know just how responsive the customers are and that responsiveness also affects the

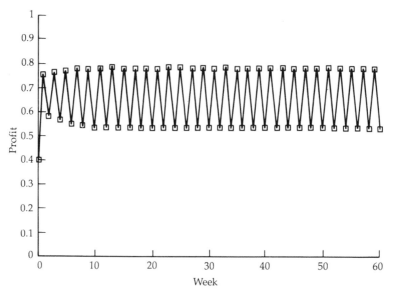

Figure 7.4 *Regular two-period cycles in profit*

parameter value. He may unknowingly therefore stray into this undesirable profit path. So, what if the parameter is tuned even higher?

As the parameter is tuned higher, the amplitude of the fixed cycle increases. This is not what the vendor is looking for and his unease rises as his son tunes the parameter up a little further, so making the feedback rule a little more sensitive. Now the final state into which profit settles is one with a perfectly stable cycle of period four, that is two peaks and two troughs. The printout of this outcome is given in Figure 7.5.

And as the parameter is tuned up further, this cycle fractures into a cycle with eight peaks and eight troughs. Another touch to the parameter gives 16 peaks and 16 troughs. As the parameter is tuned up by smaller and smaller amounts, the cycles fracture further and further until there are infinitely many cycles superimposed on each other. The vendor is astonished to notice how very small changes in the parameter are leading to completely different cyclical behaviours. But, at least, once the parameter is fixed, that cycle remains constant and stable. There is still predictable, if highly complex, equilibrium.

Then the son increases the parameter by a further minute amount, and the proportion of profit ploughed back is only increased by a tiny fraction. The result is astonishing, because the time series of profit never settles down to any regular pattern. It bounces around irregularly between upper and lower boundaries. That time series becomes inherently random for evermore and never once returns precisely to the same point it occupied before. The printout for this outcome is shown in Figure 7.6. That result is a fundamental property of non-linear feedback

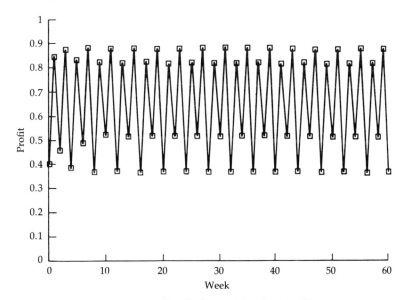

Figure 7.5 *Regular four-period cycles in profit*

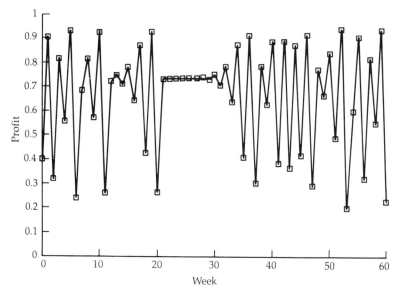

Figure 7.6 *Chaotic time path in profit*

mechanisms. No matter where the particular mechanism used to derive this graph (it is given in Appendix B) is found, the result is the same. So it could be the mechanism driving this flower vendor's business. But the same kind of mechanism has been found to apply when liquid helium is heated, when insects reproduce on a bush and a great many other instances. The resulting pattern in outcomes as you tune the parameter up is always the same. (Appendix A gives further information on where such mechanisms are to be found.)

If the vendor happens to fix just that proportion of profit ploughed back, and the customers happen to display just that degree of responsiveness, and nothing ever changes in the decision rule or the market place, then profit will move in an inherently random manner for ever. This is not simply an appearance of randomness; it is randomness. At this particular parameter value the system is attracted to a final state of behaviour which is 'chaotic'. The technical term is a 'strange attractor', or it is also called a 'fractal' and sometimes a 'chaotic attractor'. Vending flowers can be a very unsettling business, even when everything is held absolutely constant. Randomness is coming from the very structure of the business system itself. And when market conditions and decision rules keep changing things can only get worse.

But even this is not the end. For, as the parameter is tuned up further the system suddenly displays a constant profit path once again, then cycles of period three which fracture into period six and so on back to chaos. The complete pattern of behaviours, from stable paths through cycles to chaos, are repeated over and over again as the vendor looks at the behaviour of the system in more and more detail, that is, for smaller and smaller changes in the parameter value. When the behaviour of the system follows a strange attractor, we find similar patterns within patterns and this goes on forever.

It is only when the parameter is substantially increased that the vendor gets back to territory he can recognize. When the feedback rule is very sensitive then profit settles into a path of explosive growth. This is once more a state of equilibrium but this time an unstable state because explosive growth cannot continue for long.

So, we have here a rule governing a system such that the behaviour of that system settles down into stable equilibrium states of constancy, or of regular cycles, when the rule is insensitive, and unstable equilibrium states of explosive growth when the rule is very sensitive. Between these equilibrium states there is a border in which behaviour is highly complex and ultimately random, the strange attractor chaos. What is so astonishing about the complex behaviour in this border area is that it is generated by a very simple feedback mechanism in which the parameter is fixed. Nothing is changing in the markets, nothing is changing in the decision rule and yet the profit fluctuates in a random way. Profit increases occur without any specific cause and they turn into decreases also without any specific cause. The reason for the behaviour is the very structure of the business system itself. The chaos is within; it does not come from the environment. Of course the environment may be chaotic too and so add to the turbulence.

Chapter 4 has shown that business organizations are fundamentally sets of non-linear feedback mechanisms. If their control parameters are ever set at the particular values we are talking about, then their specific long-term performance outcomes will be absolutely random. If the development of a business involves changing control parameters, as it surely does, then it is possible that outcomes will sometimes be stable equilibrium states, sometimes unstable equilibrium states and sometimes highly complex patterns of cycles which easily slip into chaos.

2   Extreme sensitivity to change

The second feature uncovered by scientists is this. It takes only tiny changes in the control parameter, tiny changes in the sensitivity of the feedback mechanisms, to move behaviour over time from perfectly predictable cycles to random patterns. The changes are so tiny, for example a difference to the thousandth decimal place, that we would have to be able to measure the parameter with absolute exactness if we are anywhere near the chaos area and wish to secure a particular pattern of behaviour. Scientists call this sensitive dependence on initial conditions. And it means that if the sensitivity of the feedback mechanism is such that it is far from the equilibrium states, then tiny changes impacting on the system will escalate into major unpredictable changes over the long term. Long-term developments will be significantly affected by small chance disturbances. It is not just that there is a limit to the ability to predict the specific long-term outcome; it is absolutely and totally impossible to predict that specific long-term outcome.

Features one and two tell us that order generates disorder.

Now the street vendor's discovery of these disconcerting facts leads to a number of typical responses. Like many scientists first confronted with chaos, he refuses to believe it. It may be a mathematical fact that feedback loops behave in this manner, but this is simply a mathematical curiosity which has nothing to do with the real world. That is not a tenable position. The evidence is that most systems in nature are governed by feedback loops and do display the kind of behaviour described. This evidence is referred to in Appendix I. The properties of feedback loops provide the most useful explanations so far available of the nature of turbulence in nature. Turbulence is a chaotic state and occurs because systems are following a strange attractor. Long-term outcomes may be absolutely unpredictable but at least we can now understand more about what is going on. There is also some evidence that feedback loops and chaotic behaviour could explain the operation of economic systems such as the Stock Exchange. And in Chapter 4 above a clear case was presented for concluding that business organizations are sets of non-linear feedback mechanisms of the kind we are discussing here. They must therefore be capable of the kind of complex behaviour that the street vendor's simple feedback loop exhibits. If the vendor's description of his business is as he says it is, then it must be capable of the sequence of behaviours which this model has indicated.

The vendor now reaches two conclusions. First, if by some misfortune, his decision rules and his market conditions do ever produce parameter values which generate chaos, then there is no way that he can control his business. When behaviour is chaotic, all will occur by pure chance and he will be lost. This leads to his second conclusion, namely that he must at all costs avoid decision rules and market relationships which take his business anywhere near the chaos border. He must secure the order to be found near to the stable equilibrium states. He believes that there are systematic features in human systems which can and must be deployed to keep them away from chaos.

Further consideration, however, leads us to question both of these responses. All is not lost when the system's behaviour follows a strange attractor, for there is a 'hidden' pattern in chaos.

3   The 'hidden' pattern in chaos

The third feature of non-linear dynamic systems which scientists have uncovered is this: there is order within disorder.

Because it takes time for small differences to escalate into major changes of behaviour, the specific short-term behaviour of a chaotic system is predictable. Although we can never predict long-term weather patterns, we can predict the weather to a reasonable degree of accuracy over the next few days. And this is an important form of order within the disorder of a chaotic system. Even though we may not be able to say anything about the long-term future of a business, we will be able to forecast short-term outcomes.

The rules which generate chaotic behaviour are perfectly deterministic. They can be identified and measured. It is therefore possible, at least in principle, to identify the conditions within which the behaviour of a system will become chaotic. We can predict the occurrence of chaos itself, even though we can never predict the specific path a chaotic system will follow.

Then, there is a perfectly regular pattern in the sequence of behaviours which all non-linear feedback rules of the same class follow, no matter where they are found, in gases, chemical reactions, insects reproducing on a bush, oil markets or business organizations. They all pass through phases of stability, fixed cycles, chaos and explosive growth as the control parameter is tuned up to make the mechanisms more sensitive. We can identify the feedback mechanisms and we can predict the behaviour patterns they will follow, including when chaos will occur.

What is perhaps the most important aspect of order within disorder is rather harder to understand. In the border between the stable equilibrium and the unstable equilibrium attractors, we have the strange attractor called chaos. Now although the specific path of behaviour in the strange attractor is inherently random, that behaviour does have a 'hidden' order which is a determined, overall shape. Perhaps the easiest way to understand this is to look at a picture of the strange attractor which is the weather system, a simplified version of this is built up in Figures 7.7 and 7.8.

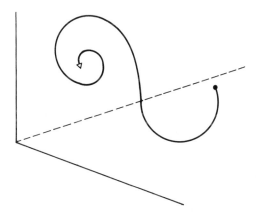

Figure 7.7 *Plotting the state of the weather system*

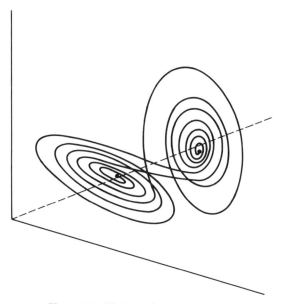

Figure 7.8   *The butterfly strange attractor*

Figure 7.7 depicts three dimensions of the weather system – say air pressure on the vertical axis, humidity on one of the horizontal axes and temperature on the other. Any point in that three-dimensional space therefore represents some combination of air pressure, humidity and temperature at some point in time. By plotting the combinations of pressure, humidity and temperature at each point in time, we can build up a picture of the time path of the weather system. So, start with the combination in Figure 7.7 which exists at this second (the dot) and then follow the changes for subsequent seconds along the line to the arrow. This shows how the weather described in terms of air pressure, humidity and temperature, is varying over time. If you plot this information for a long period, you will build up a picture along the lines shown in Figure 7.8. This is a strange attractor called the butterfly (or Lorenz) attractor. The weather system moves around one of those lines in say the left-hand lobe of the diagram and then suddenly switches to the right-hand lobe, spins around there for a while and then shifts back again. The weather system moves endlessly around this shape, never once returning to any point it has previously occupied; the lines never intersect. (They appear to do so in Figure 7.8 only because this is a two-dimensional representation of a three-dimensional figure.)

So, the specific path of the weather is inherently random and totally unpredictable in the long-term. But it always follows the same global shape. There are boundaries outside which the weather system hardly ever moves and if it does so, it is soon attracted back to the shape prescribed by the attractor. Some weather conditions are not allowed –

snow storms in the Sahara desert or heat waves in the Arctic. There is an overall shape to weather behaviour because it is constrained in some way. And if we can identify the feedback rules driving the system, then we can identify the overall shape of the behaviour, the quantitative bounds within which it moves and the general qualitative patterns it displays. Because of this 'hidden' order, the system displays typical patterns, or recognizable categories of behaviour. Even before we knew anything about the shape of the weather's strange attractor, we always recognized patterns of storms and sunshine, hurricanes and calm, and seasonal patterns. And these recognizable patterns are repeated in an approximate way over and over again. They are never exactly the same, but there is always some similarity. They are similar to what went before and similar to what is occurring elsewhere in the system. The system has the property of self-similarity.

Chaos is not simply unpredictable paths in specific behaviour. It is a combination of that disorder with a looser form of order called self-similarity. If you were to examine the time path of one of the weather variables that was plotted in Figures 7.7 and 7.8, you would see that it shows fluctuations which are never the same. But many fluctuations have a similar appearance to many others. An illustration of what is meant by this is shown in Figure 7.9.

And if you look at Figure 7.4 again, showing the random fluctuations in the street vendor's profits, you will see the same thing. It looks as if there might be underlying regular cycles being disturbed by other factors which we have not taken into account. And this is how scientists tended to look at such data. For example, economists look at output data and conclude that there are underlying, regular trade cycles disturbed by random shocks (for example, political or economic policy changes) to produce the irregular time series we observe. But we now know, at least as far as the weather is concerned, that there are no regular cycles, only this property of self-similarity. There is no proof as yet that this conclusion applies to economic behaviour in general. But there are some studies which indicate

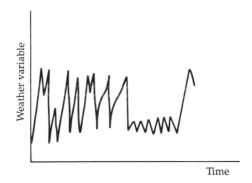

Figure 7.9 *Time path of one of the weather variables*

that it could apply to the foreign exchange and stock markets (see Appendix A.)

Recognizable categories

So, because the dynamic of the weather system is chaotic we cannot predict the specific course the weather will take in the long term. But we do get typical categories, or patterns, in the behaviour of the weather system which are repeated over and over again. The category winter follows the category autumn and within a particular winter we find typical patterns of temperature, rainfall and wind speed. As we enter a particular winter, we do not know whether the temperature will be very low or very high for that time of the year, the rainfall heavy or light, the wind speed moderate or at gale force. We cannot identify specific causes which yield specific outcomes, but we know the boundaries within which the system moves and the qualitative nature of the patterns it displays. We know that the very irregularity of the weather will itself be regular because it is constrained in some way – it cannot do just anything. We can use the resulting self similar patterns of winter weather to prepare appropriate behaviour – we can buy an umbrella or move the sheep off the high ground. We can cope with the uncertainty and the lack of causal connection because we are aware of self-similar patterns and use them in a qualitative way to guide specific choices.

Reasoning by analogy

And in Chapter 1 we saw how experts use these self-similar patterns. They detect analogies between some new situation and some other situation they have experienced before. They then develop new or adjusted mental models to design actions for the new situation. Humans are mentally equipped to deal with chaos, that mixture of unpredictable specifics within overall qualitative similarity. Humans are not well equipped to deal with utter confusion or complete randomness at all levels. But this is not chaos in the scientific meaning of that word.

When we confront the uncertain future of a particular business organization we approach the problem in two different ways. The first approach is the analytical one. Conditioned by traditional scientific methodology, we look for cause and effect. For example, we analyse the structure of the industry our particular company is operating in – the barriers to entry of new firms, the availability of substitutes for our product, the power of our suppliers and customers, the intensity of the competition we face. We then identify the particular combinations of these factors which cause successful companies to follow generic strategies of cost leadership, product differentiation or focus on niche markets. Having identified cause and successful effect, we then prescribe one of those strategies for our particular business. And there are many techniques available for use in this manner: value chain analysis, product life cycles, product portfolio analysis, learning curves and many more. Another example of this direct cause and effect reasoning is to be found in the contingency approach. Here we conclude that particular environmental features such as rapid growth and high levels of uncertainty lead to organic organizational structures, while mature markets and low levels of uncertainty lead to mechanistic structures.

This approach then is that of analytical cause and effect leading to specific predictions and prescriptions. We know that these predictions and prescriptions will only ever be approximate because we are not able to specify the model accurately enough to take all relevant factors into account.

When managers come to use the techniques and their predictions, they find it impossible to apply them in this direct cause and effect way. In fact it is positively dangerous to do so. In the 1970s General Foods used product portfolio analysis and reached the conclusion that its coffee business was a cash cow which should not be invested in. This conclusion led it almost to miss the differentiation of the coffee market into specialist types of coffee with high margins. Instead of reasoning in direct cause and effect terms, creative managers use the techniques to generate analogies to their own situation. We use categories of strategic behaviour, such as cost leadership or differentiation, to prompt questions and raise issues around the specific action we should now take in a particular company. We look at patterns of development as companies move from small entrepreneurial businesses to more bureaucratic corporations. And we use these typical conclusions to guide choices we now have to make in particular circumstances. We are then, I suggest, employing the self-similar nature of the development in strategies and structures to prompt and provoke a range of choices we should now consider in particular circumstances. What is then important is not the analysis, the cause and effect link, but the qualitative description of patterns of behaviour. When we think of a successful business as one with chaotic dynamics, we stop looking for specific causes and effects leading to prescriptions. Instead we look for self-similar patterns, and differences, as prompts to creative choices. Chaos is not a no hope situation. It is one with which we are mentally particularly well equipped to deal. In fact we have always dealt with it without being all that clear about what we were doing.

For example – differentiation in the electricity industry

An example of how we use this property of self-similarity in business is provided, I believe, by a study of changes occurring in the electricity industry in North America and Europe.[2] The author of that study puts forward the proposition that electricity suppliers will increasingly differentiate their product. There is no definitive model which allows us to predict that such differentiation will occur or what form it will take. So, the author looks for similar circumstances and translates the patterns observed there into ones which might apply to electricity. Those similar circumstances are provided by the airline industry. As with electricity, the product cannot be stored and demand moves from sharp peaks to deep troughs on a daily basis. Airlines have differentiated their products by category of passenger (business and tourist), by time of use (peak and off peak) and by level of service (first class and economy). It is argued that electricity suppliers have been doing much the same thing in terms of customer category and time of use, and that they will take this differentiation much further. For example they may introduce low cost, low service products with interruptible supply. This is not a prediction of what will happen but a guide which managers in the electricity industry might consider in forming judgements on the creative changes they are trying to make in their business.

What we are doing here is using experience of similarity in one place to draw conclusions about possible actions in another place. We do much the same thing when we form expectations of the behaviour of a group of people at some time from experience of their behaviour at previous times – we know it will not be exactly the same but there will be some similarity. As management consultants move from one assignment to another, they accumulate models of general personality types and general group interactions. When they see a highly authoritarian manager, they expect either submissive or rebellious interactions. They have no idea how these interactions will develop in specific terms, but they are not completely surprised at the outcomes.

For example – the global corporation

The controversy around the global corporation is another example of the way we explain developments in strictly cause and effect terms, but the real value is the qualitative description. One model identifies a number of causes leading to the world business satisfying the needs of the world customer. The causes are the spread of common tastes, fashions and standards across national frontiers; the reduction in national barriers to trade, investment and fund raising; and the availability of cheap information processing and telecommunication. The effect is the global corporation which locates production wherever costs are lowest, modifies product offerings to meet remaining national differences and organizes on a global scale. It becomes a stateless world citizen independent of its original nationality. The prescription for success is then for a company to become a global competitor which shakes off its national origins. One way to do so is to reduce the power of the head office which is usually dominated by local customer requirements.[3] Another model accepts all the above causes but adds that of difference between companies as the source of competitive advantage. This difference, due to innovative vitality, arises from the conditions at the company's home base. Such a set of causes leads to companies taking their home-based competitive advantage into other markets that globalization is making more similar. The prescription for success is then to preserve the national origins at almost all costs.[4]

These two models yield diametrically opposed prescriptions. But we could look at the global and multinational corporation as qualitative descriptions, the self-similar outcomes for chaotic business systems. We could then ask what insights these patterns might provoke about the issues facing a particular business. This leads not to immediate prescriptions but to possible different directions in strategic thinking.

Analogy versus cause and effect

The key point for managers about the 'hidden pattern' in the behaviour of chaotic systems is this. When the dynamic is chaotic, prescriptions resulting from direct cause and effect reasoning will be dangerous guides to choice. What are valuable as prompts to strategic thinking are the general qualitative descriptions of developments in the business world. Such useful qualitative descriptions will apply not only to categories of strategy and structure but also to categories of personality and group dynamics that will affect categories of strategic choices made. It is these qualitative descriptions that provide the regularity in the variety of specific choices and their outcomes. When the dynamic is chaotic, the degree of variation in the self-similar patterns over time or space, is constant. And this allows us to identify qualitative patterns. This 'hidden' pattern with its property of self-similarity means that the behaviour of any chaotic system will exhibit recognizable categories within which no two individual events will be the same. Because their behaviour is being driven by feedback mechanisms operating away from equilibrium, there is a category called snowflakes within which no two snowflakes are ever the same. The same point applies to oak trees, cumulus clouds, coast lines, elephants, insects and human beings. The same point may also apply to human interactions – a set of interactions may be described as conflict, but the specific course that conflict takes, even between the same two individuals, will be different on each specific occasion. The choices people make in a business may be entirely consistent over time and those observing them are never surprised. Or such choices may be completely inconsistent all the time so that those observing them are always surprised or even shocked. But there is another possibility – those choices may be a chaotic sequence, and that means regular inconsistency. Those observing such choices are surprised by the individual choices but not by the fact that they are inconsistent or by the degree of that inconsistency.

The overall pattern, the property of self-similarity, is a consequence of the structure of the feedback mechanisms. It is the constraints upon those feedback mechanisms, that which makes them non-linear, that leads to self-similarity. In the case of the flower vendor, that constraint is provide by ultimately limited demand for flowers and by the response of competitors to his behaviour. In Chapter 4 we considered the constraints in more complex business systems. It is those constraints that account for self-similarity in business. In the next three chapters we will explore more fully the implications of constraints. Without constraints we get utter confusion, but with constraints we get chaos. Constraints provide the self-similarity, the stability, that enables us to cope with chaos.

There is order within the disorder of chaos. That order is self-similarity, regular irregularity, a constant degree of variability. Scientific chaos is not about mindless confusion, it is about intertwined order and disorder. Even if the business of the flower vendor does stray into the chaotic border between equilibrium states, all will not be lost. He will be able to use qualitative descriptions of behaviour as a guide to action, even though specific outcomes are unpredictable.

But surely he should nevertheless try to stay within an equilibrium state of order and stability and strenuously avoid chaos? Perhaps one individual should. But when we come to a group of business people who must innovate to survive, then we have to think differently. So, we now leave the flower vendor behind in order to think in terms of more complex businesses. It is here that explanations of non-linear dynamics closely related to scientific chaos yield conclusions that are, if anything, even more surprising than those already discussed. These explanations, called self-organization theory, tell us that when success follows from innovation, such success requires a system to be sustained far-from-equilibrium in a state of instability. In Chapter 4, we saw how a business is a set of non-linear feedback mechanisms. We also saw that the equilibrium states for a business driven by such mechanisms are either the stable equilibrium of ossification or the unstable one of disintegration. Success for the innovative business system lies away from equilibrium, just as it does for nature's systems. Since long-term business success is so clearly tied up with innovation, successful businesses will be those that are far-from-equilibrium, those with chaotic dynamics. Successful businesses will not be those that maintain the complete order of equilibrium, or the complete disorder of utter confusion, but the intertwined order and disorder of chaos. They will be recognizable by the individual variety, irregularity and difference they utilize to deal with open-ended change, all within the stable overall framework within which they conduct their day-to-day business. The claim made by this book that the dynamic of a successful business is chaotic does not mean that as soon as we walk in the door we are overwhelmed by disorder, or that performance is completely erratic. Quite the contrary. All the more obvious signs of order and stability will be there. The disorderly aspect of chaotic dynamics refers to the variety, difference, confusion and conflict that characterize the behaviour leading to innovative handling of open-ended change.

4   Chaos is essential to innovation

Feature four is this. When the control parameter in the non-linear feedback mechanism driving the behaviour of a system is fixed so that it is in one of the predictable, equilibrium states (stable path, stable cycles, explosive growth), it is incapable of doing anything new. Our solar system is close to equilibrium (in time frames that mean anything to most of us) and the planets follow stable orbits around the sun. If a system is at equilibrium and you leave it alone, it simply goes on doing what it did before. Century after century each planet follows the same orbit around the sun. At or near to equilibrium the control mechanisms operate in a damping fashion to keep the system where it is. If it strays from equilibrium the controls bring it back. Anyone who has worked in an organization that is governed by rigidly enforced rules and precedents, where there are strong norms on how things are to be done, will immediately recognize this description of equilibrium. And if you want the system to do something different, you have to introduce a major change; you have significantly to alter the control parameters in the feedback mechanisms that drive it. Major environmental change, or very complex reaction systems, are required to shift a system out of one equilibrium into another. One human being operating in such a system cannot do anything significant to change it. A new chief executive will simply get sucked into doing things the way they are, or become frustrated and leave. Changing equilibrium systems is very difficult indeed.

However if the system is far-from-equilibrium, in a state of bounded instability, it is continuously creative. Tiny changes in its environments, causing tiny changes in the control parameters, send it off on completely different long-term time paths. They may be better or worse, but they are different. Because the system is open and highly sensitive to its environment, because the control and development mechanisms are amplifying, the whole system can easily set off in some different direction. One human being operating in such a system can have a profound impact on what happens. In such a system it matters very much who the prime minister is and what he/she does, who the chief executive is and what he/she does.

Chaos feature four therefore says that creative systems have to operate far-from-equilibrium in a state of instability. (This is discussed in more detail in Appendix C.) Now the essence of success in business is the ability to innovate and create the new. We know from experience that one individual can completely alter long-term outcomes for a business organization. Business organizations are quite clearly non-linear feedback mechanisms (see Chapter 4) and the proposition put forward here is that successful ones are therefore far-from-equilibrium. The cost of being far-from-equilibrium is absolute unpredictability over the long-term in the specific path of development. The compensating trade off is the possibility of continuing creativity. And scientists have interesting things to say about the process of creativity.

5   Innovation emerges from destruction

This is feature five. Systems pushed far-from-equilibrium are extremely sensitive to tiny changes in their environments, and the operation of their feedback loops is amplifying. Tiny disturbances in the environment are therefore amplified through the system with the consequence that existing structures, patterns and behaviours are shattered. Scientists call this symmetry-breaking. So, as a particular gas is heated, the molecules move in a more and more excited way, destroying any pattern in their relationship to each other until they move in a completely random manner. They do this just before a highly organized laser beam appears.

No new order or structure can emerge without first destroying the old and this period of destruction is one of disorder and confusion. The agents in, or the components of, a system behave in non-uniform, conflicting ways. As a chemical or gas passes through this unstable, symmetry breaking phase, all the molecules behave in a highly excited state, rushing hither and thither in different directions. People in business organizations can be observed to behave similarly in phases of transition. Managers in business organizations can be observed forming political coalitions to attract organizational attention for particular issues, so amplifying the issue and disturbing the existing order. Feature five says that an innovation, a new strategic direction, can only occur if instability is first experienced. Chaos is essential to new order.

The IBM example

This relationship between far-from-equilibrium instability and innovation is well illustrated by the manner in which IBM developed its 360 series of products in the early 1960s.[5] The dramatic move from a disparate and proliferating range of products to one compatible series did not result

from careful market research, thorough planning or even a clearly articulated vision. Despite the IBM image for chilling efficiency and logical
planning, the new strategic direction emerged from a period of instability, confusion and intense political activity. In the three years preceding
the announcement of the System/360 in 1964 the IBM organization was
substantially restructured three times. The power of different executives
rose and fell rapidly and unpredictably. The rivalry between different
divisions was intense as at least four different courses of product development vied for support. The issues of product compatibility became
intertwined, often in a confusing manner, with that of changing technology from transistors to microcircuitry, with moves from assembly to
manufacturing, and with the development of global marketing approaches. During those three years IBM accorded with the description of
a dynamic system, open to its environment, amplifying small changes to
build support for potential new directions, instability causing the destruction of existing organizational structures and ways of thinking. And
this interpretation of the first phases of innovation has been documented
in studies of the political process in business organizations (see Chapter
5).

6   Innovative choices at critical points

Feature six is concerned with the process of emerging from the symmetry
breaking turbulence. During this phase, the system is faced with a series
of choices at critical points. It either 'chooses' to continue down one
chaotic path, or several, or it may 'choose' a new orderly direction. So, as
it is heated a particular gas 'chooses' at a critical point in the random
movement of its molecules to follow a highly organized path that is the
laser beam. Managers in business organizations are similarly faced with
critical choices. Sometimes the choice leads to continued confusion and at
other times represents the start of a new strategic direction. Both the
choice itself and the outcome to which it will lead are inherently unpredictable. The laws of physics do not predict the emergence of a laser
beam. Feature six is concerned with critical points and unpredictable
choices.

7   Innovations emerge through communication and self-organization

Feature seven has to do with how the choice is made at the critical point.
The agents in, or the components of, the system communicate with each
other. They cooperate. They reach a consensus and abruptly make an
unpredictable choice. The process is one of spontaneous self-organiz-

ation. So at critical points in chemical reactions or physical changes, the behaviour of molecules becomes correlated – it is as if they were communicating with each other. And then they all abruptly and spontaneously behave in the same way. The result is a whole system transformation; the whole system moves to a qualitatively different form of behaviour. Suddenly laser beams appear as molecules communicate, and all point in the same direction. Suddenly disorderly chemical reactions oscillate with clock-like precision.

8   Fragile new structures

And feature eight is that this state of consensus, this commitment to behaving in the same consistent manner, all pointing in the same direction, is a precarious one. Without sustained inputs of energy and attention, this new more complex orderly state will be short lived. It is difficult to sustain, and if the system is to go on to innovate further, it will have to be submerged in a new wave of chaos. This precarious, difficult-to-maintain state of consensus and commitment is called by scientists a 'dissipative structure' (see Appendix C).

The IBM example

The process described by features six to eight is also well illustrated by IBM's experience with System/360. Around 1961 the IBM top executives were faced with a number of critical point choices. Should the new Stretch computer continue to be marketed or written off at a loss of $20m? Should the proposed new 8000 series be developed using transistor technology? Should the existing 7000 series be further developed? Should resources be allocated to back Scamp, a new small scientific computer? Or should the proposal to launch what was to become the 360 be backed? The last named was a highly risky proposal to replace all IBM's existing products with the new series at one fell swoop. The unpredictable consequences of these decisions was recognized by those involved – one of the chief protagonists of the 360 called it 'You bet your company'. The political process through which the choice was made can aptly be described as self-organizing. There was no overall authority organizing executives into different political factions – such coalitions were self-organized. After the 360 proposal had gained sufficient support, an informal committee was set up to develop the idea. In early 1962 the report of the committee was presented to 50 top executives. At the end of that meeting, chief executive Learson sensed sufficient support despite objections and concluded, 'All right, we'll do it.' Here we have an abrupt choice at a critical point. Two years later IBM had changed in a dramatic way. The unpredictable outcome on this occasion was success, but it may not have been. Further evidence of the applicability of these general patterns in the innovative process is provided by studies of the political process in business organizations. These were described in Chapter 5.

Chaos: a more useful model of business dynamics

Chaos is the science of the dynamic behaviour of non-linear feedback systems. We saw in Chapter 4 that a business organization is a set of non-linear feedback mechanisms. Its performance is driven by amplifying and damping feedback in sales, output, profit and all other performance indicators from one period to the next. The parameters in those feedback mechanisms are determined by relationships with the environment and by the decision-making (control) process. Relationships with the environment are driven by amplifying and damping feedback mechanisms. This follows from the fact that organizations partly create or shape their own environments through the product offerings they make and from the manner in which those product offerings spread through the customer population. The control process, the discovering, choosing and acting that drives the organization through time, is also a set of amplifying and damping feedback mechanisms. Because business organizations are so clearly feedback systems, the science of chaos must have something to say about the dynamic of business behaviour.

It has been known for a long time that feedback systems can generate either stable or explosively unstable behaviour. When the parameter values in feedback mechanisms are low, that is the mechanism is relatively insensitive or unresponsive, then behaviour is stable. At high parameter values, when the feedback is highly sensitive and responsive, then behaviour is explosively unstable. And it has always been thought that the dynamic of functional systems is to be explained in terms of an attraction or movement towards stable equilibrium positions. We know that decision making and performance in organizations can be stable and that they can also be highly unstable. But the dynamic of successful organizations, we have usually thought, is driven by movement towards stability. We saw, when reviewing today's most prominent models of management in Chapter 5, that rational models explain the functioning of a successful organization as an orderly system and present prescriptions to secure stability. The entrepreneurial models focus on environmental instability and the need for great sensitivity and responsiveness to the environment. Large numbers of trial-and-error actions are supposed to offset large numbers of random shocks coming from the environment. Any mismatches between actions and shocks should be largely cancelled out according to the laws of large numbers. This and other prescribed steps to do with visions and shared values, should keep the organization in a state of stability. In both cases the dynamic of success is the drive to adaptive equilibrium with the environment. Neither explanation takes much account of the feedback nature of organizations, nor are they able to explain why small changes escalate and virtuous and vicious circles in performance and behaviour appear. The only exaplanation they can put forward for the irregular performance we observe, is ignorance or incompetence.

Chapter 4 showed that innovative organizations are those with highly sensitive and creative relationships with the environment. For such organizations purely adaptive equilibrium with the environment has little meaning. That chapter also showed that in innovative organizations the decision-making and control process cannot be one of equilibrium. Stable equilibrium is a state of ossification in which the organization is too hidebound to handle open-ended change. Unstable equilibrium is a state of disintegration in which the organization is too fragmented to handle open-ended change. There are powerful forces pulling all organizations to ossification and disintegration. Success lies in a non-equilibrium state between the stability and instability that feedback mechanisms are capable of generating. Our existing models do not yield useful explanations of such a state and they are therefore defective models of the dynamic of management.

What the discussion on scientific chaos in this chapter has demonstrated is this: non-linear feedback mechanisms are capable of a third form of behaviour we did not know about before. In addition to stability and instability there is bounded instability called chaos. As a feedback system becomes more sensitive and responsive, as the parameter values in the mechanisms are increased, the system passes through a form of bounded instability before it reaches a state of explosive instability. This is therefore the state in which successful organizations must operate.

It is a fundamental property of this state of bounded instability that small changes escalate into major consequences, that behaviour follows self-reinforcing patterns of virtuous and vicious circles. The very feedback structure itself generates these patterns. And because they escalate from tiny disturbances, the outcomes depend upon chance and are inherently unpredictable in the long-term. But those outcomes are bounded. They move within fixed boundaries and they show self-similar patterns. These self-similar patterns are general, qualitative and descriptive; they do not enable long-term predictability of specific outcomes. They generate instead recognizable categories within which no two individuals are the same. These general categories allow us to cope with specific unpredictability through analogous reasoning. Chapter 4 has shown that it is these very features we would look to a dynamic model of business behaviour to explain.

Scientific chaos therefore provides a more useful explanation of the dynamics of management than any of today's prominent models. It explains fundamental characteristics of the feedback mechanisms that are a business organization's. It shows how escalating small changes and self-reinforcing virtuous and vicious circles are fundamental properties of a business system. It shows that long-term performance and the long-term sequence of choices a business makes are all unpredictable at a specific level. But it also indicates how we manage to cope with this unpredictability by using the accompanying self-similarity. What it tells us is that no amount of information gathering, analysis or research can remove these properties. The reason a business faces open-ended change is only partly due to random shocks coming from its environment. Open-ended change also arises partly from the very structure of the business system itself. The consequences of open-ended change are inherently unknowable and there is nothing we can do about it. Regularity and irregularity are intimately intertwined. Irregular business performance and behaviour may be due to ignorance and incompetence. But even if they are removed, there will still be that irreducible irregularity that is a fundamental property of the successful business system.

Non-linear feedback systems are also known to have other dynamic properties. They use chaos to amplify small disturbances, so shattering existing patterns of behaviour. They utilize spontaneous communication and self-organization of their components to make choices at critical points with unpredictable outcomes. At critical points they spontaneously develop sufficient consensus and commitment to behave in a new manner. Some of those choices are creative new developments – innovation. But this state of consensus and commitment to a new form of behaviour is a dissipative structure. It is far-from-equilibrium and requires continuing inputs of energy and attention if it is to be sustained. And it will be submerged into chaos as the system innovates yet further. This model provides a useful explanation of the dynamics of the political learning process through which business organizations make and enact innovative choices. Later chapters will show how this approach provides a more useful explanation than those we currently attend to, of the processes used in the political learning feedback control loop identified in Chapter 3 (Figure 3.2).

So, an organization operating far-from-equilibrium in an environment that consists of other organizations operating far-from-equilibrium will face a spectrum of change situations in which the short-term will have all the characteristics of closed change as described in Chapter 2. And it will also face long-term consequences of its present actions and the events impacting upon it, which are open-ended because of the very nature of the organization itself. It will face very many possible long-term futures. The future is not simply the currently unknown; it is the fundamentally unknowable. Chaos theory explains how non-linear feedback mechanisms are capable of amplifying small changes into major consequences. It demonstrates that virtuous and vicious circles are an inherent property of such feedback mechanisms. It explains how it is possible for systems driven by perfectly fixed rules and laws to behave in a manner affected by chance in an essential way. It explains the mixture of order and disorder we observe in business. Successful business organizations operate far-from-equilibrium, and self-organization theory explains how systems sustained far-from-equilibrium utilize instability to shatter old orders. It explains how such systems depend upon spontaneous self-organization to develop unpredictable new strategic directions. The phases of political choice making in organizations described in Chapter 5 clearly follow the rhythm of symmetry breaking, self-organization and critical point choices found in other non-linear feedback systems.

These two closely related approaches to understanding how complex dynamic systems work – chaos and self-organization – provide managers with important insights into the dynamics of their organizations. They provide insights into the mixture of order and disorder we observe in practice. This, I believe, makes them the basis for developing a more useful dynamic model ploy with which managers may design their actions. The next chapter looks more closely at the implications of the chaos approach for controlling and developing a business.

Conclusion: explaining intertwined order and disorder

Turbulent behaviour and the existence of great individual variety within recognizable categories was previously thought to result from the operation of extremely complex relationships. The chaos explanations demonstrate that such complexity is generated from rather simple rules – amplifying and damping feedback control loops – not much different from the system used to control a domestic central heating system. It is not the rules themselves, but the way in which they operate that accounts for the complexity we observe. Instead of operating in a predictable manner that maintains order, balance or equilibrium, they operate in a far-from-equilibrium state to generate disorder that turns out to be essential to continuing creation. And it is this previously unthinkable way of operating that has challenged the whole frame of reference within which traditional scientific thinking has been conducted (see Appendix A).

Although this body of science has only been developed over the past 20 years or so, it has already had a profound impact on the ability of scientists to understand and explain heretofore inexplicable phenomena in every branch of the natural sciences. In particular, it explains what turbulence is, why it occurs and how it is used in the development of a system. Scientific chaos (and the closely related self-organization theory) is being hailed, along with the theories of relativity and quantum mechanics as one of the three greatest discoveries of this century.

And since human beings employ and are governed by amplifying and damping feedback controls in their dealings with each other, in groups and in organizations, the principles of scientific chaos must be of tremendous importance to social scientists of all kinds. That importance is only just starting to be explored. Since business organizations are fundamentally a set of feedback control and development mechanisms, since they experience the continuing turbulence that is an essential property of such systems, scientific chaos must have significant implications for how managers understand the functioning of their organizations and the part they play in that functioning.

It is now an established fact that the great majority of nature's systems are driven by non-linear feedback control mechanisms and that they positively use turbulent behaviour to change and develop in a creative manner. Trees grow, snowflakes form, weather patterns develop, chemical reactions occur, species perhaps evolve, the human heart operates, diseases spread, gases follow patterns, tremors and earthquakes occur, water drips from a tap, all in a manner determined by the operation of the non-linear feedback mechanisms that control their development.

Scientific chaos together with the theory of self-organization tells us that:

- Order generates disorder. Fixed non-linear feedback rules generate a range of behaviours, some orderly and some disorderly. We can think of such a system as being pulled or attracted towards a number of predictable equilibrium states, the borders between which are disorderly and chaotic, far-from-equilibrium. Behaviour in the border is random and totally unpredictable in terms of the specific path it follows.

- There is order within disorder. The sequence of behaviours as we increase the control parameter in the mechanism is predictable and orderly. And the totally unpredictable specific outcome path has a self-similar pattern where the degree of variability is constant. It is the structure of the mechanism, the constraints that make it non-linear, that are essential to this property of self-similarity.

- Order is born from disorder. The order of new strategic direction and innovation is not a continuing possibility unless the system is far-from-equilibrium, where it experiences instability.

- The new order of innovation, consensus and commitment will be short lived, periodic and difficult to maintain in continuously innovating systems.

- Periodic new order emerges at critical points in an unpredictable way through a process of spontaneous self-organization.

And this is a revolution in scientific thinking. Traditional science, and that includes the methodology and frame of reference within which explanations of management and organization have been developed, sees order as determined by order, and disorder arising only from disorder. Traditional science is conducted within a frame of reference in which systems are thought to operate in the same manner as machines. From this tradition, prescriptions for managing and organizing are all to do with banishing disorder and establishing order as the basis of success. And it is these explanations that managers articulate when they explain how a business functions and what they should do to secure success. From a chaos perspective these are prescriptions that lead to failure. But when they actually behave successfully, managers do not follow the prescriptions that flow from the explanations they profess; they do what is more consistent with the real situation. However, the problem with explaining things in one way and doing them in another is all manner of confusing anomalies. Managers can only benefit from examining what they do in the light of the new scientific theories and developing more realistic explanations of what is going on, all as the basis for more effective action.

References

1   References to the literature on chaos can be found in Appendix B.
2   Sioshansi, F. (January 1990), *Pricing and Marketing Electricity*, The Economist Intelligence Unit.
3   Ohmae, K. (1990), *The Borderless World*, Harper Business.
4   Porter, M. (1990), *The Competitive Advantage of Nations*, Free Press.
5   Quinn, J. B. (1988), IBM (A): The System/360 Decision, in Quinn, J., Mintzberg, H., James, R., *The Strategy Process*, Prentice-Hall.

8 Implications of chaos for controlling and developing a business

In Chapter 4 we saw that business organizations are feedback mechanisms. We also saw that successful businesses do not operate in equilibrium states. They operate in a border area between the equilibrium states of ossification and disintegration. The insights of scientific theories of chaos and self-organization show that this border area between equilibrium states is in fact a chaotic one, far-from-equilibrium. The conclusion is that the dynamic of a successful business is chaotic. The following paragraphs summarize the main implications of this conclusion for business control and innovation. What these conclusions mean for control and development in open-ended situations is dealt with in the next three chapters, together with supporting case studies.

The first implication of scientific chaos has to do with the techniques we use to control and plan the development of a business. Both the short interval control appropriate to closed situations and the long-term planning form of control that can only work in contained situations, rely on quantification, the use of probability concepts, forecasting and simulating. They rely on the possibility of constructing general quantitative models to be applied in many different specific situations. The purpose of such models is to yield reasonably specific information about future states so as to guide present actions. When such quantitative models fail in practice, the entrepreneurial models advise us to rely on visions about the future. Those visions are qualitative pictures of future states which are supposed to be operationally useful.

But chaotic dynamics make all of this impossible when it comes to dealing with the long term because of the dynamic of the business system itself. The dynamic generates open-ended change with unknowable consequences. Chaotic dynamics do not affect the applicability of short interval control methods. The rational models of managing and organizing remain valid in their short-term form. Chaotic dynamics however requires us to rethink our approach to control and development over the long term because the techniques for building general models applicable to a wide tange of specific long-term situations simply break down.

The techniques break down and planning fails in open-ended change

Chaos has important implications for:

- the interpretation of the data used for control purposes;
- the practical usefulness of probability concepts used in decision-making and control;
- the possibility of forecasting and simulating;
- the possibility of having a vision of the future.

It therefore has significant implications for the form of control that may effectively be applied to open-ended change.

Long-term financial models are of little value

The idea that what you can measure you can control, that performance you measure and review is performance that improves, is firmly embedded in today's received business wisdom. And applied to the short-term control of the business, the evidence on the benefits of this approach is impressive. Since it all works in the short term, the approach of measuring and controlling performance is extended to the long term as well. To do this, meaning has to be extracted from the mass of measurements and data that is collected on the performance of a business. The data has to be interpreted and used to construct some kind of physical or financial model of the business. For example, we have to establish the relationships between profits and volumes, between prices and volumes, between volumes and material and labour requirements, between volumes and quality. The belief is that if we are able to identify long-term relationships in this way we will then have a powerful tool for the long-term control of a business. We can ask 'what if' questions and so determine the consequences of what we propose to do, before we burn our bridges and do it.

To extract meaning from the mass of data generated by a business, to identify relationships for a general quantitative model, it is necessary to employ statistical techniques. The simplest and most widely used techniques are averages, the normal distribution, regression analysis and probability. We cannot deal with a whole time series of price data but we can collapse it into an average over the period and deal with that. And we can use the assumption that the deviations of actual prices from this average are normally distributed to measure the bands within which prices are likely to move around the average. Even more sophisticated, we can use regression analysis to identify the relationship between prices and volumes demanded by customers. The problem is that when the dynamic of the system we are dealing with is chaotic, all these approaches are flawed in their application to the long term.

When we average the data generated by a chaotic system, problems arise from the lack of uniform distribution that is a characteristic of chaos:

> Engineers were perplexed by the problem of noise in telephone lines used to transmit information from computer to computer . . . although by its nature the transmission noise was random, it was well known to come in clusters. Periods of error-less communication would be followed by periods of errors . . . Mandelbrot provided a way of describing the distribution of errors that predicted exactly the observed patterns. Yet it was exceedingly peculiar. For one thing, it made it impossible to calculate an average rate of errors – an average number of errors per hour, or per minute or per second . . . Suppose you divide a day into hours. An hour might pass with no errors at all. Then an hour might come with errors. Then an hour might pass with no errors. But suppose you then divide the hour with errors into smaller periods of twenty minutes. You would find that here, too, some periods would be completely clean, while some would contain a burst of errors. In fact, Mandelbrot argued – contrary to intuition – that you could never find a time during which errors where scattered continuously. Within any burst of errors, no matter how short, there would always be periods of completely error free trans-mission. Furthermore, he discovered a consistent geometric relationship between the bursts of errors and clean transmission. On scales of an hour or a second, the proportion of error-free to error-ridden periods remained constant.[1]

So the average you get will depend upon the particular time period you happen to select. If you did not understand the dynamics you could draw very misleading conclusions from an average that reflected more about the time period your data happened to cover than anything else of real significance. A similar problem was encountered in a study of the behaviour of a population of whitefly on viburnum bushes:

> To analyse such a system it is important to do the dynamics first, and then average the results, rather than take averages first and then do the dynamics. For example if you choose a dozen patches, each with a different population density, and see how the average population size varies from generation to generation, you will not expect to see the same pattern that would occur for a uniform population of average density. This is because the dynamic is non-linear, and non-linearities don't respect averages.[2]

If data is in fact being generated by chaotic systems then the standard statistical techniques applied in economics and in business modelling become questionable – fundamental concepts such as averages, normal distribution and regression are then of doubtful value in trying to derive relationships and build models. It would be necessary to fit exactly the right relationship to the data – some other linear or non-linear approximation would not do.

Business decisions based upon financial models that are almost always linear approximations to the feedback mechanisms of an organization can therefore only have any validity for very short-term periods into the future. They can only be of any use in the short-term control of the business. The very dynamics of the business organization renders general quantitative models useless for real strategic control.

Probability only helps in the short term

Faced with a number of possible outcomes, it is common practice in business to use some measure of which of them is more likely, in order to make a rational choice. An investment may be particularly sensitive to the level of the oil price. At $3 per barrel the investment will not yield a profit, at $5 it might, but at $6 it will. If the probability of each outcome can be measured this will greatly assist in making the best choice.

The concept of probability provides a practically useful approach to randomness when events are repeatable over time or where we are dealing with large numbers of the same kind of event. It provides the measures of risk, without which there would be no insurance industry. But in any practical sense it does depend on repeatability. We can only say that some event A at some point in the future is more likely than some other event B, if we can use past experience to show that events similar to A have occurred more frequently than events similar to B. We also need to believe that the underlying structures that generate A and B will continue to operate in the same manner into the future. If you get the opportunity to repeat events A and B a great many times, the measure of probability provides you with a useful decision-making tool. However if you do not get the opportunity to repeat the rule, there is no practical value in any theoretical probability measurement. If your fortune depends on the occurrence of event A and ruin on the occurrence of event B, you may never get the opportunity to try again. In situations of true uncertainty (one unique occasion without close parallels in past experience) as opposed to risk (repeatable occasions or those were there is some precedent), probability provides no practical assistance because you only get one chance.

When the dynamics are chaotic, specific events will follow an inherently random path over the long term. There will be an infinite number of possible long-term outcomes. The probability of any event occurring is then infinitely small and provides no assistance in making a decision. Because tiny changes can escalate into major consequences, it will in practice be impossible to generate the same sequence of events twice. In practice it is therefore impossible to measure any probability. At critical points, the system faces unique choices, where the laws of large numbers and hence statistical approaches do not apply. Close to critical points, the disturbances or fluctuations become abnormally high, sometimes as high as the mean values of the system. The distinction between noise, or error terms, and means breaks down.

Many quantitative decision-making techniques in business today are based on probability. Such techniques may have short-term validity, but because of the chaotic dynamics of successful businesses, they can provide no assistance when it comes to strategic control. Instead we have to deploy reasoning by analogy, making use of the qualitative similarities in the behaviour generated by chaotic systems.

Long-term forecasts and simulations are impossible

The presence of chaos is the death knell to any form of quantitative forecasting or simulation in anything other than the short term. If a tiny change can escalate into behaviour of a qualitatively different kind, then extrapolating past trends is clearly senseless. The techniques used to make more sophisticated long-term forecasts cannot overcome the hurdle of sensitive dependence on initial conditions either.

> When the dynamics of a system goes chaotic, there's a trade off between the precision with which we know its current state, and the period of time over which we can say what – in detail – it will do. And the precision of observations has to be almost impossibly good to make even medium-term predictions.[3]

And simulation, or the use of scenarios, to get some feel for how the system might behave in the long term fares little better.

> A computer can address any problem by simulating it, rapidly calculating each cycle. But simulation brings its own problem: the tiny imprecision built into each calculation rapidly takes over, because this is a system with sensitive dependence on initial conditions. Before long the signal disappears and all that remains is noise.[4]

> For a chaotic system, however, simulation is pointless, because we only get the same amount of information out as we put in. More and more computing power is required to tell us less and less. In other words we are not predicting anything, merely describing the system to a certain limited level of accuracy as it evolves in real time . . . We cannot determine a chaotic path unless we are first given that path.[5]

However, although we can never forecast the specific quantitative path that a chaotic system will follow, we can now have a greater understanding than we did before of how that system behaves. Previously we could not explain random observable patterns of behaviour other than to ascribe them to random shocks. Now scientific chaos can identify the orderly rules that are generating such behaviour. Once these rules have been identified it is possible to establish the conditions within which chaos will be present. So those operating in the Stock Exchange or studying the weather can determine whether there is any point in trying to forecast in particular circumstances. If what we need is stability then we can identify the conditions within which that stability will occur and so avoid chaos.

Furthermore, once the feedback rules have been identified, we can determine the overall shape of the strange attractors to which the behaviour of the system may be drawn. So, in the case of the weather, we know it will follow the general pattern of the butterfly attractor (see Chapter 7, Figure 7.8). We can say something, at least qualitatively, about general categories of behaviour and we can say something quantitatively about the boundaries within which random behaviour will occur. The self-similar nature of chaotic behaviour allows us at least to perceive recognizable patterns and constant degrees of variation. From these we can build up experience to give some guidance in dealing with future uncertainty. And since it takes time for changes to build up in chaotic systems, their short-term future is predictable.

What we can do in the presence of chaos, then, is to predict the qualitative nature of the whole system and the quantitative limits within which it will move. And it is quite possible that simple methods, which appear now to have very little scientific validity, may turn out to be make more sense than much more respectable approaches. It could be, for example, that chartists capture something about the shape of the stock market's movements that has more validity than fundamental analysis, although only for the short term. It may also be that experience-based intuition is a more reliable approach to the overall shape of a dynamic business system than any analytical methods presently available to us.

Now a great many of the decision-making and control techniques employed in business today are based firmly on the view that forecasting is possible and that the use of different scenarios provides some assistance. One very senior executive quite seriously described the strategic control system he was looking for in terms of a computerized model of his business. The outputs of this model would be called up on a computer screen in the boardroom, so allowing him and his colleagues to put 'what if' questions to the computer and receive on-line answers immediately. This may be useful when it comes to very short-term control, but because the dynamics of success are chaotic, such techniques are useless for real strategic control.

Modern methods of investment appraisal employ discounted cashflow approaches. Here the cashflow consequences of an investment to be undertaken in say six months time are all projected for 25 years into the future. Different predicted scenarios are used to generate different rates of return on the investment. We then apply some idea of probability to select the most likely outcome and therefore to decide whether or not to proceed with the investment. This whole procedure is pure fantasy when the dynamics are chaotic. Because of the dynamic we cannot forecast, simulate or apply probability to long-term consequences. And in fact most managers never really use this approach. They may be required by current practice to produce the analysis. But their perfectly sensible approach is then to manipulate the figures to produce a rate of return that accords with their judgement.

A common objection to this point of view runs as follows. In, say, the pharmaceuticals industry, it takes 10 to 15 years to develop a new drug. In, say, the aerospace industry it can take 15 to 20 years to develop and produce a new aircraft. In the construction industry it may take five years or more to design and build a power station. Such businesses therefore have to plan for the future. Now planning in these cases is clearly essential where that planning means setting out, well in advance of performing them, the action steps required to develop, design, test and launch on to the market the drug, the aircraft or the power station. Many of the steps we now intend to take in order to do all these things can be set out in advance of our doing them because they depend almost entirely on what we have done before to develop products or build power stations. But the argument is usually taken further. In addition to such action steps it is also said to be necessary to set out projections of all the costs, revenues and consequent profit flows. This is in order to take the initial decision to embark on the project and to control it as it proceeds. In the case of the power station this may be possible if contractual arrangements that cover all the cashflows are entered into at the start of the project. In the case of the drug or the aircraft it is not a realistic proposition. In the absence of contractual arrangements, no one can forecast the snags that may be encountered in the development, the costs that will be incurred in year 10 or the market demand that will prevail in year 15, simply because there are too many unknowns. Such long-term projects can therefore only realistically be embarked upon on the basis of here and now judgements, on the basis of chance. The plan cannot refer to long-term outcomes of the project itself, only to the steps necessary to carry that project out. The remainder of any long-term project plan is pure fiction if change is open ended.

There is an alternative approach to making long-term investment decisions. This is to make them on the assumption that we cannot know how they will turn out. The judgement criteria are then based on retaining flexibility, on building a market position, preventing the entry of competition, or installing a facility that will last. It is curious that modern

UK governments cannot afford to construct a new sewage system – frequent collapses have to be tolerated. The Victorians who were many times less affluent than modern Britons, whose labour productivity was many times lower, constructed a sewage system that is still in use. Would they have constructed so long lasting a system if they had used discounted cashflow analysis?

Long-term plans make no contribution

The conclusion to be drawn, if one accepts the premise that the dynamic of success is chaotic, is this: all forms of long-term planning are completely ineffective as modes of controlling the development of an innovative business over the long term. They can have nothing directly to do with creating new strategic direction or with innovation. This is because when the dynamic is chaotic, long-term outcomes are inherently unpredictable. And so is the sequence of the organizational choices that lead to those outcomes. If a long-term planning exercise involves widespread discussion of ambiguous current issues, if it involves insightful interpretation and analysis of the past and present situation, it can contribute to that organizational learning that constitutes controlled behaviour in turbulent times. But its very formality and regularity mitigate against this.

And simulation, the generation of different scenarios and the selection of most likely outcomes, cannot come to the rescue of either long-term planning or quantitative techniques for investment appraisal. Given extreme sensitivity to tiny changes, there are too many long-term outcomes to make simulations a practical possibility. And in the circumstances of chaotic dynamics, statistical probability has no practical use so we cannot select a most likely scenario. There will of course be individual developments in the environment that are predictable because they are repetitions of what has happened before, or because they are the unwinding of events that have already occurred. The composition of the population of consumers over the next two decades is predictable because the events determining it have already occurred. While such predictions are useful in making judgements, they provide only a few of the many factors that will determine the long-term outcome of a business. They cannot therefore rescue long-term planning or formal quantitative techniques of long-term decision-making.

For this reason we observe that while successful companies may prepare long-term plans and conduct quantitative investment appraisals, such techniques effectively play no direct part in the choices that are made. At their most useful they provide interpretations of what has happened and is happening to assist in making judgements. At their least useful they provide symbolic myths that managers are being rational, when the dynamic means that they cannot be. They are positively dangerous when they provide false comfort by lulling senior managers into the belief that they are in control in the rational, usually accepted sense of that word. Such techniques are even more dangerous when they are believed and actually used to make decisions. Since they can take no account of the real dynamic of the business, since they are conditioned by simplistic ideas of the organization matching and fitting its resources to the environment, they can only lead to marginal adaptations that exclude really innovative moves. Furthermore they soon become rituals that waste scarce management time, distracting managers from exploring the real issues.

Short interval control is vital

But long-term unpredictability, the uncertainty this gives rise to, and the reactions it provokes in people in an organization, all make realistic forms of stability more important. Chaotic dynamics are intertwined order and disorder – there is an overall pattern or rhythm to the development of the system. Consequently, the short-term development of the organization is reasonably predictable. Planning forms of control, quantitative, analytical techniques for decision-making are then highly relevant. Scientific chaos therefore underlines the extreme importance of the whole planning approach to short-term control and the need for effective management information and control systems.

It is a contradiction in terms to call, as some writers do,[6] for tight, short interval financial control, and to couple that with the advice that everyone should be involved in everything, that job definitions should be loose and assignments ambiguous. It is also a contradiction to advise, as some writers do,[7] that power be dispersed throughout the organization and clear management hierarchies replaced by loose network, matrix and clover leaf structures. These prescriptions are supposed to lead to more effective strategic management. It is argued in this book that they do not, and that furthermore they make tight, short interval control virtually impossible. Tight, short interval control demands simple, clear cut hierarchies of managers and that means stable but unequal distributions of power increasingly concentrated with movement up the hierarchy. It also means that job definitions have to be clear and that in the normal run of things everyone should focus on specific areas of responsibility. By clearly focusing attention on where and why rational planning forms of control and development cannot work, chaos underlines where and how they must be rigorously applied. For scientific chaos is not simply about disorder, it is about the appropriate place of order and disorder.

Visions of the future may be dangerous fantasies

Because the dynamic of a successful business is chaotic, it is impossible to forecast or simulate its long-term future. An immediate response of many to this conclusion is that we knew this anyway. We knew that there was a limit to the accuracy with which the long-term future could be predicted. But we can still:

- forecast significant aspects of that future – for example future changes in the composition of the population and their implications for consumer expenditure patterns can be predicted, or we can forecast future applications of existing new technology; and we can
- determine the broad direction in which the business will go into the future – we can establish a mission of what we want the business to be at some point in the future, we can form some vision of what shape it will take in the future.

The argument is that such direction, missions and visions provide the aim for the business which is necessary to motivate people and provide continuity. As we go into the future we can remain flexible and make alterations to the course we are following. The analogy of a ship is used. The ship's course is set to reach a particular point and as the journey proceeds, adjustments to direction are made. If no particular distant point was set, the ship would simply wander aimlessly.

This view is based upon the following three assumptions:

- First, that it is impossible to act coherently in the absence of a clear long-term purpose, without something to aim for in the distant future.
- Second, that there is one future 'out there' and it is necessary to identify that future in some way in order to reach it. Seen from the here and now that future is hazy and fuzzy. But parts of it can be identified (partial forecasts) and the general hazy outline can be 'seen' (missions and visions which give direction). As that future is approached its outline becomes clearer, its detail more identifiable, enabling the direction to it to be fixed more precisely.
- Third, that the partial forecasts and the visions provide sufficient information for people in a business to discover and choose what to do in advance of the changes occurring. They allow people to learn in advance of having to take action.

This third assumption is particularly important. If the missions and visions are so vague and general that they have no specific operational content, then they cannot enable people to learn enough in advance of the change to make any difference to their actions. The visions then make no difference to what people actually do, and therefore to the outcomes of what they do. Strategic control has to be operational; it has at least to facilitate discovery, choice and action taken now having long-term consequences. Strategic control is of little use if it simply relates to a vague set of possible actions that might be taken at some future point. If missions and visions of the future have no real operational content then they are irrelevant to real strategic control.

This point can be illustrated by the situation faced by a group of divisional managers I worked with recently. The division consisted of a number of information technology companies that had been acquired a short time before. Some of these companies distributed directly to end users and others sold products to own-equipment manufacturers including their own sister subsidiaries. The direct distribution companies therefore competed with customers of those who distributed product indirectly. Not surprisingly, this use of two routes to market led to continuous conflict between the subsidiaries. Those distributing through the indirect route complained that those distributing directly were competing unfairly because of the transfer pricing rules imposed by the division. This was antagonizing the customers of those distributing indirectly, and they were therefore losing business. The problem confronting the divisional management was therefore either one of devising an organizational structure and transfer pricing policies to allow both companies to operate effectively, or to abandon one of the routes to market. To deal with the problem divisional management were advised to formulate a vision or dream of what they wanted to be in the future. The mission statement they all agreed upon was to become one of the major players in the market, using both routes to market. Given the uncertain market conditions they faced, none of the divisional managers felt that they were able to formulate anything more specific than this.

Now this mission or vision had little operational content. It did exclude the possibility of abandoning one or other routes to market. But there was nothing in it to indicate which structural form or what transfer pricing policy was appropriate. Instructing these managers to have a vision had no practical usefulness and indeed distracted attention from the real issues. The real issue had to do with conflicting ambitions on the part of the members of the team and judgements about the reactions of the own-equipment customers and competitors to different arrangements. Focusing on the here and now strategic issue agenda was possible and practical, while formulating visions was not.

Many futures

When the dynamics are chaotic then the potential futures open to the system are infinite. There is not just one future to be seen in hazy outline. Which particular potential future is realized will depend upon the many small changes impacting on the system as it moves through real time, and on the responses that are made, or not made, to them. So, in say November 1990, a particular business may face a number of choices for expansion and given limited resources it cannot pursue all of them. It is possible to allocate most of the resources for expansion in the home market, or to allocate some of them to setting up an operation in Germany or France. Or it might be better to try to take advantage of changes in Eastern Europe, perhaps Poland or Lithuania. In November 1990, then, the business faces many potential futures. Suppose its vision is to become a major player in the European Community rather than a purely UK company. Most of the effort and resource is then directed to acquisition in France or Germany. But one of the directors has contacts in Poland and the company responds to a request for a small joint venture in that country. Some backing is also given to the development of a speculative new product in the UK. It is quite possible that acquisition attempts in France and Germany will fail and that large new businesses will gradually develop in Poland or from the new speculative product development in the UK. It is perfectly possible that in the late 1990s this company will not be a major player in the European Community at all, but a significant force in some market in Poland or in a new market in the UK. How can managers 'see' which of these futures will materialize, when all depends on the detail of what will happen and be done in the UK, France, Germany and Poland in the next few years?

Which of the potential futures is realized depends upon many small actions the company undertakes now, such as sending two executives to Poland rather than to Lithuania, to explore the possibilities. Which particular future materialises is thus unknowable. Chaotic dynamics make qualitative visions and missions as impossible as quantitative forecasts. An ability to forecast a few aspects of any one of those futures, or some aspects that may be common to many of them, is simply not enough. Nor is being able to 'see' the rough outline of some of those futures through some vision. As we approach a particular point in the future we may not find a clearer picture of the vision we had before, but a completely different outcome. Because there are so many potential futures, no set of partial forecasts or visions can contain enough operational detail to inform present actions. Because the future is unknowable we cannot learn enough to make choices and to act in advance of the changes occurring. We have to learn in real time as the changes occur and as we bring them about.

And if we do find visions with specific operational content, they may well be fantasies. When the dynamic is chaotic, no view of the future can contain operational detail. If it does it must be a departure from reality and that is what we mean by fantasy. And observation confirms this. In practice, mission statements are vague and general and one company's mission statement looks very much like every other. Ask chief executives to state their vision, to say where their company is going, and you get vague statements about being big, growing rapidly, achieving market share, securing adequate returns on capital, serving the community and so on. In practice, then, direction, mission and vision really mean aspiration, not a picture of some future state.

Aspirations and ambitions

Visions make sense only as aspirations, ambitions or intentions, as a desire to achieve something, a desire which drives behaviour in the here and now. In practice people derive their realistic aspirations from what they have discovered in the past and are discovering now. Aspirations that are connected to reality arise from where we have come from and where we are now. Aspirations arising from some imagined future state are fantasies. When behaviour is driven by fantasy it is neurotic and dangerous. Where behaviour is connected to reality, we do not conjure up some vision first and then act. Instead we aspire to some achievement because of what we know, what we have done and are doing and that aspiration affects our actions. Through those actions we discover more and this may change our aspirations, which then affect our behaviour in a continuing process. Realistic vision, mission and direction are all interpretations of what is going on now, not imaginings about the future. Using the word vision creates the wrong expectation.

Does this distinction matter?

The answer is yes. If we believe that we cannot proceed to do anything without first setting a specific purpose in terms of some future desired outcome, we start to use vision, mission and direction in their meanings of fantasy. Fantasies have either a misleading or a paralysing effect on behaviour. If you advise a group of managers to fix their purpose, set out their future direction before they do anything else, then they do not know what to do. All they can do is fantasize, or, just as dangerously, pick some future and pursue it with tunnel vision. The behaviour is different if we believe that we can proceed without fixing a specific purpose, without a future direction. We then proceed on the basis of interpreting the past and the present, on the basis of how we judge and feel. We are then able to discover purpose as we go along. We would then give different advice to a group of managers. You cannot know anything operationally useful about the future, so you should examine where you have come from and where you are now. Interpret this as the basis of your next actions. Base your aspirations on this interpretation. And examine the effectiveness of how you are interpreting and interacting as a group. With such advice, managers then know what to do and it is firmly based in reality. And it is not simply reacting in a blind manner. It is reflecting and searching for creative solutions to real problems rather than speculating about an infinite number of futures. It is attending to realistic agendas of here and now issues which will have long-term consequences.

The debilitating effect that a false belief in the ability to specify future direction has on managers can be illustrated by the following incident. The managing director of the information technology division referred to earlier decided to use a workshop approach with middle managers to surface their views on what form the reorganization should take. I was asked to facilitate this workshop. The first meeting of this workshop did not reach agreement and one reason for this was the different assumptions people were making about the future direction of the business. In particular, one group was assuming that the major future impetus would be through sales of their products direct to the end users, while another was assuming that the main thrust would be through indirect sales to own-equipment manufacturers. They looked to top management to make a decision about future direction. Unusually in my experience, the top management team stated that they did not know where the future direction lay – it was all too uncertain. At the next workshop, some of the middle managers found this completely unacceptable; they could not see how any further work on reorganization could continue without first defining future direction. In fact, the group as a whole was able to put forward sensible proposals about reorganization to deal with the here and now. But some members were demotivated; their contribution declined because of their belief in the need for future direction.

Selective interpretation

Some, however, will argue that there are clear cases where individuals have had a vision. They have had some picture of a realizable future that has been expressed in a simple, realistic and understandable way, so inspiring others to believe in and enact it. For example, in 1914 David Sarnoff heard an experimental broadcast of phonographic music and in 1915 wrote a memo on 'Radio Music Boxes'. In this memo he described a vast market for wireless sets as household utilities. This vision became RCA. Ray Croc had a vision of assembly-line efficiency applied to fast foods and that vision became McDonalds. Walt Disney had a vision of people's need for fantasy worlds and this was realized as Disneyland.

The interpretation of these events is that some individual formed a picture of the future and inspired others with it. Because it was the 'right' picture, the one that matched a given set of future requirements, those individuals were successful. The prescription for others is that they should develop a vision and persuade others to follow it. They should do this by analysing opportunities and then making some creative leap of the imagination. But such interpretations are made with the benefit of hindsight. Looking back it is all too easy to take some successful outcome and then identify preceding statements and actions which indicate clear fore-sight. In doing this we are ignoring all the other ideas, suggestions, statements and actions that people such as Walt Disney and Ray Croc had, many of which will not have shown any foresight at all. This point has already been made in Chapter 1 and in the example of successful and failed 'visions' of Federal Express.

The other danger of this 'man with a vision' interpretation is that we focus all the attention on one charismatic personality and ignore the many contributions that others make to the success story. No one develops a huge business alone. The folk heroes of business have colleagues who help to shape what happens. The 'vision' interpretation of success is one in which inspired colleagues follow the vision. In fact, often in unob-trusive ways, colleagues contribute to the shaping and development of the outcome. The way in which they do this together and the manner in which they interact with the charismatic leader has a powerful effect on what happens. The development of Apple Computers, for example, is a story of conflict and cooperation between its two founders.

A more useful interpretation of what happens in entrepreneurial suc-cess stories runs in terms of an unfolding sequence of aspirations and challenging formulations of ideas based on what is happening now. There is not one fixed vision, but a flow of many, often conflicting, issues and creative ideas that are surfaced by people like Ray Croc and Walt Disney. Other colleagues make contributions too and together they ex-plore and learn about the issues, discarding some and proceeding with others as they go along. It is only with hindsight that we can attach outcome to preceding statements or plans.

This interpretation focuses attention on the continuing, creative surfac-ing of ideas, on political processes for attracting attention to those ideas, on group learning behaviour to develop those ideas, on the organiz-ation's dynamic issue agenda. And in this process, different perspectives and conflict around issues is all important. The focus then is on how groups of managers behave, not simply on how one charismatic individ-ual acquires an idea. The vision interpretation is dangerous because it places an onerous burden on one individual to create a vision. It is also dangerous because it emphasizes the need for very early commitment to one fixed view of the future, when the dynamics mean that there are many.

Trial-and-error action cannot ensure stability

The point has been made a number of times before that entrepreneurial models of managing assume that the successful business can maintain stability through trial-and-error action. The idea is that a business that undertakes large numbers of trial actions in response to unpredictable changes occurring in the environment will find that mismatches between those unpredictable changes and the actions taken in response to them will cancel out. If we undertake a large enough number of experiments then the errors will largely cancel out. According to the laws of probability, we will be left with only a small percentage of mismatches or errors. Irregular performance should then be a very minor component of the total unless managers are incompetent, or they do not undertake a sufficient volume of trials. Excellent companies will be highly active ones.

Now all this can only work if the unpredictable changes and the consequent actions occur in large numbers and are largely repetitive. Furthermore they must not be small changes that escalate into large outcomes. If they are, we cannot rely on errors cancelling out. It will be important to get the right response for that small change that might escalate, otherwise the consequence could be disaster. Where the dynamic is chaotic all these conditions for the cancelling out of mismatches between trial actions and unpredictable changes fail to be met. Chaotic dynamics generate long-term situations that are open-ended. Here the changes are unique not repetitive. And small changes do escalate with large consequences. Stability can then only be maintained if we act in a manner that matches each specific change. We will always have to detect the change and get the timing right. That is, we will have to be able to forecast specific long-term outcomes. This is impossible in chaos. It follows that no matter how competent managers are, performance and behaviour will always display irregularity combined with regularity.

Scientific chaos, then, raises very serious questions indeed for current widely accepted approaches to interpreting data, to the use of statistical techniques, to the use of forecasting and simulation, to the role of visions, as part of decision-making processes directed to issues with long-term consequences. Taken together these questions require a reappraisal of how we actually control business organizations when it comes to the strategic issues. And that reappraisal requires examining what managers actually do. Although many say they need future direction, although many prepare long-term plans, successful managers actually do something completely different.

Building strategic issue agendas is the key to strategic 'control'

In practice, when managers are confronted with open-ended change, they utilize political learning processes. Effective political learning processes occur within a context that encourages people to detect and select small disturbances in the environments and the functioning of the organization. The point is to surface ambiguous and equivocal issues. These issues are then amplified through political support-building processes so that they gain organizational attention. Those issues that gain attention become the organization's strategic agenda. This agenda is the pivot of effective strategic control. It is the heart of the strategic control loop depicted in Figure 3.2, Chapter 3. An innovative organization is one with a lively, ever changing agenda of issues that are being clarified through discusion and reflection, that are being enacted in exploratory ways and backed with resource as they succeed. The process of building agendas is an amplifying, not a damping one. It is one in which small changes are blown up into large consequences that will shatter existing ways of doing things. In common with all other systems where the dynamic is chaotic, this amplification process has to be one that shatters old perceptions, relationships and structures. It will therefore be confusing and arouse conflict. During the confusion that flows from the dynamic, the organization reaches critical points and the choices made at these points will depend upon the spontaneous self-organization of those involved. The sequence of choices made in the political learning process is unpredictable and the process itself requires spontaneity and cannot therefore be installed and controlled in the rational manner we usually take control to mean.

But the process is not lacking in control in the wider meaning of coherent behaviour, because there is a pattern or rhythm to the process; a sequence of phases from detection through amplification to spontaneous choice and the possible emergence of innovation. There is also, in successful organizations, that other aspect of order within chaos, the 'hidden' pattern of self-similarity or regular irregularity in behaving and choosing. It is this that provides enough stability for controlled behaviour.

At one extreme we could have pattern and order in which the political and learning behaviours, as well as the choices and actions they produce, are completely coherent and consistent. They follow some clearly logical form and sequence; they always hang together and are never contradictory. Then there is no chaos. This situation can be illustrated by the managing director who defines your job, tells you he will monitor your performance once a month and then leaves you do to the job, never interfering until he monitors your performance. There is no variation in his behaviour or choices; it is completely consistent. The situation is easy to cope with.

At the other extreme there is no pattern in the sense that one behaviour is followed by another, one choice is followed by another, each of which is a total surprise to those involved or affected. No behaviour or choice bears any resemblance to what has gone before it; each one in the sequence shoots all over the place without any perceptible bounds or constraints. This is utter confusion, devoid of all form and it is not chaos. So the above managing director may say that you will be left to do the job and then one day leave you to do it, interfere in the next issue, leave you alone for the next week and then interfere for the next 10 days, always in a different way on different issues, reversing what he told you to do the day before. There is nothing constant about his interference; it is completely inconsistent. Few of us can cope with this.

However, we can and do get sequences of behaviour and choices where each element of the sequence is not predictable from what went before, but nevertheless bears some resemblance to what went before. Each event is a surprise but not entirely because there is some similarity. There are perceptible boundaries within which the sequence moves, perceptible constraints. In other words there is some regularity in the irregularity of behaviour and choice. So, the managing director may say he will leave you to do the job, but then interfere now and again on issues that bear some resemblance to each other, reversing his prior decisions only on some occasions that have something to do with perceived circumstances. Here the behaviour and the choices are unpredictable. They are irregular, but there is a constancy to that irregularity. The inconsistency of this manager is regular. We can then cope because we are not totally surprised and we have similar patterns on the basis of which we can reason by analogy.

Constraints

The regular irregularity in political behaviour and choice flows from the structure and operation of the feedback mechanisms, just as the randomness and confusion does. Key to the important order-breaking randomness is the extreme sensitivity to tiny changes and the amplifying nature of the mechanism. Key to the regular irregularity is the constraints placed upon the operation of the feedback loop. The loop is non-linear in the first place because of these constraints – it is the constraints that prevent it from being proportional. And in the case of political activity there would be no constraints, the sequence of choices could shoot just anywhere, people could behave in just any haphazard fashion, if there was no hierarchy, an equal distribution of power and no difference in people's values and cultural norms. Quite clearly, both hierarchy and the closely related unequal distribution of power place a constraint on the behaviour of people and the choices they make; some behaviours and choices are simply not allowed. Highly centralised and widely distributed power both remove this constraint. In the former case one or two people can do whatever they please and in the latter everyone can. But power that is unequally distributed places constraints upon everyone.

Different values and cultural norms are just as important as power distribution in providing boundary conditions. If everyone in a group has the same values, that group of people could just continue to behave in exactly the same way, making the same choices from period to period. Or they could just as easily all go shooting off together in some different direction for a considerable period of time. For example, in August 1990, the highly cohesive cultural values and concentrated power in Iraq made it possible simply to abandon all the claims that had been fought for in the Iran–Iraq war and set off on a path of confrontation with the rest of the world over the invasion of Kuwait. In France the strongly held belief in nuclear energy at Electricité de France made it possible for that organization to continue building nuclear power stations even after serious questions about costs had been surfaced. The result is an over-supply of expensive electricity. The Italian electricity industry with its diversity of values and lack of common policy is today the beneficiary of that over-supply in the form of cheap imports of electricity. Different values and norms will prompt different individual behaviours and choices and so constrain any common direction in those behaviours and choices. Because of unequal power and different values a sequence of choices will not be able to move outside certain bounds. The constraints of difference provide stability in chaos.

However, chaos is never simply one thing or another. The necessary difference in values and degrees of commitment relates to issues that have ambiguous long-term consequences. They are values about how the organization should respond to those issues. There are of course other values, those to do with a few simple ethical beliefs, for example. An organization cannot function if some members have the values of marauding bandits and others the values of philanthropic saints. Sharing values at this very basic level is therefore required. When it comes to the predictable day-to-day conduct of the existing business, then shared values around, for example, consistent quality and customer service levels are also vital. However, when the requirement for shared values is escalated from a few simple commonsense requirements to do with ethical conduct and day-to-day tasks, to become a fanatical demand for total commitment to the organization, to some plan, or some vision, the essential constraint that provides constant variation in behaviour and choice disappears.

Different cultural norms within the same organization are of major importance because, at the deepest level, they generate different perceptions. And innovation depends on different perceptions. All of this is impossible without conflict around issues. And conflict around issues inevitably becomes part of conflict around personalities, organizational ambitions, goals and individual desires. Conflict itself is not harmful if it has at least some connection with issues. What is harmful is the suppression and avoidance of conflict. On one of my consultancy assignments, a top management team had just been formed to take a particular enterprise from the state to the private sector. Some members were from outside the industry, others were from the old enterprise. That group strenuously avoided confronting the deep-seated conflict which existed between them on how the business should be managed. The only way they could avoid the personal conflict was to avoid discussing the issues as a group. Issues were dealt with in groups of two or three people only. That simply increased the underlying conflict. Suppressing and avoiding the personal animosity when they were together as a group was simply resulting in ineffective handling of the issues. Once they confronted each other with personal issues, it became possible to work on organizational issues. They did not become a cohesive like-minded band of brothers, the conflict did not disappear, but they were able to deal with the important issues.

New models for each new situation

As soon as we think of a successful organization as one which operates far-from-equilibrium in chaos, we see that the irregularity and disorder it has to contend with is not just due to random shocks from the environment. The problem is not as simple as a series of changes in government policies, technologies and customer requirements. Those unpredictable changes are important, but just as important is the irregularity and disorder generated by the very structure of the business system itself. Open-ended change is to an important extent a fundamental property of the feedback nature of a successful business organization itself. Even if there were no random shocks coming from the environment, the business would still face open-ended change. The long-term performance, and the long-term sequence of choices leading to that performance, would still be inherently unpredictable within the boundaries of recognizable categories. The dynamic of a successful business is such that it inevitably unfolds in the form of self-reinforcing virtuous and vicious circles, often touched off by small chance disturbances.

Two important conclusions follow from this view. The first is that there is no general model or set of prescriptions that managers can acquire in advance to enable them to design appropriate actions for each new open-ended situation they encounter. They continually have to construct new mental models to deal with each new situation as it unfolds. Managers are able to do this, despite the completely unpredictable nature of what they are doing, because they are able to reason by analogy. They can utilize the self-similar nature of chaotic paths in performance and choice to develop analogies from which they can obtain new insight, construct new mental models and design innovative actions. And this is what we mean by learning – our existing mental models are altered and new ones are developed. The process of building strategic issue agendas and taking action on them is therefore a learning one in which we are continually developing new mental models to create new responses to new situations.

And the second conclusion is this. The instrument managers use to control and develop the business in open-ended change is not a constant. In closed and contained change situations, we can embed the objective setting, planning and monitoring feedback loop into an institutionalized system, with clear rules and procedures. We can do this in advance of the action we have to take in response to a change and it will remain relatively constant as we use it to handle the change. But the political learning feedback loops required to handle open-ended change are fluid and ever altering. We are designing the control and development instrument itself, the mental model itself, as we use it to handle the change. For this reason we observe that when managers handle open-ended change, they expend even more time and energy on identifying matters internal to the organization than they do on what is happening in the markets. They spend more time on discussing who should run a new business venture and how it is to be controlled than they do on discussing its market prospects.

Conclusion: rethinking the approach to strategic 'control'

If the dynamic of a successful business is chaotic, as this book argues it is, then managers cannot rely on plans to handle their open-ended long-term futures. Nor can they rely on visions, shared values and trial-and-error actions to secure stability in open-ended situations. To retain these things in the belief that most people could not cope if they are abandoned is to run the risk of not dealing adequately with open-ended change. Holding on to illusions of ineffective control forms, simply to provide people with false comfort, will obstruct the innovation upon which survival today depends. There is a more realistic alternative for effective control and development. This more realistic alternative is to understand and make more effective the political learning process through which managers continually develop new mental models, build strategic issue agendas, and take action to create their own environments. The whole process is unpredictable in specific terms but there is the order of recognizable categories of events, choices and actions.

This does not mean that planning forms of control and rational forms of decision-making are of no importance. The effecitve day-to-day conduct of the existing business depends critically on these processes. And at some point open-ended changes reach a degree of clarity and predictability in which they too must be handled in this way – they move from the category of open-ended to the categories of contained and closed, in which rational control forms apply. And the development of new mental models with which to handle open-ended change does not occur in a vacuum. Information gathering and analysis play some part in provoking new insights.

What the chaos perspective means is that we have to arrange our affairs on the basis that:

- The short-term future is predictable and requires rational forms of control.
- The long-term future is completely unknowable in any specific sense, but we will be able to use qualitatively similar patterns to develop new mental models when we encounter it. In this way we can behave creatively and innovate.
- Small changes will escalate into vicious and virtuous circles and therefore what happens will depend significantly on chance. From this we do not withdraw from any action with long-term consequnces and behave in a purely short-term fashion. To survive through innovation we expose ourselves to chance and deal creatively with whatever happens.
- There are often no clear cause and effect links in what happens to the business.
- It is these very features of the system in which we operate that enable creativity and innovation.

When we take a chaos perspective we behave in a way that is open and sensitive to our environment, we take a chance, we do creative things with long-term consequences we cannot foresee, we work at understanding and at developing new understandings; and we create a part at least of what happens to us, accepting that the rest is a matter of chance. And this is a more exciting perspective on the role of managers than that in which they only formulate and implement plans.

The next three chapters explore this process in more detail. They first consider the learning aspect, then the political aspects and then the path of creative exploration that is strategic control.

References

1   Gleick, J. (1988), *Chaos*, Heinemann, p. 91, reprinted by permission of William Heinemann Ltd.
2   Stewart, I. (1989), *Does God Play Dice: The Mathematics of Chaos*, Basil Blackwell, p. 273.
3   Stewart, I., op. cit., p. 286.
4   Gleick, J., op. cit., p. 44.
5   Davies, P. (1987), *The Cosmic Blueprint*, Heinemann, p. 54, reprinted by permission of William Heinemann Ltd.
6   Peters, T. (1988), *Thriving on Chaos*, Macmillan.
7   Moss Kanter, R. (1985), *The Change Masters*, Simon & Schuster.

9 Strategic 'control' is organizational learning

The form of control an organization is able to practise in open-ended situations is fundamentally different to that which it can apply to closed and contained changes. In the latter case it is possible to clarify preferences and objectives in advance of taking action and then search for solutions using step-by-step, algorithmic techniques. It is possible to apply rational modes of thinking, learning and choosing because outcomes are to some useful extent predictable. But in open-ended situations control can only mean learning about preferences, objectives and aspirations as action is taken, because outcomes are unknowable. People have to discover and learn, in groups, about changes as the organization moves through real time – it cannot be done in advance. And not only that, as this chapter will argue, control in open-ended situations also requires a different way of thinking and learning to that appropriate in closed or contained change situations. How managers think and learn is the key to effective strategic choice, not what they plan or what visions of the future they are somehow supposed to develop. This chapter is concerned with the fundamental nature of strategic thinking and learning.

Thinking and learning proceeds step by step to a goal

Managers rarely have the time or the inclination to ponder on how they think and learn, either as individuals or in groups. But my own observation of many managers suggests that their behaviour is conditioned by a widespread view on the nature of effective thinking and learning. This view is that as individuals and in groups, we think and learn using orderly, step-by-step procedures just like the algorithmic software programmes utilized by computers. That the behaviour of many managers is conditioned by this view is evidenced by commonly encountered management behaviour of the following kinds:

- On being confronted with an issue the first questions asked are: 'What is our objective? What is the purpose of this meeting? What is our goal?' And very soon into any discussion there is a statement: 'We must fix the criteria the decision has to satisfy.' Or a question: 'What criteria are we to use in judging whether our long-term plan is any good or not?' And the replies tend to run along the following lines: 'consistency', or 'fit with the environment', or 'the difference it makes to the bottom line'. Such managers are working on the assumption that thinking, learning and choosing can only be driven by some clear purpose and clear criteria for success. Computers require some purpose and clear criteria if they are to reach a conclusion.
- At the end of a meeting on some ambiguous issue managers frequently say: 'That was a waste of time, we simply went round in circles and failed to reach a conclusion. There was no action plan.' The assumption here is that immediate action is an essential outcome, that exchanges which clarify people's positions or provoke thoughts that might affect actions much later on are a waste of time. The assumption is that it is always possible to reach a conclusion, and not doing so is a failure. We are only impressed by software programmes that produce answers.
- Meetings that provoke the comments just reported are frequently blamed on the incompetence of the chairman: 'He should have organized it better. We did not have enough information to have a positive discussion. He is not much of a leader. We need to develop a more cohesive team and stop conflicting so much.' Such comments indicate an assumption that effective choices require more information and that this is available if enough money is spent on acquiring it. They also indicate assumptions that groups learn more and make better choices when they strongly share cultural norms, when they all pull together. The assumption is that the whole learning and choosing process can and should be highly organized. The procedures computers use are highly organized.
- After a management seminar managers may say: 'That was interesting, I suppose, but there was no clear message. There were no techniques or relevant data that we can go back with and apply to our work.' The assumption is that learning is the acquisition of relevant data and software programmes of techniques to be loaded into the mind. The assumption is that effective thinking and problem solving requires techniques and models that set out the steps to be followed to reach a conclusion. The assumption is that there are clear links from any effect we observe back to some specific cause. There is also a follow-on assumption that it is possible to develop general models

that can be applied to a large number of specific situations. Somewhere there is a recipe and we should be trying to find it – it is not good enough to reason in a general qualitative way using analogies with other situations.

Such statements imply that it is always possible, given enough time and resources, to break a problem into its parts and find the techniques, or the experts, to set out the steps to reach the goal. Reflection is rather a waste of time and intuition is a second-best option often derogatorily called 'seat of the pants' management. Underlying assumptions of this kind lead to a particular view of the nature of strategic thinking. It is the analytical processing of information that is relevant to long-term goals and long-term outcomes. Managers should not be making choices based on analogies and past experience, because such analogies and experience could be wrong. What they should be doing is applying logical, rational, cause and effect reasoning. Strategic learning is then the build-up of shared knowledge about the potential long-term outcomes derived from analysis in advance of action. Such learning is thought to be effective when individuals are part of a cohesive team pursuing the same long-term goal in an organized manner.

Chaos provides another perspective

When one views the successful business as a chaotic system a very different perspective on thinking, learning and choosing in open-ended situations is indicated:

- There are propositions which are undecidable by algorithmic means. That is, there are occasions in which no step-by-step rules and procedures, no technique, can be used to make a decision. Such occasions relate to the finding of new meanings and new truths, and they are associated with turbulent and chaotic conditions. In open-ended situations algorithmic thinking breaks down. Humans then discover new meanings through intuition. Intuition is not a step-by-step procedure. Open-ended situations are about unique changes with unpredictable outcomes requiring creative and innovative responses. Intuition is not a second best, 'fall back' method of making choices in open-ended situations; it is initially the only method.
- Open-ended change means that long-term outcomes are totally unpredictable in their specific form because the feedback system generating it produces random outcomes. And small changes escalate with major consequences. It will then often be impossible to identify direct cause and effect links. Rational, analytical thinking will break down. But open-ended change is also qualitatively similar patterns, making it possile to apply reasoning by analogy derived from past experience. That analogous reasoning may be wrong or it may be right. The point

is that this is the only way to reason in conditions of open-ended change.

- In open-ended situations, learning is essentially the discovery of new perspectives and meanings. Such learning requires reflection and experimentation in order to discover purpose. And this is seriously restricted by the early imposition of goals and objectives. People can and do interact with each other without knowing a great deal about each other's preferences and goals. They can do this if certain other conditions are satisfied. One person must know that what he or she is trying to discover or achieve depends upon the contributions of some other people and that he or she can rely on them and trust them. Those others must have similar views. Then they can all function together as a group. What holds them together is not a goal, but mutual expected contributions. They can function together without prior purpose, in order to discover purpose.[1]

- It is quite possible for a group of people to operate effectively in learning about open-ended situations if each individual plays a fairly small part and can rely on others to make helpful contributions in the same way. In this manner each deals with a part of something too complex for any one of them to understand in full. They may then build a complex structure between themselves which none of them fully understands. Such a pattern of 'loose coupling' may well be more effective for learning about open-ended situations than highly structured tight coupling.[2] The point is that it may be better not to organize the learning. It may even be impossible to do so. Artificially simplifying the complexity involved and pressing people to work towards consensus could handicap rather than help a group. Members could evolve a more complex structure capable of coping with more complex inputs if they did not have to be explicit about how they plan to cope with the future. Attempts to make a structure understandable to everyone could lead managers to introduce excessive simplification and limited linkages between people.[3]

- Sharing values strongly, blocks the emergence of the new perspectives that are required if there is to be innovation. Innovation requires that people be different, think differently and learn differently. And this inevitably means that they will disagree and conflict. Attempts to avoid the conflict, or overcome it at too early a stage, could kill the innovation.

- What people learn in groups depends upon how they are interacting. It depends upon the group dynamic. Understanding that dynamic becomes far more important than acquiring techniques.

- In open-ended change there is no set of techniques or general model that can be applied to a large number of specific open-ended situations. Therefore groups have to develop new models for each new strategic situation. They have to use intuition and analogies based on experience to change existing mental models and develop new ones. That is, they have to learn afresh each time and they have to learn how to learn as they do it.[4]

In open-ended situations effective thinking is all about the discovery of new meanings and the development of new perspectives. It is not simply information processing. It requires thinking by analogy with other situations to develop new insight. It is thinking that makes use of the self-similarity in the development of chaotic systems. It is about the discovery of new goals in situations that are unique in specific terms but similar in overall terms. This makes it impossible to learn in advance of action. Such thinking and learning utilizes intuition and is provoked by personal interactions that are in many respects disorderly.

Now all of these points have been made in the management literature before, some of them a long time ago. But they have not been absorbed into the explicit models or thinking of most practising managers. It has been possible to dismiss many of them as slightly weird psychoanalysis. Talk of people not having a purpose, of propositions being undecidable and groups displaying bizarre behaviours that affect their ability to work, has seemed to many to be inapplicable to business conditions. But since the dynamic of a successful business is chaotic, strategic control is a political learning process. For cold scientific reasons that have to do with the feedback nature of the business, the ideas set out above can no longer be ignored. The question of how managers think and learn in open-ended situations is thus of great practical importance. The view we take on this matter will determine what it is we are trying to encourage when we call upon managers to think strategically. What we believe about the nature of thinking and learning in open-ended situations has a profound impact on how we try to practise the strategic control of the business.

This chapter first summarizes the prevailing view on the nature of thinking that seems to drive the behaviour of many managers. This is the artificial intelligence view. The chapter then provides a critique of that view. After that it explores control in open-ended situations as a learning process. The political dimensions of this process are dealt with in the following two chapters.

Thinking and learning in closed situations

According to the artificial intelligence school, the human brain is a physical symbol system.[5] It receives inputs from the environment (visual, audio, tactile) that it translates, using a set of rules and procedures, into symbols or data (chemically induced electric pulses). It then stores the data in either the rapid access (short-term) memory or in the long-term memory banks. The act of thinking involves retrieving data from the long-term memory, which is then processed, again using set rules and

procedures also retrieved from the memory banks. The rules and procedures are realized as on–off electric pulses, passing through synaptic
connections between one neuron and another in the brain. The processing rules and procedures applied to the data result in a thought
output that is then translated, again using rules and procedures, into
sound or movement of some kind.

The key point about all the coding, storage, processing and decoding
steps is that they are algorithmic. That is, they consist of precisely defined
steps described inside the brain by the presence or absence of electric
current. An algorithm is a systematic procedure for calculating, a set of
instructions, in fact a software programme. And the above description of
the human brain applies exactly to a computer. The only difference is that
the hardware of the brain is flesh and blood, while the hardware of the
computer is silicon and metal. In terms of software programs, the input
and output of data and the manner in which the data is processed, there is
absolutely no difference at all. They both use electric currents and they
both use algorithmic processes. Both think serially, they process data
step-by-step, one step at a time.

The brain and the computer are different in some non-fundamental
aspects however. The algorithmic software of the 'meat' machine is
immensely more complex than any currently available for electronic
machines. The range over which the brain can think, and the new
thoughts that it can produce, far exceed those of any computer. The brain
is also capable of sudden 'flashes' that allow people to arrive instantly at
answers, apparently without processing – what we call intuition. Those
who see the brain as a computer, however, say that there is every reason
to believe that computers will soon be made to equal the complexity of the
brain. They also hold that intuition is simply a very rapid retrieval from
the memory banks of previously processed thoughts:

> Intuition is a genuine enough phenomenon which can be explained rather
> simply: most intuitive leaps are acts of recognition.[6]

Although the brain is more complex than present-day computers, and is
therefore in some senses superior, it is in other senses inferior. We all
know that computers process data far more rapidly than we can. We all
know that our memory storage capacity, at least the short-term rapid
access capacity, is less than that of a computer. Our long-term memory
apparently has unlimited storage capacity, but thinking requires transfer
to the short-term memory before the data can be processed. The limits to
our thinking therefore lie in short-term memory storage capacity and the
processing speed we are capable of. Experimental evidence shows that
we can only hold four to seven items in short-term memory at any one
time and it takes some seconds to transfer this to the long-term memory.

When both the brain and the computer think at anything approaching a
high level, both utilize heuristic search routines. These are selective

trial-and-error procedures. The procedure requires a goal to be achieved, a solution, and it requires criteria by which progress towards the goal can be judged. The goal however might not be a specific solution. Heuristic search can be applied to the search for some interesting concept. But then criteria must be set for judging what is interesting and what is not.

> The more difficult and novel a problem, the greater is likely to be the amount of trial-and-error required to find a solution. At the same time the trial-and-error is not completely random or blind; it is in fact rather highly selective. The new expressions that are obtained by transforming given ones are examined to see whether they represent progress towards the goal. Indications of progress spur further search in the same direction; lack of progress signals abandonment of a line of search. Problem solving requires selective trial-and-error.[7]

The selectivity is provided by feedbacks of current information from the environment, or from data of previous experience stored up in the memory.

Learning

Learning for both brains and computers is the adaptive change of the long-term memory banks. Learning is the updating of knowledge already stored, the addition of new knowledge, the improving of existing processing procedures and the addition of new processing procedures. Learning here is purely algorithmic and the memory is a vast library in which what has been learned is catalogued so that it may be retrieved. Learning is more rapid and is retained for longer periods when it is accompanied by understanding and meaning, when it is not accomplished by rote. It seems that meaningful material is then indexed in a way that is more rapidly accessible. Meaningful material appears to be stored more in the form of procedures than data, also making it more rapidly accessible and applicable at a later date. In effect, then, learning is a matter of acquiring and loading into the memory as much useful software as possible.

This artificial intelligence view of the nature of thinking and learning now has a very powerful hold on the minds of many managers. In closed and contained change it is an adequate description of thinking – here there are goals and there are criteria for success. We can proceed step by step towards the goal according to the criteria for success.

If we accept that this is how human beings always think and learn when they are effective then we will prescribe algorithmic procedures for strategic thinking. A large corporation will then establish procedures for its managers. They will be encouraged to set out their visions and long-term objectives. They will be required to analyse the structures of their market segments to determine the source of competitive advantage and identify

generic strategies such as cost leadership or differentiation. Having identified that, say, large-scale capital expenditure is the major entry barrier to
new firms, that low cost is the prime source of competitive advantage,
they will conclude that the appropriate generic strategy is that of securing
a dominant market share. When it comes to developing a new product
they will carefully identify customer needs and wants, and technological
options open for meeting them. They will establish critical success factors. These procedures will be what we mean by strategic thinking. The
focus will be on analytical techniques. Or alternatively we might see
strategic thinking as continuous action based trial-and-error – the heuristic search of the entrepreneurial models. But is this view of strategic
thinking appropriate to the open-ended situation where the real cutting
edge of strategic thinking and control lies?

Thinking and learning in open-ended situations

The whole mechanistic artificial intelligence view is firmly based on the
proposition that all thinking and learning is algorithmic. There are several
reasons for concluding that this is not so.

Algorithms require some purpose to be achieved, even if that purpose
is as vague as finding any new or interesting idea. And they require some
criteria by which progress, or the lack of it, towards the purpose can be
determined. Furthermore, there must be a finite number of steps after
which the algorithm yields the conclusion that a particular series of steps
does indeed constitute progress towards the goal, or not, as the case may
be. In other words the algorithm must stop at some point in a particular
series of steps and reach a conclusion to continue with that series or try
some other. If it does not halt in any particular circumstance, if it just goes
on forever with the same series of steps without ever reaching a conclusion, then thinking algorithmically obviously breaks down. Thinking
that simply continues in an endless loop forever is of no use at all!

Now human beings do sometimes think in ways that initially involve
no purpose. That is, they start off thinking without having any idea of
what they are trying to conclude. They also sometimes think without any
criteria as to what constitutes progress. They do this in open-ended
situations when they face anomalies and ambiguous issues. Here people
perceive some discordance between what they expect and what seems to
be happening. The result is confusion in which it may not be possible to
be clear, at first, on what they are trying to explain. Existing step-by-step
procedures, existing mental models, may then break down. People may
reach conclusions, or have ideas, in situations in which it can be shown
that no algorithm will halt. There are some situations where step-by-step
procedures just go on forever without reaching a conclusion. Some other
approach is required. Human beings sometimes think in non-algorithmic

ways. And they do this when they are searching for new meanings, when they are confronted by open-ended change. Consider the evidence for these statements.

The properties of non-linear feedback mechanisms suggest that, in some circumstances, algorithms do not stop. In some circumstances it will not be possible to reach a conclusion in a finite number of steps. One of the most famous non-linear feedback mechanisms in mathematics is that which generates the Mandelbrot set (see Appendix B). This feedback mechanism generates a large number of events, each of which can have either of two outcomes. For each event we can use an algorithmic procedure to decide whether the event will have the first or the second outcome. For most events the algorithm works. That is, after a finite number of steps it indicates which of the two outcomes will occur as a result of a particular event. But there is a borderline between all those events having the first outcome and all those events having the second outcome. As we approach this border, the algorithm takes longer and longer to make up its mind on which side of the border to put the event. Right at the border it apparently cannot make up its mind; it just goes on forever trying to make up its mind.[8]

If our only mode of thinking were algorithmic and we were confronted by a choice of this kind, a border choice in a situation of chaotic dynamics, then we would have no way of reaching a conclusion. The human and the computer would both have to go on trying to reach a conclusion forever, or give up after a given number of steps and make a purely arbitrary choice. If we can think only in algorithmic ways and we ever find ourselves having to make a choice in a chaotic situation, we will be incapable of distinguishing that which is false from that which is true. When we get close to the borders between equilibrium and chaos states, we will end up stuck in a cycle of indecision or we will behave in a totally haphazard manner. Unless that is, we are able to think in some other way. Successful business organizations operate in a chaos border so they will encounter situations where algorithmic methods of thinking break down. Other modes of thinking will be required. Real strategic thinking will occur in ways which have little to do with step-by-step procedures.

Undecidability and intuition

The Mandelbrot set seems to be telling us that there are dynamic situations in which algorithmic, heuristic modes of thinking are no use at all. We would have to think and choose either in a purely arbitrary manner or we would have to use some non-algorithmic mode of thinking. Now while there is no proof that the algorithm does not stop in the case of the Mandelbrot set, there are other mathematical proofs that have a bearing here. Appendix B gives a brief summary of these and the key points made there are as follows.

There are a number of mathematical proofs that there is no general algorithm, no general set of rules and procedures, which can generate specific rules and procedures for solving all mathematical problems of a specific class. There is no general set of rules and procedures to decide what specific rules and procedures to adopt in all specific cases. There are always some statements in a mathematical system that are neither provable nor disprovable using step-by-step procedures. But the very ability to prove these propositions shows that the human mind is able to see whether a proposition is true or false even when an algorithm cannot. And it does so by intuition, common sense, insight and reflection. In other words, there are fundamental mathematical problems that cannot possibly be solved using step-by-step procedures, the algorithms of computers, but humans can do it nevertheless.

If this applies to mathematics, the most precise and fundamental area of human understanding, the area to which it should be the easiest to apply computer algorithmic thinking, it must also apply at the level of management and organization. There are occasions where there is no system of rules and procedures which would allow us to make a decision. The most difficult have to be dealt with in the same exploratory manner as new mathematical ideas, employing the same processes of intuition and insight, employing reflection principles. This applies to open-ended situations and the strategic thinking such situations call for.

This leads to an important conclusion. Human understanding, thinking and therefore learning is algorithmic for much of the time. But, at certain critical points in open-ended situations, non-algorithmic processes of intuition are employed. We reason by analogy utilizing the self-similar properties of chaotic patterns. No rules and procedures, no matter how complex or sophisticated can lead to truth, meaning, or coherent choice at these points. At such points computers, and those with minds like computers, will not be able to deal with the situation. There will be no general model we can apply to such situations. We will have to develop a new specific model in order to choose and act. In open-ended situations the business organization will have to rely on the experience-based intuition of individuals, on reasoning by analogy, if it is to innovate and discover new strategic direction.

If we accept this view of the nature of effective thinking in open-ended situations, we will then not focus on algorithmic type procedures to encourage strategic thinking. We will be much more concerned with how we can provoke people within an organization to pay attention to anomalies and ambiguities. We will be concerned with establishing conditions within which they may develop new perspectives. This happens when people counter the received wisdom; when they try to expose and critically examine the submerged basic assumptions governing their behaviour; when they try to surface their implicit mental models. It happens when people go against the recipes of the company or industry they work for. It is this searching for new ways of doing things that leads to innovation. And in business, people do all this in groups.

The need for this changed focus on strategic thinking is well illustrated by a company with which I recently worked. This large corporation has run a series of management development programmes for all senior managers. They have all been trained to apply to their business the techniques of mission statements, market segmentation, industry analysis and many others. But after three years of this kind of training in strategic thinking, one major division spent nearly a year unsuccessfully trying to reorganize itself. The cause of this difficulty lay quite clearly in the lack of effective learning and interaction between members of the top divisional management team. Considerable attention had been paid to a form of thinking that is not all that helpful in open-ended situations, while real learning difficulties received no concerted attention. An inability to handle open-ended issues followed.

When we turn to open-ended change we need to shift the focus of attention away from highly organized step-by-step procedures to how people learn and interact politically in groups. The rest of this chapter will concentrate on the learning aspects and the next two chapters will be concerned with the political aspects. The key question is how to get real strategic thinking to occur without causing organized anarchy. The easy solution is to call for widespread participation in strategic choice, the empowering of people. But this solution leads so easily to organized anarchy with no improvement in group learning ability. This point was made in Chapter 8 and will be returned to in Chapter 10. We need to consider more carefuly how people think, learn and interact in groups if we are to prescribe conditions within which they will question everything and yet preserve some form of order.

Chaos and other mathematical insights, then, question widely prevalent views held by many managers on thinking, learning and thus choosing and acting. For an individual mind, learning is partly the acquisition of data and algorithmic procedures. The action context is particularly effective here. Firstly because the carrying out of an algorithm by doing something reinforces memory retention. Perhaps more importantly, action provides concrete experience that can be questioned and reflected upon. Individuals discover meaning by reflecting on and questioning action of some sort. But, learning, the discovery of meaning, is not entirely a matter of acquiring algorithms and storing them in the memory. It is not entirely consequent upon action, where that means some overt action outside the brain itself. Insight, intuition, commonsense connections, reasoning by analogy, all non-algorithmic in nature, can create new meaning through reflection upon what has already been learned without any overt new action. There is an important aspect of learning that is non-algorithmic, creative and not necessarily related to action. And it is this more complex form of thinking and learning that is required in open-ended situations.

Organizational learning takes place in groups

The process of learning is not entirely or even predominantly, an individual matter. People in business organizations learn most frequently and most effectively with other human beings in groups. Such group learning can be algorithmic. Then members in the group proceed in questioning and discussing bodies of knowledge, or actions of individual members in a step-by-step manner. They can do this when they are operating in closed and contained situations. But in open-ended situations, the processes of discussing, questioning and reflecting on matters that cover existing bodies of knowledge, individual experience and recent action proceeds in a random manner. And it is this learning in groups that is most relevant to strategic control. This follows inevitably from the ambiguous and ill-structured nature of the issues thrown up by the unique changes characteristic of open-ended situations.

An example of this learning process is provided by a group of top managers in one of the UK's electricity companies that was about to be privatized. Those managers were exploring ways of improving the margins they could earn on their electricity product. Since it is a commodity they were discussing possibilities for differentiating it. The situation they found themselves in was open-ended in just about every respect. The kind of electricity market they were having to operate in had never existed before and did not exist anywhere else in the world. The chief executive started the discussion by drawing attention to a study that drew parallels between differentiation of airline products and possible differentiation in electricity. Two other colleagues then joined in and started talking about the technology that would be necessary to differentiate electricity by time of use. The discussion proceeded for some time before one of the quietest members of the group suggested that the whole basis of the comparison between airlines and electricity was invalid. That interjection opened up the way for colleagues who had not expressed their views. Then one of the more vociferous colleagues suggested that differentiation could best be secured by adding customer features such as installation of appliances. And he attached this issue to the need for coordinated marketing. This was seen by the others as a bid for increased power and the discussion switched to organizational matters. A later meeting then resumed the discussion on the very ambiguous and ill-structured issue of differentiation. The discussion this time was backed by market research evidence on customer wants, the required shape of which had emerged from previous discussions. More concrete proposals for product differentiation were then made.

These managers were learning, in a group context, about a very complex strategic issue. The somewhat random process of discussion was serving the valuable function of bringing different perspectives to bear on the issue. Eventually, out of this process would come concrete proposals attracting support, or the abandonment of the idea after wide-ranging discussion. In my experience this example is typical of the early stages of handling strategic issues. Out of initial wide-ranging and random discussion, there emerges more precise requirements for information and proposals for action. And that initial random stage can go on for a long time – there is nothing predetermined about it.

The group learning experience depends on who participates by making comments, asking questions, donating interpretations. Learning depends on the content of such contributions. It also depends upon the context and sequence in which contributions occur. There may not be, and there frequently is not, one individual consciously and successfully guiding the process to a predetermined end. What each individual learns in such situations depends only partly on his or her own reflections and thinking processes – it depends significantly on how he or she and the other members of the group are interacting with each other. It depends upon the combination of personalities in the group. Learning then becomes dependent on the dynamics of the group, on the emotions contributing to and provoking those dynamics, on triggers to the unconscious mind. High levels of uncertainty, lack of structure and insecurity are all known to lead to bizarre group behaviours that can prevent that group from functioning as a working learning group.[9] The learning that occurs within a group will also depend significantly on the culture that group has developed. Culture is that body of basic assumptions that the members of that group share on how to proceed, on how things are to be done, on what is important and what is not.[10] This shared culture is the retained memory of the group and it has a powerful effect on how the group proceeds.

The next two sections briefly examine the impact of personality, group dynamics and culture on organizational learning.

Organizational learning: personality composition and group dynamics

It is possible to instruct a group of people to learn some simple rote task, technique or body of data and ensure that they do it by testing them and then rewarding or punishing them. It is not possible to compel any group of people to learn anything more complex than this. To succeed and innovate, an organization requires groups of people who perform complex learning through which they discover and choose new perspectives, new ideas, new ways of doing things. This process has to be spontaneous and whether or not it occurs depends on the context within which the group is working. Such complex learning processes also cannot be organized in some step-by-step, orderly fashion. This is because in complex situations no one can know what the group is trying to learn, to discover. The learning process starts without a clear specific purpose of what is to be learned, or even of how it is to be learned. What purposes the group develops, what it learns and how it learns all depend on the context in which its members are working. The process is spontaneous and self-organizing and part of what the group learns is its purpose and the method through which it should be learning.

Interactive thinking, learning and choosing in a group context is governed by feedback loops that have amplifying and damping properties. A comment made by one member can irritate another who responds, perhaps by attack on some other front or by withdrawal from the discussion. In this way consequences are amplified and what is learned, what the outcome of the group interaction turns out to be, is therefore frequently a matter of chance. The properties of chaos, it seems, apply to learning in a group context. Complex learning only occurs when the nature of the feedback loops governing the learning is such that they are far-from-equilibrium. People spark new ideas off each other when they argue and disagree, when they are conflicting, confused and searching for a new meaning. Far-from-equilibrium instability is a precondition for the kind of learning that provokes new meanings. And in these circumstances people display categories of behaviour that we all recognize. One category of behaviour might be avoiding the issues and another might be conflict around the issues. These categories are recognizable, but the specific course they take is unpredictable. This is the nature of chaos – disorderly specific behaviours occurring within recognizable categories of behaviour. People do not provoke new insights when their discussions are characterized by orderly equilibrium states of conformity and dependence on the one hand, or completely disorderly states of rivalry and avoidance on the other.

Because the learning system of a successful group is far-from-equilibrium, it is highly sensitive to the context within which it occurs. And among the most important elements of the context are the personality composition and dynamic of the group.

Personality type

Some personality types are comfortable with open-ended issues. Other personality types look for high degrees of analytical security before they are willing to progress an issue. Some personality types prefer to keep options open, while others always look for immediate closure. Some personality types think intuitively and others rely heavily on formal logic. Some rely on feelings while others always want the facts.[11] The learning styles of individuals consequently differ markedly. The kinds of issues a given group will deal with, what they will try to avoid, the manner in which they deal with issues they do attend to, how successful they are, will then depend significantly on the composition of the group in personality terms. Small changes in personality composition, the removal of one person or the addition of another, can have a major impact on the outcome of their work together. One person behaving in a neurotic manner can completely disrupt the work of the group. Because of this sensitivity to who is there and how they behave, the outcomes of group work, when open-ended change is being dealt with, depend on chance and are unpredictable in specific terms.

But there are recognizable patterns in individual behaviours. This is the property of self-similarity possessed by all chaotic systems. We can recognize the personality category types, even though we cannot predict specific behaviour. And the same point applies to categories of interaction between people.

Categories of group dynamic

Some typical patterns of group dynamic have been identified by researchers. One well-known study explains the behaviour of a group in terms of two levels.[12] At one level, the conscious apparent level, the group is focusing on the work in hand, the tasks it has come together to perform. But at the unconscious level, the behaviour of individuals in the group is affected by a basic assumption, an atmosphere which affects how they work together. They may be unconsciously affected by the fight–flight assumption. Here the underlying dynamic is either one of intense conflict or one of the complete avoidance of conflict. Or the assumption may be one of dependence, where the group is looking for leadership. Or it may be one of pairing in which most of the group is observing an interchange between two of their number, hoping that this will yield the answer they are looking for. And different basic assumptions are appropriate to different tasks. Where the group is concerned with closed change, a basic assumption of dependence and the compliance that accompanies this will make it more effective. Where it is concerned with open-ended issues a basic assumption that results in some conflict is more likely to be helpful. When structures are removed and the group faces considerable uncertainty, the basic assumptions can come to dominate behaviour in the group so that it is incapable of any work at all. And a group can switch in a volatile manner from one basic assumption to another.

Groups may respond to great uncertainty by showing a high level of dependence on a leader, or they may seek security in smaller coalitions. Or they may simply conflict with each other and avoid the uncertain issue. Or they may sit and listen to the managing director and an 'expert' consultant, waiting for their exchange to produce the solution to the problem. And it is open-ended change situations that are those most likely to provoke group dynamics which are obstructive to dealing with the issues. It is not unusual for managers to abandon meetings trying to deal with open-ended issues because they simply do not function. One of my clients in the electronics industry called an informal meeting of top executives to discuss reorganization proposals. That group accomplished nothing in two days of meetings because they did little but fight over the proposals. That chief executive thereafter avoided such informal meet-ings. On another occasion, the first two strategy workshops I facilitated with a top management team involved little but the others listening to a discussion between the chief executive and myself. It was only when we brought in other people that the dynamic changed. On another occasion in the same industry faced with massive changes, the top team did little but avoid any serious issues for three meetings. The underlying conflict between them made it too dangerous to talk about any of the issues in a serious way.

Such dynamics show the essential properties of chaos. There are recog-nizable categories of group dynamic, but the specific behaviours over time are unpredictable.

The same points apply to another explanation of the group dynamic where four stages of group development are identified: forming where members develop acceptable behaviours; storming where conflict arises because of the restrictions the group imposes on the individual; norming in which a strong group identity emerges; and performing where energy is channelled into tasks.

Labelling group interactions in this way does oversimplify them, but it also makes the point that what happens to an issue will depend on highly complex interpersonal relationships in groups. Groups to which one might apply, at a particular time, the labels of 'storming' or 'fight–flight' will obviously not deal with open-end issues at that time. Groups show-ing a high level of dependence, or even those that have reached the performing stage may not develop wide enough perspectives to handle such issues effectively. What happens during meetings will therefore often be very difficult to explain. A well timed remark, or even a purely chance remark, could divert the whole course of the discussion and the approach to the issue into completely different and unexpected direc-tions. Small interventions could escalate and have a major impact.

Key point

The key point is this. The cutting edge of strategic control can most usefully be described as the discovering, choosing and acting in open-ended situations that yield innovation. Because open-ended change generates ambiguous issues with unknowable consequences, that discovery, choosing and acting has to take the form of organizational learning in real time. Such learning is intimately connected with personality and group dynamics. It consequently displays chaotic dynamics and it has the potential for innovation because of these chaotic dynamics. We will promote effective strategic thinking and thus secure more effective strategic control by establishing groups with appropriate personality composition and by creating conditions for functional group dynamics. The focus should be on group behaviour rather than techniques of analysis. We cannot secure an outcome using some techniques when change is open ended, but we can create favourable conditions for groups to explore and innovate. The prescription is for much less attention to trying to manage outcomes and for much more attention to managing process. Get the process right and the outcomes will take care of themselves. The next point is to consider the role that group culture plays in this chaotic learning process.

Group dynamics have a time dimension. We remember them and we share memories of them as a group. That retained memory of the group constitutes its basic cultural assumptions. These basic cultural assumptions are developed through the past experience and education of each individual. In particular they are developed by the experience which those individuals have had in working together as a group. Some forms of behaviour will have been found acceptable in the past and these forms tend to become part of the culture. These basic assumptions are largely below the level of awareness as far as each individual is concerned. They are rarely questioned, examined or discussed. It is consequently difficult to identify what they are and what effect they are having. It is even more difficult to change them if it turns out that they are dysfunctional.

Strongly shared cultures block group learning

There seems to be an almost universal current received wisdom among practising managers and management consultants, as well as management teachers and writers. This is that widely shared, strong cultural norms are required if people are to cooperate and work together in organizations. The belief is that such strong sharing creates conditions of trust, integrating people into an organization and so securing their adherence to organizational goals. Strong cultural sharing then creates the feeling of belonging, where mutual gain and contribution are seen in terms of achieving organizational goals together. This emphasis on belief, sharing and belonging, coupled with that on missions and visions, gives a mystical, religious dimension to a modern business. But religious communities have throughout history been notable for their reluctance to change, and without change a business dies. So, it is widely recognized that strongly shared cultural norms do block change. The prescription for such sharing is therefore accompanied by one requiring a culture that loves and thrives on change.[13] But what does this mean?

Apparent culture

The culture of any group of people exists on two levels.[14] At the most apparent level it is embodied in artifacts, buildings, sounds, stories, informal rules of conduct and statements on ethical values. We draw conclusions on the culture of a business when we first visit it. In some companies we notice the plush carpets, separate elevators and dining rooms for the senior executives on the top floor who are guarded by secretaries and closed doors. In other companies we see senior executives seated in open-plan offices surrounded by staff in their shirt sleeves and secretaries in denim jeans. We immediately expect different behaviours and different ways of making organizational choices.

Unconscious culture

The apparent manifestations of the culture are often reflections of the basic assumptions upon which people behave. In the first company there is a basic assumption that decision making is most effective when it is compartmentalized. So the top levels focus on major strategic choices, which they make in an 'expert' and secretive manner. Those lower down in the management hierarchy deal with the day-to-day matters. In the second company there is an assumption that major strategic decisions involve a wider group of people. Such choices are best made through discussion and being close to the action. The important point about these basic assumptions is that most of them have slipped below the level of awareness. In both the example companies people simply accept that their way of making decisions works. They do not consider each day how best to make choices. They simply go ahead and make them. Because the basic assumptions are below the level of awareness, they are very rarely questioned or examined. They are consequently both powerful drivers of behaviour and very difficult to change. They constitute the unconscious mind or unconscious shared memory of the group. They are assumptions about conduct that have been developed from previous experience of being part of the group. They reflect those behaviours that secure group approval and assistance.

Culture then exists at an apparent level and at a group unconscious level. And when we say that cultural norms are strongly shared, we must mean that sharing occurs at the group unconscious level. If the sharing is simply at an apparent level, then it is relatively easy for an individual in the group to conform on the surface but to think and behave in ways that do not accord with the rest of the group. Where a number of individuals are doing this, they will have to keep explaining what they are doing so that others understand and agree. When however there is sharing of norms at the unconscious level the need for communication and the need to search for consensus is greatly reduced. Commitment and consensus is more likely to be continuously maintained and conflict levels reduced.

But cultural norms that are shared at the unconscious level are very difficult to change and they block new perceptions. Real learning and real change occur when we alter the submerged norms that govern the way we think and behave. The more strongly we hold on to those norms as a group, the deeper they are submerged in the unconscious, the less we are able to examine and question them. We are then less capable of learning and change. It is therefore a contradiction in terms to talk about strong sharing of cultural norms and then say that one of those norms should be a mutually shared love of change. A culture that loves change is by definition one in which individuals in a group do not strongly share the same cultural norms. A culture open to change must be one where there are different cultural norms, one where there is only weak sharing. And weak sharing means sharing at the apparent level rather than the unconscious, or sharing only a very narrow range of norms at the unconscious level. It then becomes important to say something about what kinds of norm we are trying to encourage people to share.

Cultural norms at both the apparent and the unconscious level can be classified into what we might call performing norms and learning norms.

Performing and learning norms

Performing norms have to do with the actions a group is taking together at the present time. They are about what people judge to be the criteria for successful outcomes of those actions. So, people in a group producing electronic components will have a set of cultural norms around the production process, the service levels and the quality they believe leads to successful sales and customer satisfaction. They may believe that it is acceptable for the percentage of customer returns to run at 5 per cent. Or they may believe that any level of returns represents failure. Performing norms also cover how it is acceptable to treat people both within and outside the group – basic ethical values. Such norms include shared beliefs on how it is acceptable to control the current activities in which the group is engaged.

Learning norms on the other hand are concerned with how the group should discover, choose and take action in relation to changes in what it is doing now and what is happening around it. They are concerned with what it is acceptable to question and to seek to discover. They are concerned with what the group is fundamentally there for, and what those outside it are really looking for.

For example, in one group open conflict may be taboo, while in another vigorous discussion and the exposure of strong differences of opinion may be permissible. In one group it may be required to show deference to the chairman's views and in another this may not be necessary. In one group individuals may not feel free to conjecture in the absence of well-thought-out arguments; points may only be raised after careful analysis. In another group it may be acceptable to introduce bizarre ideas for the consideration of others. The basic cultural assumptions will also determine what matters are undiscussable in a group context. For example the behaviour and style of the chairman may be undiscussable. In a family-owned company, the possibility of raising capital through share issues that dilute family control may be undiscussable.

Furthermore, cultural norms, apparent or unconscious, learning or performing, can be either narrow or widespread in terms of coverage. Widespread performing norms at the apparent level mean a high level of detail in how, for example, one person should treat another. The norms may require addressing a superior as 'sir', or bowing to a certain depth. The norm then has a high ritualistic content. Or the performing norms may have a narrow coverage so that they only require avoiding abuse and leave the detail of the behaviour to the individuals involved.

Sharing norms

Clearly if a group is to work together at all there has to be some level of sharing norms. And that minimal level must be sharing performing norms over a narrow range. The more strongly such focused performing norms are shared, that is the more they are submerged into the unconscious, the more efficient the work of the group will be. Such sharing cuts down on the need for information exchange and more formal controls. On the other hand, the strong sharing of learning norms over a wide range is the characteristic of a group of fanatics. Such a group is highly resistant to change because they all in effect agree never to question taboos on what they should discover. They all believe the company or industry recipe without question.

Trust amongst members of a group, holistic perceptions of their roles in the group and mutually perceived gain and contribution can be secured where there is strong sharing of performing norms over a narrow, focused range. This means a few basic ethical values and a common view of acceptable performance of existing tasks. Widespread sharing of learning norms, particularly at the unconscious level, is not necessary for trust or mutual gain. It is quite possible to accept the contribution of someone who thinks in a different way and focuses attention on different issues to ourselves. When learning norms are only weakly shared, people feel free to question the fundamental purpose of what they are doing together, why they are doing it and how they are doing it.

The effective functioning of the existing business of an organization only requires strong sharing of a narrow range of performing norms. Learning norms should not be strongly shared. The presence of weakly shared learning norms means first that the chances of new perceptions emerging are enhanced. Second it means that there is some constraint on the sequence of choices made. Where learning norms are strongly shared, the group sharing them can continue for a long time down a particular path of choices. Tin can manufacturers continued to offer the same paint can product long after customers expressed dissatisfaction with it. Groups of like-minded executives did not question their industry and company recipes. When some path becomes clearly inappropriate it is possible for all members of that group to follow a major swing in another direction. Where the learning norms are only weakly shared, where people have different ideas on what to discover and how to do it, a sequence of choices will be stopped from going in one direction for long. The sequence will show more reversals. But there will be bounds. The variation may be greater but the degree of variation is more likely to be constant. And this is the constant variation that provides the self-similar patterns we find in chaos. Without constraints in a sequence of choices we get pure instability. With constraints we get the bounded instability that is chaos. And weakly shared norms provide an important constraint.

If we do succeed in securing strongly shared learning and performing norms over a wide range we ensure that we do not get the dynamic we are looking for in spontaneous learning in open-ended situations. We do not get the questioning that is vital to successfully handling open-ended change. Strong sharing of a narrow range of selected performing norms is important for dealing with closed and contained change. Weak sharing of a wide range of unconscious learning norms is required in open-ended situations.

The learning process is therefore infinitely more complex than any simple analogy with algorithms and computers might lead us to believe. Such learning is not always a step-by-step orderly process. In fact it more usually is not. It is far more realistic to think of it as a chaotic system that is highly sensitive to the context of personality type, group dynamic and culture (retained memory). The consequence is that the specific path the learning takes is unpredictable but there are patterns in that learning. There are recognizable general patterns in the impact that personality type and group dynamic have on the learning process. The constraints of different personality types, different cultures are essential to provide the

boundaries within which discoveries and choices are made. Such difference is the source of stability. Current received wisdom is that we get
stability if we promote strongly shared cultures. From a chaos perspective
we get both the prompt to discovery and the stability of boundaries
around these discoveries from different cultures.

The unpredictable specific path of learning about open-ended situations has a very important consequence. Since the learning itself is
unpredictable we have to learn how to learn as we go along. We cannot
decide on some technique we are going to follow in advance and then
simply follow it. All the time we are learning about open-ended change
we will have to be aware of how we are learning. We will have to be aware
of the impact that personality type, group dynamic and culture are having
on what we are learning and how we are doing it. Such learning is not one
simple feedback loop but a double one.[15] Following one loop we do the
learning but at the same time we have to follow another loop that involves
observing, and discussing with each other how we are learning. And that
means continually questioning the basic assumptions that govern our
behaviour.

Learning how to learn in real time

If we put together two key facets of the context within which learning
takes place – whether it is in an individual or a group context, whether it is
in a closed / contained or an open-ended change context – we can identify
a number of crucial differences in the kind of learning that occurs. This is
done in Figure 9.1 which shows how the two-dimensional context determines four different forms of learning appropriate to each context. Appropriate forms may be:

- learning about outcomes;
- learning about outcomes and cooperation;
- learning that is the discovery of meaning;
- learning that is the discovery of meaning and the discovery of the
  process of learning itself.

Take an individual learning within a change context that is either closed
or contained. Because outcomes are predictable, the activities of thinking
and learning during the course of performing some sequence of actions
can focus primarily on the content of the outcomes of those actions. So, as
we manage the day-to-day existing business we simply focus on what is
happening to sales and profits. In such contexts the individual can acquire
the algorithmic procedures and the data that he or she requires to perform, in advance of the performance. We prepare the budget. Learning as
one performs is then simply a matter of checking outcomes against
expectations and making relatively minor adjustments. We monitor the
budget and take corrective action. Learning here is about what is going on
and it is algorithmic.

	Closed/contained change	Open-ended change
Individual	Learning about outcome	Learning = discovery of meaning
Group	Learning about outcome and cooperation	Learning = discovery of meaning + discovery of process

Figure 9.1 *Learning during performance*

When that individual moves into a group context, still within a closed or contained change situation, then a new dimension is added to the learning process. Each individual in the group can still acquire, in advance, all the algorithmic procedures and data required to perform. But these now have to include procedures relating to cooperation with all the other individuals in that group. And cooperation in conditions close to certainty can be secured by rules and bargains to which all the individuals agree in advance. As the group performs, therefore, learning is confined to checking outcomes against expectations and checking individual contributions against accepted norms. Learning here is still essentially about what is going on and it is still algorithmic.

As soon as the individual is placed in an open-ended change situation, he or she can no longer acquire, in advance, all the algorithmic procedures and data required to perform. The situation is unknowable and there will be undecidable critical points where algorithmic procedures break down. The bulk of the learning cannot be achieved in advance of performing the sequence of actions. The individual will then employ intuitive thinking processes and reasoning by analogy. Learning, as performance proceeds, becomes an important process of discovering not only what is going on, but why. The individual will be searching for new meanings, developing new perspectives, discovering and clarifying preferences and objectives. But individual learning in this context does not demand explicit attention to how one is learning. The individual can be, and is, highly effective in open-ended situations, even when he or she is proceeding to think and learn in new ways without being fully aware of what those ways are. The procedures and the basic assumptions upon which they are based are below the level of awareness and they can remain so without necessarily impairing effectiveness. An explicit examination of how one is learning, of the basic assumptions one is making, may aid the learning process, but it does not usually seem to be vital. So an individual scientist may intuitively discover some new meaning without continually examining the manner in which he or she is doing so.

When groups of individuals find themselves in open-ended change situations then the learning process becomes highly complex. Those individuals are unable to acquire, in advance, algorithmic procedures and the data necessary for performance. They are also unable to establish, in advance, the necessary rules and bargains required for cooperation. They cannot do any of these things because they cannot know what is important or unimportant, what will happen. Learning as performance proceeds must then cover outcomes and the processes of performing and learning themselves. In open-ended change situations we must discover not only what to do, and why to do it, but also how to do it. And the process, the how, is now of vital importance because of the group context. If individuals in a group are to work together effectively as a group, then they have to make explicit, to some extent, how the group is proceeding and the basic assumptions upon which it is proceeding. Failure to do so, leaving such matters below the level of group awareness, creates the risk of confusion and lack of constructive cooperation among group members. It will lead to the application of increasingly inappropriate processes, given that the change context is essentially unpredictable and characterized by chance.[16]

And it is particularly in the highly uncertain and anxiety provoking conditions of open-ended change that group dynamics are the hardest to understand and make sense of. To be effective, the learning process must also incorporate the discovery of important characteristics of the group dynamic.

In one company I was involved with over a number of years, the top management team repeatedly announced the intention of diversifying its activities into new businesses closely allied to its core business. None of those managers openly disagreed with this intention – they all supported acquisition as the route to diversification. Considerable effort was devoted to analysing a number of suitable market segments and many potential acquisition targets. Proposal after proposal was put to top management meetings, but they all came to nothing. One delaying tactic after another was devised to avoid making a decision because a number of powerful executives were actually against diversification although they never publicly said so. But no one ever suggested that the fruitless activity of looking for an acquisition should be abandoned. The strongly shared culture made it impossible openly to discuss this vicious circle and explore the underlying assumptions and group dynamic causing it. Consequently that group of managers could not learn or do anything about diversification. We often find the same kind of vicious circle when decisions are actually taken and embodied in plans that are then never implemented. This is usually seen as a problem of implementation which sends people looking for prescriptions for better implementation. In fact the problem usually lies with the learning process in the first place.

Learning as politics and control

Now what has been described as a group learning process in conditions of open-ended change could just as easily be described as a political process. Throughout, learning in these conditions depends upon and employs power and influence; the interactions occurring between members of the group, interactions from which they learn, are clearly political. Not only is there an equivalence between learning and political process in these conditions, they also amount to a form of control – it is through this complex political learning process that the group develops coherent behaviour; it is through this process that it discovers, chooses and acts.

It is this highly complex form of group learning that is the only form of control available to business organizations when it comes to handling the disturbances generated by open-ended change. It is the only way to develop some form of coherence in behaviour when we do not know what we are doing.

The process that is at one and the same time organizational learning, politics and control in open-ended situations is summarized in Figure 9.2.

This diagram depicts two feedback loops in the learning control process. At any one time a number of events are occurring; outcomes of previous actions; new occurrences; reactions to previous events. At the most basic level the organizational actors have to discover what is

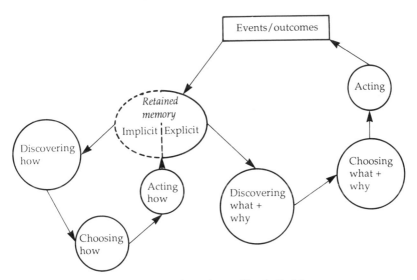

Figure 9.2 *Learning and controlling feedback loops*

happening and why. This discovery, or interpretation, is conditioned by the retained memory of the organization, the shared memories of the organizational actors, their cultural norms. Part of that memory is explicit – it is the set of articulated models, views, beliefs, company and industry recipes that individuals use in common to explain and understand what is happening, why it is happening and how they should deal with it. But part of the retained memory is below the level of awareness. These are the implicit models, the basic cultural assumptions, rarely examined but driving behaviour nonetheless. Retained memory in both its explicit and implicit forms also conditions the next link in the learning and control loop – choosing what to do. Having chosen, the organization then acts. Those actions have outcomes which must be discovered and so we go around the loop once more. And as the organization continuously moves around this loop, it alters the retained memory both explicit and implicit, to reflect its experience. This loop on its own is adequate to deal with closed and contained change because nothing uniquely new happens here.

When it comes to open-ended change, effective learning and control must involve the second feedback loop shown in Figure 9.2. While the organization is learning about the what and the why, it must also learn about the how. It must continuously discover how to discover, choose and act. This means explicitly identifying and questioning the procedures it is using to deal with strategic issues. There may be insufficient time to discuss such issues. There may be few occasions on which they can be discussed. When they are discussed, the chief executive may dominate each discussion. All such practices need to be frequently reviewed and questioned.

A group of managers must continually choose how to discover, choose and act. And the managers must implement the choices on how to discover, choose and act. This loop too is conditioned by retained memory in both its explicit and implicit forms. Indeed the 'how' loop is very much a process of reflecting upon and amending that retained memory, particularly the implicit content, the basic cultural assumptions that govern how things are done.

Learning in open-ended situations is primarily a matter of questioning the retained memory of the organization. The basic cultural assumptions, the memory, condition what managers perceive, what they ignore and what meanings they attach to what is going on. All these determine what they do. Inevitably as the world around them changes, that unconscious retained memory becomes a liability because it leads to inappropriate interpretations and actions. If they are not to wait for some crisis that makes it quite evident how far the real world has drifted from their previous experience, managers have to keep surfacing and questioning their basic assumptions as the platform from which to develop new perceptions.

Conclusion: innovative strategic choice depends on group learning

This chapter has been concerned with interpreting some important aspects of the feedback control loop managers apply in open-ended situations. That loop was depicted in Figure 3.2 of Chapter 3. The concern has been with the thinking and learning processes managers apply to detect and select open-ended changes for organizational attention. It has also been concerned with the thinking and learning processes they utilize to handle issues on the strategic agendas of their organizations.

The learning political control loops relevant to open-ended change, in any organization, are amplifying and damping feedback mechanisms. From practical experience we all know that they can and do generate behaviour that is random and disorderly, the outcome of which depends significantly on chance. But received wisdom tells us that these properties of disorder and chance are to be removed if the organization is to succeed. It stresses the damping aspects of learning and control loops. The insight of chaos theory is that success requires these properties of disorder and chance, that successful organizations utilize them to innovate and develop new strategic directions. Chaos theory stresses the essential need for the amplifying operation of the learning and control loops.

The message for managers is that real innovation, real strategic choice depends upon how effectively groups of managers learn about open-ended situations. They can do much to improve their ability to manage strategically by working together to understand the effects that personality composition, group dynamics and cultural assumptions are having on their ability to learn. Expenditure of time on this endeavour is more realistic than preparing long-term plans, drawing future visions from thin air or working assiduously to get everyone facing in the same direction. And working together in this way is difficult for many reasons. The focus of attention it involves is highly personal. The group dynamic has much to do with the manner in which power is used and it is uncomfortable to discuss this topic publicly.

Organizational learning in open-ended situations is a political process. It is one that uses power. The way power is used has a major impact on the group dynamic and thus the quality of the organizational learning. The next chapter turns to the question of power and politics in business organizations and their relationship to the organizational learning form of control in open-ended situations.

References

1   Bion, W. (1961), *Experiences in Groups, And Other Papers*, Tavistock Publications.

2   Weick, K. (1979), *The Social Psychology of Organizing*, Addison Wesley.
3   Weick, K., op. cit., p. 103.
4   Argyris, C. (1982), *Reasoning, Learning and Action*, Jossey-Bass.
5   Simon, H. A. (1981), *The Sciences of the Artificial*, MIT.
6   Simon, H. A., op. cit., p. 105.
7   Simon, H. A., op. cit., p. 205.
8   Penrose, R. (1989), *The Emperor's New Mind*, Oxford University Press.
9   Bion, W. (1961), *Experiences in Groups and Other Papers*, London, Tavistock Publications.
10 Schein, A. (1985), *Organizational Culture and Leadership*, Jossey-Bass.
11 Weick, K., op. cit., p. 151.
12 Bion, W., op. cit.
13 Peters, T. (1988), *Thriving on Chaos*, Macmillan; Moss Kanter, R. (1985), *The Change Masters*, Simon & Schuster.
14 Schein, E., op. cit.
15 Argyris C., Schön, D. A. (1978), *Organizational Learning: A Theory of Action Perspective*, Addison-Wesley.
16 Argyris, C., op. cit.

10 Strategic 'control' is spontaneous political choice

Since the dynamic of a successful business is chaotic, its management faces the continuing problem of behaving coherently in the face of changes having absolutely unpredictable long-term consequences. When managers are confronted with such change it is impossible for them to establish immediate clarity on specific aspirations, preferences and goals. Instead they are presented with ambiguous and ill-structured challenges of which they have to make some sense. Consequently, neither the rational goal-driven method nor the inspirational vision mode of making strategic choice can cope in the early stages of developing new strategic direction. The only way to do this, the only form of control available to managers in this situation, is a complex one of learning in real time about the developing path of the business as it unfolds. They discover and choose preferences, aspirations and goals as they discover and choose what to do. Control in open-ended situations is learning through reflection and undertaking experiments which themselves affect that unfolding path. It is through such learning and experimentation that managers play a creative part in the development of the organization.

The last chapter made a number of points about this real-time learning in chaotic conditions. Step-by-step, algorithmic thinking and learning, that which employs predigested techniques and software programs of the mind, breaks down in open-ended situations. Instead, managers have to rely on insight, intuition, analogy, reflection and common sense, all non-algorithmic forms of thinking and learning based on experience. It is as much hard work as analytical reasoning. It is a sophisticated ability to use analogies with other situations to provoke new insights into current challenges. This is made possible by the fact that chaotic dynamics generate unpredictable new situations that have qualitatively similar patterns to previous ones. Learning is altering existing models and developing new ones for new situations.

And organizational learning takes place within groups of people. It produces a sequence of discoveries, meanings and choices that flow from the interaction between people. Those interactions, the group dynamic, are the most important determinant of what is learned and therefore of what choices are made. Those interactions are themselves generated by non-linear feedback loops operating away from equilibrium. Consequently the interactions are inherently unpredictable in specific terms, although in general terms they fall into recognizable categories. We recognize a category of group dynamic called conflict, but we never know what specific course that conflict will take and what impact it will have on choice and action. Because the process of learning in open-ended situations is itself unpredictable, managers have to learn how to learn in real time as the learning proceeds. And the key to that learning is the surfacing and questioning of the underlying assumptions that are driving the way we think and act. The message for managers is this: devote time to understanding how you are learning together, instead of wasting that time on long-term plans and visionary propaganda. The key to innovative outcomes lies in strategic thinking in groups of managers. Real strategic thinking does not proceed step-by-step to a goal – it questions and challenges existing structures and received wisdom from many unexpected directions.

This chapter examines why group interactions in the learning situation are amplifying and damping feedback loops. It points to patterns of the group dynamic flowing from such loops and the impact this has on the sequence of choices made by an organization. Interaction in a learning group within a business is essentially political. It is a process of developing a viewpoint and persuading, or compelling, others to adopt that viewpoint and agree to a choice. Control as learning is also political control, and politics is about the use of power.

Power form and group dynamic

Power is a relationship between individuals and groups which determines how one affects or responds to the other in making an organizational choice when there is conflict or great uncertainty. Where there is neither conflict nor uncertainty then all those involved in making a choice can have clear preferences about the outcome and clear goals on what they want to achieve. They can know what the potential range of outcomes is. They can therefore proceed to analyse the situation in a rational manner and make a choice based on rational criteria. Where they conflict in such a situation, then the choice has to be made by the more powerful applying their power.

But where there is great uncertainty, those involved in making the choice cannot initially have clear preferences as to what they want or clear goals on what they are trying to achieve. The problem becomes one of determining what to consider in the first place, how to consider it, and what are the most important questions to ask. Since purely analytical and rational modes of making the choice then break down, people have to resort to the use of power to choose what to explore and how to explore it so as to clarify preferences and goals. Power is then employed in a way which is far more complex than simply settling a difference between two opposed choices. The kind of power that can effectively be used in one situation is different from that used in the other. Power used as authority can effectively settle conflicts between clear goals. But it cannot provoke insight into new goals. Power as influence is required for this. We can distinguish between different forms of power by looking at the source from which the more powerful derive it and the basis upon which the less powerful consent to its use. Power is an interaction and always requires both a source and a basis of consent.

The ultimate source of power lies in the ability of the possessor of power to impose sanctions of some sort. Power increases with the ability of one person or group to reward or punish another in terms of prestige, status, money or career progression. But sanctions may be more subtle than this. One person or group can reward or punish another by simply making or withholding some contribution that might benefit the other. The ability to impose sanctions of any sort arises from:

- structural or situational interdependence – one individual or group is relatively more powerful than another if the former controls more resources, has greater access to information, performs critical activities upon which others depend for their performance, has greater access to communication channels, has access to more powerful people or groups, has control over communication agendas or decision-making situations;
- personal contribution. Relative power increases with the personal skills and expertise of particular individuals and their ability to interpret ambiguous situations, so reducing uncertainty for others.

The form in which power appears on any given occasion in a business organization depends upon the relationships between those with relatively more power, the leaders, and those with relatively less, the followers. A leader derives power, the ability to apply sanctions, from the formal rules, procedures and hierarchical structure of the organization, and from the contribution which the leader is able to make in a given situation. And in any given situation the leader may or may not choose to exert that power. These factors are set out on the horizontal plane in Figure 10.1. Followers are either unwilling to accept the power of leaders or they consent to it on some basis. This basis may be duty and obligation flowing from the formal structures, procedures and rules of the organization, or belief flowing from the organization's strong cultural norms. Or the consent may be based on followers' expected gains or contributions. Or it may be based on fear and that is close to not giving consent. These factors are set out on the vertical axis of Figure 10.1.

Different combinations of these factors results in different forms of power. Different forms of power provoke different categories of group dynamic. That group dynamic creates a context that has a major impact on what a group of managers discovers, chooses and enacts. A top management team whose behaviour is characterized by acceptance of the authority of a leader will take actions that are very different from another group in which intense rivalry flows from unwillingness either to apply or to accept power. No matter what the rational consideration, these two groups of managers will end up going in very different directions. The most sophisticated prescriptions and procedures for strategic analysis and planning will have little impact if the group dynamic of the management team is not conducive to complex forms of learning. The most effective way of impacting on strategic direction is to operate on the context for organizational learning that is generated by political interaction or group dynamics.

Figure 10.1 describes how the interaction between the leader and the followers determines the form in which power appears.

	Power not exerted	Exertion of power based on:	
		Contribution/gain	Structure/rules
Duty, obligation, strong belief	Vacuum	Authority	Authority
Contribution + gain *me*	Vacuum	*S. B.* Influence	*D. L.* Force
Fear No consent	Impotence	Impotence	Force

Consent to power based on: (vertical axis label)

Figure 10.1 *Determinants of the form of power*

Authority and compliance

The leader may apply power derived from structural and situational interdependence as set out in the organization's rules and procedures. For example, the leader normally has relatively greater control of resources or access to information. Power is derived from the need of followers for this resource or information. The leader may also exert power because of his or her own personal ability. If these applications of power are consented to by followers because they are legitimate according to the structures, rules and procedures of the organization, or because of widespread strongly shared performing and learning cultural norms, then power takes the form of authority. Authority is the vertical flow of discoveries and choices. And authority provokes a distinctive type of political interaction, or group dynamic. That interaction is one of compliance. Followers willingly and unquestioningly do what the leaders want. They suspend intellectual and moral judgements about the appropriateness of the superiors' choices and actions. They act as if they subscribe to these.[1] And this is the normal situation to be found in the day-to-day running of a business. The workload on a particular department or business unit rises, the manager requests additional resource and a superior manager decides whether to accede to the request. But this form of power with its consequent group dynamic is not conducive to the probing and questioning attitudes on which complex organizational learning and therefore strategic control depend. It is required for the day-to-day control of the existing business but is lethal to effective strategic control.

Influence and volatile group dynamics

The leader might apply power derived from his or her own personal skills and experience. If followers consent to this on the same basis then power takes the form of influence. Influence is a vertical and horizontal flow because followers also have contributions to make. And influence also provokes typical kinds of interaction or group dynamics, but of a wider variety with greater changeability. Here subordinates do not suspend their critical faculties or their willingness to act on their own judgements. Here people offer advice, enter into discussions, make suggestions, persuade. A whole range of interactions can emerge, from conflict to cooperation, from avoidance to commitment, from compliance to dissatisfaction with the leader, from questioning and consensus seeking to game playing and making issues undiscussable. And this is the form of power that will be most noticeable when successful organizations deal with open-ended change, for example, when developing a new product. This form of power and its consequent disorderly dynamics is a necessary condition for complex organizational learning and thus effective strategic control.

Force, submission and rebellion

Where there is no consent on the part of the followers, and leaders apply power derived from interdependence, then power takes the form of force. Force is also accompanied by typical group dynamics, either submission or rebellion. For example, the manager of one business unit within an organization may obtain business from the customer of another, against the agreed policy criteria. That other may appeal to a superior to put a stop to the practice. The superior may arbitrarily decide in favour of the one not adhering to the criteria. The other manager either has to submit, ignore the instruction or leave the organization. Force and its consequent dynamics are clearly not conducive either to day-to-day control or to strategic control, but may nevertheless be necessary in extreme circumstances.

Impotence

Where neither leader nor followers are willing to use or consent to power, there is a state of impotence. The typical group dynamic here is intense rivalry. This powerless state may be observed when a chief executive devotes the greater part of his time to public duties, leaving a number of equally powerful, strong minded and ambitious subordinates to run the business. This form of power and its consequent group dynamics hinders all forms of control.

Power vacuum

Finally, where the leader is unwilling to apply power while followers are willing to consent, we get a power vacuum. Typical group dynamics here are passive loyalty, searching for a new leader, frustration. This situation occurs where a chief executive is weak or unsure of what to do, but there are no powerful subordinates willing to step into the vacuum. This form of power and its consequent group dynamic is also lethal to all forms of control.

Power then is derived from a number of sources and it is consented to on a number of bases. Power may not be exerted or consented to at all, or it may be exerted and consented to with different degrees of willingness. The range of possible combinations produces a spectrum of forms of power ranging from brute coercion to helpful influence, with authority and shades of pressure and imposition in between. The way in which the power form is applied may be overt or covert. Or it may be unobtrusive in the sense that the leader structures the decision situation to prevent the exposure of followers to certain alternatives.[2] And each of these different forms of power, and the manner in which they are applied, provokes recognizable types of group dynamic. The manner in which power is used and responded to creates the group dynamic. The form of power and the accompanying group dynamic create the context within which the group learns. And that context has an important bearing on the sequences of discoveries, choices and actions that emerge. The key to affecting the strategic direction of a business lies in operating on the power form and group dynamic context within which groups of key managers make strategic choices. It is then of great importance to understand this context.

Political interactions as feedback loops

Political choices are the outcomes of relationships between individuals and groups having and using different levels of power in the form of force, authority or influence. By using some form of power, one party is able to get others to conform to a choice they are unwilling to conform to or do not really agree with. Or that party may enable others to make a choice they could not otherwise have made because they did not possess the resources. Or that party may enable others to make a choice they would not otherwise have made because they lacked the information or perspective. The application of power is therefore serving the purpose of enabling the organization to make a choice about changes whose outcomes are certain but where people conflict about the choice – authority or force determines the choice. And the application of power enables the organization to make a choice, even where there is no conflict, about changes whose consequences are highly uncertain – influence helps to clarify the situation and guide the group to a choice, while authority and force may resolve any conflicts along the way.

Amplifying and damping loops

When the relatively more powerful A exerts power in some way (or B perceives that he or she will), then B reacts in some way and an organizational choice may result. This may be the end of the matter; the interaction may be damping. So, the chief executive instructs the managing directors of two subsidiaries, one large and one small, to make all their export sales through a new international subsidiary, which has been set up because of the overlaps between them. They carry out his instructions. This may work and that sequence of choices comes to an end.

However, on the other hand it may not be the end of the matter. The managing director of the smaller subsidiary may subsequently fail to meet his export sales plan and argue that he cannot be held responsible – the new managing director of the international subsidiary is to blame because she is directing most of her effort to meeting the needs of the larger subsidiary with the more powerful managing director. The chief executive decides to resolve the conflict by changing the reporting structure so that the managing directors of the smaller company and the international company both report to the managing director of the larger subsidiary. The managing director of the smaller company refuses to accept this and leaves. The performance of that company then declines. The strategic direction of the corporation is different to what it might otherwise have been. This time the interaction loop between the players is an amplifying one. One choice is feeding into the next over time in an amplifying manner.

Political interaction between individuals and groups in business organizations is such that A's political actions are related to B's and B's are related to A's in a loop over time. The loop sometimes produces damping choices and outcomes and sometimes amplifying ones. Because of this kind of interaction, A's political activities and choices now are related to those that he took in a previous period and so are B's. And these relationships are non-proportional because people overreact and underreact. They are non-proportional because any sequence of political choices and outcomes is constrained in some way. One constraint is provided by the power that others have. Because of the distribution of power, one party cannot simply carry on doing what he or she wants. Another constraint is provided by the fact that cultural norms are never completely shared. Sooner or later, a series of political choices and actions will be constrained by the disagreement of others. The organization's political system is therefore a set of non-linear feedback mechanisms relating political choices to each other over time.[3] And consequently one of its inherent properties is that it is capable of generating virtuous and vicious circles in certain conditions. The principles of scientific chaos must therefore apply to the political systems of business organizations. Depending upon the values of the parameters connecting a political action now to a subsequent one, we will find either stable, explosive or chaotic final states of behaviour for the political system of a business.

The parameters

Now exactly how damping and amplifying the relationships between political actors in the organizations will be, what the parameter values in the relationships will be, depends upon human behaviour in the political context. That behaviour is conditioned by the willingness and ability of the relatively more powerful actor to apply power. And behaviour in a political context is also determined by the willingness of the less powerful actors to accept the application of power. It is also determined by the basis upon which such consent is given.

In general, if A's ability and willingness to exert some form of power is very high and the willingness of B and C to consent to that power on a given basis is also very high, the interactions between them are damped. The leader gives instructions and the followers immediately accept them. This amounts to reducing the sensitivity of the political feedback loop, to reducing the value of the parameter connecting a choice in one period to choices in later ones. But if willingness on the part of all parties to exert and consent to power is very low, then the interaction will be amplifying. For example, B and C will conflict with each other as to which choice is to be made and this will affect A, their leader. Since A does little to resolve the conflict, B and C continue to conflict. This is the situation where leaders do not effectively exert their power and the followers have no inclination to accept that power anyway. This is equivalent to fixing a very high parameter value for the feedback mechanisms. The mechanism is then highly sensitive leading to vicious circles of choice and action.

If A's willingness to exert power is increased, while B's willingness to accept it is decreased, then A and B will conflict and the pattern of interaction will be amplifying. The same amplifying consequence follows if A's willingness to apply power is reduced while that of the subordinate to accept it is increased. Here the subordinate is looking for instruction, which is not forthcoming, so leading to dissatisfaction and consequences that keep going around the loop. These moves to greater amplification are equivalent to increasing the parameter values in the feedback mechanisms.

We have then a set of non-linear feedback loops, the parameters of which are varied by the willingness with which power is exercised and responded to. Willingness to accept the exertion of power is highly correlated with the extent to which cultural norms are shared. Where both learning and performing cultural norms are strongly shared over a wide range, then people willingly consent to the application of power. When cultural norms are hardly shared at all then people are unwilling to accept the exertion of power. Willingness and ability to apply power is highly correlated with the way in which power is distributed and the nature of the organizational structure. Where power is highly concentrated at the top and hierarchical structures are clear cut and simple, we are likely to find high ability and willingness to exert power. Where power is widely dispersed and structures are complex, then both the ability and willingness to exert power will be low. Complex structures will mean that people are not all that clear on what power they have. Widespread control over resource allocation has a similar effect.

Business political systems and chaos

In Chapter 7 (see also Appendix B) we saw that when the parameters in a non-linear feedback mechanisms are such that the mechanism is rather insensitive or unresponsive, the final state of behaviour settles into a stable equilibrium. It requires a major change to shift behaviour to a qualitatively different type. When the mechanism is highly sensitive, then the final state of behaviour is an unstable equilibrium that is not constrained by the operation of the mechanism itself. Behaviour here is unstable in an explosive way, but it is still an equilibrium state. It still takes major change to shift the system to a qualitatively different form of behaviour. Between these equilibrium states, there is what we can think of as a border area – this is far-from-equilibrium. At certain intermediate levels of sensitivity and responsiveness, the system is held far-from-equilibrium where it produces behaviour that is chaotic. This behaviour is unstable but bounded by the operation of the system itself. There are constraints on the instability which lead to recognizable categories of behaviour in a qualitative, descriptive sense. But within those categories, behaviour in a specific sense is dependent on small chance differences in context and is hence unpredictable over the long-term. Here we can get qualitatively different behaviour as the result of tiny changes. This makes it possible for the system to develop new complex forms of behaviour easily, but those new forms are unpredictable.

We also saw in Chapter 4 that a business is a set of non-linear feedback mechanisms. It is therefore capable of the full range of behaviours described above. If it is to be innovative then it must be sustained in the far-from-equilibrium border area where it is easy to develop new strategic directions. This chapter has so far argued that the development of new strategic direction depends upon political activity and that the political system within a business is also a set of non-linear feedback mechanisms. The sensitivity and responsiveness of this system is determined by the willingness of people to exert and accept power. The business political system must therefore also be capable of generating stable and unstable behaviour, with a far-from-equilibrium border between them, in which behaviour displays the characteristics of bounded instability. We now go on to explore possible equilibrium states for a business political system and the far-from-equilibrium border between them.

The question to consider is that of the final states of political interaction at different parameter values, at different combinations of willingness to exert and consent to power.

Attractors in political systems

An organization characterized by strongly shared cultural norms and concentrated power in clear hierarchies is one where willingness on both sides is high. Power then takes the form of authority and the interaction pattern is one of unquestioning compliance. Because all organizations are powerfully pulled by the forces of integration (see Chapter 4), all political systems in business organizations will be powerfully pulled to a political state where power takes the form of authority and the group dynamic is compliance. As organizations try to take advantage of synergy and inter-connection, as they drive towards commonly accepted goals and build shared cultures, they move to political systems where authority is the predominant form of power and compliance the predominant group dynamic.

Chapter 4 presented the example of a UK fuel processing company that had adopted a clearly defined, simple functional hierarchical structure. Its rules and procedures were formally set out and highly integrative – decisions of any importance were brought to the centre. There was a strongly shared culture in which priority was always attached to matters of safety and avoidance of conflict with the trades unions. Authority was quite clearly the dominant form of power and the dynamic at top manage-ment level was clearly one of compliance. Top management meetings were conducted in a highly formal manner according to long agendas. The managing director conducted these meetings so that other members replied to his questions only in their own areas of expertise. Members always came carefully prepared with staff papers and large bundles of files to which they referred when questioned. Informal meetings of top managers were not all that common. In meetings I had with those managers they did not readily reply to questions of a general nature outside their own functional areas. They saw the strategy of their busi-ness as a matter for the managing director.

An organization in which power is widely dispersed and cultural norms are little shared will be one where willingness to exert power and to consent to it are both very low. This is a state of political impotence in which the predominant group dynamic is one of intense rivalry. Since all organizations are powerfully pulled towards disintegration by the forces of division and differentiation (see Chapter 4), all political systems in business organizations will be pulled towards a state of impotence ac-companied by intense rivalry. As the organization tries to deal with high levels of uncertainty and benefit from the division of tasks and the segmenting of markets, it develops many different units with different cultures. The power of the centre weakens and rivalry breaks out between the units.

Chapter 4 also referred to an example of an agricultural company that contained a number of subsidiaries operating in different but overlapping market segments. The most powerful figure in that company was the chairman. He had withdrawn from the role of chief executive, leaving each subsidiary to be run by strong-minded, powerful managing direc-tors. Each subsidiary had developed its own culture. This created a power vacuum in which intense rivalry between subsidiaries occurred. The managing directors hardly ever spoke to each other and met only at formal board meetings. Not surprisingly, matters of strategic importance to the whole group of companies were never addressed.

Another example of the state of power vacuum is provided by the way most universities are run at least in North America and the UK. Here we find a number of faculties each with their own culture. Power in these institutions is widely dispersed and decision making highly participative. The rivalry that occurs between faculties and even between academics within the same faculty is well documented and has provided fertile ground for the novelist. And studies of decision making in these organizations has shown how strategic decisions depend almost entirely on chance – this kind of organized anarchy or 'garbage can' decision making will be returned to later on in this chapter.[4]

There are two other possibilities for the final state of a business political system. These are created by the response of leaders to the forces pulling the organization in the two different directions described above. Organisations and their leaders may respond to weak sharing of values by imposing greater order, by concentrating power at the top. Willingness to exert power is thus great but willingness to accept it is low. Power then takes the form of force and the predominant group dynamic is either submission, or resistance, or alternation between the two.

One company I worked with had experienced some years of rather weak leadership in which power was increasingly assumed by powerful divisional barons. These divisions developed distinctive cultures of their own and cooperation then became increasingly difficult. When the company experienced a profit and cashflow crisis, a new chief executive was appointed. His reorganization and reconstitution of the management team resulted in a substantial concentration of power in his own hands. The dynamic that followed was one of submission in which even the most senior manager would not put forward any suggestion that was thought likely to attract the disapproval of the chief executive. The game became one of second guessing what the chief executive wanted. But there were also pockets of resistance and after some time this led to the replacement of the chief executive.

Another response to the consequences of division and differentiation may be to offset the effects of widespread distribution of power by promoting the strong sharing of cultural norms over a wide range. Ability and willingness to exert power is then low and willingness to consent is high. This creates a power vacuum in which the typical dynamics are ones of passive loyalty, or frustration, or search for leadership.

Figure 10.2 depicts these four final states.

The political system of a business organization is then pulled in four different directions. These are equilibrium states. Once an organization has been drawn into one of these, so that it becomes the predominant, continuously experienced state, it is very difficult to move way from it. It

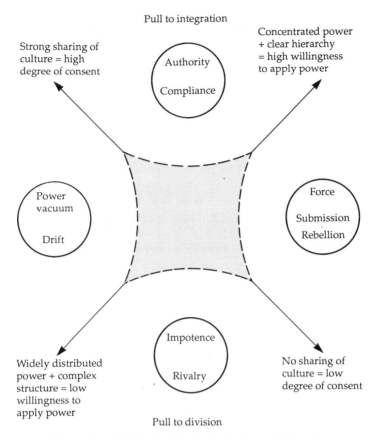

Figure 10.2 *Equilibrium states for the business political system*

requires some political coup in which the leader is removed. It also usually requires major restructuring, installing new management teams and altering systems and procedures. And none of these equilibrium states can successfully deal with open-ended change. The group dynamics provoked by all of them simply obstruct the questioning and complex learning that open-ended change requires if it is to be effectively dealt with.

Success is far-from-equilibrium

Successful political systems are therefore those that are sustained far-from-equilibrium, by preventing the:

- Strong sharing of cultural norms over a wide range and avoiding a state in which they are hardly shared at all. Organisational political systems are sustained far-from-equilibrium by weak sharing of cultural norms. Weak sharing means that people have different unconscious assumptions on what and how to learn. It means that any strong sharing is confined to a limited range of performing norms. Difference in cultures is an essential characteristic of the far-from-equilibrium state.

• Widespread distribution of authority over strategic resource allocation and the confusion of hierarchical structures. The far-from-equilibrium state is one where authority is distributed, but not widely. It is one where hierarchies are clear, not confused. Difference in power distribution is an essential characteristic of the far-from-equilibrium state.

Successful political systems are those that avoid the continuous application of power as either authority or force and that avoid continuous power vacuums and impotence. It is in this border area between the equilibrium states of authority, force, power vacuum and impotence that we find power in its form of influence. Influence is incompatible with all these states but will be exercised when values are weakly shared and power is unequally distributed. And this makes common sense. The possibility of influence arises when there is difference. Influence implies that the parties are open to persuasion, that they welcome questioning and the consideration of new perspectives. They are by definition not open to such persuasion when they strongly share a wide range of cultural norms or when they share none at all. They are also by definition not open to persuasion when power is so highly concentrated that those at the top do not need to listen, or when it is so widely distributed that there is not much they could do even if they did listen. The predominant form of power is influence when the political system is far-from-equilibrium. And influence provokes a range of group dynamics, only one of which may be consensus seeking. In the border area between the equilibrium attractors of non-linear feedback mechanisms, behaviour is more complex than one form of interaction can describe.

In the border between the equilibrium attractors of the system, behaviour is fractal. Behaviour fractures into self-similar patterns that have a recognizable shape but are never exactly the same. And those patterns include ones similar to those found in the equilibrium states of the system. Translating this into organizational political terms this means that we will find interactions, or group dynamics, that are similar to compliance, submission and resistance, rivalry, passive loyalty, frustration and dissatisfaction with the leadership. In other words, we will find forms of power that include authority, force, influence and the absence of power applications. And we will also find interactions that are specifically related to the exercise of power as influence – cooperation and consensus seeking, but also conflict, avoidance, game playing, making issues undiscussable, manipulating decision situations and many others. In the far-from-equilibrium state, power is not continuously applied in form – it is alternately applied in different forms. In the far-from-equilibrium state the group dynamic is volatile. Small changes in the group dynamic can escalate into large differences in discoveries, choices and actions. The next chapter will give examples of this.

Scientific chaos establishes a number of principles relating to the behaviour of non-linear feedback mechanisms that are far-from-equilibrium. First, long-term outcomes are unpredictable. Second they are self-similar. Third, such systems positively utilize far-from-equilibrium chaos to develop new, more complex forms of order. In this chapter the properties of unpredictability and self-similarity are considered. The next chapter looks at order from chaos.

Unpredictable political choices

A central characteristic of the far-from-equilibrium, chaotic border area is that of extreme sensitivity to small changes in context. Translating this into business political terms, it means that there could well be major changes in the nature of the interaction between people as they:

- switch from one type of issue to another;
- move from operating in one type of communication arena to another;
- experience changes in their workloads;
- shift the type of power they exert and to which they consent;
- move from operating on the basis of strongly shared to weakly shared cultural norms.

Small changes in the willingness to exert and consent to power in any of its forms could escalate into major changes in the group dynamic. Groups can and do move quickly from a dynamic of compliance to one of covert resistance or overt rivalry. The timing of any intervention made by one party can completely change the group dynamic. For example, one person may arrive at a meeting with a completely worked up proposed solution to a problem. If that proposal is introduced right at the start of the meeting, before colleagues have had time to thrash out their own views, they could respond with hostility and ignore the proposal. However the same proposal introduced later on in the proceedings could be greeted with gratitude and accorded serious attention.

This sensitivity of political interaction to small changes in context means that the sequences of discoveries, choices and actions that emerge from that interaction will also be highly sensitive to the context. Small changes in context could lead to very different sequences of choices. As with all other non-linear feedback mechanisms operating far-from-equilibrium, the sequence of behaviours and choices is affected by chance, and specific long-term paths are inherently unpredictable. No one involved in the political process can know what the long-term outcomes of that one process will be. Order and control as we normally understand those words, are not properties of political systems that generate innovation, despite the stable distribution of power over time and issue that we find in them.

To fix ideas on what is meant by the impact of context on the strategic choices that groups of managers make, consider a common problem. In my consultancy work I have frequently encountered the following situation. Members of top management teams in a company believe that it is their prime role to deal with the strategic issues facing their organization. But when they meet as a board or as a top executive team, they find their time is dominated by what they see as operational matters. As individuals, they question the purpose of their meeting and are highly cynical about its usefulness. There is confusion as to the role they are performing together, but they all avoid raising these concerns when they meet together. In private, they blame their failure to deal with strategic issues on the style of the chairman. They call for greater delegation of power and point to the fact that the real strategic issues are handled informally by smaller groupings outside their meetings. We might conclude that such behaviour is irrational or incompetent, but it happens so frequently to groups of managers who are quite clearly intelligent and competent that there has to be some other reason for such behaviour. It is suggested here that the reason lies in the context within which managers are politically interacting.

How then does the context of political activity affect the sequence of strategic choices it makes?

The context of political activity in businesses

Political activity is interaction and communication between people involving the use of power in some way to produce a flow of discoveries, choices and actions in response to change. It is a learning form of control. The interaction and communication takes place through the medium of exchanges of documents, through electronic and telephonic exchanges of information and through meetings. Each occasion on which any such exchange takes place can be thought of as a communication arena. Those arenas may be regular and predetermined in time terms, or irregular and spontaneous; formal or informal (spontaneous) in conduct; restricted or open in access terms; fluid and changing, or consistent and regular in participation terms. Whatever kind of communication arena it is, the amount of communication and interaction that can occur is limited by the availability of the time participants have available. Every communication arena can be thought of as a receptacle with limited capacity for handling whatever has to be handled.[5]

The most obvious arenas in any business are those that may be described as institutionalized. These are created by intentional design flowing from the structures, formal systems, rules and procedures of the organization. They are usually regular in time terms, formal in conduct and restricted in access. For example, such arenas taking document form cover budgets, plans, schedules, policy statements, manuals, information bulletins, company newsletters, capital expenditure requests, purchase requisitions, minutes of meetings, reports and accounts and many more. Those communication arenas taking the form of meetings include shareholder meetings, social functions for employees or customers, retirement or leaving functions, special meetings to explain policy changes, board meetings, monthly management meetings, daily production scheduling meetings and many more.

Our prime concern here is to understand what part such communication arenas play in handling the issues that arise in open-ended change situations; what part they play in discovering, choosing and acting in relation to strategic matters. There are four important points to make in this regard:

- Making a choice is not the only function that institutionalized arenas perform. And even where making a choice is one of the functions, taking and implementing a decision is not the only possible outcome.
- Since the capacities of communication arenas are limited, only some of the range of functions will consistently be performed.
- Which of those functions are performed will depend on why people were invited and agreed to participate and how busy they are.
- Where choice is one of those functions, the outcome will depend on what type of issue it is.

The argument is this. Communication and the choice it leads to, are both highly sensitive to the context within which they occur. That context is the type of arena, the type of functions it performs, the workload on the arena and its participants and the combination of issue types presented to it. Because of its context, an institutionalized arena will not attend to strategic, open-ended issues. By its very nature the board meeting will rarely be the forum in which strategic issues are developed and progressed. Such issues will be developed and progressed in informal, spontaneous communication arenas because the context is more favourable. Institutionalized arenas will attend to issues arising in closed and contained change situations. What an arena deals with and what the outcome is, depends on context even where the relative distribution of power is stable over time and issue. Consequently if we want to improve the handling of strategic issues we have to create a context within which informal spontaneous arenas can thrive.

Each of these points and the conclusions they lead to are now examined in more detail.

Communication arenas fulfil many functions and implementing a choice is not the only outcome

The functions of communication arenas in general can be grouped into six categories:

- Conveying symbolic and ritualistic meaning. Almost all communication arenas reinforce symbols to do with organizational purpose and the status of individuals. Arenas provide the means of legitimizing views, values, beliefs, plans and decisions already taken. And often they are used to create the impression that logical, rational decision making is occurring even when it is not. Symbolic functions provide comfort, security, legitimation and the promotion of belief.
- Attending to administrative matters: this covers discussions and information exchanges on pension arrangements, safety requirements and the many other standard operating procedures of the business. Administrative functions maintain the orderly functioning of the formal systems.
- Reviewing past performance: Explaining the past through the many budget, plan and performance reviews that are regularly conducted can take the beneficial form of interpreting what has happened and why. It can be searching for and understanding errors made or factors which led to success. Such reviewing, or past explaining, can also take the less beneficial, and frequently harmful, form of creating self justifying myths about what happened in order to raise comfort levels.
- Learning through exploring issues: participants here are exploring and learning about the meaning of changes to the business and its environments. They are testing values, beliefs, purpose, domain and direction. The concern here is with qualitative information, meanings and perspectives.
- Learning through team building: many communication arenas provide occasions for the development of friendship, trust and liking. Almost all meetings have some social aspects that are vital to knitting people together into teams, to learning about each other and their functioning together as a group.
- Making a choice.

When participants in an arena are presented with a choice they may:

- Transfer it to another arena that is thought to be more appropriate. Some vague or contentious issue is raised at a meeting and the chairman rules that it should be dealt with outside that meeting.
- Postpone it to be dealt with on a later occasion in the same arena. During a consultancy assignment, I attended monthly meetings of the top management team of a particular company and observed how

each month they postponed dealing with issues around the 1992 single European market.

- Redefine it as another issue to be dealt with at the same arena or some other. A specific conflict between two business units may be redefined as a reorganization issue for the whole company.
- Resolve it some way. Resolution may occur because, after proper consideration, the issue is either rejected or an affirmative decision is taken and followed by appropriate action. But the issue could also be resolved, and this will normally be only a temporary resolution, by a decision that is never implemented. In one company I worked with, the top team repeatedly made decisions to diversify but never implemented these. Or the issue could be resolved by oversight; it may not be fully considered, the consequences may not be well understood and resolution may then take the form of some hasty decision. This too is likely to be only a temporary resolution. On one occasion, I observed a hasty decision taken by a busy top management team to buy a hover barge to relieve port congestion in the Middle East. Since the blockage was in fact not due to physical capacity but to administration problems, the management team was faced one year later with the issue of what to do with an idle barge.

The point to note here is that communication arenas are not solely concerned with taking decisions, and implemented decisions are not the only outcome. This is the function and outcome that is so often talked about as if it were the only useful result of communication – meetings are often held to be a waste of time if there is no decision followed by action. The fact is that in many communication arenas, decision making is either absent or of relatively little importance. But other important functions are being performed.

Communication arenas perform a wide range of functions in addition to making a choice and when they are confronted with a choice, a decision followed by an action is not the only outcome. Which of the functions will institutionalized arenas perform, given that they have limited capacities? What happens to open-ended issues brought to such arenas? The answer is that institutionalized arenas will quite predictably transfer or postpone open-ended issues because of the context within which they operate.

Institutionalized communication arenas tend to shelve open-ended issues

Individuals are invited to attend institutionalized arenas because of their status and position in the hierarchy; because of the formal rules and procedures of the organization. The degree to which an individual shares the culture and is a member of the team is also relevant. The chief executive officer is invited to board meetings because of the position he or she holds, and because he or she is acceptable to colleagues. Whether particular individuals accept the invitation or not depends upon whether their perception of their own power in some sense matches the perception of those inviting them. The individual will accept an invitation to an institutionalized arena primarily because the arena is important and there is a duty or obligation to attend arising from the rules, structures and procedures of the organization or a common cultural allegiance.

Those managers invited because of their position in the hierarchy must be the more important managers in any situation. And the more important the manager is, in these terms, the more he or she is looked to for the legitimation of the proposals and decisions of others and the confirmation of administrative matters – this is the essence of the hierarchical principles of delegation. The more important the manager, the more he or she takes responsibility for the performance of the organization, or a part of it, and consequently the more he or she is required to review and explain the past. This is the essence of properly functioning management and information control systems. Invitation by status is in fact an invitation to contribute symbolic, administrative and reviewing the past functions. An acceptance of the invitation that has to do with the perceived importance of the arena, to do with obligation, duty and role expectations implies an acceptance on the part of the manager that he or she will fulfil those symbolic, administrative and past explanation functions. It is therefore these functions that will be accorded primacy in institutionalized arenas.

Furthermore, communication arenas have limited capacities. Capacity is limited by the time that participants have available. Arenas are like receptacles into which only limited amounts of function can be placed. Regular, formal arenas, attended for status and procedural reasons will, we have seen, focus on the symbolic, the administrative and explaining the past. They are highly likely to be filled with these functions. The load factor will be such that the learning functions will be crowded out. On many occasions now I have had the opportunity of observing boards of directors and senior management teams at work in their regular meetings. With great frequency they spend about 80 per cent of their time together on these occasions on symbolic, administrative and past reviewing functions. The remaining time is devoted to issues. But, institutionalized communication arenas occur at regular time intervals and have standardized agendas. They therefore tend to deal with foreseeable matters, those with short-term consequences and high levels of clarity, characteristic of closed and contained change. The very nature of such issues guarantees that they will have high perceived importance and relevance and so receive attention. When in addition they are raised by a participant of high perceived importance, then the issue stands a very high chance indeed of being resolved. It will be properly considered and either rejected on good grounds or decided by affirmative decision followed by action.

If the issue is generated by open-ended change it will have long-term consequences that are inherently unpredictable. Because of this and the fact that so many of the changes giving rise to such issues are small, the issue will have a low level of clarity and high novelty in terms of past experience of participants and the organization. These inherent features of open-ended issues provoke reactions of confusion in people and hence such issues are likely to be perceived as low in importance and relevance. This immediately mitigates against open-ended issues receiving high levels of attention. If such issues are brought to an arena by a participant of low perceived importance (and this is likely to happen quite frequently because the lower levels in the hierarchy are closer to the source of the change), if the workload of the arena itself is high, if participants are distracted by numerous other issues and high workloads, then it is a virtual certainty that the issue will not be resolved. And if it is resolved at all, it is highly likely that the form of resolution will be outright rejection, affirmative decision with no action following or an inappropriate decision made by oversight. Such resolution is then only temporary and almost guarantees that the issue will surface again in another guise, perhaps in another arena, perhaps raised by another participant.

There will therefore be a predictable tendency for institutionalized arenas in efficient organizations, those with near optimality in the short-term utilization of resources, to focus on short-term closed change. There will be a predictable tendency not to attend to, not to resolve, a great many of the important open-ended, strategic issues. And this will apply particularly at the top level of the hierarchy, the very level which is traditionally supposed to be most concerned with the strategic, with open-ended change. This is a consequence, not of some short-sighted incompetence on the part of senior managers, but of the very nature of the functioning of the organization. It results from the existence of hierarchy so necessary for the handling of closed change. It also results from the logical, common-sense principle of attending first to that which is most pressing and easiest to dispose of.

If we focus on the formal distribution of power as hierarchical authority, we expect that power distribution to remain relatively constant over time and over issue. We expect the same people to exert their power in relation to the same kinds of issue whenever they come up. It is logical to expect that the most powerful will attend to and exert their power in relation to the most important issues, that is, those strategic issues arising in open-ended change. We therefore expect strategic choices to be made at the visibly most important meetings. And we expect those choices to follow in an orderly manner, predictable from the distribution of power. Once we know the relative distribution of power and the preferences of the most powerful we ought to be able to predict the choices that will be made. What this interpretation omits, however, is the importance of context. Contextual factors such as time pressures, the reasons for participation, the kind of group dynamic, will all have an impact on what happens to open-ended issues, despite the relative stability of power distribution.

The outcome of an open-ended issue is thus highly dependent upon context: the type of arena, the functions it performs, the combination of issue types it has to deal with, the load on it, the values its participants share. Because the context of institutionalized arenas is unfavourable in almost all respects for dealing with open-ended change, a business organization will have to rely on other arenas for that function. It will have to rely on spontaneous arenas to handle open-ended issues to the point where they are sufficiently clear and require legitimating and resource allocation decisions. The ability of an organization to make strategic choices will therefore depend critically on how easily spontaneous arenas are formed. Examples of what is meant by spontaneous arenas are: special interest groups that form around particular issues and their champions; task forces that undertake the active progression of selected issues; workshops where broad ranging issues are discussed and interpreted; informal one-to-one meetings between two managers in a car at which they exchange views on the latest reorganization proposals. It becomes a matter of great importance to understand what conditions lead to the emergence of spontaneous communication arenas.

The emergence of spontaneous communication arenas

Spontaneous communication arenas in an organization usually emerge informally. Or if they are intentionally created, their conduct displays a high degree of informality and spontaneity. They lack well-defined operational purposes and they are not specifically about achieving prearranged clear goals. In fact they are a response to a lack of clarity in preferences and goals. Spontaneity in either creation or conduct has little to do with status, rules or procedures. The minimal conditions for spontaneous attention to open-ended issues to occur are:

- Holistic perceptions of roles: if people in the organization see their roles entirely in terms of the function and business unit they are most directly concerned with, then they will not concern themselves with open-ended issues which inevitably span many functions and business units.
- Trust between participants: people do not necessarily have to like each other all that much to work together on some issue concerning their organization. But without trust they are unlikely to do so.
- Mutually perceived gain and contribution: the motivation to join with others in identifying and progressing open-ended issues does not necessarily have to do with financial rewards. Gain may take the form of personal career progression, or the advancement of the function or business unit of an individual, or even the good of the organization as

a whole. The opportunity to make a contribution may itself constitute sufficient motivation to participate in progressing open-ended issues.
- Workload: the interaction required to handle open-ended issues at spontaneous communication arenas takes time. If the management resource is tightly stretched, managers will be forced to attend to the most pressing day-to-day issues only, and spontaneous arenas will not form.

Without appropriate role perceptions, resource slack, trust, and mutually perceived gain people will not spontaneously group to deal with some actual or potential issue. The leaders of an organization cannot install or control spontaneity; it is no longer spontaneous if they do. But they can affect the context. They can foster particular role perceptions and create conditions of sufficient management resource slack, trust and mutual gain. The most immediately obvious ways of doing this are through training and development programmes, career progression and reward systems. But perceptions on roles, trust, perceived gain and contributions are primarily matters of attitude and behaviour. And they follow not from specific, clearly identifiable individual causes but from the total situation created by the cultural norms of the organization, the manner in which power is used and the form the organizational structure takes. These combine to provoke particular kinds of group dynamic. Such dynamics, for example compliance or rivalry, may obstruct the formation of spontaneous communication arenas. Or such dynamics, for example questioning and consensus seeking, may promote the formation of spontaneous communication arenas. Whether spontaneous arenas form, how they are conducted and what emerges from them is highly sensitive to a host of contextual factors. We can create conditions within which spontaneous communication and organizational learning may occur. But because it is spontaneous we cannot organize or predetermine the outcome. As soon as we try to do this, the spontaneous becomes institutionalized and we encounter the predictable tendency of the institutionalized to shelve open-ended issues. Because of this, whether open-ended issues are handled or not, how they are handled and what choices emerge, are all significantly dependent upon chance. The long-term sequence of choices that emerge are therefore unpredictable.

The practical implications of this argument are as follows. We have to accept that it is not the role of the board meeting or the formal top executive meetings to develop and progress strategic issues. Their role is primarily to review the past and legitimate new strategic directions that are emerging. Their role is primarily one of backing new strategic directions, once they have been sufficiently clarified, by allocating strategic resources to their pursuit. It is through this authority to allocate resource that formal top management teams can shape the organization's strategic issue agenda and secure what are judged to be appropriate levels of consistency. But the identification of strategic issues, their progress and clarification will depend upon much more informal and spontaneous processes, not necessarily related to hierarchical position. The ability to build strategic issue agendas in the first place will depend upon spontaneous political learning activity. Because that activity is so sensitive to the way managers interact, the dynamic development of the strategic issue agenda will depend significantly on chance. This relationship between chance and the unpredictability of new strategic direction will be returned to in the next chapter.

Recognizable patterns in political choices

The first property of the chaotic dynamics of a business political system is thus that the specific patterns of political interaction over time, and the specific sequences of choices they generate in response to open-ended issues, are inherently unpredictable in the long-term. But those sequences also display self-similarity. And this second property of chaotic dynamics constitutes a more sophisticated concept of order in political systems. Self similarity means that patterns of behaviour and sequences of choices show a constant degree of variation, or regular irregularity. They are not haphazard, but move within boundaries.

Regularity

In a sequence of choices that any organization makes over time, one choice might follow from another in a perfectly logical manner apparent to all. This will causes no surprise to members of the organization because the reasons for any reversal of a previous decision are clear to all. Preparing, reviewing and acting upon an annual plan can have these characteristics. For example, the plan may be based on sales and cost forecasts, derived in ways that all those involved agree with. That plan may set out the actions to be taken to achieve the objectives. Such actions may include a level of capital expenditure. On reviewing the first quarter, the loss of a large customer may lead to a decision to place a moratorium on capital expenditure. Two quarters later additional sales revenue may justify reinstating the capital expenditure programme. The sequence of choices involves reversals of decisions for clear reasons understandable to all involved. We can then say that there is complete regularity in the choice sequence. Anything approaching such a sequence is only possible close to certainty.

Irregularity

Any realistic sequence of choices will show irregularity, where this means that choices made today are reversed tomorrow for reasons that are not clear to, or agreed upon by all. Such a sequence might fluctuate wildly, with choices made today bearing absolutely no perceptible, consistent connection with those that went before, thus causing continual surprise to members of the organization. Here there is irregularity and the degree of that irregularity is not constant. A choice today may be followed by a complete reversal tomorrow, or no change at all even though circumstances have changed. Lengthy periods may pass with no reversals followed by periods of continual reversal for reasons that most cannot connect to the circumstances. There is complete irregularity. A choice yesterday to enter a new market is followed by a choice today not to, but to enter some other market instead. An instruction from the chief executive to the chemical plant production manager yesterday to produce a particular combination of chemicals, is followed today by an instruction to produce a different combination. For some time periods the chief executive interferes hardly at all and at others he suddenly interferes frequently. These decisions are not only different from period to period, they have no perceptible connection and swing wildly from one direction to another. They do not move within perceptible boundaries. This is utter confusion, old-fashioned chaos, not scientific chaos.

Regular irregularity

Between the one extreme of complete regularity and the other of complete irregularity there is another possibility. That possibility is irregularity within boundaries. Here choices are consistently reversed. For example, they are either usually completely reversed; or they are usually only partially reversed; or they are reversed with some regularity in time terms. There is, in other words, some similarity over time in the manner in which the choices swing about. The chief executive intervenes in ways that are unpredictable on each specific occasion, but they do relate to similar circumstances and similar types of issue. The irregularity has some degree of regularity over time. Subordinates are then surprised by the specific choice but not by the intervention itself. They half expect it. The chief executive does not completely reverse yesterday's decision. He amends it in ways that are similar to, but not exactly the same as the past. And people can and do cope with this situation. There is a pattern that they can perceive. This is chaos, disorder within a pattern.

The point is that people are able to perceive patterns even if the connections cannot be described as logical or even thought to be sensible. Where some pattern is perceived in the sequence, members of the organization can be heard to say that the organization has direction, that top management knows what it is doing and has vision. When choices swing wildly, when members cannot expect anything about today's choices from what went before, they will report that the organization lacks direction, that the people at the top do not know what they are doing, that they have no vision. People's perceptions about vision and direction relate not to some future knowledge, but to how easily they are able to detect some pattern in the organizational choices they see emerging.[6] People react well to the first situation and badly to the second, thus affecting the overall performance of the organization.

Constraints

Far-from-equilibrium then, both the patterns of behaviour and the choices they produce are self-similar. And this property follows from the structure of the feedback mechanisms themselves. It occurs because they are constrained in some way. The choice sequence has a self-similar pattern because there are constraints that prevent it from shooting all over the place, that prevent the sequence from moving outside given bounds. And the tendency to some form of regular irregularity will be greater when:

- Power is unequal but distributed. Where all members of a group have equal power, that power provides no constraint on any of them. Choices can therefore swing wildly from day to day, depending upon who happens to participate and who happens to support whom. Where power is widely distributed and conditions are highly uncertain, a greater range of views and preferences will have to be taken into account. But, purely personal goals will carry more weight, communication difficulties will increase, personality differences will be more prominent. So, the possibility of any pattern in the sequence of choices declines. Where power is hardly distributed at all, but concentrated in the hands of an autocrat, then power also provides no constraint. The autocrat has all the power and is constrained by no one. Highly concentrated power makes it likely that few different perspectives are applied to making the choice. Choices are therefore more likely, when uncertainty is high and pure rationality cannot be applied, to stray from a path connected to the changes actually occurring. As the organization moves either to widespread distribution or to very little distribution of power, the constraints which provide some consistency in irregular choice sequences, are weakened. Power which is both unequal and distributed will provide the necessary boundaries.
- Hierarchies are simple and clear cut. Simple, clear hierarchies set bounds within which choices have to be made. And the line of authority they establish, the clarity of communication they enable, makes it difficult for choices to swing about wildly over time. But the more complex the structure, the more people there are engaged in making organizational choices and the less clear cut their relationships with each other are, the more likely the choice sequence is to swing wildly.
- Values are shared, but in a weak sense. Where people do not share

cultural norms at all, where their views on what is important and how they should proceed hardly ever coincide, then there are likely to be few constraints on the choices they make. It will be possible for them to swing about wildly, as one or another's preferences are acceded to. Strongly shared values also provide few constraints on the degree of variability. People with predominantly the same views on what is important, and on how to proceed, can quite easily all move off together in the same direction away from what is required by the situation. With strongly shared values they can quite easily all suddenly change that direction. Mobs and groups of fanatics are characterized by strongly shared values at the time and the degree of variation in the choices they make is not constant. Weakly shared values do however provide a constraint. A wide range of views and preferences has to be taken into account, but wild swings away from what the situation requires will be inhibited by opposition from some members of a group.

- Workloads are low enough to allow time for reflection and discussion. Reflection and discussion provide constraints upon the extent to which a choice sequence can depart from that which the situation requires. But these activities use the scarce resource of time. Organizations that are highly efficient in the short-term sense of full utilization of the management resource will therefore weaken a constraint that tends to produce boundaries around irregular choice sequences in open-ended situations.

The point of this concern with the constraints and boundaries around irregular sequences of choices is that it is this that produces self-similarity in the choice sequence. We cannot have the actual choice sequence always matching that required by the situation when the level of uncertainty is very high. We cannot have complete regularity. But we must then have self-similarity in that sequence if we are not to face complete and utter confusion. We have to have a recognizable pattern in the sequence of choices, which people in the organization can perceive. We have, in conditions of great uncertainty to abandon the hope of order as a stable sequence of choices always matching the situation and settle for recognizable patterns within disorder, for chaos.

Structure and the distribution of power

When it comes to the question of power distribution in business organizations we do not find the monolithic agreement we find on the question of shared cultures. Most senior managers, in my experience, regard the concentration of power at the top of an organization as essential to effective control. Many popular writers on management, however, equate the wide distribution of power with increased ability of an organization to innovate.[7] Closely tied to the matter of power distribution is that of hierarchical structure and role definitions. Those who believe that success is related to concentrated power usually also believe that simple hierarchical structures and clear role definitions are requirements for success. Those who call for the widespread distribution of power usually also call for intersecting job areas, ambiguous assignments, people involved in everything. Some accompany this with the advice to install simple, decentralized structures[8] and others advise complex centralist network structures.[9] The belief is that promoting widespread participation in decision making, empowering more people to choose and act, leads to higher levels of innovation.

When discussing the distribution of power we need to be clear on what kind of power we are talking about. A previous section in this chapter has distinguished between power as authority, force and influence. Different forms of power provoke different kinds of group dynamic, and that dynamic has much to do with the choices people will make.

Distributed authority

Consider first what the more widespread distribution of authority means. Those who advise the widespread distribution of power maintain that ability to allocate resources and gain access to the institutionalized communication arenas of the organization widens the number who can expect to contribute to and gain from innovative activity.[10] But distributing authority means that the structures, rules and procedures of the organization establish the conditions within which more people may legitimately allocate resources and apply sanctions. Widespread distribution of authority is simply delegation to reallocate resources in predefined circumstances. But the circumstances are predefined. There are performance standards to be met. Such delegating can therefore only apply to closed and possibly contained change situations. Authority, by definition, cannot be delegated to handle open-ended situations, to make substantial reallocations of strategic resources in unforeseeable circumstances. Authority is always exercised, even when dispersed, in institutionalized arenas that show an inevitable tendency to shelve open-ended issues. The dynamic provoked by authority is compliance, the opposite of the dynamic required for the spontaneous arenas which must handle open-ended change. Distributing or delegating authority is a part of the response to the complexities of controlling large organizations in conditions of closed or contained change. It has little to do with the innovation with which we are concerned in open-ended situations.

Part and parcel of the delegation of authority is the structural form which defines what is being delegated. That delegation is at its clearest when it is done through simple hierarchies and clear job definitions. Complex centralist structures, matrix and network structures confuse the distribution of authority in the hope that this will encourage what that distribution itself cannot do. And that is the encouragement of more holistic approaches, the attention to open-ended changes. But this is essentially an attempt to institutionalise the mechanism of searching for and making choices about open-ended issues. It will therefore follow the inevitable fate of institutionalized arenas. All structural approaches essentially deal with power in its authority form. Because authority is institutionalized, and because of the dynamic it provokes, it cannot deal with the open ended until it has been clarified to the point of being a concrete proposal.

Wide distribution of authority and formal participation mechanisms cannot improve ability to make strategic choices. Indeed it will be harmful. For, the unequal distribution of authority has a beneficial impact on the variability of choices emerging from the political process. The unequal distribution of authority provides important constraints. Suppose an organization did distribute authority to allocate strategic resources in unforeseeable circumstances to a large number of units in the organization. It would then be possible for choices to shoot all over the place. Suppose it highly concentrated authority in the hands of one or two people at the top. Choices would also be able to shoot off in one direction for lengthy periods of time or to shoot all over the place. Authority that is both distributed and unequal therefore provides an important constraint on the sequence of choices. It provides the boundaries within which the inevitably irregular choice sequences of open-ended situations have to move. When authority is either highly concentrated or widely dispersed, one of the constraints on the irregularity of sequences of discoveries, choices and actions is removed. This can create so high a degree of instability as to block innovation. Chaos is constrained instability. Because of constraint there are recognizable patterns in the disorder. Such patterns provide security and allow innovations to be identified through analogous reasoning.

Participation

If widespread distribution of power as authority cannot yield the spontaneous dynamic so essential to handling the open-ended issues facing the business, can the widespread distribution of power as influence do so? It is held that power as influence is distributed by setting up complex centralist organizational structures, by defining jobs loosely so that people involve themselves in many matters, by setting up consultative forums, all encouraging widespread participation in decision making.[11] None of these steps is either necessary or sufficient to secure innovative behaviour. Influence operates when leaders are willing to apply power derived from personal ability to contribute to the handling of an issue and followers consent by themselves making contributions. How widespread this is depends upon the context within which managers operate. It depends upon the levels of mutual trust, the way people perceive their roles, the way they use their power. The widespread distribution of influence is the same thing as the emergence and operation of spontaneous communication arenas. This follows from a set of attitudes, ways of behaving which can accompany either concentrated or delegated authority, either simple hierarchical structures or complex centralist ones. Distributing influence means being willing to listen and seek advice.

Simply setting up loose systems and structures and defining jobs ambiguously, so inviting widespread participation, will not in themselves establish the effective spontaneous interactive learning that innovation requires. Studies of decision making in universites and other public bodies,[12] show how widely dispersed power, widespread participation in decision making, unstructured access to communication arenas and unclear job content, all lead to 'garbage can' decision making. Here the sequence of choices that emerge depend entirely on chance. (The chance model was discussed in Chapter 6.) In universities and other public-sector bodies, widespread distribution of power and open participation actually make it harder to make choices in open-ended situations. These organizations are not noted for continuing innovation. This is not to say that the decision-making processes used in these organizations are inappropriate to what they are there for. Those processes preserve individual freedom and allow individual innovations. But business success requires continuing innovation at an organizational level and dispersed power and widespread participation manifestly do not secure this result.

Studies on organizational learning also question the appropriateness of dispersed power and widespread participation. These studies[13] show how subordinates suffer from the same learning problems in surfacing the basic assumptions underlying their learning process as do their superiors. Simply widening participation therefore has little to do with more effective learning in an organizational context.

Instead of prescribing dispersed power and widespread participation, we should be focusing on how key groups of managers function together, starting with the top team. It is when these people interact and apply their power effectively that we get effective strategic control. This leads to the building of dynamic strategic issue agendas, to effective organizational attention to open-ended issues. The top team must communicate with and be open to suggestions from those lower down, but this does not require everyone to participate in everything.

The implication, then, is that business organizations cannot improve their ability to make innovative strategic choices by distributing power in the sense of simply widening participation and trying to freeze informal networks into organizational structures. Ability to handle open-ended issues depends upon spontaneity. That cannot be installed or structurally designed. Whether or not it occurs depends upon the context created by the manner in which power is used and the impact this has on organizational learning, not on the widespread distribution of power.

Furthermore, effective short interval control demands clear job definitions and well specified hierarchical levels of management. It requires formal rules and procedures, quantification and analytical processes. Interestingly then, a chaos theory of managing and organizing leads to the placing of just as much importance on tight short interval control and formal management hierarchies as the rational explanations of management and organization do. The difference is that a chaos theory recognizes this as one form of control only, a vital stabilizing form in the short-term, but only one form nevertheless.

From this perspective, the current trend to change organizational structures from formal hierarchies to loose networks in line with the prescriptions of the entrepreneurial explanations of management and organization, is misguided. Nowadays, some major organizations are restructuring to strip out a number of management layers and replace rigid formal structures with structures based on loose networks of managers. The reason for doing this is to enable them to cope more effectively with today's turbulent environment. A structural solution is being sought for the problem of open-ended change. A chaos perspective suggests that open-ended problems require continuous political learning processes, not frozen structural solutions. Structure is there to cope with closed and contained change. It also provides sufficient stability to enable the organization to reduce anxiety levels to the point where people are comfortable enough to cope with open-ended change. Networks should not be seen as structural replacements for formal hierarchy, but as political process additions to that formal hierarchy. Because managers simultaneously face both closed and open-ended change, they have simultaneously and alternately to operate in highly stratified formal hierarchical and loose political network terms.

Conclusion: strategic choice depends upon political context

This chapter has been concerned with an interpretation of aspects of the feedback control loop that managers use to handle open-ended change (see Figure 3.2 in Chapter 3). It has been concerned with the political processes managers use to gain attention for strategic issues through building political support for them. It has been concerned with the importance of the context provided by personality, group dynamics, types of communication arena and time pressures for the political choices made to attend to strategic issues. Those contextual factors also influence the process of dealing with the issues on the strategic agenda, the choices to progress them and ultimately back successful experiments with resource.

Scientific chaos directs our attention to the feedback nature of business organizations. It places at the centre a concern for the vicious and virtuous circles such loops are capable of generating. It points to unpredictability in specific outcomes and to the importance of constraints in providing recognizable qualitative patterns in unpredictable disorder. Those patterns make it possible to deal with unpredictability. And it highlights the importance of spontaneity in dealing with unpredictability. Thinking in this way represents a revolution in our understanding of the role of political control in business organizations. To see this, consider first the current received wisdom on the role of politics in business organizations.

In received wisdom predictable business political choices flow from stable power

Managers do not often pay explicit attention to the manner in which the political systems in their organizations function, or to the contributions that political activities make to strategic choices. Nevertheless they all engage with great frequency in political activities internal to their organizations. Most hold much the same, rarely examined views on the part that such activities play. In my consultancy and teaching experience, in conversations with managers in both the UK and the US, I have come across the following views with great regularity:

- Some managers, especially those in the middle ranks, regard the resort to political modes of making strategic choices as a failure of rationality. Or they see it as a breakdown in team consensus and commitment. Or they see it as the elevation of personal convenience and career progression above the needs of the organization as a whole. Strategic failures are so often blamed on senior executives who are seen to have imposed their will before they gathered all the facts or carried out an adequate analysis of the consequences. When an acquisition fails it is because those at the top did not take the advice of their colleagues; they should have been able to see that the acquisition would not work. Or the decision on the new location for the head office was based on the travel convenience of the chief executive. Or a particular subsidiary managing director is backing a project because it will enhance his prospects of succeeding the chief executive. Politics on this view is the dysfunctional imposition of the will of a few to satisfy their own personal desires. Power is force which disrupts team work and rational choice.
- Other managers see political activity as an inevitable method of making a choice when there is conflict around which choice to make, most often in conditions of uncertainty. Here the application of power

by those higher up in the hierarchy is the last resort in resolving conflict. It is power as authority or force, a realistic recognition that the team does not always work.

- Yet others regard political activity as charismatic leadership through which followers are inspired to believe in a vision for the future of the business and share the strong cultural norms of the organization. Power here is persuasion and inspiration which builds teams and maintains continuing consensus and commitment.

- Many, especially those in the senior ranks, see political interaction as a two-way process in which they influence subordinates who also influence them. Many senior managers do not want obedient subordinates who do as they are told, but seek those who will argue back and contribute to the best choice. Here politics is a functional contributor to strategic choice and as such is often labelled as something other than politics. It is called a consultative or participative management style. Here power is influence, a contributor to strategic choice flowing from participation, contribution and effective teamwork.

- But almost all managers see the top most powerful executives as those who drive the political process. It is they who 'own' it and ultimately control it. And they are able to control the process because they guard the distribution of power to allocate strategic resources. Prescriptions calling for widespread distribution of such power, for forms of industrial democracy, are widely regarded as impractical 'leftist' ideology. Many writers on the other hand imply that managers rejecting these views have a 'rightist' ideology.

- Almost all managers see successful politics as the application of power to build, preserve and utilize teams and common cultures so producing a state of continuing commitment and consensus. Successful politics in business organizations is disciplined teamwork which leads to orderly strategic choice. It is recognized that differences of viewpoint are necessary stimuli to the search for appropriate choices. But, conflict and dissension are not seen as central players in the political process. Attempts to explain, and prescriptions to explore, the disorderly impact of group dynamics on the political process are often regarded as organizational behaviour 'rubbish' or dangerously threatening group psychoanalysis.

- Consequently, great numbers of managers believe that successful political systems can be identified and installed. The necessary teams can be built and appropriate cultural changes made, although with great difficulty. It is not an essentially spontaneous process and it does not lead to unpredictable outcomes.

Underlying these beliefs is the assumption that political activity occurs because there is actual or potential conflict between people who have clear goals and clear preferences on how to achieve them. They derive this clarity from rational analysis and forecasting and the conflict is overcome in an orderly manner because the distribution of power is stable over time and issue. In the end, politics is about overcoming, suppressing and avoiding conflict because it is dysfunctional. This whole, widely adhered-to conception of the nature of successful politics in business organizations is clearly based on a deep seated assumption that success flows from the maintenance of order in the sense of internal harmony. Success is pulling together and facing in the same direction to achieve the same goal. Order is a state of sameness, of consensus. And an orderly state of sameness leads to an orderly state of success. Small deviations from cohesive team work, the inevitable messiness of real life, do not lead to major differences in the choices made. But introducing anything as disorderly as conflict and dissension on a significant scale leads to disorderly outcomes in terms of strategic choices. The frame of reference is that of the traditional scientific method in which approximately given causes lead through given rules to approximately predictable results.

Scientific chaos provides a completely different perspective

The new science has abandoned the traditional frame of reference and developed a revolutionary new understanding of how dynamic systems work. We in business have yet to catch up with that revolution and adjust our ways of thinking to take it into account. Cold mathematical analysis and scientific examination now demonstrate that innovation depends critically on disorder; in terms of organizations this means dissension and disagreement. Disorder can lead to order. Cold analysis and examination shows that innovative systems are highly sensitive to small deviations. That sensitivity means that they will display inherently random and unpredictable behaviour in terms of the specific paths they follow. But that random behaviour has a pattern of self-similarity. The behaviour of the system is never the same but always similar. Order takes on a new meaning; it is not sameness but similarity.

And cold mathematical analysis and scientific examination shows that we cannot control the specific unpredictable paths that dynamic systems follow. All we can do is affect the context within which they operate, either blocking or allowing, but never controlling the path of innovation. And this means that we cannot afford to dismiss a concern with group dynamics as organizational behaviour 'rubbish', because small differences in behaviour can have major impacts on choice. Nor can we afford to dismiss different views on the effect of power distribution as suspect ideology. The basic conclusions on how dynamic systems work have nothing to do with ideology, or principles of motivating people, or weird psychoanalysis. They are the factual consequences of the properties of non-linear feedback control mechanisms; they are scientific discoveries that business people cannot afford to ignore. They represent a radically different way of thinking.

This chapter has argued that the political system of a business organization is a set of non-linear feedback mechanisms. Politics is interaction between people based on power, and that interaction sometimes follows an amplifying and sometimes a damping loop. This chapter has further argued that successful political systems are those operating far-from-equilibrium where they are open and sensitive to small changes. And the next chapter explores how a business organization utilizes this far-from-equilibrium state of instability to innovate and develop new strategic direction. These two chapters demonstrate that scientific chaos establishes important principles about the dynamic properties of such systems that point to the following conclusions:

- Political activity in a business may be a dysfunctional failure of rationality. It may simply be a way of overcoming conflict when consensus breaks down. It may be a way of inspiring others with a vision and building teams. But when the dynamic is chaotic it performs a far more important role. Rationality cannot apply and consensus is an obstacle to learning when the dynamic is chaotic. Political activity then provides the interaction through which people in organizations learn.

- Political interaction is unpredictable in specific terms and so, therefore, is the specific sequence of discoveries, choices and actions that emerge from it. This is because even where the distribution of power is stable, the outcome of political activity is highly sensitive to the context within which it occurs. Small changes in context can lead to substantially different patterns of interaction. So, managers behave in certain ways at formal meetings that tend to lead to the postponement of open-ended issues. But they tend to behave in other ways at informal meetings that result in attention to open-ended issues. And at these informal meetings the interaction, the group dynamic, is volatile. Small changes in the group dynamic can have major impacts on the discoveries and choices the group makes. The context, the formality or otherwise of the meeting, the form in which power is used, may well significantly affect the outcome.

- But the pattern of such interaction and its outcomes is not only unpredictable in specific terms, it is also self-similar in general terms. This means that there are recognizable categories of interaction that are repeated over and over again. Patterns are there for those who wish to see them. So, each time a particular top management team meets to discuss an acquisition, we observe that the same two colleagues always take slightly opposing views on the issue at hand. Sometimes the first colleague expresses this as a joke, sometimes as a cynical aside, sometimes as an opposing statement on some aspect of the proposed acquisition. The other colleague sometimes responds to a joke with another joke, sometimes with an opposing statement and sometimes with a riposte bordering on anger. The chairman then usually intercedes. Or a third colleague steps in on one side or the other. The point is that this particular group dynamic has a recognizable shape, which comes as no great surprise to anyone, but on each occasion it is different. The particular aspect of the issue on which it focuses is unpredictable. Because of this, one colleague may marginalize the contribution of the other, and in this way the group dynamic has an impact on the course the discussion of the whole management team takes. When one of the two colleagues is absent the discussion takes yet another course. Because they prefer to avoid each other outside the meetings whenever possible, neither colleague puts forward proposals that require mutual collaboration. The sequence of discovery, choice and action of the whole organization will then be different from what it could otherwise have been. Specific choices are affected by chance but they have a recognizable pattern.

- The sequence of choices emerging from political interaction displays self-similarity because the political interaction does. Another way of describing the property of self-similarity is in terms of a regular irregularity. A sequence of choices has regular irregularity when the pattern of reversals, the erratic jumping about of the choices, does not come as a complete surprise to those affected by them, if they are perceptive enough. There are bounds within which the choices move, a detectable pattern in their irregularity. We detect this when we know that the managing director will fairly regularly intervene to change the work priorities he set yesterday, but he will not normally completely reverse all of them in an haphazard manner. This requires constraints preventing those choices from shooting all over the place. The managing director is constrained by the power of a subordinate or a colleague and by the difference in how much and what kinds of reversal in priorities is acceptable. Where there are no constraints provided by different levels of power or different cultural norms, choices can shoot all over the place. Difference provides the constraint that generates perceptible self-similarity. And it is self-similarity that provides order within disorder. Choice outcomes then have a manageable level of surprise, which makes it possible for people to cope with the unpredictability. Promoting innovation is more complex than simply redistributing power. Common cultural norms and widely distributed power destroy the only order there is in chaos.
- Organizations identify strategic issues because individuals use their initiative and intuition, not because of analysis and forecasts.
- All business organizations have to rely substantially on spontaneous communication to handle open-ended issues up to the point of significant resource allocation.

- A lack of consensus and commitment to particular issues is vital to the process of destroying old perceptions and creating conditions in which the new can emerge. Strongly shared cultural norms are positively harmful to the effective functioning of the political system and conflict has positive benefits. It is harmful to suppress or avoid it. Success requires different cultural norms and different perspectives. Innovation is hindered by closely knit teams.
- The normal state of political activity in an innovative organization is one of turbulence where there is a lack of consensus and commitment around issues and how to deal with them. The successful political process is one in which a fragile, temporary state of consensus and innovation emerges from chaos through spontaneous self organization.
- Consequently no one 'owns', drives or can control the successful political activity that leads to innovation. Such systems cannot be installed because spontaneity cannot be installed. But the context within which it can all happen may be created.

The key concepts in this way of thinking about political activity in business organizations are the sensitivity of outcomes to the context within which that political activity occurs; the importance of differences in viewpoint and cultural norms in shattering old perceptions; the role of unequal power distribution and different cultural norms in constraining political activity so as to produce self-similar patterns of behaviour and choice.

Further important conclusions are reached when we consider the phases through which systems far-from-equilibrium pass as they change and innovate. The next chapter examines these phases.

References

1 Bacharach, S. B., Lawler, E. J. (1980), *Power and Politics in Organizations*, Jossey-Bass.
2 Pettigrew, A. M. (1986), Some Limits of Executive Power in Creating Strategic Change, in Srivasta, S., Barrett, F. J., eds., *Executive Power*, Jossey-Bass.
3 Weick, K. (1979), *The Social Psychology of Organizations*, Addison-Wesley.
4 Cohen, M. D., March, J. G., Ohlsen, J. P. (1988), A Garbage Can Model of Organizational Choice, in March, J. G., *Decisions and Organizations*, Basil Blackwell.
5 Cohen, M. D., March, J. G., Ohlsen, J. P., op. cit.
6 Stacey, R. D. (1990), *Dynamic Strategic Management for the 1990s*, Kogan Page.
7 Moss Kanter, R. (1985), *The Change Masters*, Simon & Schuster.

8   Peters, T. (1988), *Thriving on Chaos*, Macmillan.
9   Moss Kanter, R., op. cit.
10 Moss Kanter, R., op. cit.
11 Peters, T., op. cit; Moss Kanter, R., op. cit.
12 March, J. G., Ohlsen, J. P. (1976), *Ambiguity and Choice in Organis-ations*, Bergen, Norway, Univeritesforlaget.
13 Argyris, C., (1982), *Reasoning and Learning*, Jossey-Bass.

11 Strategic 'control' is creative exploration

Among the most important principles of complex system dynamics are those that relate to the process through which feedback systems innovate. Since political systems in business are non-linear feedback mechanisms, it is argued here that these principles apply to political choices. And since innovation is by definition some significant change in what people do in a business, it requires political choice. We would expect therefore to find that innovation and the political choices leading to it are governed by the general principles applying to dynamic feedback systems. In order to innovate efficiently and continuously feedback systems must be sustained far-from-equilibrium where they are highly sensitive to small changes in the context within which they operate. Chapters 4 and 10 have demonstrated how these principles apply to business organizations as a whole and to their political systems.

Far-from-equilibrium systems in nature pass through a number of phases as they move from one complex form of order through chaos to another. These phases have already been presented in Chapter 7 and a more detailed description can be found in Appendix C. Chapter 5 summarized studies of political systems in business organizations. These studies describe a political process that bears a remarkable similarity to those found in feedback systems in nature, supporting the conclusion that the general principles of dynamic feedback systems apply. It is the purpose of this chapter to examine the phases dynamic feedback systems pass through in the context of the business political system.

In summary, the steps involved in the general order from chaos model in nature are as follows:

- Small fluctuations, or disturbances in the environment of a non-linear feedback system are detected and selected, according to some selection principle, for response by the system. The system is open and sensitive to its environment. A gas may be sensitive to heat or a chemical may be sensitive to the level of a catalytic agent. At some level of heat or catalytic agent the molecules in the gas or the chemical are arranged in a particular pattern.

- The selected disturbances are amplified through the system by the amplifying properties of the feedback rules that govern the system's behaviour. That is, the behaviour of more and more components of the system are affected by the disturbance. The disturbance spreads through the system. So as the level of heat is raised or the level of the catalytic agent is increased, the behaviour of more and more molecules is affected. The gas emits a dull glow.

- Amplification breaks symmetries. This means that existing behaviour patterns of the components of the system are disrupted. The old order is shattered and during this phase the behaviour of components of the system is one of instability and might be chaotic. The molecules in the gas or the chemical become excited and move about in an unstable manner, so destroying the pattern they formerly displayed. This phase of instability is vital to symmetry breaking, without which new order cannot emerge.

- As it proceeds through the unstable phase, which may be chaotic, the system meets critical points. At these it makes a choice, so to speak, between different options for further development. The choice is made by spontaneous self-organization among the components of the system. In effect, they communicate with each other and reach a consensus and a commitment to a choice. The particular option chosen is inherently unpredictable. Some options, which might well be chosen, represent yet more instability or chaos. Yet others lead to more complex, higher forms of order called dissipative structures. So, the molecules in the gas may suddenly all point in the same direction to produce a laser beam, or the molecules in the chemical may all suddenly move from one position to another with the absolute precision of a clock. The system has passed through instability or chaos to produce patterns of molecular behaviour that are more complex than they were before. The system has created a new form of behaviour. It has innovated.

- The new state of order, or dissipative structure, is a state of shared commitment to a new behaviour pattern, an innovation or a new strategic direction for the system. It is a state of consensus. And the key point about dissipative structures is that they require continual attention and energy if they are to be sustained. Heat has to be pumped into the gas if the laser beam is to continue. If the system is to develop further, then the dissipative structure must be short lived. To reach an even more complex state, the system will have to pass through instability or chaos once more.

So, the behaviour of the system is generated by fixed deterministic feedback rules and passes through fixed phases. But the developing path it follows is not predetermined in any specific sense. The system is experimenting, discovering and learning as it moves through real time. The process involves randomness in an essential way and the system makes unpredictable choices. The specific path of the outcomes depends upon chance. But throughout there is also a pattern. The sequence of phases through which the system passes has a predictable rhythm. The conditions required for the process to occur are predictable.

The keys to the process are: openness to the environment; sensitivity to tiny changes selected for response according to some principle; randomness and confusion; spontaneity and self-organization. And constraints or boundary conditions are essential if there are to be recognizable qualitative patterns in the unpredictable behaviour of the system. The process is highly efficient in terms of producing innovation because it requires less energy and information than that required by a shift from one equilibrium position to another.

All of this is only possible if the system is sustained in an unstable far-from-equilibrium condition. The process applies to most chemical and physical phenomena in nature and possibly to the evolution of species (see Appendices A and C). But what evidence is there that it applies to business organizations, apart from the fact that it all sounds uncannily familiar? Very strong indications that it does, are provided by studies of the sequence of political activities involved in making choices in organizations. These have already been referred to.

But the manner in which political activity is interpreted in those studies differs from the order-from-chaos explanation in important respects. Those studies pay relatively little attention to what scientists call the symmetry breaking phase; the phase during which the behaviour of the system's components is random. In current studies of the political process in organizations, the confusion and conflict required to shatter existing perceptions play a shadowy role in the background. The focus is on how consensus is sustained and on the importance of maintaining strongly shared values. Commitment and consensus are seen as the normal states of successfully functioning political systems to be attained by strongly shared cultural norms. A chaos approach to understanding how the political system functions leads to just the opposite conclusion. Current explanations of political choice are based on stable distributions of power producing predictable choices. A chaos explanation stresses the importance of context even where the power distribution is stable. Because successful political systems operate far-from-equilibrium, small changes in the choice context render political choices unpredictable.

Current explanations of the functioning of political systems also conclude that success requires a widespread distribution of power so that people are empowered and can make contributions to the political process. A chaos approach also stresses the need for contribution on a wide front but points to the conclusion that unequally distributed power provides necessary constraints. Such constraints provide the regular irregularity, the recognizable patterns, that make it possible for us to deal with unpredictability. It is how power is used, how it is skilfully alternated from one form to another, that produces success, not simply its widespread distribution. It was pointed out in the last chapter that this conclusion is supported by studies of the decision-making process where power is widely dispersed. Such decisions then depend entirely on chance.[1] The conclusion is also supported by studies on the learning process in organizations. These show that subordinates suffer from the same learning difficulties as their superiors. Widening participation is then not a sufficient condition for improving decision making.[2]

The rest of this chapter uses the order from chaos framework of the process of innovation to explain why these conclusions are reached.[3] It shows how organizations innovate through the same phases followed by non-linear feedback systems in nature.

Detecting and selecting open-ended issues

For systems in nature, the beginnings of innovation lie in small fluctuations in the environments of those systems. Some of these are selected for response by the system. In much the same way business organizations detect and select for attention small open-ended changes in their markets, technologies and methods of control.

At the start of one of my consultancy assignments, with the UK subsidiary of an international express delivery company, a number of potential disturbances to the operation of that company had been quite clearly selected for attention. That UK subsidiary provided a number of services, on a next-day-and-later basis, primarily for parcel deliveries to and from manufacturing companies. One issue had been raised around the changing composition of demand – manufacturing industry had declined in the UK while the service sectors had expanded. Some of the managers had selected issues that had to do with the changing composition of the customer base. Others saw the issues in operational terms. The volume of the larger, heavier parcels was in decline while that of the smaller lighter parcels was growing. Smaller, lighter parcels require different kinds of depots, sorting facilities and vehicle fleets. Yet other managers saw the issues in terms of cost structures. Others were more concerned with changing information technology and were talking about paperless systems. And there were those who were concerned with marketing issues and with the image the company was portraying in the changing market place. It was by no means clear which of all these and many other issues were the most important or how they were interconnected. Managers throughout that company were actively selecting open-ended issues for attention by their organization.

Open-ended disturbances cannot be detected or understood by any formal analytical process set up in advance of the disturbance occurring. Such disturbances are ill structured and unclear, small and ambiguous, giving rise to confused preferences and objectives. It is not clear what open-ended disturbances are, where they will occur or when. It follows that there can be no prior identification of, or obligation placed on, any individual to detect them or do anything about them. Neither organizational structure nor analytical process can be designed to do this job of detecting and selecting. So, the issues being selected at the express delivery company were not the result of some formal process of analysis. Who selected what issue did not relate to the existing roles of those managers in any strictly formal way. Marketing managers were concerned about the paperless system issue and operations managers were paying attention to the questions of market image. There was little information available on just how the market was changing, and such information was difficult and expensive to obtain. Information within the organization on volumes and costs was not gathered or analysed in terms of parcel size. That had not been an issue until recently, and the systems had been designed to address performance monitoring needs as they were perceived some time ago.

Intuition

In these circumstances, organizations have no option but to rely on the spontaneous willingness and ability of individuals to exercise intuition in detecting and understanding open-ended change. But intuitive thinking is not a sudden flash of genius that leads to a fully fledged definition of a problem and the solution thereto. It starts with some dim insight into a problem or opportunity that is perceived to be of potential importance. Intuitive insight comes from hard work. So, active discussion around the selected disturbances in the parcels delivery company was taking place among managers at the operational and sales levels as well as higher up in the hierarchy. Managers were drawing on their experience and intuitive judgement on how the business was changing.

In this process of intuition, the first step has to be observation of the disturbance. Individuals therefore have to be in contact with what is going on. They have to be provoked to observe some contradiction or ambiguity. Totally isolated individuals cannot begin the process of intuition, and the more open an individual is to his or her environment the more likely he or she is to develop intuition. What is required therefore is contact with others, conflict, contradiction, anomaly, stimulation and observation. The issues in the express delivery company were being provoked by the observation that smaller lighter parcels were rising in volume in a business where everyone thought of the company's strength as lying in the delivery of larger, heavier parcels. There were conflicting views as to whether small parcels were being handled at a profit or a loss.

The second step in the intuitive process is that of individual attention to the observed anomaly. Those with rigidly dogmatic approaches to the world, highly analytical straight-line thinkers who are uncomfortable with ambiguity, will block out any observed contradictions of what they already believe. Any observed discrepancy will not be amplified in the mind. Those lacking confidence or interpersonal skills are also likely to be ineffective intuitive thinkers. They will avoid, or be ineffective at the interpersonal contacts that are also necessary to amplify the disturbances to an individual's perceptions. A group of individuals who fanatically share values, who cling to common cultures, will also block the intuitive detection and selection of what is anomalous and ambiguous.

The managers at the express delivery company were not wedded to existing ways of doing things. They were open to the possibility that their business would be completely changed by what they were observing. They did not all share the same approach to resolving the issues. Some were calling for a more analytical approach based on market research. Others were suggesting special surveys to ascertain what volume of smaller parcels they were actually delivering and what the costs of doing so were. Others suggested the need to work together as a group to thrash out the issues. Yet others were calling for a strategic plan. Some were suggesting an immediate start on a small scale, setting up smaller depots and offering a letter delivery service without wasting time on extensive analysis.

The third step in this process of selecting open-ended issues is that of attracting the attention of others in the organization to the particular disturbance. The support of others in the organization has to be obtained to deal with the issue. Right at the beginning therefore, handling open-ended issues becomes a political process.

Access to communication arenas

Whoever in an organization exercises the kind of initiative and intuition called for will depend on the context within which political activity takes place. The first contextual factor is access to appropriate communication arenas and the perception that there is some chance of the issue receiving attention at such an arena. An individual will only feel this if previous experience, or observation of others, suggests that at least some of the disturbances detected are likely to receive organizational attention. Since institutionalized arenas have limited access, the ease with which the organization forms spontaneous arenas will have a major impact on whether individuals bother to use their initiative and intuition. The degree to which the institutionalized arenas are supportive or obstructive of intuitive initiatives will have a similar impact. At the point when I first became involved with the express delivery company, the discussion around most of the issues mentioned was taking place informally. But the chief executive of the UK subsidiary and the managing director of the business unit most concerned with the changes, as well as other members of the board, were all actively participating in discussions around these issues. Such discussion extended down the hierarchy. One of the more prominent protagonist of the paperless issue and the impact of smaller parcels was at the middle management level in the operations function. Managers at all levels had no doubt that those at the top were receptive to their input.

This was not an organization in which power was dispersed. There was a clear hierarchy and there was no questioning the superior power of the most senior managers. There was no formal mechanism for widespread participation in decision making. It was the attitudes and behaviour of the most senior managers that in effect invited contributions from middle managers.

Form of power

The form in which power is exerted, and the behavioural dynamic it provokes, is the second major determinant of the extent to which individuals pay attention to open-ended changes. States of impotence, power vacuums and force all seriously discourage the detection and selection of changes. There is either no point because it is clear that there can be no effective response to any issue raised for attention, or resistance, submission, passive loyalty and rivalry all distract attention from what is going on. The continuous use of power as authority clearly discourages intuitive initiatives. Such initiatives are likely to fall outside the rules that are the source of authority. The political interaction provoked by authority is one of unquestioning obedience that will block the raising of issues that question the existing order. Power exercised as influence clearly provokes the kind of dynamic required. But it is actually the skilful alternation of power in different forms that provides the most provocation for individuals to exercise intuition and initiative. We are more spurred to do things when we are alternately encouraged with helpful suggestions (influence), cajoled to perform (authority) and left to do it (power vacuum). And it is this alternation of power form, and consequent behavioural dynamic, that is a feature of the far-from-equilibrium state in a political system.

The express delivery company had a clear hierarchy. There was no question of widely dispersed authority. Any resource allocation outside the budget required the approval of the business unit managing director, the chief executive and indeed the international holding company. The business unit managers and their functional managers had delegated power in clearly defined terms that did not include authority to make significant changes to the way in which the business operated. But the more powerful were open to the participation of those lower down in developing open-ended issues. Power as influence received recognition. But there was no participation in the sense that those lower down would have much say in any decisions that would eventually be taken. All were clear on that. The key motivator to participate at all seemed to lie in the realization that those lower down would be listened to sometimes. And the manner in which the chief executive used his power was interesting. He sometimes encouraged those with contributions to make by listening to them and seeking their views. At other times he withdrew from the discussions while others thrashed around the issues. At some of the meetings he made almost no intervention at all. Many he did not even attend. Then at some points he imposed his authority on the direction in which work on the issues was proceeding, even threatening to remove one of the participants who was felt not to be making sufficient contribution.

Simply distributing power and making rules about open participation is no guarantee at all of widespread contribution to the political process or of effective organizational learning.

Workload

The third important contextual factor that affects the attention paid to open-ended issues is the workload on individuals and on communication arenas. Thought, energy and time are required if small open-ended changes are to be given definition as a problem an opportunity or even a solution without a clear problem. (For example the 3M glue was a solution searching for a problem and when it eventually found the problem, it became the familiar yellow 'Post It' note.) Time is required to sustain such attention. Without resource slack, open-ended issues will not be attended to. If the organization is running at maximum efficiency with little resource slack, the load factor will be too high to permit attention to the vague and the open-ended. This will seriously damage an organization's ability to innovate and manage change. The express delivery company did not have all its managers working on day-to-day business until late into every night. There was time and resources to devote to the discussion and exploration of open-ended issues.

That which blocks the detection and selection of open-ended disturbance follows quite clearly from these context requirements. Those organizations that concentrate power in all its forms entirely at the top, that have few communication arenas with open access and have dissatisfied members lower down in the hierarchy, in effect determine that only a few

My situation is that ... open-ended disturbance ... detect ... but not shared. Power - Small amounts are relevant by D.O's at Lo.

at the top of the organization detect and select open-ended disturbances. The real problem with such restriction to the top levels of the hierarchy is that those at the top are less able to respond effectively, simply because they are far away from the source of the change. Strong sharing of cultural norms will obstruct any individual focus on the ambiguity and contradiction on which the intuitive detection of open-ended change depends. It will also obstruct support for responding to such contradiction on the part of others.

Soon after working with the express delivery company I moved on to another assignment with a manufacturing and merchanting company in the agriculture sector. The contrast with the express delivery company was striking. The agricultural company had a confused structure. In a sense power was dispersed since the chairman had largely withdrawn and left power in the hands of three directors. But in another sense power was highly concentrated because none of the directors delegated much authority to those below. There were no opportunities for people to meet and discuss issues. Even the directors did not have much to do with each other, except for formal board meetings. The dynamic was one of rivalry between business units and compliance within each of them. Not surprisingly, that organization was in effect ignoring the many changes occurring within and around it.

On another occasion I worked with a company in the construction industry. Here authority over day-to-day matters was effectively delegated within a clear hierarchical structure, and authority to allocate strategic resources was concentrated at the top. This organization was characterized by very strongly shared cultural norms tied to methods of operating that had succeeded in the construction industry. Learning norms were strongly shared and based on the assumption that the best way to make strategic choices was that which relied on the judgement of the top two or three people in that organization. Whenever the issue of diversifying into related activities was raised, it was blocked without much serious consideration by those top few, widely supported by other senior executives. Strong values on what the business was best at and how strategic choices should be made prevented any real exploration of this particular issue.

But no organization, no matter how open it is to its environment, can detect and select for response all the open-ended changes that could potentially affect it. There is an infinite number of such disturbances. Without some selection criteria the organization would do nothing but explore open-ended issues to the detriment of its day-to-day business. The selection criteria are provided by that which determines the nature of the political system – the distribution of power and the cultural norms that are shared.

e.g. not a learning company.

Selection principles

Individuals select disturbances and build issues around them if they perceive that those with power are likely to attend to them. Highly concentrated power means that relatively few disturbances will be selected; only those likely to attract the support of those few with the authority to progress them will be selected. Widely distributed power may mean that very many issues are selected because many possess the authority to progress them. Or more likely, very few will be selected because no one possesses enough power to progress them. Power that is distributed but unequal is more likely to provide manageable selection criteria.

Even more powerful as selection criteria are those cultural norms that are shared. Such norms in effect constitute the retained memory of the organization. People remember the kinds of venture that worked for the organization in the past and those that did not. They remember the kinds of market response that were provoked in the past and those that were not. They remember those approaches to making decisions that worked in the past and those that did not. They remember those ways of treating people that worked in the past and those that did not. Where there is very little sharing of norms then there is little limitation on what is selected for attention. The organization is inundated with suggestions on what is to be done, and cannot cope. But strong sharing is just as harmful. Strong sharing means deeply embedded received wisdom, widely adhered-to company and industry recipes that provide very tight selection criteria. The weak sharing of a small range of performing norms required for the effective conduct of the existing business is likely to provide the most useful set of selection criteria.

Amplifying issues and breaking symmetries – champions and special interest groups

When most of the context factors are favourable, individuals will detect disturbances and formulate them into personal issues. Those individuals then become champions for particular issues. The principal function of the issue champion is to amplify the disturbance through the organization in order to clarify it, interpret it, continuously redefine it and gain organizational attention for it. The individual with an issue will try to persuade others of the importance of that issue. In so doing he or she is either establishing a new communication arena, a special interest group, or utilizing a previously established, loose network of allies who constitute a special interest group. Together they will work to amplify the issue, so gaining attention for it. They are faced with a great array of permanent, purpose designed arenas, a set of hastily designed arenas for specific issues and a fluid shifting set of arenas with the possibility that others may be created. Some exist by prior design while others occur by spontaneous self-organization, given that the context is favourable. Workshops on strategy, meetings called to discuss reorganization or select key managers or explore the company's aims and objectives could all provide occasions on which to promote the issue.

Building support

What is quite clearly happening is the building of support for open-ended issues through a largely spontaneous, self-organized process. The process however has a clearly and necessarily destructive aspect. Open-ended issues threaten existing structures and shared values. They require changes in perspectives if innovative responses are to be developed. Amplifying new issues through the organization therefore challenges old perceptions and existing positions, giving rise to conflict and confusion. This whole stage is one that necessarily creates confusion and disorder. Without this, the old perceptions and positions will survive and innovation will be impossible. And it is a dynamic process in which the issues are redefined, in which they change shape and emerge as rather different issues. During the process some issues are dropped and others emerge.

As it explored the issues provoked by market and technology changes, by the internal drive for growth and greater profitability, the managers in the express delivery company experienced just this confusing stage. Those pressing for the application of new technology to provide a paperless delivery system attached this issue to that of capability to deliver smaller parcels in a cost-effective manner. They produced evidence that smaller parcels now accounted for higher volumes than larger ones, and that the smaller ones were being delivered at a loss. Not all agreed with the validity of the evidence or the conclusion drawn from it. And this evidence gave rise to new issues. Was the high proportion of small parcel deliveries due to the market or to the company's pricing policies? An argument was presented which pointed to the pricing policy. That was countered by arguments that pricing policies had already been changed to prevent the taking on of small parcel deliveries at a loss. The argument was that it was all due to the market and that anyway it was desirable to develop a small parcels service. Underlying many of these arguments was the realization that changes in the nature of the business were going to change structures, systems and roles. Some would benefit and some would lose. Pressing a particular business issue was often tied up with personal ambitions.

Despite diversions, the arguments presented by the group most concerned with small parcel operation and paperless delivery issues continued to dominate the discussions. Proposals were put forward to develop a separate business unit to handle small parcel deliveries, with its

own sorting facilities and depot system. That led to discussions on
whether such a new system should be based on a national or a number of
regional sorting facilities. And costings based on existing practices raised
questions as to the efficiency of those existing practices. Arguments were
then conducted on the adequacy of the management control systems for
sorting facility, depot and vehicle utilization. These were dismissed as not
being central to the issue of developing a small parcels business. At
various points the options of focusing more on international deliveries or
same day letter deliveries were raised. And the managing director of
another business unit injected his concern that the focus of discussion
was leading to the ignoring of possibilities for business units to take
opportunities through joint action. Then others introduced a more
market oriented approach. Would customers' needs be met by one business delivering large parcels and another delivering small parcels?

For months on end then, this company was experiencing a political
process of exploring and learning about a large number of interconnected
issues that were difficult to structure. At one time the problem was
framed primarily as an operational one. At another time it was framed
mainly in technological terms. At yet other times it was framed as a
marketing opportunity. It was a period in which there was no consensus
or commitment to any one solution by the management as a whole. There
was conflict between those espousing one approach and those putting
forward another. Part of my consultancy assignment was to organize a
number of workshops to progress these issues. It was never possible to
predict how those workshops would go in specific terms – what new
issues would emerge or how already identified ones would be dealt with.
The group dynamic swung from rivalry between those with different
views, to dependence on the chief executive to articulate a direction, to
consensus that some new line of enquiry should be conducted. For
example, market research was commissioned. Patterns in the group
dynamic and the manner in which the chief executive and the managing
director of the business unit applied their power could be discerned. The
pattern of suggestion and withdrawal, encouragement and imposition of
authority, allowing conflict to develop and then intervening to end it, was
noticeable throughout. It was a pattern of similarity in which no two
occasions were exactly the same.

Shattering existing perceptions

Throughout this process, old perceptions about the business were being
destroyed: the perception that the business was a large parcel delivery
service; the perception that its management and information controls
were adequate; the perception that there was nothing wrong with the
pricing policy; the perception that the optimal operating configuration

required a national sorting facility. The dissension, the conflict, the confusion created by questioning everything was performing the essential
function of shattering old views and conventional wisdoms. And all of
this was occurring at some times and some levels in a total business that
was being conducted in a highly orderly day-to-day manner. There were
no visible signs of chaos to anyone outside the groups of managers
exploring the issues.

In other companies I have been involved with, most below the top
management level were denied access to communication arenas, including a one-to-one with superiors on open-ended issues. Here issues
fell into a pool of latent issues, which lay about until they were picked up
by one of the top executives, if they were ever picked up at all. Those
below the top level were discouraged from developing issues at all. The
tendency is for such individuals simply to 'switch off' and concentrate on
the 'job'. In these organizations, most communication arenas are filled
with symbolic, administrative and reviewing-the-past functions. This
effectively denies access for open-ended issues. Those organizations
displayed continuing consensus and commitment to their existing business. Those organizations did not display lengthy periods of confusion
and conflict around issues. And those organizations did not develop
significantly different, innovative businesses. They are still doing what
they were doing long before.

The principal mechanism for amplifying new perspectives through an
organization is its issue champions and the special interest groups that
form around them. It is through such political feedback mechanisms that
issues receive organizational attention. That is, they reach the strategic
issue agenda of that organization. And the process is essentially disorderly, characterized by confusion, conflict and dissensus. Its specific
outcomes are unpredictable, but patterns of behaviour and choices that
emerge are self-similar. People can deal with the chaos because they can
recognise categories of behaviour and choice even though each specific
instance is different from all others. They can deal with the new open-
ended situations presented to them because they look for analogies with
similar situations in the past and elsewhere. And they use these analogies
to develop new mental models to understand what is going on and to
choose what to do.

Amplifying issues and breaking symmetries: experimenting with open-ended issues

The process of detecting and selecting disturbances to the existing business is primarily spontaneous, as is the subsequent phase of amplifying it
through the organization to shatter old perceptions. Both are conducted
through spontaneous communication arenas. At various points,

however, an open-ended issue will have to appear on the agenda of one of the institutionalized arenas. It is here that attention to the issue is legitimated and resources made available to pursue it. Part of the organizational process of exploring an issue, part of the process of changing perceptions on how to conduct the business and what business to conduct, is the carrying out of some experiment. The vehicle for carrying out such experiments is a task force, a multi-discipline project team of some sort. And this requires resources which it is the prerogative of institutionalized arenas to allocate. During the process in which the express delivery company explored the issues confronting it, some of those issues appeared as formal agenda items at the regular, formal management meetings. One such item related to the authorization of expenditure on market research. Another involved the setting up of a task force to develop proposals on paperless delivery systems and small parcel delivery capability. And yet another was authorization of an experiment to test the market for same-day letter delivery at one or two of the more suitable depots.

Task forces

Task forces are also communication arenas, ones designed with greater clarity of purpose and tighter focus on choice and action than the special interest groups and workshops discussed so far. But they are concerned with experiments. They are concerned with activities and ways of doing things that are in some sense new to the organization. Task forces conduct prototype product or production process developments; trial advertising campaigns; small trial operations in new markets and new countries. A high degree of spontaneity is required in the conduct, if not the creation, of such arenas. Initially task forces are not part of the institutionalized set of arenas, although they may later become so. Normally a task force is temporary and calls for a wide range of skills and functions, cutting across the existing organizational structure – it is a multidiscipline project team.

Successful task forces require continuing attention and support from top management and their institutionalized arenas. Task forces are all about experiments, about trial-and-error, so there will be errors and they are part of the learning process. The functioning of task forces will be blocked unless there is permission to fail. Inability to establish, conduct and support task forces will mean that the organization cannot experiment and so cannot learn about highly uncertain change. The express delivery company had a successful tradition of establishing and running task forces to explore open-ended issues. The formal management team maintained a continuing interest in their progress and called for regular reports on that progress. Another company I worked with did not. If some new business venture put forward by someone well below the top level was ever authorized, the top management team lost interest in it. None of those ventures, with which I am familiar, ever succeeded.

Strategic issue agenda

The detection and selection of ill-structured issues arising from open-ended change depends on the spontaneous exercise of initiative and intuition by individuals, the issue champions. The amplification of that issue so that it gains organizational attention depends upon the spontaneous formation of special interest groups, the building of political support and the formation of coalitions. But this is not simply a political process, the application of power to make a choice. It is also a learning process to discover what choice to make. Such learning proceeds through discussion and group interaction, through testing potential consequences of the issue by experimental, trial-and-error actions. And these are conducted by intentionally designed task forces with a high degree of spontaneity. The organization is in effect building an agenda of strategic issues; an implicit list of items that managers judge it important to attend to if the organization is to innovate and develop new strategic direction. That agenda is dynamic and changing; issues on that agenda are continually redefined, new ones are added and old ones disappear. The process of amplifying disturbances and building strategic issue agendas is one that threatens existing ways of doing things and changes existing perceptions of what should be done and how. It therefore cannot occur without creating confusion, generating dissension and weakening commitment to the existing order.

So, a business moves towards innovation through a process of political learning that has four important phases. The first is selection of disturbances to attend to. The second is amplification of the disturbance through the organization to gain attention for it. The third is confusion, dissensus and lack of commitment to the old, which shatters existing forms of order and paves the way for the new to take their place. The fourth is a process of spontaneous self-organization that yields a fragile state of consensus for a particular choice. The process is essentially the same as that observed in other systems driven by non-linear feedback mechanisms, those to be found in nature.

Fragile state of consensus and commitment

At some point during the discussions, the learning, the political manoeuvring and the experimentation, sufficient consensus and commitment is reached to enable a choice. Potentially successful proposals or experiments may be legitimated and substantial enough resource allocated to them to realize an innovation, a new strategic direction. And legitimation, decisions to allocate resources, are matters for the organization's institutionalized communication arenas. Prior to this point the role of the institutionalized arenas in a business is primarily one of symbolic support and encouragement for the process of reaching a consensus.

Institutionalized arenas (board meetings, top management meetings, formal one-to-one meetings) make their most important contribution to the handling of open-ended issues through the symbolic, past interpretation and decision functions. Symbolic support of the work of task forces is vital to their continuing operation. Interpreting and judging the likely success or failure of experiments being conducted by task forces leads up to legitimating what they are doing. It leads to deciding whether to back potential success with energy and resource. This resource allocation decision leads to business innovation and new strategic direction for the organization as a whole.

So, after months of exploring the issues described above, the express delivery company put together a set of coherent proposal, for expanding its total capability on a national scale. The proposals were designed to handle both small and large parcels and to develop same-day letter services. These proposals were approved by the international holding company. Work then began on identifying new depot sites and designing the expanded operational capability. But the world does not stand still. The international holding company increased the emphasis it was placing on expansion into the European market and the UK managers became involved in that. Then the opportunity arose for the express delivery company to acquire another company with whom it had been running a joint venture. That company had its own small parcel delivery capability. It was acquired and the problem then became one of integrating the two operations. And each new development raised anew what the changes meant and how they should be responded to. The particular strategic direction that involved building new depots and sorting facilities had by this time been replaced with one of expansion by acquisition. And managers were in a better position to deal with that acquisition because of the work they had put into developing proposals for expansion by organic growth.

The point is that the consensus achieved around one direction, and the commitment to that direction, had rapidly dissolved into the dissensus required to continue the process of innovation. In nature's systems the new complex orderly states, which emerge by spontaneous self-organization from chaos, are dissipative. They require continuing inputs of energy if they are to be sustained. In just the same way, the consensus and commitment, the innovation and new strategic direction that emerges from a largely spontaneous process in a business is fragile.

Change continues to occur. The need to continue innovating means that dissensus and lack of commitment to any one innovation and direction have to be the norm for successful businesses.

The express delivery company example illustrates another important point. The outcomes of the innovation process, the consequences of choices made at critical points are inherently unpredictable. When the small parcel issue was first identified it was not possible to predict the form of the consensus that would be reached. When that consensus was reached and the implementation was embarked upon it was not possible to predict the other changes that would occur to take the company in a rather different direction. And this too is a characteristic of the innovative development of nature's systems that are far-from-equilibrium. Strategies emerge unpredictably, they are not planned.

The important conclusion to be reached from this explanation of how successful businesses innovate is this: systems and procedures, specific management controls, cannot be installed to ensure innovative outcomes; it is impossible to install a political learning system that is essentially spontaneous; it is counterproductive to install a system to maintain continuing consensus and commitment when the very nature of innovation requires the opposite; innovation and change themselves cannot be managed; spontaneity cannot be built into structures.

What managers can do is operate on the context within which innovative learning occurs. This amounts to removing obstacles that block the spontaneous, unpredictable process from occurring. Operating on the context means: skilfully alternating the form in which power is applied; promoting trust; maintaining workloads at levels that allow enough time to learn about open-ended issues; creating communication opportunities where spontaneous interaction is possible; supporting champions and task forces; not filling institutionalized arenas with purely symbolic functions. Above all it means promoting difference, not sameness. This means abandoning today's excessive concern with strongly shared cultures.

A study of Japanese companies (NEC, Nippon Telegraph and Telephone, Sharp, Ricoh, Pioneer, Seven Eleven, Honda, TDK, Canon, Matsushita, Epson)[4] demonstrates how they practise self-renewal by sustaining non-equilibrium, promoting several counter cultures, presenting creative but equivocal challenges, exploring contradictions, conveying a sense of crisis, making a decision in the morning and changing it in the evening. The purpose of all this is continuously to provoke the new perspectives upon which innovation depends. But it is all done within the constraints presented by clear hierarchies and unequally distributed power.

Conclusion: how organisations proceed when they do not know what they are doing

Throughout the journey of an issue from a small open-ended change to a new strategic direction, there are a number of critical points at each of which the outcomes cannot be predicted. Those critical points are depicted in Figure 11.1. One such point lies at the detection and selection stage – point A in Figure 11.1. Will an individual detect a disturbance and understand enough of it to take it up? Since we do not know what we are looking for, we cannot prearrange the selection. Whether it happens or not is unpredictable. All an organization can do is create the conditions that facilitate detection. For example, one company I worked with made a decision to expand its existing building block capability by investing in a new factory. It did so after thorough analysis of the market and the costs. It dismissed a potential threat from an alternative way of building houses using the timber frame method. The costs of the timber frame method were not significantly different and people in the UK preferred block and brick houses. But a new competitor appeared and promoted timber frame housing. Consequently the market for blocks declined. Some years later, after a television programme attacking timber frame methods, this technique went into decline and the block market boomed. Whether or not such small changes are detected and taken seriously at the critical time depends upon chance. So at point A in Figure 11.1 we may go on to point

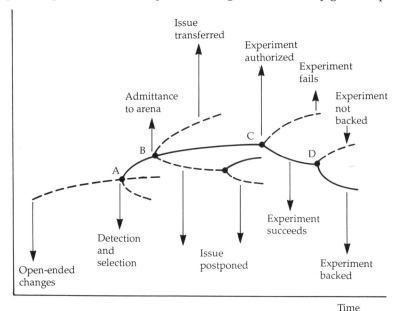

Figure 11.1 *Unpredictable choices at critical points*

B or continue along the unstable dotted line of ignoring the small changes.

The amplification stage is characterized by a critical point – B in Figure 11.1. Will an issue be admitted to the agenda? Will it be postponed or rejected? Will it be resolved by experiment? Given all the other issues confronting the business, attention to any one issue is to a significant extent a matter of chance. We may therefore continue along the firm line to another critical point at C or we may move along the unstable dotted line that represents latent issues not being attended to. Since we cannot know which issues will turn out to be really important and which will not, we cannot design a system to ensure that the really important issues are attended to. All the organization can do is establish the conditions that are conducive to the creation of arenas and the authorization of experiments.

Another critical point is confronted when we come to the backing of a potentially successful experiment – point D in Figure 11.1. Will it really work on a large scale? Is it really the basis of a new strategic direction? Will the experiment attract enough backing and support? Since we cannot know in advance how experiments will turn out we cannot prearrange the answer. All the organization can do is to create an environment in which backing is not obstructed.

At each critical point, detecting and selecting a change for attention, attracting attention for it, backing it with resource, the organization faces a choice. The outcome of that choice depends upon the context in which it is taken at the time – the workload on people and communication arenas, the other functions to be performed, the other issues requiring attention, the form in which power is applied and the group dynamic it provokes. Because the choice is sensitive to context its outcome cannot be predicted. The organization may make a choice that leads to some innovation or new direction, or it may continue down paths of confusion.

And this is how organizations have to proceed when they do not know what they are doing. That is, when they are managing open-ended change. The whole process is essentially one of organizational learning, one with consequences that are not really all that surprising, but that we resist explicitly accepting. Innovations and new strategic directions emerge from a process involving abrupt, spontaneous self-organization at critical points, very like that now known to characterize many of nature's systems. Afterwards we rationalize it, claim that it was 'decided', that we have been pursuing a strategy.

The difficulty many have in accepting this view lies in the fact that it means admitting that we do not really know what we are doing; we do not really know where we are going. This would indeed be a shocking thing for the chairman of a major corporation to admit. It would hardly be acceptable to the financial markets to proclaim the real truth that, although we do not know where we are going we do have in place learning mechanisms to find out. We cannot control the outcome, but we are very much in control of context within which complex learning can take place. Instead of applauding ex-post-rationalization, financial institutions should be backing honest attempts to improve the learning process.

The really important question for innovation is not how well ordered the organization is. The question is whether the organization has enough inbuilt acceptance of the disorder through which it must continuously pass if it is to develop the more complex order that is innovation and new strategic direction. It means sacrificing some short-term efficiency to create the management resource slack which allows spontaneous communication arenas to form and operate so that the organization may learn. It means seeing training and development, not simply as training people in functional skills, but as a vital part of the control system, in all respects as important as the latest computerized system or investment in the newest technology.

This political process, one of creative, interactive learning, is essentially one of generating and spreading new perspectives. It is about creating new meanings and therefore improving the qualitative aspects of information. Such new perspectives arise in conditions of contradiction, conflict, confusion and ambiguity. They are provoked by exciting challenges. All this is chaos and without chaos there can be no qualitative improvement of information, no new meanings, no reformulation of problems. Such chaos is vital for the symmetry breaking process, in which old ideas are shattered and new ones emerge. Without chaos there can be no innovation, nothing creative. The recognition of chaotic dynamics is not a cause for alarm. Organizations are capable of discovering, choosing and acting when the dynamic is chaotic. And more than that, such a dynamic makes it possible for an organization to be continually innovative and creative. It means that individual managers play a major part in creating the futures of their organizations.

This chapter has been concerned with an interpretation of the feedback control loop that managers deploy in open-ended change situations. That loop was depicted in Figure 3.2 in Chapter 3. The interpretation given here is one of a number of phases that constitute a creative journey of exploration into an unknowable future.

The final section of this book considers how managers might intervene to prompt and encourage the spontaneous, self organizing learning and political processes through which the business organization builds strategic issue agendas and copes with open-ended change.

References

1   Cohen, M. D., March, J. G., Ohlsen, J. P. (1988), A Garbage Can

Model of Organizational Choice, in March, J. G. *Decisions and Organization*, Blackwell.

2 Argyris, C. (1982), *Reasoning, Learning and Action*, Jossey-Bass.
3 Prigogine, I., Stengers, I. (1985), *Order out of Chaos*, Flamingo; Nonaka, I. (Spring 1988), Creating Organisational Order out of Chaos: Self Renewal in Japanese Firms, *California Management Review*; Gemmill, G., Smith, C. (1985), A Dissipative Structure Model of Organisational Transformation, *Human Relations*, vol. 38, no. 8.
4 Nonaka, I., op. cit.

Part Four
Dynamic Management, Choice and Action

The choices managers make and the actions they design all depend upon the mental models they use to understand the operation of their business. The conventional belief is that successful businesses are those that maintain an orderly, dynamic internal and external equilibrium. With this mental model, managers will foster strong adherence to a uniform view of the future and a common culture. They will follow strategies to fit their capabilities to given market requirements. Chaos is a revolution for managerial action because it requires us to reappraise that conventional wisdom for purely scientific reasons. These reasons have to do with the factual nature of the feedback loops that govern the behaviour of a business.

Continuing success in business today depends on the ability to innovate and develop new strategic directions. This flows from the ability of people in an organization to see things differently, to develop new perspectives, to amplify small changes so that they become major innovations. New perspectives can only emerge if we question old ones, if we shatter old ways of looking at things. That process of breaking old orders must be confusing at first. Questioning old values is bound to cause conflict. Ambiguity is bound to be generated. And all of this is disorder and chaos. Disorder and chaos are prerequisites for the generation of the new in organizations. Continuing innovation arises from continuing confusion and conflict. The traditional model that focuses thinking on order and stability is therefore at odds with the requirements of innovation. What we need is a model that focuses on the nature of disorder and instability. And this is what chaos explanations do. Instability and conflict are at the forefront of a chaos model, not in the shadowy background they usually occupy in explanations of managing and organizing.

From a chaos perspective we come to see equilibrium as failure and the dynamic of success as:

- Creative interaction between a business and the other organizations and people that are its environment. Successful managers create their own environment. They do not simply adapt to it.
- A normal state of dissensus and disagreement between people in an organiz-

ation, people having weakly shared cultures, all of which is vital to innovation.

- A difficult-to-sustain and ever changing position between the forces of division differentiation and adaptation on the one hand, and integration and isolation on the other. These forces pull the organization to equilibrium states that are failure; success lies in the chaotic border between them.

And the consequence of seeing the organizational dynamics of success in chaos terms is a profoundly different approach to designing actions to 'control' the organization in a strategic sense. We need to arrange our affairs on the basis that we cannot know specific future outcomes at all. If we do this we take significantly different actions to those we take if we believe that we can know something useful about the specific future. The chapters in Part Four explore those differences.

12 Chaos: a different perspective for action

The purpose of the final project of one of my students was to identify, and make recommendations to improve, the strategic decision-making process of that student's organization. The organization is a significant division of a major multinational company. The student conducted interviews with the division's top management team and with a large sample of the next level down in the hierarchy. These managers were asked if the company had a strategy, what the strategy was and how specific strategic decisions were made. The student was somewhat surprised at what emerged from the interviews. Every manager thought that there was a strategy, but the majority did not know what it was, and that included some members of the top management team. They believed that managers at the level above them knew where the company was going. The remaining managers claimed to know what the strategy was but their expositions were rather vague, and furthermore they differed significantly from each other. And this organization had a formal planning process and a long-term corporate plan. The top team also occasionally went on weekend retreats to discuss strategy in general. When asked how strategic decisions were made, the managers described the formal planning process and the programme of formal meetings that were regularly held. But when asked to describe how some specific decision had been made, they talked about individual personalities and how powerful they were.

Variations on these same themes have run through all my interviews, during consultancy assignments and in seeking to obtain them, with managers in some three dozen companies over the past five years. There was a universal belief that top managers either do, or should, know where the company is going. But in fact they did not, in any usefully specific sense. There was always the same inability to articulate anything very specific and the same diversity of views on what the strategy was.

Sometimes the top team did all make the same very general points, which had little operational content. But they were surprised to discover that those below them did not know what the strategy was, even after much effort had been put into formal communication. General discussions on how strategy should be formulated focused on formal procedures and organizational structures. But reviews of how specific decisions had been made always referred to informal discussions, personalities and power, with very little reference to the plans and strategy formulation procedures.

There is a widespread gap between what managers say they do, the explicit explanations they put forward on how to achieve success, and what they actually do when confronted with open-ended strategic issues. It seems that explicit explanations break down and they fall back on implicit understandings of how to do things. How is it that this occurs?

When we articulate an explanation of what we are doing, we always do so within a particular frame of reference. That is, we always do so using implicit models we have developed through past experience and education. The frame of reference, the implicit models, determine what we look for and how we construct an explanation. This book has put forward the proposition that the frame of reference we use to explain managing and organizing businesses has been imported from the traditional scientific method in which we have all been educated. This is a machine frame of reference in which a given cause leads through fixed laws to a given effect. Establish the causes, identify the laws and the outcomes are determined and fixed. There is only one possible future and the world works like a machine to produce orderly outcomes. The problem is that we have not so far been able to identify all the laws and all the causes. What we observe therefore is underlying regularity in the behaviour of any system determined by the laws we have identified. But superimposed upon this, and separate from it, is irregularity caused partly by our inadequate knowledge of the laws governing the system (noise or error), but primarily by random shocks coming from the system's environment. The random shocks are the main part of what we cannot yet explain. They are the source of the open-ended change we face. Also within this machine frame of reference is the belief that the behaviour of a system may ultimately be either stable or explosively unstable. Since nature's systems are clearly not in a state of explosive instability, they must be in an underlying state of stability. Since successful human systems are not normally in a state of explosive instability either, they too must be at least tending to stability. And the dynamic of a system is then thought to be driven by the forces leading to stability and equilibrium. The dynamic can be described in terms of systems adapting to changes in their environments so as to maintain a continuing match or fit. These implicit understandings are normally below the level of awareness and are therefore rarely examined and questioned. We simply use them; we do not examine them every time we articulate an explanation.

Dynamic equilibrium

Conditioned by this frame of reference, all the predominant explanations of managing and organizing see business success as a state of dynamic equilibrium. Here the successful business organization:

- Maintains a continuing balance between its internal capability and the requirements of its markets. As the markets change, successful companies change in step to maintain the moving balance that is dynamic equilibrium. Success follows from – innovation is – a continuing adaptation to the environment. The criteria for judging strategies is that they should fit the market and be internally consistent. Successful businesses design control systems, management styles, types of strategy and organizational structures to be appropriate to their size and the environments they operate in. In this sense, organizations are seen as contingent upon their environments, leading to prescriptions for mechanistic organizations in stable environments and organic ones in volatile environments. When we try to explain why different structures, styles, systems and strategies exist, we look for the reasons in the environment.
- Establishes and sustains continuing internal harmony. In the face of change, people within the successful organization remain committed and consensus between them is the normal state of affairs. Success is a state of equilibrium between personal and organizational goals secured through strongly shared cultural norms.
- Maintains a continuing balance between the forces requiring division of tasks and differentiation on the one hand, and integration and synergy on the other. As markets and technologies change, successful organizations continuously sustain the equilibrium balance between division and integration.

On this view, there are clear causes and clear effects. The problem is to identify the laws connecting them. Success in business flows from stability and regularity. It is an orderly state that can be secured through discipline, leadership, structure, culture and motivating people. It is this state which generates the underlying patterns of performance, choice and behaviour in the business. The dynamic of success is order. The erratic movements we observe around the underlying patterns are due to random shocks from the environment. The successful organization responds to a shock by adapting and returning to equilibrium. And thinking in equilibrium terms leads to the view that there is only one future for a business, or at least only a limited number. Success comes from specifying the direction to that identifiable future.

The prescriptions

Now if, below the level of awareness, managers assume that a business works like a computing machine, they will articulate explicit explanations of business success along the following lines:

- There is always a purpose and it should be fixed in advance of acting. Hence the concern with setting immediate objectives, formulating missions, expressing dreams and visions;
- There are identifiable criteria for success which should be fixed in advance of acting. Hence the prescriptions for fit between strategies, structures and style on the one hand and the markets on the other. Success is the equilibrium adaptation of the business to its markets.
- Decision-making should be a rational process in which the data is gathered and analysed in a step-by-step procedure leading to a definite solution. Or decision-making should be an emotional, exciting process, which leads to trial-and-error search for a definite solution.
- Orderly decision-making processes should be maintained through organizational structures and through binding people together into cohesive teams that share strong cultural norms.
- Finding a solution quickly, either in advance or as a result of the action, is the key to success.
- There are general recipes and appropriate systems that can be installed to deal with a wide range of specific new situations.

The result is then a highly rational view of how a business should work – it should work utilizing objectives, criteria and orderly step-by-step procedures just as a computer does. But most managers are ambivalent about this. The world is messier than this and when we are too obviously confronted with the mismatch between rationality and reality we retreat into mysticism. Modern managers then maintain a myth of rationality – someone up there knows what the strategy is. Or there is an almost religious approach and managers then talk about bands of brothers in adversity, inspired by visions and missions for the future.

The problem with dynamic equilibrium

So far we have talked about the frame of reference, the implicit mental models, that managers use when they articulate what they are doing. And much of the time they use these articulated models to design their actions. But, a central proposition put forward in this book is that the frame of reference leads to explanations of managing and organizing that ignore very important aspects of the dynamics of the business world. The frame of reference itself blocks explanations that incorporate the effects of disorder, instability and chance on the dynamic development of a business. Those explanations do not then account for amplifying feedback, for escalating small changes, for self-reinforcing vicious and virtuous circles, all of which are extremely important in open-ended situations. Consequently today's explicit models are defective when it comes to designing actions in open-ended situations. When managers come to design their actions in those situations, they therefore automatically turn to different implicit models. They have to turn to implicit models outside the machine frame of reference if they are to design successful actions in open-ended situations. These models are also below the level of awareness and are therefore rarely examined or questioned. The reason that managers say one thing and do another, so particularly noticeable in open-ended situations, is that they are sometimes using implicit models to explain that are different to the implicit models they use to design their actions. The result is conflicting behaviours, anomalies and unintended actions. Because we are then not sufficiently aware of what we are doing, we may well design inappropriate actions. To deal with this problem we need a more useful frame of reference within which to explain what we actually do, so that we may design more appropriate actions. And this book argues that chaos theory provides this more useful frame of reference.

Before scientists discovered the chaotic properties of feedback mechanisms it was believed that the behaviour of any system was ultimately either stable or unstable. We now know that as non-linear systems move from stability to instability, they pass through a state of bounded instability which is chaos. There is another choice. In addition to that between stability and instability there is the chaos choice. When systems operate in chaos, they generate patterns of behaviour that are random at the specific level, but qualitatively self-similar at a general level. This means that the specific behaviour cannot be decomposed into a uniform part and another part which is irregular noise or error. The whole pattern is generated by the same law and it is erratic at one level and similar at another. The very structure of the system itself generates the irregularity and similarity we observe in its development. The underlying laws do not generate uniformity as was previously thought. Variety and uniformity come from the same source, the structure of the system, not simply from random shocks arising in the environment. The development of the system is affected by chance in an essential way because of the sensitivity to small changes, not simply because it is affected by random shocks from the environment. A fundamental property of systems operating in chaos is amplifying feedback which leads to the escalation of small changes and the development of virtuous and vicious circles. This means that there is often no clear link between a given specific cause and a fixed specific effect. It is then quite possible for systems to generate unintended outcomes, even if we fully understand what is going on.

It is the chaos choice that explains the creative combination of order and disorder we observe in nature. The dynamic of such creative systems is not driven by forces leading to stability, but by forces sustaining the system far-from-equilibrium.[1] Because most of nature's systems do not operate in orderly equilibrium states, because they operate in states of instability far-from-equilibrium, they are capable of exciting variety and continuing creativity. And because of this dynamic, many of nature's systems are capable of abrupt transformations of the whole system through a process of spontaneous, unpredictable choice.

Reviewing central beliefs about success

This book has argued that a business organization is driven by non-linear feedback mechanisms. It is therefore capable of chaotic behaviour. And to be innovative, it has to operate far-from-equilibrium in chaos. Because of this understanding, we need to review many of the central beliefs we hold today about the nature of business success. For it means that the long-term future of any individual business organization is absolutely unpredictable, making strategic proaction impossible; that innovation and strategic direction depend significantly on chance; that a lack of commitment and consensus is vital to innovation. But it also means that the initiatives and actions of single individuals can have a profound, if unpredictable, effect on how an organization develops over time. It means that what an organization does can have a significant impact on the environment in which it operates. Simple reaction to given environmental change is then not a meaningful concept because in a sense the environment also adapts to the organization. The environment is not given, but partly created by what the organization does. Since neither proaction nor reaction are possible responses to issues having long-term consequences, the business is left with real-time creative exploration of those consequences as the only alternative. If the dynamic of a successful business is chaotic, then we have to abandon long-term plans and visions, uniform cultures and the search for predictive models and prescriptions which lead directly to some specific form of success. Instead we have to concentrate on establishing conditions within which people in an organization can create, explore and learn as they act in real time. And this chaotic view of the business world is far more exciting than long-term plans or visions and the predictability upon which such plans and visions depend.

It is then a matter of considerable importance for managers to decide whether their business requires a chaotic dynamic if it is to be successful.

If the answer is yes, then that has major implications for the whole understanding of managing, organizing and controlling. This book has presented a number of arguments indicating that the dynamic of business success is indeed chaotic. The contention is that if managers think about their business in these terms, they will be directed to more useful actions in conditions of great uncertainty.

Chaos, the science of feedback mechanisms, challenges a whole way of thinking. Since business organizations are driven by feedback mechanisms, it has direct relevance to the world of business. But it does not provide some universal new management technique. It is a different way of thinking about how the world works, within which to design more effective actions in conditions of great uncertainty. This way of thinking is based not on ideology of any sort, but on the factual nature of feedback control loops. Where a system is governed by such loops, a given cause can lead, through fixed laws, to totally random, inherently unpredictable behaviour. There is not one future for such a system, but infinitely many futures. Perfectly orderly systems can generate chaos, which is a far-from-equilibrium state. And furthermore, if systems are to innovate, they must be sustained far from equilibrium, in a state of instability. This book has maintained that innovative businesses work in that way too, because they are governed by feedback mechanisms and because the equilibrium states of those mechanisms are ones incapable of coping with open-ended change. The principal conclusions to be drawn from scientific chaos for the functioning of business organizations over the long-term are:

- Long-term purpose in a specific operational sense cannot be fixed in advance. It is part of that which is to be discovered.
- Criteria for success that have to do with equilibrium and adaptive fit of the organization to its environment lead to failure, not success.
- Decision-making about issues with long-term consequences cannot be a rational process. It is impossible to gather the data in advance and perform analytical step-by-step procedures. Neither can it be some visionary, almost religious process. Managers have to rely instead on individual initiative, intuition and experience; on working to learn together in groups. Solutions are discovered through groups of people discussing and reflecting upon what they have done and are doing; discussing and reflecting upon how they are doing it.
- Maintaining orderly decision-making processes, relying on structures, strongly shared cultures, continuing commitment and consensus, are all death to innovation. Innovation requires dissensus, not consensus. It depends on people having different cultural values. It is a spontaneous process which cannot be created through inevitably frozen structures.

Scientific chaos is a revolution because it shifts the whole way managers should think when it comes to explaining and designing strategic actions, for purely scientific reasons. It shifts the emphasis:

From	*To*
order	disorder
sameness	difference and similarity
discipline	spontaneity
structural solutions	political and learning interaction in groups
information processing, techniques and action	meaning, reflection and discussion
myths and mysticism	self-examination

This different way of thinking makes it more likely that we will use the same implicit models to explain and to act in open-ended situations. We will then not sometimes apply our explicit models and at other times turn to implicit models that are different to those we use when we articulate what we do. This will reduce conflicting, confusing, wasteful and unintended actions.

A chaos model of managing and organizing is summarized in the next section. It is then compared with today's most prominent explanations.

A chaos explanation of managing and organizing

A chaos model for designing management action focuses on what we have always done to manage and organize when we do not know, and cannot know, what we are doing. It focuses on explanations of organizing and managing to which practitioners have so far paid relatively little attention. This different focus may enable us to cope better with such difficult situations.

Scientific chaos provides the framework for a revolutionary explanation of how innovative businesses are managed dynamically in turbulent times. The key steps in this explanation are as follows:

- The performance over time of any business is driven by amplifying and damping feedback loops. Profits are fed back into investment, research and development, advertising and promotion, all of which feed back in turn to profit. The amplifying and damping nature of the loops is a consequence of constraints, financial, capacity, skill, the laws of diminishing returns.
- The parameters in those performance feedback loops are determined partly by the organization's relationships with other organizations and people (the environment) and partly by the whole decision-making process

- The forces of task integration, market and production process synergy, orderly motivation of people and organizational goals, pull the organization to the equilibrium of ossification. This occurs when the parameters in the feedback mechanisms are low. That is, when the decision-making process is unresponsive. The forces of task division, market segmentation and production process separation, emotional motivation of people and personal goals, pull the organization to the equilibrium of disintegration. This occurs when the parameters in the feedback mechanism are high. That is, when the decision-making process is highly responsive. Ossification and disintegration are equilibrium positions because strong forces keep the organization in those positions once they are reached. It is difficult to change such organizations. Neither of these equilibrium states allows innovation and they are therefore states of failure in open-ended situations.
- Innovative organizations are consequently those sustained by their management in the border area between two fatal equilibria. Such a border area is far-from-equilibrium: chaos.
- The relationships of a business with other organizations and people in the environment are also amplifying and damping loops. Where the organization is highly unresponsive to its environment, the parameters in the feedback are low and it is in an equilibrium state of isolation. Where that organization is highly responsive to the given requirements of its environment, the parameters in the feedback are very high and it is in an equilibrium state of adaptation. Innovative success, where the organization interacts to create partly its own environment, lies between these two equilibrium states. It is far-from-equilibrium in chaos. This conclusion is supported when we observe that small changes can escalate and there are self-reinforcing vicious and virtuous circles in the development of markets.
- The long-term decision-making process of a business is a political learning one. Political and learning activities are amplifying and damping feedback loops. Interaction here is drawn to states of compliance when power takes the form of authority, rivalry when there is a power vacuum, dependence and frustration when there is impotence and submission or rebellion when power is applied as force. None of these equilibrium states makes innovation possible. Successful long-term decision-making processes are therefore chaotic and far-from-equilibrium. Here the form of power is alternated and the group dynamic is volatile. This creates a context within which small changes can escalate with unpredictable consequences. Control in open-ended situations is amplifying feedback.
- The short-term control process is a planning and monitoring loop that utilizes the possibility of making short-term forecasts of the behaviour of chaotic systems. It is a damping feedback control loop.

The dynamic of the innovative and thus ultimately successful business, is chaotic in performance, chaotic in long-term decision-making and chaotic in terms of relationships with the environment. The principal characteristics of the far-from-equilibrium, chaotic state are:

- Extreme sensitivity to selected small changes in the environment and the context of the decision-making process, with the consequence that long-term sequences of strategic choices and consequent performance depend significantly upon chance. They are inherently unpredictable in terms of specific long-term paths.
- Self-similarity in strategic choice sequences, relationships with the environment, and long-term performance. Self-similarity applies at a general level. It means that patterns of performance, environmental relationships and choice sequences bear a recognizable resemblance to each other. They fall into categories that are always similar but never the same in specific terms. It means that choice sequences, environmental relationships and performance all display regular irregularity that people can recognize if they are perceptive. Self-similarity arises when choice sequences are constrained by different cultural norms, different levels of power and clear hierarchies. It provides the order and stability without which people could not cope with unpredictability. It provides situations in which we can reason by analogy, using recognizable qualitative patterns to develop new specific models to design our actions in new specific situations. We can recognize the patterns because of our past experience. The instrument of control in open-ended situations is then the changing of mental models that constitutes learning and political activity. The instrument alters with the changes being dealt with. The instrument of control is not fixed in advance of the change.
- Strategic choice sequences depend upon the context within which they are taken. The manner in which power is used affects the interaction between people – the group dynamic. The group dynamic in turn affects how a group of people learns together, what they learn and thus what choices they make. Small changes in the way power is used can have major impacts on the group dynamic, the learning process and thus the choice sequence.

The innovative business organization uses the above characteristics of the far-from-equilibrium chaos state to innovate in the following manner:

- Because the context of the formal, institutionalized meetings of the business dictate that they will shelve open-ended issues, the organization relies upon a spontaneous process to make strategic choices.
- It relies on individual initiative and intuition to detect and select often small disturbances in the environment and the decision-making process itself. The particular disturbances that are selected depend upon

the retained memory of the organization, its unconscious cultural norms, what has succeeded or failed in the past. Selection also depends upon what the powerful are likely to pay attention to.

- Selected disturbances are amplified through the political process of support building, the formation of special interest groups. They are further amplified through experimentation conducted by task forces.
- The effect of amplification is to shatter existing perceptions and develop new ones. It is a state of chaos in which there are differences of opinion, conflict, dissensus and lack of commitment to a particular way forward.
- At critical points strategic choices may be made if sufficient consensus and commitment develops spontaneously. This state of consensus and commitment is a dissipative structure, requiring continual inputs of effort and attention. The long-term outcome of choices at critical points is unpredictable.
- The whole process is partly dependent upon chance in a significant way, partly dependent on determined individual effort, intuition and reasoning power, and partly dependent upon the effectiveness of relationships between individuals.
- The open-ended future of an innovative organization is only partly generated by random shocks from the environment. It is also partly generated by the very feedback structure of the business system itself. An open-ended future is a fundamental feature of an innovative business system. The consequent unpredictability cannot be cured by any amount of information gathering or research. Even the most successful organization will display irregular performance in addition to that which might be generated by the environment or by management incompetence.

Given this chaos explanation of how innovation proceeds in creative systems driven by amplifying and damping feedback loops, there are a number of implications for managers:

- It is impossible to establish in advance the future direction of an innovative business. The words 'direction', 'vision' and 'mission' can only realistically mean aspirations or interpretations of the present. Outcomes cannot be managed or controlled.
- Strategic control is a political learning process in real time. Managers cannot 'own' it or 'drive' it to some conclusion decided in advance. Control comes to mean control over the context within which the process of learning takes place. Control is intervention to create the conditions within which spontaneous self-organizing learning can occur. This is the development of new mental models by individuals working with each other.

- A context of strongly shared cultural norms is fatal to innovative learning.
- The manner in which power is used has a substantial effect upon the context of organizational learning through its impact on the group dynamic. Skill in using power means the understanding and judgement of how to alternate the form of power used, from authority to influence to pressure and back again. Widespread distribution of power is neither practical nor useful in this process.
- The innovative process is not one of simple adaptation to, or fit with, the environment. It is neither simple anticipation nor simple reaction. It is a process of continuing, creative interaction with other organizations and people in the environment.
- There is no general recipe, no widely applicable list of prescriptions, that can be applied in a wide range of open-ended situations to ensure success. Each business must develop a new model each time it handles a new strategic situation, as it handles that situation. Teams of managers develop new models using analogous reasoning from past experience and this is made possible by the self-similarity of chaotic dynamics.

The message of chaos for managers is this. Trying to manage outcomes through visions and plans is an illusion which distracts attention from the real processes. Strategic choices require groups exploring different perceptions, working together. The role of the top managers is to establish the context of power form, sufficient management resource slack and trust to allow this to happen. The role of top managers is to encourage key groups of managers to explore and understand how they learn and interact in groups. Control in highly ambiguous and uncertain circumstances is indirect. It is about establishing the conditions within which coherent behaviour can spontaneously occur to handle the new and unknowable.

It is being suggested here that explicit models of managing and organizing along the lines outlined above provide a more useful model of what managers actually do and how organizations actually develop in open-ended situations. This should bring explicit and implicit models closer together, so enabling the design of more effective actions.

Explanations of strategic choice compared

The conclusion we reach then, is this. Because of its chaotic internal dynamic and the continual fluctuation in its external environmental conditions, the successful business organization faces different change situations in the here and now. Managers in the organization have to make choices in relation to events occurring and actions taken which have largely predictable short-term consequences, largely probabilistic consequences a little further out into the future and completely unknowable consequences over the longer term. Successful managers recognize this fact, usually not explicitly, and adopt different forms of control in different change situations. They use different modes of discovering issues, making choices about them and acting on those choices depending on the kind of change they are dealing with.

Chaos and the rational model

The appropriate process of managerial choice in closed and contained situations is well explained by the rational models of management and organization discussed in Chapter 5. These models yield highly useful general prescriptions for the effective short interval control of a business. They are applicable in a wide range of closed and contained situations. There is ample evidence that the practice of this form of control, in these kinds of change situation, is a precondition for success. Here the preferences and objectives of individual managers can be clarified and determined by analytical means in advance of action, as can the changes they have to deal with. Choices can be made through purely logical, step-by-step reasoning and embodied in plans that are sets of actions to be taken at future points in time so as to realize known future objectives. Where there is conflict between individual preferences and objectives, these can be settled by simple forms of bargaining. Most of the learning is done in advance of the action and embodied in the plan. The framework required to promote this mode of making choices is clear. The prime requirements are simple hierarchies where power is unequally distributed and stable, as well as clear job definitions. Strongly shared cultural values around the performance of defined tasks relating to the conduct of the existing business are also necessary.

The result of adopting this mode of choice-making is an orderly sequence of choices leading to a predetermined path into the short-term future, disturbed only by random shocks coming from the environment. Here the organization is an information processing machine which adapts to a given environment through proactive and reactive mechanisms. Here the control loop is the traditional damping one. The instrument applied to the changes is fixed in advance of those changes occurring.

However, when it comes to open-ended situations where consequences of events and actions are inherently unpredictable, this rational model of choice-making and action is completely inadequate. All the analytical techniques used in rational short interval control forms break down. This is because of the very nature of the organization itself, its non-linear feedback characteristics, and because of the unpredictable fluctuations in its chaotic environments. Rational models of conventional strategic management are therefore of little use. Successful managers actually switch to an alternative mode of making choices and designing actions, which they rarely examine explicitly.

Chaos and entrepreneurial models

Modern entrepreneurial models of management and organization put forward explanations of how strategic choices are made and enacted, based on observations and studies of managers at work. These were also discussed in Chapter 5. But the most prominent entrepreneurial interpretations of strategic choice, those to which practising managers pay attention, have been developed within a traditional scientific frame of reference. They are heavily conditioned by Darwinian evolutionary theory. They interpret the strategic choice-making process of an organization in terms of an organizm adapting to its environment in an orderly evolutionary manner. Chaos insights lead to a different interpretation of what is going on when managers make strategic choices.

To clarify the difference, consider how the entrepreneurial and chaos explanations each describe the making of a strategic choice, the nature of those choices, the outcome of those choices and the framework required to make them.

Making a choice

Modern entrepreneurial interpretations of strategic choice start with the galvanizing events and anomalies that highly volatile environments create for a business. Such volatile environments provoke political activity by champions who seek to build support for particular choices of which they are in favour. The assumption is that such champions know what they want; that they have clear preferences and objectives which take the form of vision. The choice that is made then depends upon the stable distribution of power that exists in business organizations – the more powerful champions are those who prevail. The context within which a particular choice is made is not seen as important. Factors such as the other issues facing those making the choice, differences in their personalities, the dynamics of the interaction between them, are all ignored as essential parts of how and what choice is made. Small chance differences in these contextual factors play no significant part in the explanation of the choice. The purpose of the political activity that generates the choice is to secure commitment and consensus to a choice. Such commitment and consensus is a necessary condition for effective political activity. Successful political systems quickly overcome initial disagreements between the clear preferences and objectives of individuals in the organization.

A chaos interpretation is concerned with the same political process but sees it in a substantially different way. Strategic choice is applied to issues of an open-ended nature, arising both from environmental volatility and from the essentially chaotic nature of the internal dynamic of the successful business. The feedback rules that govern an organization themselves generate volatility in addition to that arising in the environment. The control system responding to environmental volatility is itself in a state of flux. An immediate consequence of such open-ended situations is that organizational actors cannot have clear preferences, objectives or visions. Instead of trying to build support for some clear choice, champions are trying to gain support for organizational attention to an incompletely perceived issue. And the champion's perception of that issue is likely to change during the communication and interaction that is the political learning process. The perceptions of different people determine the shape that issue is given. Those perceptions are conditioned by their personalities, preconceptions and the received wisdom of the organization and the industry they work in. The ambiguous, ill-structured nature of open-ended issues, the changing shape of these issues as they are discussed, the manner in which different people apply their power to shape the issues, all provoke patterns of interaction that can change rapidly. The manner in which power is applied in open-ended situations provokes volatile group dynamics that feed back into how the issue is shaped and what choice emerges. The choice made therefore depends partly on stable power and partly on the context of the group dynamic, the personalities involved and the manner in which they learn. The choice itself is affected by small differences in context and therefore depends partly on chance.

In this interpretation, political processes are performing the role of amplifying different perspectives through the organization. In doing so these political processes are undermining and breaking down existing perceptions and ways of doing things. It is through political processes that the issue champions are clarifying and exploring their preferences, aspirations and objectives. The process is spreading dissensus, not consensus. It is this dissensus that is the precondition for successful learning. Without it the old perceptions could not be shattered and therefore the new could not emerge. From time to time, some critical point is reached at which some pressure, internal or external, requires a choice to be made. Sufficient clarity may then be reached on preferences, aspirations and objectives, as well as the nature of the issue, to enable a choice. Such consensus and commitment is reached in a spontaneous self-organizing way. This state of commitment and consensus is a fragile and temporary one. It requires effort and energy to maintain it. It is, in scientific terms, a dissipative structure. The resulting choice is unpredictable because it is so highly dependent upon the context at the time.

Communication and discussion is then the key to strategic choice. Since that communication is concerned with open-ended issues that are ill-structured and ambiguous, it has to be spontaneous in some sense. We cannot set out in advance how it should occur, because we cannot know in advance what we are dealing with. We can set up a general purpose discussion forum, but we cannot prearrange the agenda or the manner in which the discussion should proceed – conduct of the discussion has to be spontaneous. Since we cannot say in advance what issue needs to be addressed, the coming together of people to discuss it will often depend upon spontaneous individual effort. Attention to the issue will be self-organizing in the way it occurs and in the way it develops. It is a consequence of spontaneous self-organization. The picture this interpretation paints is that of lengthy periods of thrashing about without any action, dependent on individual initiative, spontaneous communication. These periods are followed by periodic, unstable states of commitment in which an unpredictable strategic choice is possible.

Orderly entrepreneurial choice

The picture presented by the entrepreneurial interpretations is one of a continuing series of random shocks arising in the environment. The entrepreneurial response is a sequence of orderly choices leading to trial-and-error actions. Here chance plays little part in the choice; it depends on the vision and the stable distribution of power. But chance does play a role in the action, in the sense that some of the trials will work and others will not. But that chance is not an essential part of the explanation. This is because of the high probability that mismatches between trial actions and random shocks will cancel out, it is assumed, because of the large numbers involved. The key to success is then frenetic action. Frenetic action, guided by vision, makes it highly probable that the vision will be achieved because of the laws of large numbers. The organization is engaging in trial-and-error search of its environment in order to adapt to that environment, a process sometimes called logical incrementalism. The search is guided by the vision and the criteria for success are provided by fit with the core values and by some logical connection with the existing business.

This is a fast moving process, requiring continual action, all within a continuing state of commitment and consensus – consensus is the predominant state of the successful choice process. The outcome then is one of an organization continuously feeling the shape of its environment and fitting itself to that shape. Since the environment is highly volatile, the organization must be able to produce a large number of potential responses to match it – large numbers will cancel out mismatches between change and response to it. To provoke this behaviour, jobs must be loosely defined and intersecting. Structures must be simple and decentralized with tight financial controls. Or on another view, complex centralist structures are required to benefit from synergies. It must all be held together by visions and strongly shared cultures which produce a normal continuing state of consensus and commitment. The key aspects of the process are action and continuing cooperation. But in the end we get movement to a predetermined vision in which the organization is adapted to its environment. And we can get this predictable movement because of the laws of probability.

Unpredictable choices in chaos

The chaos interpretation is one of periodic unpredictable choices made at critical points leading to actions that change the environment in some way. That change feeds back into the organization so creating fresh open-ended issues. Just as with an entrepreneurial interpretation, we start with a volatile, fluctuating environment. But now we recognize that there is feedback between managers in the organization and people in the environment. Managers are playing a part in creating their own environment. What they do determines what subsequently happens to the organization. Adapting to that environment through trial-and-error search is then meaningless because we cannot be clear who is adapting to whom. We cannot rely on the laws of probability to cancel out mismatches between large numbers of trial actions and random shocks. This is because the changes are unique, not repetitive, and because small changes escalate. Instead we have to think about creative interaction between organizational actors and actors in the environment.

Such creative interaction, or innovation, depends critically on people having different perspectives, thus inevitably conflicting with each other. Part of the strategic choice process has to be the continuous discovery and clarification of preference and objectives. Strategic choice then emerges from a process in which dissensus shatters old order and spontaneous self-organization may lead to unpredictable choices at critical points. These may be abrupt and revolutionary, causing the whole system to change. Looking back we may be able to interpret it as adaptive trial-and-error search, even though that is not what happened. The strategy is not a movement towards a vision. It emerges from smaller numbers of individual trials at critical points when successful ones are backed. The outcome then depends upon chance in an essential way and it is inherently unpredictable over the long-term.

This interpretation of what managers actually do when they make strategic choices immediately focuses attention on the chaotic nature of the political process and its sensitive dependence on the context within which it occurs – that is, on the impact of personality differences and group dynamics. The keys to strategic choice are attitudes and behaviour, communication and discussion. And the framework required is weakly shared values, clear hierarchies and unequally distributed power. Empowering people on a wide scale and promoting widespread participation are not in themselves necessary or sufficient conditions for effective learning that produces strategic choice. This can be seen by comparing the power and chance models of political activity that were discussed in Chapters 5 and 6 above.

Chaos explanations of political activity

The chaos explanation of political activity takes account of constraints upon the choice-making process necessary to generate regular irregularity in choice sequences. These constraints are unequally distributed power, clear hierarchies and weakly shared cultures. The chance model of political activity applies where the power and hierarchical constraints are not present. As a result, choice depends entirely on the context within which the choice is made. The choice becomes unpredictable. The chaos model takes account of this sensitivity to context, but within power and hierarchical constraints. The power models of political activity assume away the importance of the context and focuses on stable distributions of power. The choice is then predictable.

In the chaos model, the constraints are provided first by simple, well-defined hierarchies of managers with reasonably clear job definitions. The second constraint is provided by the unequal distribution of power this implies. The third constraint is provided by differences in individual values and cultural norms. These constraints mean that sequences of choices cannot move in the haphazard manner predicted by the chance models, because some organizational actors have more power than others and will not permit it. Nor can that choice sequence move in the stable manner predicted by the power models, because differences in values and perspectives prevent it. The constraints provide boundaries within which choices move; they provide regularity to the irregularity with which choices jump about in ambiguous open-ended situations.

The context within which the choices are made from a chaos perspective is determined by: the form in which power is used on any particular occasion; the consequent impact on group dynamics on that occasion; the personalities of individuals taking part in the choice-making activity on that occasion; the other functions the group confronted with the choice has to perform on that occasion; and the workload of those individuals at the time. And all these contextual factors will vary to some extent from occasion to occasion. Since the dynamic of the successful political system is chaotic, small differences in contextual factors can have a major impact on what choice is made, or whether a choice is made at all. Political choices are then affected by chance and any sequence of choices is unpredictable over the long run because of small changes in the contextual factors, even though power is stable over time and issue. But the chance or random aspect of such decisions is bounded. Unlike the chance models of politics, we are talking about bounded instability, not pure instability. Chaotic choice sequences, and the behaviours associated with them, exhibit overall recognizable patterns because of the constraints placed on the choice-making process. We will observe recognizable patterns of avoidance, dependence, consensus seeking, temporary commitment, deferring choice, resolving it by oversight, and sometimes making choices and implementing them. And there will also be a rhythm, or phases, to the pattern of political activity. The phases are those of selecting issues, amplifying them to shatter the existing order, reaching temporary consensus and commitment that arises spontaneously from confusion at critical choice points. At every stage those involved are learning, in the sense that they are striving to formulate and clarify preferences and objectives.

A chaos explanation of managing clearly differs from a rational explanation because it sees strategic choice as a learning political activity, not an analytical plan. A chaos explanation also differs from current entrepreneurial explanations of managing. First because of the primary emphasis it places on political activity and the manner in which it regards political activity as a learning form of control. Second, it differs significantly because of the way in which it views that political form of control, seeing it as a dynamic process that is highly sensitive to context, thus generating an unpredictable sequence of choices. Third, it differs in that it stresses the need for constraints on this choice-making process. Those constraints are provided by unequal power, clear hierarchies and weakly shared cultures. Modern entrepreneurial explanations on the other hand advocate widespread distribution of power and participation, unclear job definitions and strongly shared cultures. Entrepreneurial explanations see uncertainty arising from the environment and the dynamic as one of equilibrium adaptation to that environment. The chaos approach places as much emphasis on the great uncertainty generated by the internal dynamic of the business itself, the behavioural interactions within it. The dynamic is one of creative interaction in which adaptation does not have any clear meaning.

Different prescriptions for strategic management

The differences outlined above lead to very different prescriptions for successful management.

First, while modern entrepreneurial explanations frequently reject rational explanations of management and the prescriptions they lead to, a chaos approach does not. Because the short-term future of a chaotic system is predictable, the rational prescriptions must be applied to the management of events and actions having short-term consequences. A chaos explanation sees the rational models as yielding valid special case prescriptions which must be applied in their entirety to the management of the short-term outcomes of the existing business. This provides a vital element of stability in an otherwise highly uncertain situation. Without effective short interval control, budgets and analytical information systems, there will be no information on the current situation from which to develop strategic choices. There will be no time to deal with the strategic because ineffective day-to-day control will consume management time. And there will be no instrument to implement strategic choices. Effective short interval control means clear job definitions, well-defined and simple hierarchical levels, and unequally distributed power. It also requires the strong sharing of a narrow range of performing cultural norms relating to the carrying out of existing tasks. Given that the dynamic of success is chaotic and the long-term future is unknowable, we must establish stability wherever it is realistically and beneficially possible if we are to avoid total confusion. This is one of the reasons for rejecting the entrepreneurial call for loose job definitions, complex structures, widespread distribution of power and widespread participation.

Second, modern entrepreneurial theories prescribe a mechanism of adapting to the environment through trial-and-error action search for the path to a vision, guided by criteria for success that require actions to be consistent with strongly shared core values and the existing business. The mechanism relies on the laws of probability in which mismatches between large numbers of actions and unpredictable changes will cancel out. The chaos explanation makes it clear that it is impossible to have any vision of the long-term future that has sufficient operational content to guide actions taken in the here and now. These explanations make it clear that fanatically defended values with any operational content will obstruct the emergence of new perspectives and the destruction of the old ones, all of which is vital to innovation. And these explanations make it clear that the laws of probability break down at critical points in open-ended change. In chaos then there are no visions or criteria to guide managers through the laws of probability towards some fixed point in the future. Instead, managers have to create and explain the development of their business as it occurs, using their initiative, intuition and experience, all exercised in a group learning context driven by difference and conflict. There is trial-and-error action, but it is not a step-by-step procedure, using a large number of small chance steps to reach a given vision or goal. Instead trial-and-error follows from unpredictable choices relating to unique events taken at critical points. The consequences of these choices are unpredictable and could constitute a major transformation of the business. And the choice made at critical points depends not upon vision and goals but upon the context within which the choices are made at the time, and upon the spontaneous self-organization of those involved. The strategy emerges partly by chance and partly by determined creative effort.

Because of the importance of the context within which strategic choices are made, chaos explanations direct immediate attention to matters for which entrepreneurial models have little regard. These matters are to do with group behavioural dynamics; the impact of different personality types; the manner in which power is used; the nitty gritty of how meetings are conducted and what functions they perform; the workload being placed on managers. It is these matters that will determine how effective an organization's political system is in producing that organizational learning which is strategic 'control' in open-ended situations.

The model determines the action

What steps a manager takes to improve the strategic management of a business will depend crucially on which explanation of the dynamic of success that manager believes in. A manager may believe that success comes from rational predictive adaptation to the environment; from proaction and reaction where proaction fails. That manager will then set about installing long-range planning systems, analysing markets and employing SWOT and portfolio planning techniques. The belief will be that the manager can control strategic direction, can control the sequence of strategic choices and their outcomes. The strategy will be something set out in advance, the first step taken in advance of any action. The manager will believe that he or she can own and drive the strategy.

Or, a manager may believe that success flows from entrepreneurial trial-and-error adaptation to a rapidly changing and hence unpredictable environment. That manager will seek to formulate visions, enthuse others, promote and fanatically defend core values, empower people, distribute power, loosen job descriptions and install network structures to benefit from synergies. The strategy will then be seen as a consequence of the vision and of the trial-and-error actions taken to realize it. But the belief will still be that the manager controls the process in the sense of owning and driving it.

A manager who approaches business from a chaos perspective will realize that all he or she can install is a short interval control system with its clear job definitions, simple hierarchy and unequally distributed power, to ensure the effective day-to-day control of the existing business. Having done that he or she will be concerned not so much with long-term outcomes, but much more with how key groups of managers are working and learning together to make strategic discoveries and choices and then act upon them. The concern will not be with proaction or reaction, or even so much with trial-and-error action, but with creativity. The concern will be with the effect of managerial action on other organizations and people in the environment. Managers will be concerned with how they can create their own environment. The focus will be on here and now relationships between people, the dynamics of groups, the way meetings are conducted, the manner in which power is being used. Such a manager will encourage informal meetings to explore the strategic issues inevitably shelved in the institutionalized management meetings. Such a manager will use his or her power in different ways at different times to prod, push, encourage and challenge others to explore ambiguous issues with long-term consequences, and with the effect of surfacing conflicts and developing different values and perspectives. This is operating on the boundary conditions, creating the atmosphere within which that creative learning that is strategic 'control' in turbulent times can occur.

Conclusion: a different model for designing action

This book makes the claim that scientific chaos requires a revolution in the way most managers currently explain the successful long-term development of a business and therefore in much of what they do. It requires a review of the prescriptions for success to which most managers subscribe. Long-term success in business flows from innovation, creativity and the ability to develop new strategic directions. From my own consulting experience, working with managers in Europe and North America, and judging from what the best-selling management books say, I suggest that most managers would agree with the following statements on how this creative success is to be achieved:

- Long-term success is significantly enhanced when the organization is future directed. Managers must think about the future and establish future direction for the business. This means setting long-term objectives to be achieved by following a strategic plan, recognizing that such a plan has to be flexible and will be continually changed. 'Here's the paradox: there needs to be a plan, and the plan has to acknowledge that it will be departed from.'[2] As well as, or perhaps instead of a plan, managers need to develop a vision of the future, an inspirational idea of where the business is going to and what it is to be in the future. The organization then moves towards the vision by a series of incremental, trial-and-error steps. The belief is that it is possible for managers to make significantly useful statements about long-term outcomes and control the movement of the business to those outcomes. Success follows from future objectives and visions and an orientation to action.

- Harmony in organizations is vital to long-term success. People must 'pull together' and 'sing off the same hymn sheet'. There must be 'conviction that everyone in the organization is at least facing in the same direction ... Even though the plan is not a guarantee, and deviations are an important part of realising it, a plan helps provide unity ... The second form of unity is cultural ... a sense that there is a whole and there are clear principles guiding it.'[3] Internal harmony is widely seen as vital to success. It can and should be secured by shared plans, strongly shared cultural norms, reward systems, participative management styles and other motivational devices.

- Success requires a predominant state of commitment to the organization and consensus on the choices being made. The point here is that the order provided by harmony needs to be the 'normal' state, if success is to be secured. There is a need for different perspectives and this will sometimes provoke conflict, but innovative 'organizations reduce rancorous conflict and isolation between organizational units; create mechanisms for exchange of information and new ideas across organizational boundaries; ensure that multiple perspectives will be taken into account in decisions; and provide coherence and direction to the whole organization. In these team oriented cooperative environments, innovation flourishes. There may be differences recognized and even encouraged, – an array of different specialities, a diversity of people – but the mechanisms exist for transcending differences and finding common ground.'[4]

- The formal structure can be used to promote innovation. Complex centralist structures of the matrix type, or those that institutionalize a network of contacts across business units and functions, promote the orderly exchange of ideas upon which innovation depends. The widespread distribution of power to allocate resources and the job intersections that complex structures promote, motivate people to cooperate on innovative ventures. Not all managers accept this. Some focus on short-term control needs for simple decentralized structures where power is concentrated and stable.

- The framework required to achieve long-term success can be installed. It is possible to set up planning procedures, design structures, formulate future visions and change cultures to those which produce continuing success. The prescriptions for success can be identified in advance.

Clearly, the underlying understanding of how successful businesses operate is one in which success, and thus innovation, is seen to flow from a continuing state of order. And order means continuing consensus and commitment secured through strongly shared values and appropriate

structures. Some hold that such consensus also requires the wide distribution of power, and others that it follows from the application of concentrated stable power in the form of authority. Order in all cases is achieved
by following step-by-step procedures and is essentially to do with sameness. Different perspectives are of course seen as necessary to innovation,
but the differences are submerged by harmony, with conflict appearing
only periodically. The successful organization is flexible, always in flux,
but only exceptionally to a point that can be described as disorderly.

   If the reader agrees with these points then scientific chaos represents a
revolution at a very fundamental level, in explaining business success.
For, if the dynamic of business success is chaotic, as this book argues it is,
then innovation flows from disorder, closely intertwined with a more
subtle, more difficult to comprehend form of order than that described
above. Chaotic dynamics mean that:

- It is impossible for managers to say anything that is operationally
  useful about the long-term outcomes of a successful business. Its
  long-term development over time cannot be controlled, in the sense
  that we now use that word. The long-term outcome can only be
  discovered and control, defined more loosely as coherent behaviour,
  then takes the form of learning about outcomes in real time. This
  means that future visions and strategic plans are simply illusions.
  Long-term forecasting, simulation, preparing scenarios, using quantitative techniques such as discounted cash-flow analysis for making
  investment decisions, are all pointless games. Instead success flows
  from reflection and from the organization's ability to learn from its
  actions.
- It is not harmony which is vital to innovation, but discord and conflict.
  It is when people are not 'singing off the same hymn sheet' that they
  develop different perspectives. Innovation occurs when people are
  not all facing in the same direction, when they hold different cultural
  values. It is from this state of chaos that innovation unpredictably
  emerges.
- The predominant state of a continuously innovating business is thus
  dissensus rather than consensus. Consensus and commitment to a
  new direction are periodic and very difficult to sustain. They are
  consequently not the 'normal' state of a successful business.
- Innovation emerges from a process of spontaneous self-organization,
  and that spontaneity cannot be frozen into any organizational
  structure.
- The framework required to produce long-term success cannot be
  installed. Periodic states of consensus around innovations are
  achieved through a process of spontaneous self-organization. Spontaneity cannot be installed, but the conditions in which it may happen
  can be created. Senior executives cannot control the outcomes, but

they can take part in the spontaneous process and they can helpfully intervene in the context within which that process occurs. There is no set of prescriptions available in advance. Each new open-ended situation must be dealt with by developing new models.

Chaos is a revolution because the underlying understanding of how dynamic systems operate is one in which success and innovation are seen to flow from disorder. But that disorder has a pattern, one of self-similarity; patterns of behaviour and choice that people can recognize and use to reason by analogy, so creating new mental models. Self-similarity is a recognizable category within which individual events follow a random course. And it exists because the system is constrained. In a business organization such constraints are provided by difference – different levels of power, different hierarchical levels of manager and different cultural norms. Chaos explanations stress both spontaneity and constraint, both difference and similarity. Step-by-step procedures of thinking and deciding break down in chaos, and people have to use their intuition and their ability to reason by analogy.

For managers the message is:

- Forget your long-term plans and future visions, they are illusions.
- Stop trying to turn the people in your organization into a bunch of fanatics who all share the same values.
- Instead create the conditions in which they can explore their differences and work at understanding how they function as a group, so as to develop new perspectives on the business with which to design more effective actions.
- Accept that long-term outcomes are inherently unpredictable, that innovative responses to them rely on spontaneity of people. Attempts to impose order, to freeze relationships into complex formal structures are counter productive.

And this message is not derived from any 'political' ideology, 'soft' organizational behaviour philosophies or 'weird' psychoanalysis. It is the logical consequence of the nature of feedback control loops. It is the new scientific method of management.

References

1 Progogine, I., Stengers, I. (1984), *Order out of Chaos*, Bantam Books.
2 Moss Kanter, R. (1988), *The Change Masters*, Unwin Hyman, p. 305.
3 Weick, K. (1979), *Organizational Psychology*, Addison-Wesley.
4 Moss Kanter, R., op. cit., p. 28.

13 Management intervention and strategic 'control'

This chapter first summarizes the central argument put forward in previous chapters. It then goes on to make key points about the role of managers in the strategic control of a business.

Changing the models for designing action

The great majority of managers in the business enterprises of Western societies were educated within a common scientific tradition. This provides a common framework used to understand and explain just about everything from physics and chemistry to economics and business organizations. Most of today's managers consequently share a number of 'self evident' basic views, which are rarely questioned, on how the world of business works and therefore on how to manage. In traditional science, the world is a given reality 'out there' to be observed, measured and explained. No matter what world it is, be it the solar system, an atom or a business organization, its development is governed by fixed deterministic laws. Once the structure of such laws has been identified and fixed values assigned to the parameters and variables of those laws, then they generate only one perfectly predictable pattern of behaviour. At school or university, we did not encounter fixed equations into which we plugged fixed numbers to get answers that were completely random. If we subsequently observe what looks like random behaviour, it is because something is changing, the parameters or the variables, or because we have not found the right law. And tiny changes in a parameter or a variable do not completely alter the qualitative nature of the behaviour generated by the laws.

In traditional science there is another important but rarely questioned assumption: systems, be they pendulums or markets, tend to a normal state of orderly equilibrium. The underlying idea is that all systems are drawn to a state in which the laws governing them will keep them in that state, unless some powerful outside change disturbs it. So, the laws of economics establish conditions in which the forces of demand and supply will be balanced at a particular price. Any move away from that price will set in train automatic forces of supply and demand to restore the price to its equilibrium position. The system returns to equilibrium unless we put some obstacle in its way. The system moves to substantially different behaviour only when some significant change outside it alters the forces of supply and demand.

In much the same way the laws of business organizations are concerned with establishing a continuing dynamic equilibrium, a state of balance between the capability of an organization and the requirements of its markets. Success is where the business continuously matches its performance to the requirements of its customers. If it were able to achieve this equilibrium and there were no further changes in the market, it would stay there – its structures, systems and common cultures would see to that. Unfortunately the markets keep changing and so the organization has to keep adapting. And at or near to equilibrium, small changes do not matter – they have small consequences so that we do not have to bother much with them. It can all be summed up by saying that the really important thing to be explained about any business system is its orderliness and what leads to that orderliness. Having understood such a system and identified its laws, it can be controlled. It is possible to 'own' or drive the process of control and the outcomes of control.

Given these very basic, commonly shared views on how the world works, it is not surprising to find the great majority of managers subscribing to the following views:

- We have to establish what direction we are going in, where we want to be, what we will be in say five years time. We need objectives, missions and visions if we are to make orderly progress. But of course, we have to be flexible about it because the world is so uncertain.
- We all have to face in the same direction and pull together. This is what team work means. We have to like each other, we have to have the same values and maintain continuing consensus and commitment.
- We have to maintain order and discipline through structures and system, while motivating people through appropriate reward systems. We have to use structural devices, perhaps complex ones, to bring ideas to the centre.
- We have to be rational. Intuition is a last resort when we have no choice.
- We have to act as quickly as possible.
- The structures and techniques required to achieve success can be

identified in advance and can be installed. The techniques and the data are available if we spend time and money finding them. There is a general recipe that can be applied in a wide range of specific situations.

- Top management is in control. They know where we are going. Someone must own and drive the process that leads to strategic direction. We can manage the outcome.
- Success is achieved by matching the capability of the business to the demands of the environment.

The underlying belief is that the role of management is to secure order as sameness.

But the new science is dramatically different from the traditional. The idea of a given reality 'out there' to be observed, measured and explained is too simple. For what we observe depends on our position when we observe it (Einstein's relativity at the solar level); the act of measurement can be an intervention that disturbs what we measure so making precise measurement impossible (Heisenberg's uncertainty principle at the level of the particle); some truths cannot be determined by means of step-by-step rules and procedures (Gödel's undecidability). Simple deterministic orderliness has dissolved into relativity, uncertainty and undecidability. And now the chaos, unpredictability, self-similarity, symmetry-breaking, self-organization and dissipative structures of far-from-equilibrium states in dynamic systems. The essence of the world is now seen as disorder and irregularity, not simple order. The world is continuously destructive and creative, hence following unpredictable, not preordained, paths of development.

Chaos and self-organization theories present a revolution for managers at a most basic level. They are powerful new insights because we have purely rational, scientific discoveries which tell us that inherent randomness, complete unpredictability, unique uncertainty is generated by purely rational deterministic laws. Systems can behave randomly even when nothing outside of them changes. The very structure of the system itself generates the chaos that makes continuing creation possible. Chaos is the science of feedback controls and a business is quite clearly driven by feedback controls. Chaos must surely then be part of a new scientific management, just as it is part of the new science of physics and chemistry.

Contradictions in what we say

Chaos is a powerful revolutionary insight for managers because it brings us face to face with the internal contradictions in what we say today about successful management. A system driven by feedback controls is innovative, not when it is at or near to equilibrium, but when it is sustained far-from-equilibrium. This is a state of dissensus and randomness at the individual component level, which is unstable in a bounded sense. There the system is highly sensitive to small changes, making it possible for it to take on new forms more easily. But the price to be paid is that the new forms depend on chance and are unpredictable – there is not one future for the system but many potential futures. And which future is realized depends upon small changes and individual choices along the way. Given that this is how innovative systems develop over time, it is completely illogical to say that managers must choose one of these futures in advance and then be flexible. This advice implies that there is only one future and as we get closer to it we will see it more clearly. We will then bend, stretch and twist in order to reach it. But the reality is that the one future we select will not be the one we see as we get closer – it will be a completely different one. Bending, stretching and twisting will not be enough. We will have to tear up the future we chose and go in a different direction. This is not flexibility; it is more drastic than that. In a world that has many futures it is illogical, restricting and dangerous to fix on a vision of one.

It is no counter argument to say that some investments and product developments have long lead times and therefore you have to look ahead. Of course it is then necessary to plan the actions required to install the investment, erect the building or develop the product. But building a new plant simply means that you can say that in five years time we will have such and such a plant. Developing a new product means that we can say that in 10 years time we should have such and such a product. You still cannot say whether the market will be there for the output of that plant or that product, or whether the price will be high enough to repay the investment.

A system driven by feedback loops innovates by amplifying small changes, spreading them from one component of the system to another, so as to destroy existing structures. The components have to experience randomness and instability if they are to break with the present and move to a new future. Given that this is how innovative systems develop over time, it is completely illogical to say that the key to business success is building teams that have strongly shared values, a continuing state of consensus and commitment. Old perceptions cannot be shattered and innovation emerge, unless cultural norms are weakly shared, people are different and have different values and views. Difference and dissensus is vital to innovation and they are the normal state for successful business organizations, because successful businesses innovate continuously.

A system driven by feedback mechanisms innovates through a process of spontaneous self-organization at critical points during chaos. The outcomes are inherently unpredictable. Given that this is how innovative systems develop over time, it is illogical to believe that successful systems can be installed in advance. It is illogical to believe that organizational structures can incorporate innovative processes or that some senior manager can 'own' or 'drive' the process of innovation or strategic direction. The individual initiative and intuition required to select and amplify small changes and the spontaneous self-organization required to develop strategic direction cannot be installed. By definition the processes that generate innovation cannot be 'owned' or 'driven'. Spontaneity cannot be frozen into a network structure. What senior managers can do is create conditions favourable to individual initiative and intuition, as well as spontaneous self-organization. These conditions have to do with learning. Senior managers can intervene in the process, but they cannot control the outcome. Strategic direction emerges and depends upon chance.

The strategic role of managers is then seen not to be managing an outcome that is the match of capability to the market. The role of managers is to sustain the organization in the challenging, disorderly state far-from-equilibrium, where creativity is possible. There are no powerful automatic forces which keep systems far-from-equilibrium, as there are at equilibrium. Instead intentional effort and attention is required to sustain the atmosphere and attitudes of challenge. The outcome is not simply a match with the environment but a creative interaction with other organizations and people in the environment to develop new things.

Chaos presents a powerful revolution for management thinking because it provides a scientific basis for the following conclusions. The strategic control of a business organization is a complex political learning process that has nothing to do with long-term plans. Nor has it much to do with mystic visions of the future to which the troops can be bound by strongly shared values. Complex learning occurs when people come together to discuss what they are doing, why and how they are doing it. Complex learning occurs when people in groups explore how and why they are interacting in the way they do. Strategic control and development is spontaneously creative exploration by groups of people in real time. No one controls it in the conventional sense of that word, but managers can create, through their own behaviour, the atmosphere in which it may all happen. That atmosphere is one that creates challenges to existing perceptions and hence uncertainty. It is one that encourages spontaneity. But that atmosphere is not some free-for-all loose form of widespread participation in making strategic choices, which is held together by strongly shared values. Nor does that atmosphere arise from the widespread distribution of power. Chaos is random behaviour at a specific level within an overall pattern – it is bounded instability. It is constrained. In business those constraints are provided, first, by clear hierarchies and simple organizational structures where power is unequally distributed, and second by weakly shared values.

Creating the atmosphere has to do not just with spontaneity but also with constraint.

Facing open-ended change

The insights of chaos theory lead us to start our explaining by identifying substantially different change situations within which we have to manage simultaneously and alternately. Chaos provides a general theory of change. With this starting point we are logically driven to understanding control in two fundamentally different forms. The first is the planning, monitoring and corrective action control loop which we all immediately identify as control. This simple, stable form of control is appropriate in conditions close to certainty. In business that means short-term consequences of events and actions taken in the here and now. It is rational decision making. It is the same thing as learning about outcomes, and the only form of political activity needed for it to function effectively is that of simple bargaining. Learning is all done in advance of taking action. In fact learning and political activity are so unimportant, in relative terms, that it is legitimate to ignore them. Probably most political activity in these conditions is dysfunctional, self-seeking 'politicking'. The control loop here is essentially a damping one. The effects of unforeseen changes are automatically detected and adjustments are made to accommodate them rapidly. This keeps the organization on its predetermined short-term course. Such damping is the essence of control in closed and contained change situations. Control as a feedback loop that damps down disturbances from a desired state is the predominant understanding we currently have. Once we have decided what to do, nothing much new happens – the damping form of control sees to that.

The chaos contribution to managing and organizing is that it uncompromisingly forces us to face open-ended change at the same time as closed change and its conventional control form. Open-ended change consists of turbulent environmental change, as well as that turbulence generated by the internal dynamic of the business itself and by the complex interaction of the organization with its environments. Here we cannot know in advance what to do and chaos theory directs attention to a form of control that is essentially amplifying. The purpose of control in open-ended situations is that of amplifying small changes so that we can discover what to do, so that continuing creativity and innovation become possible. In a sense we come to see control in terms completely opposed to the traditional view.

And this focus provides us with a framework within which to combine a number of important developments in the thinking about management and organization that have so far received little attention from most practising managers. An understanding of control in open-ended situations, as an amplifying political process of learning and discovering, requires the incorporation of sociological, psychological and political perspectives. For control in open-ended situations is nothing other than a voyage of discovery, a group learning process that utilizes political activity and is significantly affected by group dynamics. In the end it is a process of spontaneous self-organization, the outcome of which depends significantly on chance.

Greater insight into this political learning form of control is provided by considering it in the context of scientific chaos. Human systems, like most of those in nature, are non-linear feedback loops. Nature's systems can only innovate and create in conditions far-from-equilibrium. So too can business organizations only innovate and generate new strategic directions if they are operating within chaotic conditions at certain levels, in relation to certain time frames. Nature's systems utilise spontaneous self-organization to move periodically, at critical points, out of chaos into more complex forms of order. So too must business organizations rely upon spontaneous self-organization if they are to innovate and develop new strategic direction.

In human systems that spontaneous self-organization is a political process through which organizations continuously learn what to do when conditions are ambiguous and confusing. This learning process is a highly complex one in which the learning is not simply about the 'what' and the 'why', but about the 'how'. It is not just about outcomes but about process. And learning about process requires digging below the level of awareness. It requires carrying out uncomfortable procedures of questioning basic cultural and behavioural assumptions. It requires clarifying the implicit explanations driving behaviour, and developing more appropriate explicit explanations of what is going on.

The chaos insight into how successful organizations innovate and develop new strategic directions has major implications for managing change. Since the dynamic of business success is essentially chaotic, it follows that long-term outcomes are significantly conditioned by chance. And this means that we cannot manage the long-term outcome itself. Control is a form of learning when the dynamics are chaotic. This includes learning how to control as we go along in conditions that are unforeseeable. We cannot develop models of the processes to be installed, in advance of dealing with change in a wide range of specific circumstances. All we can do is intervene in a manner which creates the conditions within which continuous complex learning can occur. The rest we have to leave to spontaneous self-organization. And that learning is the development of new mental models for each new situation.

Although we cannot manage change itself, then, we can prompt a move from one set of conditions to another by some form of managed intervention. If such intervention is to be managed, then we must be clear on what conditions we are trying to move from and what conditions we are trying to move to.

Moving from managing outcomes to managing process

In turbulent conditions the grand designs for future outcomes, generated by conventional strategic management, fall apart. When it comes to dealing with the open-ended long-term, managers therefore need to move from the conventional planning mentality to creating the conditions in which organizations can benefit from self-organization. Dynamic strategic management is a process of creating favourable conditions for self-organization because that is the effective, scientific way of dealing with the unknowable. This prescription is not derived from ideological beliefs that democracy and empowering people is a 'good' thing. It does not look for justification in the psychological proposition that participation is required to get the best out of people. Such ideological beliefs and motivational propositions may well be true, but the requirement for self-organization is based on scientific effectiveness. Systems characterized by chaotic dynamics, and a business organization must be one of them, are dependent upon self-organizing forms of control for their creative development. Companies that do not create the conditions for this form of control will not be able to deal effectively with open-ended change. When key changes are small ones with unforeseeable consequences, we have no option but to rely on individuals spontaneously detecting them and spontaneously organizing themselves to handle such change.

Moving from conventional to dynamic strategic management means moving:

- *From* control forms appropriate for closed and contained change only
  – *to* control forms appropriate for closed, contained and open-ended change
- *From* strategic management as a separate type of management where future direction is established in advance and structures, roles, systems and cultures are then designed to deliver that future direction
  – *to* management as an integrated process where the form of control matches the change situation. Here different forms of control are simultaneously and alternately applied. Structures, roles, systems and cultures are established to secure tight short interval control in advance of short-term change. And conditions are established to enable the political learning which produces new strategic direction as changes occur.
- *From* writing strategic reports, setting long-term objectives and devis-

ing long-term plans – *to* facilitating and encouraging the emergence of appropriate political and learning systems on a wide scale.

- *From* that damping form of control in open-ended situations which relies on the individual expert – *to* that amplifying form of control which relies on group activities and widespread discussion and reflection.
- *From* the group harmony of sharing the same cultural norms and values – *to* the creative challenge of different people having different values and perceptions.
- *From* a concern with the distribution of power – *To* a concern with how power is used.
- *From* looking for structural solutions to open-ended challenges – *To* creating conditions for spontaneous group processes.
- *From* a focus on explicit explanations only – *To* a focus on implicit explanations, on basic cultural assumptions and group dynamics, as well.

In essence we are talking about intervening in the functioning of an organization to create conditions in which strategic thinking and learning can occur. And this means moving from a situation in which we explain what we are doing in one way and then do something rather different, to a situation in which we continually examine what we actually do, learn from that and then do what we say. This required move is summarized in Figure 13.1 and each box in that figure is then discussed in the following sections.

What we say we do (or should do) about control (box A in Figure 13.1)

The main explicit explanations put forward by practising managers on what they do or should be doing, are essentially those of the rational and entrepreneurial models of management (see Chapter 5). These views are important driving forces in the behaviour of managers and they may be thought of as the conscious mind of the organization. The principal features of each of these explanations is summarized in Figure 13.2. They present radically different views on how a business should be managed for long-term success. But the overall aims of both of these sets of pre-scriptions on how to manage are the same, namely to secure:

- internal organizational equilibrium of harmony among people so as to enable.
- continuing equilibrium adaptation of the organization to its changing environment (matching resources/capability to the environment, securing fit) which leads to

- success, excellence, continuing and stable flows of profit, achieving objectives, missions and visions.

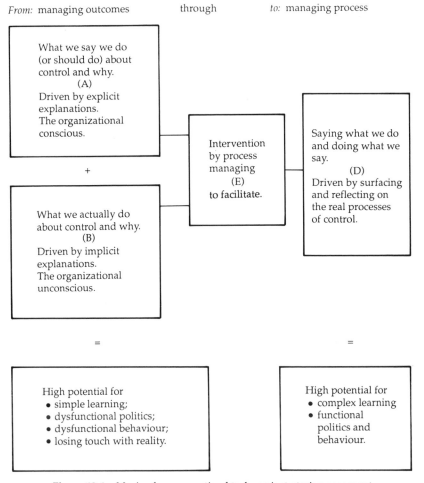

Figure 13.1 *Moving from conventional to dynamic strategic management*

What we actually do about control (box B in Figure 13.1)

But managers, in company with people in all other walks of life, actually do something quite different from what they say they do on many occasions. And this is particularly noticeable when they deal with open-ended change.

Sometimes they scan the environment analytically, sometimes they listen informally to customers and suppliers. But frequently the analysis and the listening yield ambiguous results and so they invent and create the environment. For example in one company I have worked with,

Rational	Entrepreneurial
Formal, analytical scanning of environment and forecasting.	Informal listening to customers and alliances with suppliers and competitors.
Fixed objectives and future missions set by leaders or experts.	Visions generated by heroic leaders.
Decision-making modes which are step-by-step rules and procedures to generate alternatives and make choices to achieve optimal or satisfactory objectives (Algorithm).	Decision-making mode that is a trial-and-error search according to criteria on error to achieve vision (Heuristic).
Heavy focus on action plans, tasks, to achieve known objectives.	Heavy focus on (random) action to discover how to achieve vision.
Imposed discipline through hierarchies of managers, objectives, plans, policies and rules. People seek security of being told what to do.	Self-discipline through being enthused by the vision. People are creative, responsible and seek excitement. Tear up the rule book.
Harmony through clear structure, motivation, team building, common culture, all designed to fit the strategy. Conflict settled by bargaining. Politics are disruptive. 'All sing from the same hymn sheet.'	Harmony through fanatically shared values, family-like belonging. Politics is orderly application of power to produce motivation. Conflict avoided by belief and loyalty. 'All pull together.'
All adds up to a regular process utilizing analysis, quantification, formal rules. Institutionalized communication.	All adds up to irregular process utilizing intuitive, qualitative judgement and informality.

Figure 13.2   *What we say we do*

managers invented rust as the most important reason for their customers' switching from tin plate to plastic paint cans. In fact customers were switching because of poor service levels. Managers often create a competitive environment through advertising and price cuts. Managers often ignore small changes in their markets because they conflict with some preconceived notion. They take fixed positions on what their customers should be wanting. They manage according to the company and industry recipes that were developed in past situations and may well not apply today.

Sometimes managers fix objectives and sometimes leaders have visions which enthuse others. But frequently no one knows what the objectives or vision should be. Frequently the real difficulty is to find out what they should be. Different businesses have different learning systems and some will therefore discover objectives more effectively than others. Frequently things happen that no one really intended. For example that famous yellow 'Post It' note started as a glue for which no one could think of a use.

Sometimes we use rational, step-by-step decision-making modes. Sometimes we use trial-and-error search. But we can only do these things when we have objectives and criteria to distinguish success from failure. Frequently we find ourselves in a situation where these are absent. The choice is made in a political manner determined by individual initiative and the context within which the choice is made. Different businesses have different political systems and will therefore notice different changes and make different choices. Frequently the nature of the political system will block the amplification of detected changes.

So, sometimes we focus on plans and tasks, sometimes on experimental action, but frequently the focus is on political processes and learning in ambiguous situations. Different businesses use different control methods and have different types of political learning systems. They will therefore develop different strategic directions, even in the same environments.

Sometimes discipline is imposed through hierarchy, sometimes it is secured through shared values, but frequently discipline is absent and power struggles take pace. They determine outcomes. Sometimes businesses will block the development of new perspectives by imposing too much discipline.

Sometimes harmony is secured through structures, sometimes through shared values and we all pull together and sing from the same hymn sheet. But frequently we pull in different directions. Sophisticated political activity is the only way we have of coping with the ensuing conflict and confusion required to generate new perspectives. This is often characterized by group dynamics which are dysfunctional.

In practice then we find processes that are sometimes regular and orderly in the rational or entrepreneurial sense, but frequently they are disorderly in a chaotic sense. We end up relying on individuals to detect and select change, political activity to amplify it, experiments to test it and provide material to reflect upon. So we discover objectives and develop new strategic direction. We frequently shelve issues because of the time pressures on institutionalized communication arenas and top levels in the hierarchy.

The consequences of saying one thing and doing another (box C in Figure 13.1)

Because we frequently do one thing while we say we do another, we create conditions for organizational fantasy in which we may lose touch with reality. The real explanations of what we are doing slip below the level awareness into the unconscious mind. This creates high potential for:

- Failure to understand the real dynamics.
- Obstacles to learning about the effectiveness of the process. When we avoid examining what we are actually doing, when we say one thing and do another, we are by definition learning only about outcomes. We are not examining and reflecting upon the real processes being used. The results are undiscussable issues; avoidance of threatening but important issues in order to preserve harmony; lack of public testing of interpretations; win/lose dynamics; polarization and destructive warfare; games of deception; non-tolerance of failure; focus on immediate goals and objectives and shelving open-handed issues; shared beliefs that are out of date and obstruct new perspectives; roles rigidly defined in all circumstances so that people are discouraged from detecting and doing something about the new; basic cultural assumptions which are no longer appropriate to the situation being faced.
- Dysfunctional political processes and group behaviour, with poor upward flows of new ideas and a consequent low rate of innovation.
- Inability to tolerate the vagueness and ambiguity without which new perspectives are impossible.
- Too narrow and orderly an approach to be able to cope with open-ended change. Those who demand that control should be orderly in all respects, at all times, are unable to flow with events when this is necessary.
- Losing touch with reality. We depend on myths. We use comfort-raising symbols and rituals instead of confronting the confusion of change. We rationalize the past instead of learning from it.

The total consequence of all the above is dysfunctional control.

Saying what we do and doing what we say (box D in Figure 13.1)

Effective control in open-ended, turbulent conditions requires a form of learning which is about process as well as about outcome. That form of learning can only occur if managers examine and reflect upon what they are actually doing and why. It means continuously saying what we do, examining it, revising the way we explain and then doing what we say. It means going through the more complex learning and control loops that involve examining the implicit models driving behaviour.

Figure 13.3 sets out the control and learning loops. The simpler, more conventional learning and control loop moves from changing events through the interpretation of what they mean using the explicit models we subscribe to, making a choice and acting upon that choice. Such action has consequences that will then require interpretation and reflection upon the explicit models being used to explain what is going on. Part of the control learning loop is to revise the explicit models in the light of

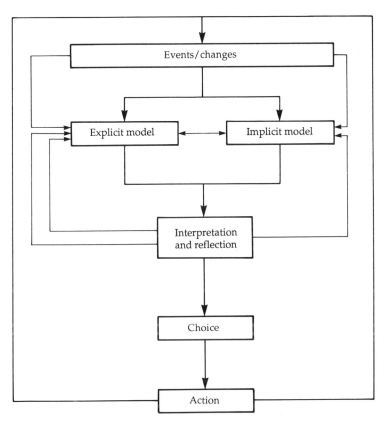

Figure 13.3 *Control and learning loops*

experience. But when conditions are turbulent there is an additional need. And that need is to interpret and reflect upon the implicit models as well; those assumptions which are submerged below the level of awareness but are nevertheless driving behaviour.

The conditions we are trying to create by some form of managed intervention, therefore, are those within which this more complex learning and control can occur.

The intervention process (box E in Figure 13.1)

Some form of management intervention is necessary to move an organization from a situation in which it is trying in vain to manage long-term outcomes, to a situation in which it is concerned with managing a complex learning process. It is such intervention which is the realistic contribution of top managers to the strategic 'control' of their organizations.

Managers and strategic 'control'

Strategic control is the process by means of which the managers of an organization discover strategic issues, make strategic choices and act to realize those choices. If strategic control is to be effective then the processes deployed must bear some realistic relationship to the nature of strategic issues.

Strategic issues

The really important strategic issues are open-ended. They often arise from small, hardly noticeable changes. They are ambiguous, ill-structured and accompanied by inadequate information. Such issues have significant long-term consequences for a business that are inherently unpredictable. How those consequences evolve depends upon what actions managers take, or fail to take, from period to period. How they evolve also depends on what other events occur from period to period, as those consequences unfold. All this follows from the dynamic of a chaotic system with its continuing self-reinforcing feedback. The consequences of strategic issues are not an independent given that exists outside the business organization quite independent of what it does, to which it must adapt. As a result there is no fixed future point. Instead there are many futures. The consequences of strategic issues have widespread impact on the organization and for this reason they threaten any existing order.

The nature of strategic issues as described above has a direct impact on human behaviour. Because the consequences of such issues threaten the existing order, they arouse states of anxiety. Since those consequences are inherently unpredictable and uniquely uncertain it is impossible for people to immediately clarify their preferences or establish objectives. And this causes even further anxiety. The ill-structured nature of the issue means that it can be interpreted in many ways. Individual interpretations will be heavily conditioned by the existing perceptions and beliefs of those individuals. They will also be conditioned by pressures to conform to interpretations that are acceptable to others in their group. Strategic issues will therefore give rise to fluctuating and alternating behaviours of conflict and commitment, confusion and consensus, avoidance and attention, misinterpretation, conformity and dependence on others who seem to have better interpretations.

The very nature of strategic issues and the behaviours they provoke means that when they handle such issues, managers cannot know what they are going to do, or even what they are doing, until they do it. Realistic strategic control must therefore be a process which generates sequences of discoveries, choices and actions in circumstances where people do not know what they are doing in advance of doing it. In such circumstances we have to respond by exploring, inventing, creating the new and destroying the old. Strategic control is the same thing as creating, innovating or managing complex change. They always involve destruction too. It is a process of continuously destroying old perceptions and developing new ones, abandoning existing ways of thinking about and doing things in favour of new ways. And how to do all this also has to be discovered chosen and acted upon as we do it. The nature of strategic issues means that we can neither decide in advance what to do, nor can we decide in advance how to decide what to do.

Strategy

The strategy of a business emerges from the process of strategic control it adopts. Strategy is the continuing, unfolding flow of consequences of the actions managers take and the reactions they provoke in customers, competitors and suppliers. These actions are to do with product offerings, market positions, technology and so on. Strategic direction and innovation are the same thing. They cannot be predicted and given the processes from which they emerge they depend significantly upon chance.

Strategic control

The nature of strategic issues means that strategic discovery, choice and action has to be generated by a process of organizational learning. Groups of people have to work together, using intuition and experience, to discover, choose and act in real time as they go along. Analytical processes contribute to this by aiding the understanding of the current and past situations. Such processes help people to structure their thinking and discussion but they do not directly yield the answer. They provide analogies from previous situations which may or may not be useful in a new situation. How a group of people performs this complex learning in open-ended situations is very sensitive to:

- How they perceive changes, how they explain those changes and what they believe about the functioning of their system. Organizational learning is thus dependent upon what the cultural assumptions actually are and how strongly they are shared. Fixed perceptions and strongly shared cultures effectively block organizational learning in open-ended situations because they block changing perceptions.
- What the personalities of the individuals involved are and how each approaches learning tasks. Groups composed of very similar personality types and hence similar learning styles are less likely to generate different perceptions.
- How the individuals involved interact with each other. The dynamic interaction of people in a group is characterized by recognizable patterns of behaviour, some of which obstruct learning, for example, excessive dependence on a leader, dominant behaviours of conflict or avoidance. The group dynamic will depend upon the manner in which power is used.
- What political processes of persuasion and coercion are used by people in the group. For example, power exercised as authority provokes typical group dynamics of dependence which will obstruct learning in open-ended situations.
- The time pressures upon people in the group and the other functions and issues they have to attend to. Highly efficient organizations in a short-term sense with fully stretched managers will have no time for effective learning in open-ended situations.
- The spontaneity or formality of the arena in which they are communicating.
- The reasons for the involvement of people in a group, whether it is symbolic and based on status or based on mutual gain and contribution. Invitations based on expected contribution provoke more effective learning behaviour than invitations based on status.

The process of political learning is a feedback one that is very sensitive to the contextual factors mentioned above. This means that the sequences of discoveries, choices and actions it produces will be unpredictable. The process is spontaneous and self-organizing. Consequently senior managers cannot control the process or its outcome. What they can do is operate on the contextual factors listed above to make the process more effective. What kinds of intervention help to establish a supportive context?

Management intervention

In my experience as a strategy consultant to a number of companies I have found that the most helpful top management intervention is establishing what one might call a strategy workshop.

Strategy workshops

These are meetings held once or twice a month which are concerned entirely with discussing and exploring strategic issues. Normal institutionalized meetings of managers will with predictable regularity fail to deal with strategic issues because of the very institutionalized nature of those meetings. Such meetings are about running the existing business, about short interval control in closed change situations. By setting up workshops, top management is in effect installing a special communication arena that is spontaneous in terms of conduct. This means that the meeting is conducted in a highly informal and rather unstructured manner. It means that people are invited to attend those meetings because of the contributions they have to make, not because of the status they have. Such meetings should not simply be a replication of the formal top management meetings – to generate spontaneity it must include people lower down in the hierarchy and it must not be run according to fixed agendas. Note that managers are invited to attend for a specific reason, namely that they are judged potentially to have significant contributions to make. This is not widespread participation and it is not empowering people in the sense that those people will make decisions about resource allocation. The purpose of the meeting is not to take decisions but to explore issues. When such meetings are effective, those taking part work on the assumption that their contributions will be accorded serious attention. They do not necessarily assume that such contributions will be acted upon or that some kind of majority or consensus view will be taken. When it comes to making a choice about resource allocation that will be done through the operation of the normal procedures within the authority power structure. The whole purpose of the strategy workshop is to create an opportunity to raise ill-structured issues, explore them, reflect upon them and pool different insights. The most important sense in which such meetings are spontaneous is in terms of the attitudes and behaviour of those who participate.

Workshops that fail

To illustrate this point consider one case with which I am familiar. The managing director of a smallish service company decided for the first time to hold what he called a strategy meeting with his middle managers. He outlined a strategy for the expansion of the company to that group of middle managers and then asked them for their views on it. One of the managers pointed to the problems being caused by allocating increased resources primarily to the sales and marketing functions. This was leading to expansion but creating severe difficulties in delivering the levels of service required to retain customers. The consequence was the loss of existing customers at almost the same rate as the acquisition of new ones. The managing director's reaction was one of irritation and defensiveness. He made it quite clear that the middle manager was being 'negative'. The other middle managers knew better than to offer any comments that could be construed as being critical in any way. A very dispirited and isolated middle manager decided never to make comments at such meetings again. A few months later the same managing director organized an 'away day' at a hotel for his board and middle managers. At this meeting he spoke for nearly four hours, again outlining the company's strategy. The others listened and reported that they found it all very interesting. Two months after that a weekend trip was organized for the same group to a foreign holiday resort at which they all took part in team-building exercises.

There is no sense in which these meetings can be described as spontaneous. The managing director had no intention of listening to anyone else. He was simply exercising his considerable selling skills to get everyone else to 'buy in' to his ideas. The purpose was to get everyone 'on board', aiming for the same thing, sharing the same culture. It was a propaganda exercise. The behaviour of the managing director was such that he ensured that there would be no contribution, no discovery and no exploration of strategic issues.

I have attended a number of such meetings at which managers are gathered together at hotels. Top managers inform them about what is going on. Visiting speakers lecture them on some interesting management topic. And they are exhorted to 'pull together'. On one occasion I heard the chief executive end such a weekend gathering with a threat that those who did not believe in, and work assiduously to implement, a proposed customer care programme would not be a welcome members of the team.

Whatever purposes such gatherings may serve, they do not constitute strategy workshops in the sense that the term is used here. If they are to be effective then behaviour at strategy workshops should not be governed by any attempt to sell any top management idea, promote any common culture or even make any decisions. Strategy workshops fulfil an essential function when top management behaviour invites critical examination of issues and of the approaches being adopted to deal with such issues. In this sense the behaviour of top managers creates the context within which spontaneous learning and political processes can occur.

Workshops that succeed

In one of the companies I am currently working with, the chief executive holds strategy workshop meetings on approximately two afternoons a month. Membership includes managers from the top two levels of the hierarchy and others are invited to attend where this seems appropriate. There are occasions when one of the members simply invites one of his subordinates without needing to ask the permission of the chief executive. A loose agenda of issues to be discussed is set out in advance and background information is usually provided. The kind of conduct at those meetings is indicated by the following example. One of the managers put forward a suggestion to expand the range of services provided with the main product. The suggestion had not been comprehensively thought through; no advance warning had been made that the suggestion would be put forward and there were no papers setting out or justifying the argument. The suggestion provoked considerable discussion in which the chief executive adopted a highly probing attitude and asked a number of uncomfortable questions. But at the end of the discussion he encouraged the manager to give further thought to the matter despite his own freely expressed scepticism. Despite receiving a 'hard time' on that occasion, the manager concerned put forward other suggestions at subsequent meetings. Behaviour here encourages people to surface and explore ideas and pursue them with some rigour. And it is this kind of behaviour which leads to useful strategic learning. The company just described receives favourable press for the imaginative manner in which it is dealing with very difficult circumstances.

When such general strategy workshops throw up ideas which attract sufficient interest and support, it is then useful to set up task forces to develop those ideas further. Once again membership should be based on potential contribution, and conduct should be informal. One company I have worked with was faced with a pressing need to reorganize its activities but it was proving difficult to secure sufficient support from the top management team for any proposed reorganization. The chief executive then set up a task force of middle managers to make suggestions on reorganization. These task force meetings were conducted in an informal manner and produced ideas, many of which were subsequently incorporated into reorganization proposals to which top managers eventually agreed. The task force was not treated as some kind of selling exercise in which middle managers would be encouraged to commit to a new organization because they had played a part in developing it. It was a genuine request for an input of ideas without any guarantee that any of them would be heeded. There was no question of removing the final decision from the normal procedures or power structure. Instead it was a genuine learning exercise that inevitably had some political impact and did have some influence on the choice that was ultimately made. And it is this process that is realistic strategic management.

The quality of the learning which occurs at strategy workshops and task forces can be enhanced by including outsiders to the organization at such meetings. One of the major obstacles to effective organizational learning in open-ended situations is the operation of the group's retained memory, its cultural assumptions or received wisdom. An outsider who does not share this, who has no commitment to the organization or to any issue or position, is frequently able to make others aware of the restricting impact their assumptions are having on how they are approaching the issues.

While the primary focus in workshops and task forces will normally be on the issues, it is usually beneficial to devote some time to surfacing and discussing views on process. This would cover the nature of organizational control and the impact that personality differences and the group dynamic are having on the way the group learns together. Managers usually enjoy completing non-threatening personality tests and then discussing the implications of their differences for the way in which they approach problems, make decisions and learn. And the benefits of doing so usually show up in the way they work together.

Management development

Participation in workshops and task forces is in itself a form of management development and education. The effectiveness of such activities can be enhanced by undertaking more explicit management development as well. While there is now considerable effort devoted to management development programmes for middle managers, those at the top of the organization usually receive much less attention. In my experience there are few members of top management teams or boards of directors who take time off to discuss and explore the nature of senior management, philosophies of control, the meaning of strategic management. A newly appointed board member is rarely prepared for his or her new role by any form of management training. It is then easy for top managers to base their actions on explanations of management that they rarely question and that could well be inadequate. An effective management intervention in the strategy process would then be to organize specific senior management development programmes.

Climate of challenge and questioning

Another important top management intervention has to do with creating a climate of challenge and questioning. To do this top managers themselves have to keep questioning received wisdom and hold themselves

open to the questioning of subordinates. Instead of propaganda to promote the same values, effective strategic control requires continual questioning of those values.

Thinking about the dynamic of successful businesses in chaos terms
moves top managers away from installing systems to deal with strategic
issues; away from rational techniques and 'religious' visions, dreams and
common culture propaganda. It moves them towards a direct concern
with behaviour and its impact; to power and the connection between the
form in which it is exerted and the behavioural responses that provokes.
Leaders then are creators of challenging, questioning atmospheres. They
are players in the political learning process. They exert considerable
influence on strategic direction through intervening in the context of
strategic discovery, choice and action. And they ensure sufficient stability
in what is a confusing and uncertain process through applying rational
management to issues with short-term predictable consequences,
through stable unequally distributed power and clear simple hierarchies
of management. Successful leaders continually judge how to combine
order and disorder.

The message for managers

Accepting that the dynamic of business success is chaotic does not mean
giving up on the long-term and focusing on the short-term. It does not
mean becoming reactive. Long-term unpredictability does of course
mean that we cannot anticipate long-term consequences; we cannot
therefore be proactive. But neither can we be reactive. You can only be
purely reactive if you are trying to deal with given change that occurs
whatever you do, or do not do. Reacting is simply adapting to what will
occur whatever you do. However in chaotic systems what you do, or fail
to do, will affect the long-term change that occurs; what you do matters
and is itself a change. The appropriate response is then to be continuously
creative. The response is to do something, to explore, to discover the
consequences of what you have done and then undertake further creative
action to deal with it. In chaotic systems, both proaction and reaction are
impossible – the choice is between creative exploration, action and discovery on the one hand and simply being buffeted by change on the
other. The message of chaos for managers is the exciting one of the
endless scope for creative discovery. And the chaos property of general,
qualitative, self-similar patterns is one that we are peculiarly suited to
dealing with. We have the flexible mental model-building capability provided by our ability to use analogies derived from previous experience.

The message of scientific chaos for managers is this:

- You cannot control, in the normally accepted sense of that word,
  either the long-term development of your business, or the sequence

of choices that generates such development. Both are inherently unpredictable in specific terms. All forms of future mission, long-term planning, simulations and quantitative models are therefore simply illusions of rational decision making. In the journey into the unknown you cannot have a reliable vision of some future state around which you can rally the troops by promoting a widely shared culture.

- You should therefore vigorously practise what is normally understood as control where it is possible. You can control the short-term consequences of actions taken and events occurring now because they are by and large predictable.

- When it comes to ambiguous and unpredictable long-term consequences of actions taken and events occurring now, you have no option but to rely on the spontaneous, self-organizing propensity of people in your organization. You have to rely on the political learning system through which agendas of strategic issues are continually built, through which choices are creatively made using the qualitative similarity of business patterns, and then acted upon. The long-term development of the business emerges unpredictably from a spontaneous political and learning process of groups of people. That process is dependent upon the different values, perspectives, goals and perceptions of those people. In this process, continuous commitment to and consensus on which strategic issues to deal with, and how to deal with them, is short lived and periodic. It cannot and should not be sustained for long if the organization is to innovate. But such constructive spontaneity cannot emerge in the face of uncertainty if there is an absence of perceptible boundaries or constraints to provide the security people need to function as work groups. And these constraints on wild variability in behaving, learning and choosing are provided by difference: difference in power distribution and difference in values. They are also provided by the propensity to reflect on what is happening and the time available in which to do it.

- The prime role of managers in this spontaneous process so dependent on difference is threefold. The first role of managers is to intervene in the context within which spontaneous political learning occurs. It means tolerating and encouraging difference, encouraging reflection and ensuring that there is time for it to happen. It means bringing people together informally in work groups. It means creating opportunities for open-ended discussion. The second role of managers relates to the use of the greater power those managers possess. The form in which that power is used is part of the context within which the spontaneous learning process occurs. If power is always used in its form of authority, that will kill difference and spontaneity. What is required is switching the form of power from authority, to loose influence, to strong pressure and back to authority, in order to prod and assist an otherwise spontaneous process. Spontaneity is not killed by unequal power, but by inappropriately used power. And how and when to switch its form depends on intuition based on experience. Third, the role of the manager is to participate as a significant actor in the spontaneous process of learning and political activity. Top managers exert strategic 'control' by creating the conditions within which coherent behaviour may occur. The concern is then not with driving the direction but with what enables people to learn.

- There is no recipe or general model to yield specific choices in new situations. Each new strategic situation requires us to construct new mental models through a process of reasoning by analogy. And in business we do this in groups. The key to success is conscious examination of how groups of people are learning and making choices in uncertain conditions and trying to make these processes more effective. On confronting each new strategic issue managers have to learn afresh what to do about it.

- Managers have in short to practise the art of hanging on and letting go as the circumstances require and for that they have to rely on intuition, judgement, common sense, insight and experience.

Scientific chaos is a revolution for management because it emphasizes the importance of difference and spontaneity as the keys to successful long-term development of a business. It emphasizes the manager, the leader, as a key interventionist and player, rather than a rational objective setter or a visionary former of common cultural norms. It moves to the background that is almost religious preoccupation with shared values which dominates current prescriptions for success. It suggests that current moves to abandon clear hierarchies and build loose networks is misguided. Networks are essentially spontaneous, informal and fluid and cannot be incorporated into frozen structures. To do so destroys the spontaneity. The chaos perspective suggests that prescriptions to distribute power through the organization and get everyone involved in everything could well reduce the organization's ability to cope with uncertainty, rather than increase it. The important point is not so much the level of power key managers have, but the form in which they use it and with what consequences they apply it.

Conclusion: establishing conditions for effective strategic control

The central argument presented here is this. Most managers today explicitly explain the functioning of a successful business within a rarely questioned frame of reference that sees businesses as information processing machines or adapting organisms. They consequently seek to apply forms of long-term control based on forecasts, plans, missions, visions, common cultures, continuing commitment and consensus. They see control as order and strategic direction as the consequence of that order. They believe that they are, or should be, in control of the process and the outcome. They believe that they must 'own' and drive the process in some sense, to an outcome that competent people ought to be able to see. When they are confronted with reality they cannot do these things, because the reality is one of chaotic dynamics. What successful managers do instead is to employ political learning processes to build strategic issue agendas and so discover what they are to do. The outcomes emerge and in fact managers are not in control of the process. They are prime contributors to a creative development process. But it seems many are not explicitly aware that this is what they are doing. They then try to apply inappropriate planning and visionary forms of control in open-ended situations. And when managers try to apply inappropriate forms of control they do two harmful things.

First many of the inappropriate aspects of the control forms they adopt interfere with the spontaneous political learning process. So managers may block new perceptions by insisting that those with different values are being 'negative'. They may avoid conflict situations and play political games. They may suppress conflict and so damage their ability to work as groups on organizational issues. They may impose high workloads in the interests of short-term efficiency and so reduce the possibility of spontaneous processes to deal with the unpredictable. They may waste time on planning rituals instead of addressing issues.

The second harmful consequence of espousing unrealistic explanations of how a business can function is that very little attention is paid to the processes that in reality have to be applied to dealing with the unpredictable. Little attention is paid to how a particular group of managers is learning and how effective the political interaction between them is. The group dynamic that affects the choices made is rarely explored.

By espousing one explanation while in fact behaving according to another, managers can damage the ability of their organization to cope with chaos. The view that more attention should be paid to political processes and group dynamics could previously be rejected because it was ideological or weird psychoanalysis. Scientific chaos is a revolution because it factually demonstrates, quite independently of ideology, that chaos is a consequence of the nature of the feedback control loops which drive a business and that plans, vision and common cultures cannot cope with chaos.

The perspective suggested by chaos is that it is the strategic role of top managers to establish through their own behaviour, through the manner in which they use their power, the context within which they and their colleagues can learn about open-ended change. Such learning does not follow from installing structures or systems, from dispersing power or encouraging widespread participation. It follows from establishing occasions where communication can be spontaneous among those who have real contributions to make to strategic issues. It also follows from establishing conditions within which those with contributions to make can organize themselves to make those contributions. The problems of strategic control revolve around how groups of people learn effectively so as to discover appropriate things to do. The problem is not to do with implementing plans, as is so often stated. Plans and visions are unrealistic responses to open-ended change and that is why they are so often not implemented. The real management problem is not one of implementation. Managers are good at that. The real problem is one of discovering what to do in the first place. And it is to this that scientific chaos usefully redirects our attention.

The conclusion we reach, then, is this. There are no general sets of prescriptions on how to manage and what to do in a wide range of open-ended situations because they are generated by chaotic dynamics. Each team of key managers has to develop new mental models for each new open-ended situation it encounters. You discover afresh each time what to do and how to do it, using analogies with those self-similar past patterns that chaos generates. This is the essence of the innovation upon which success in business depends today. This is what you do when you arrange your affairs on the basis that the future is not simply presently unknown, but will always be unknowable. What will happen will be the result of a complex intertwining of chance and creative individual and group efforts. Because of this you cannot simply wait for it to happen and then react. Nor can you be proactive. Instead, to be successful, you have to learn continually as the future unfolds. This means developing new mental models to design creative actions which bring about new environments. You cannot know the long-term outcomes of these actions or what that new environment will be like. But something will happen and you will deal with it as it unfolds.

If it is impossible to decide what to do in advance of the change, if you cannot list the prescriptions, you can prepare yourself in another way. You can create conditions that make it easier for key groups of managers to develop new mental models to design their actions. You can reduce time pressures. You can encourage people to retain different perspectives instead of strongly sharing cultures. You can provide the stability necessary in great uncertainty through clear hierarchies and the appropriate use of unequally distributed power. Above all you can encourage changes in the way people think. And chaos provides a highly useful new way of thinking, not a list of general prescriptions.

Appendix A
Scientific chaos: a new way of thinking about dynamics

The purpose of this appendix is to put chaos and self-organization theory into context by comparing it with the general approach adopted by scientists, including management and organization theorists, to explain how their worlds work. The appendix is concerned with the general frame of reference within which we have been educated to think about the dynamic behaviour of phenomena ranging from insects reproducing on a bush to traders operating in a market, from the behaviour of the weather system to the behaviour of economies and business organizations. And a central problem encountered in just about every area of understanding is that of explaining and coping with turbulence and randomness.

Problem of turbulence

The difficulty of understanding turbulence in business

Today's business world is commonly described as turbulent or chaotic. But the current explanations of the functioning of the business world that most clearly influence managers all fail to deal adequately with the nature of, and required response to, extreme uncertainty. All those explicit explanations and prescriptions that have attracted the attention of the business community are concerned with securing order, discipline and regularity in the conduct of business; or at least with neutralizing the impact of external disorder on a business organization through attaining some form of internal harmony. As a consequence, we find comprehensive bodies of advice on how to organize, control, manage and make decisions in orderly conditions near to certainty. And this advice commands widespread agreement and support.

But when it comes to very rapid change and high levels of uncertainty, when it come to managing strategically, there is far less consensus on how to proceed. Managers then act upon their own implicit, unconscious understanding of how a business works. It consequently becomes quite easy to proclaim that one is doing one thing while in fact doing something completely different. So we find top executives going to great lengths to prepare orderly strategic corporate plans, only to make somewhat disorderly decisions that may be entirely determined by the exercise of political power. Or they may even make decisions where it is not at all clear what has determined that decision. We find competent senior executives proclaiming the importance of thinking and acting strategically, only to observe them constantly shelving strategic issues, avoiding the confusion and anxiety that great uncertainty brings.

But it is not just managers and management scientists who find it difficult to explain what happens, or how to control, when conditions are turbulent.

The difficulty of explaining turbulence in nature

The classical sciences have for centuries encountered similar difficulties in explaining and predicting the behaviour of turbulent phenomena in nature. Newtonian dynamics can explain and predict with great accuracy the movement of the planets. But it is at a loss to explain and predict the pattern of movement of a pendulum that is pushed past a certain limit. Equilibrium thermodynamics presents precise laws on the exchange and conversion of energy, but it cannot explain and predict what happens as steam condenses to water and as water freezes to ice. It cannot predict the patterns of turbulence in fluids or gases. Darwinian evolution explains how biological systems adapt to their uncertain environments, but has considerable difficulty in accounting for the increasing complexity of those systems.

Scientists have therefore encountered similar difficulties in explaining and dealing with turbulent phenomena as those encountered by social scientists and students of management and organization. The basic approach adopted by natural scientists in building the great body of scientific knowledge has always been one of searching for the laws that will explain the inherent order in the apparent disorder we observe around us. And it is this basic approach that management and organization theorists have imported to explain their world. Can it be that the difficulties both natural and management scientists have in dealing with turbulence and chaos are consequences of the basic approach which all adopt to explaining what is going on?

Traditional approach to explaining turbulence

In seeking to explain, predict and ultimately control nature's systems, scientists have for centuries traditionally thought and worked within a frame of reference in which:

- The aim of scientific endeavour is to discover the fixed, immutable laws which govern all natural behaviour in the universe. If a given force is applied to a body of a given mass, then that body will move at a speed which is precisely determined by a scientific law, provided that there is no friction. Increase the force and the speed increases in a perfectly predictable manner. So, having specified the initial conditions of force and mass, within the boundary conditions of no friction, then the law determines what happens to that body for evermore. Thus once the initial conditions for the creation of the universe were established, the laws of Newtonian dynamics prescribe the movements of all the bodies in space for ever. There are fixed deterministic rules and relationships in which a fixed initial condition leads to a fixed, precise outcome. There is a cause for every effect we observe.
- Tiny differences in the initial conditions or the border conditions have a negligible impact on the outcome. Minute errors of measurement, very small variations in causal factors, can thus be regarded as 'noise' that does not undermine the validity of any explanations or predictions.
- Complex behavioural outcomes are determined by complex rules and relationships. Where great variety is observed, where the behaviour of systems follows many different patterns, then the scientist looks for complicated rules and relationships, in order to explain and predict all those different patterns. Complex laws enable a limited, manageable quantity of information to be transformed into predictions of tremendous variety. Complexity of the rules and relationships means that we are able to feed in less information in the form of causes than we generate in the form of predictions. If we were required to provide as much input information as we received in the form of output information, then we would not be able to provide much in the way of useful explanation of detailed patterns of behaviour. We would not be able to say in advance what would happen. So the weather, it was thought, could be predicted over the long-term if we could sample conditions on a practical scale all over the globe now and feed this information into a complex model of the weather system. The processing power of computers would then transform

the limited inputs into the tremendous variety we know we will observe in future weather conditions.

- Any observed disorder, turbulence or chaos is apparent, not real. What looks like disorder is in fact due to human ignorance of the full complexity of the laws of nature. Increased effort would in the end uncover those complex laws and what looked like disorder would then come to be seen as order. Thus, greater investment in research would enable mankind to expose fully the laws governing the weather. This together with more intensive data gathering would enable long-term weather predictions, upon which basis the earth's weather could be controlled by man.

- The appropriate scientific method is analytical reductionism. That is to say, the behaviour of systems can be explained by examining them in more and more detail, looking at smaller and smaller parts of the system in order to identify the deterministic laws that govern their behaviour. So, we can understand the behaviour of matter by examining the behaviour of atoms and the particles of which those atoms are composed.

- The behaviour of systems in nature can be controlled by man once their behaviour is predicted. So, once we have gathered enough detail on weather conditions now, and specified the laws governing weather systems, we will be able to predict conditions in the long-term future. Knowing what the weather will be at a given future point without human intervention, and knowing the consequence of any human intervention, we can then change some conditions now to yield the required weather conditions in the future.

Order from order

This whole frame of reference for scientific enquiry focuses on order and equilibrium. Nature works with the precision of a machine; a machine having a powerful attraction towards stability and balance. Explanations are then always cast in terms of the forces leading to the conditions under which stability and the balance between one thing and another will be established. Scientists search for order and that which explains order. And order is brought about, order is explained in terms of, logically predetermined step-by-step rules and procedures. In other words, an algorithm or computer program. Orderly causes lead through orderly laws to orderly outcomes and that disorder called turbulence is basically a perception of human beings based upon their own ignorance.

In this underlying view of how the world works, the machine paradigm, there is no place for unique chance in any essential sense. Outcomes may appear to occur by chance, but this is simply an appearance. Chance may play some part in the mechanisms governing the behaviour of a system, but never in the outcome. So, in the evolution of a biological species, the rules are chance (random) mutation and natural selection. Nature is in effect using a trial-and-error search procedure, a step-by-step search towards a goal where criteria for success and failure of each step are predetermined. This is the heuristic search procedure that computers also utilize. Nature uses this heuristic search to discover the adaptation a given environmental change requires in order that a species will survive in those particular environmental conditions. But the outcome is in no way a matter of chance. The change in the environment determines what is required for survival and the experimental process of evolution ensures that the required mutations occur and survive, leading to better adapted species.

Order leads to order and although the orderly rules may employ chance the outcome has nothing to do with anything as disorderly as chance. We may perceive outcomes to be a matter of chance, but this is simply our ignorance and it has nothing to do with reality.

Disorder from disorder

And scientists can deal with ignorance, with the appearance of chance outcomes, until such time as further knowledge is obtained. They can do this using the science of chance, probability theory and statistics. Where the full complexity of the deterministic laws cannot yet be identified, we can use simpler approximations and accept explanations and predictions that are not precise, but to which some probability can be attached. The approximate rules and relationships can be thought of as being subject to random shocks or error terms. So we can model our ignorance, we can model the appearance of chance and instability, by incorporating a random element in the causes of some behaviour, or by inserting a random element into the structure of the rule we are using to explain that behaviour. And these random inputs will generate the random elements we observe in the outcomes. So disorder can lead to disorder. And when large numbers of events, repetitive behaviours, are being dealt with we can identify the manner in which the random elements, the shocks to, or errors in, the system are distributed. This allows the application of a very sophisticated body of statistical techniques which basically allow us to extract the fundamentally orderly relationships hidden in the apparently disorderly data.

To model the turbulent reality we observe, we add random inputs to the orderly relationship to get a pattern of outcomes with the appearance of disorder.

This traditional scientific frame of reference also excludes the possibility of ongoing creativity. Once the initial conditions are set, the deterministic laws take over and the outcomes are for evermore determined. Creation was a once-for-all act. Nature does not, and given the laws it cannot, innovate. It changes of course, but throughout it maintains dynamic equilibrium in a predetermined manner. Man can intervene successfully if he understands the fundamental laws, which he cannot alter, and then operates on some of the conditions in which nature's systems operate. Successful intervention is based on predictability or upon small experiments that are trial-and-error search. Intervention in the absence of predictability, or in the absence of the possibility of trial-and-error search is simply blind groping that could have disastrous consequences.

The point reached by classical approaches to scientific explanation, in all disciplines adopting the pure scientific method, was one where turbulence was simply a perception based on ignorance. It was possible to go some way towards identifying the underlying orderly laws that generate what appears to be turbulence, but a full explanation was not yet possible. In the meantime we could model and simulate turbulent systems such as the weather, or a market, or a business organization, in order to make probabilistic predictions as a basis for approximate control.

Now while the scientists' underlying machine view of the world has been questioned for centuries by philosophers concerned with the matter of free will, it is only in the last two decades that it has been seriously questioned by scientists themselves.

New approach to turbulence: chaos

During the 1980s a revolution in the way scientists in many different fields view the world has been gathering pace. An intellectual revolution, with potentially far reaching implications for the way in which practitioners in almost every area of human endeavour make decisions, is spreading rapidly and yet is largely unknown to most of those practitioners.

This revolution has its origins in highly abstract theoretical mathematics, but its applications are of immense practical importance. The phenomena with which it is concerned were apparently first glimpsed by the mathematician Henri Poincaré around the turn of the century, but neither he nor the rest of the scientific community pursued the matter – it was far too inconsistent with the received wisdom on the way in which the world works; the machine paradigm. It was not until the mid-1960s that the first explicit description, which was to herald a new approach, appeared in a paper by Edward Lorenz[1] in an obscure meteorological journal. Other aspects of this new way of looking at the world emerged, often independently of each other and Lorenz, until by the mid-1980s what we may call a new approach to science had emerged. The name it has acquired, perhaps unfortunately, is chaos. And this new approach is not just a set of specific discoveries; it is an insight that goes to the heart of the rarely questioned assumptions we make when we explain. It changes a whole frame of reference.

Order can generate disorder and there is order within disorder

Scientific chaos provides a frame of reference within which to explore and understand the behaviour of nature's systems; one that differs dramatically from the traditional machine view of the world. The chaos view of the world is one in which:

- Fixed, immutable laws do indeed govern the behaviour of nature's systems. But those deterministic rules and relationships are now known to be capable of generating very complex behaviours, including under certain circumstances, inherently random outcomes. At some temperature a liquid in a container may be perfectly static. If the base of the container is heated slightly, then that heat is simply transferred in a perfectly orderly and predictable manner through the liquid. But as the heat is increased, movement in the liquid occurs, taking the the form of perfectly stable convection rolls. Then as further heat is applied, the liquid becomes turbulent and this turbulence is now known to be a chaotic state in which the pattern of movement is absolutely random and inherently unpredictable. Perfectly deterministic thermodynamic laws produce a complex range of outcomes, some of which are truly random. A fixed initial condition (a given level of heat) without any random shock or error term, together with a deterministic law also without any random element whatsoever incorporated into it, can yield the very opposite of a fixed, precise outcome. Complete order in all the inputs, complete order in the structure of the rule generating all the outcomes, can lead to complete disorder in those outcomes. And this means that there is not always a specific cause for the changes we observe.
- Tiny differences in initial conditions will, in certain circumstances, lead to major changes in the behaviour of a system. It requires only a small change at the critical heat points to alter the behaviour of a liquid from a stable state to one with convection rolls, or from a state of convection rolls to one of turbulence. Minute differences in the temperature and air impurities experienced by two snowflakes as they fall to the ground result in very different shapes. A small change in air pressure in one part of the globe can escalate up through the weather system to cause a storm many thousands of miles away. This sensitive dependence on initial conditions means that errors of measurement, no matter how small, are extremely important and cannot be dismissed as noise. For, an error even to the thousandth decimal place can lead eventually to a completely different prediction. In chaotic

conditions, an impossibly infinite degree of precision is required to enable long-term prediction.

- Complex behavioural outcomes are determined by relatively simple rules and relationships of a non-linear feedback form. The rule may be very simple, but provided that it relates cause and effect in a non-proportional way, and provided that the outcome of that rule is fed back into the rule to determine the next outcome, then complex behaviour results, despite the simplicity of the rule. In other words, simple rules with these characteristics can generate complicated amplifying and damping loops which sometimes lead to random behaviour. The rule may then be simple, but the precision and degree of detail with which causal factors must be specified is immense if outcomes are to be predicted at all. The quantity of information required as input to the rule so as to specify outcomes is equal to the quantity of output information itself. There are no benefits to be obtained from prediction or simulation. To be able to predict the weather we require an impossibly high level of input information.

- Disorder, turbulence and chaos are observed because they actually exist. They are not simply a manifestation of human ignorance. This may not sound like revolutionary stuff, but it dramatically alters the way we think about the behaviour of systems and what we are able to do to control them. No amount of research can ever remove the random behaviour in chaotic systems – it is inherent in the simple laws governing them and their sensitive dependence on initial conditions. No practically attainable level of information is of any use in predicting the outcomes. We are able to intervene in the course the weather takes, but we will never know what course it would have taken had we not intervened.

- There is a global order or structure to the complex behaviour that non-linear feedback rules generate. The same category of rule produces the same sequences of behaviour no matter where it applies and the relationship between one sequence and the next is the same. Because the same category of rule turns out to apply to a liquid being heated and insects reproducing on a bush, they both display the same sequences of stable behaviour, followed by regular cycles, followed in turn by chaos, as the intensity of a particular causal condition is increased. The conditions in which random patterns will emerge can be determined. The boundaries within which that random behaviour will occur can be discovered. It also turns out that all rules of the same category have the same constant degree of irregularity. The extent to which their behaviour fractures into different forms is constant. They have a constant fractal dimension. And this means that the outcomes of a particular rule are self-similar. Outcomes are similar in general qualitative terms, but never the same in specific terms. So there is an overall shape, or rhythm, to the behaviour of a system at a macro-level, even though at certain times, behaviour at the micro level is totally random. It is because of this property, together with sensitive dependence on initial conditions, that we can identify a category of phenomena or species, no two individual members of which are ever the same.

- It follows that the traditional scientific method of analytical reductionism is inappropriate to formulating explanations of turbulent phenomena, since detailed explanations are in fact impossible. Appropriate explanatory methods are those which focus on the macro-level, on synthesis and understanding the system as a whole.

- Control over the behaviour of a system comes to have a different meaning. And this follows from the impossibility of long-term prediction. Where there is no sensitive dependence on initial conditions, where the rules governing behaviour are such that fixed causal factors yield fixed outcomes, we can operate on the causal factor and so change the outcome in a manner that we can predict. We can use the logically predetermined step-by-step rules and procedures governing the system to alter its behaviour. Or, we can utilize an evolutionary approach of trial-and-error search, that is examining the outcomes of small experiments to see whether they are taking us towards the control goal. But when there is sensitive dependence on initial conditions and the rule is an amplifying or damping one, then control over specific outcomes is impossible. We cannot predict those outcomes over the long-term by applying predetermined step-by-step procedures to a set of starting conditions, because we cannot specify those conditions accurately enough. We cannot discover those long-term outcomes, in advance of their occurring, by using trial-and-error search. This is because we cannot know what we are searching for. As the system moves through real time, tiny differences in the conditions it experiences can totally alter its behaviour and we cannot discover those differences in advance of their occurring. In such circumstances control is reduced to the possibility of creating the boundary conditions, or context, within which certain kinds of behaviour will or may occur. We can alter the level of heat applied to the base of a container of liquid to the point where convection rolls will appear. But there is no way we can determine the direction of spin of any particular roll.

The way in which we view the working of the world from a chaos perspective is thus completely different, in all major respects, from the machine frame of reference within which traditional science was developed. Turbulence turns out to be the most important aspect of reality. It is reality, not simply a human perception born of ignorance. Consequently, instead of focusing on order, attraction to equilibrium and balance, the chaos perspective is concerned with disorder, with the properties and consequences of non-equilibrium. Far from playing no part, chance differences in initial conditions play a vital role. Outcomes can occur by chance even when they are generated by deterministic laws. Sometimes events do not have a cause.

And an important consequence of the chaos view of the world is that creativity is not a once-for-all act; it is an ongoing process. Nature innovates continuously, creating variety and unique new phenomena. Small individual actions can make major differences.

Now we know that turbulence is real; it is a chaotic state of inherently random behaviour. Now we know that we cannot predict or control in the way we thought we could when confronted by turbulence. But are we any better off? Before we can judge, we need to consider further developments in the theory on non-linear dynamics called self-organization theory. This demonstrates how disorder is essential to the emergence of higher, more complex forms of order.

Disorder is essential to complex order

The laws that govern most of nature's systems are now known to be relatively simple non-linear feedback mechanisms; simple rules that relate one point in space or time to another; simple rules that are repeated over and over again to trace out complex patterns in space and over time. They are fixed and deterministic, but they yield complex behavioural outcomes and under some conditions these outcomes are inherently random at the detailed level, but with an overall global pattern. This global pattern provides a 'hidden' order in the real disorder. The 'hidden' order is provided by the feedback rule itself, by the regularity in the sequences of behaviour that it generates, by the constant degree of irregularity that outcomes display. Chaos is the disorderly pattern in detail, within global order, all of which results from fixed orderly rules and regular repetition.

The random, disorderly pattern of the detail results from the fact that in certain circumstances repetition using non-linear feedback rules magnifies tiny differences in the starting positions or initial conditions. As the rule is repeated, tiny disturbances or fluctuations in the context within which the system is operating are amplified so as to completely change the detailed behaviour and eventually the total outcome. Such tiny differences in initial conditions are a matter of chance. Two snowflakes falling to the ground each experience tiny differences in temperature and air impurities which are amplified to produce different individual shapes.

So, randomness results from the amplifying properties of the structure of the rule, the act of repetition and the operation of chance. Nature uses chance and the amplification properties of the rules to generate variety at the individual level within a particular generic category. And that variety, that continuing innovation depends in an essential way on chance. Nature creates and innovates; it generates new patterns and differences using simple rules, repetition and chance. If we can identify the rule then we can generate individuals within the category. But no two of these individuals will be the same, nor will any of them be the same as those that actually occur in reality. Even when we know all the laws we cannot produce exact copies, only something similar. We can simulate patterns in space and time that clearly belong to the category we are interested in, but we cannot simulate the patterns within that category that will actually occur in real time.

The key conclusions that turn out to be of importance to the question of how to control a business in conditions of true uncertainty, to the question of how to promote innovation, are these:

- Nature innovates at the individual level, it generates variety, using a process of dynamic interaction that depends upon chance.
- Tiny changes in initial conditions are amplified to yield the new at an individual level and that new cannot be predicted or controlled in advance of its occurring.
- All this innovation at the individual level occurs within a global pattern that provides stability. That pattern provides the characteristics of a particular category of phenomena. This global pattern can be predicted.

But what about changes in whole categories? Scientists refer to a change in a whole category as a phase transition. Some phase transitions are changes from one equilibrium state to another. Examples are the phase transition from ice to water, that from water to steam, that from no magnetism at one temperature to magnetism at another. At the point of phase transition the behaviour of the system is chaotic. Phase transitions are turbulent. So, in order to change a system from one predictable state to another, nature uses a period of random behaviour in which the symmetry of one form of order is broken and another emerges. Instability is an essential feature of change from one state to another in nature.

Changing from one equilibrium state to another requires complex mechanisms, or large changes in the boundary conditions of the system, and that means storing large amounts of information. Small changes, limited amounts of data and simple rules will not do if there is to be continuous creation for equilibrium systems. For this reason, most of nature's systems exist in a state far-from-equilibrium, essentially an unstable state where simple rules and small changes dependent upon chance can generate major change. Far-from-equilibrium, small changes are rapidly amplified into major alterations of the behaviour of the system. Small changes are amplified to break easily the symmetry of existing order. It is now known that at some critical point during this chaotic symmetry-breaking phase a process of self-organization occurs, leading to abrupt changes in whole categories of behaviour. The outcome at each critical point is inherently unpredictable. That outcome could be further chaos, or it could be a new more complex form of order known as a dissipative structure. And it is called a dissipative structure because it requires continuing inputs of energy to sustain it. An example is provided by laser beams. As energy is pumped into a gas it first emits a diffuse glow because the molecules move in a chaotic manner, all pointing in different directions. At a critical level of energy input, the molecules abruptly self organize and point in the same direction to produce the laser beam.

Nature uses chaos and disorder to create on a major scale, to transform whole categories of behaviour. Chaos is vital to the breaking of the old order and self-organization is vital to the emergence of the new. Continuing inputs of energy are vital to sustaining that new. Nature does not manage the change, it moves through conditions of disorder within which change can emerge. But the new is not a foregone conclusion. The form of the new is unpredictable. Change itself is not managed, the boundary conditions are. And this is a simple and highly efficient way of producing continuing change – it requires less information and far simpler rules than a completely orderly approach would.

The key points that turn out to be of great relevance to the control of organizations in conditions of true uncertainty, to the promotion of innovation, to the management of change, are:

- small changes can lead to the transformation of whole systems;
- turbulence, ambiguity, confusion, conflict create the conditions within which old orders can be shattered and new perspectives can emerge;
- self-organization is the process through which new more complex order emerges when a system is far-from-equilibrium;
- the outcomes of major system changes are inherently unpredictable;
- change itself cannot be managed but the conditions within which it will occur can;
- significant continuing change is only possible for systems pushed far-from-equilibrium.

Summary

The propositions of chaos theory fundamentally contradict the most deep-seated views we have been educated to have on the working of the world. So much so that many natural scientists at first refused to accept them as anything more than mathematical curiosities. On first exposure to these ideas many managers react in exactly the same way. How can chaos in a business system possibly have anything to do with innovation and control? How could one possibly cope with chaos?

But chaos in its scientific sense is not as bad as it sounds. It does not mean utter confusion, complete formlessness, total disorder, the complete lack of principles and laws governing behaviour. It does not mean that we have to draw back in horror and give up trying to establish conclusions about anything. The science of chaos is concerned with the newly discovered fact that simple deterministic rules governing dynamical systems, which are as far apart as the human heart and the market for oil, are in certain circumstances capable of generating behaviour that is to all intents and purposes random, totally and inherently unpredictable. Disorder can arise from the operation of deterministic laws in certain circumstances. Chaos theory is concerned with establishing what those certain circumstances are and what properties this random behaviour has. Chaos is concerned with an orderly approach to disorder, with the manner in which order and disorder are intertwined and coexist, with the part disorder plays in generating order.

Our deeply received wisdom has been that the world is ultimately governed by order and that the purpose of scientific endeavour is to uncover the laws governing that order – the legitimate search was one for the conditions that establish equilibrium. The science of chaos challenges that deeply held view and draws our attention instead to the exciting, creative and realistic possibilities of orderly disorder, of far-from-equilibrium states.

Many with any experience of say the oil, foreign exchange or stock markets may be tempted to find this a trivial conclusion – it would be quite difficult to operate in those markets on a daily basis without coming to the conclusion that their behaviour is in practical terms unpredictable, that they simultaneously display characteristics of both order and extreme disorder. The surprise that the theory of chaos supplies is not so much the unpredictability, but the reason for it.

Most of us believe, or used to believe until we heard about chaos, that the reason for unpredictability lies in the complexity of the laws that govern the behaviour of a market or any other dynamic system for that matter. The oil market is influenced by so many factors, many of them to do with the behaviour of human beings, tied together in such complex causal ways that in practice we cannot at the present time reliably forecast what will happen. But in principle if we could only do enough research, gather enough information, apply enough analytical and information processing power, then we ought to be able to generate predictions which would yield at least some improvement in the decisions we make. The effort we put into information gathering, analysis and planning in one market after another and in one aspect of business operation after another, in one economy after another, demonstrates quite clearly that most practical business people and politicians make decisions on exactly this supposition.

But the science of chaos puts forward another, almost shocking, reason for unpredictability. And that reason lies in the nature of the system itself

– the very decision rules, even the most simple, that we use in business, economics and politics could have within them the seeds of inherent, irreducible unpredictability. And no amount of research and analysis could ever remove that. Simple rules can generate complex, random, chaotic behaviour. The creative functioning of the dynamic systems in nature, the human body, the economy and the business enterprise may all depend, to a significant extent, on chance. It may all fundamentally be a game in which God throws the dice. But it is a game that has rules, and we can understand those rules. Our endeavour then becomes one of understanding how God throws dice; we become far less concerned with complex laws and the conditions for equilibrium.

The science of chaos puts forward an even more shocking proposition. It is that turbulence, chaos and randomness are vital to true creativity, to significant change. It is that significant change is unpredictable and occurs through a process of self-organization.

It is therefore of immense practical importance that those who are involved in the business world, as practitioners, consultants and academics, should understand what the science of chaos has to say and judge whether the dynamics of our economies, markets and business operations are chaotic. If we are persuaded that such chaotic dynamics do in fact exist, then we have to consider what this means for the manner in which we currently make business decisions, what it means for the advice we give as consultants, what it means for the theories we have developed and teach to explain the behaviour of markets and the operation of business enterprises.

But what evidence is there that chaos actually exists in natural and human systems?

Chaos is not a mathematical or philosophical curiosity

Chaos is a fact of nature

The first demonstration that chaos existed outside abstract mathematical equations, and is in fact to be found in nature, was Lorenz's simple set of three differential equations that model the weather.[2] To predict the weather it is necessary to measure forces such as pressure, temperature, humidity and wind speed at a particular point in time, at regular vertical intervals through the atmosphere from each of a grid of points on the earth's surface.

Rules are then necessary to explain how each of the sets of interrelated measurements, at each measurement point in the atmosphere, change over time. This requires massive numbers of computations. The fundamental laws relating each variable to all the others over time had already been well established by 1963 and they took the form of a set of non-linear differential equations. What no one had ever done, up to that point, was to explore the nature of the dynamics those rules implied; the patterns in pressure, temperature and so on, over time. Lorenz simplified the set of equations down to three key equations that he showed still generated typical weather patterns. He used them to show that the weather always follows what is called a strange attractor, a chaotic pattern.

> The modern weather models work with a grid of points on the order of sixty miles apart, and even so, some starting data has to be guessed, since ground stations and satellites cannot see everywhere. But suppose the earth could be covered with sensors spaced one foot apart, rising at one foot intervals all the way to the top of the atmosphere. Suppose every sensor gives perfectly accurate readings of temperature, pressure, humidity and any other quantity a meteorologist would want. Precisely at noon an infinitely powerful computer takes all the data and calculates what will happen at each point at 12.01, then 12.02, then 12.03 ... The computer will still be unable to predict whether Princeton, New Jersey, will have sun or rain on a day one month away. At noon the spaces between the sensors will hide fluctuations that the computer will not know about, tiny deviations from the average. By 12.01, those fluctuations will already have created small errors one foot away. Soon errors will have multiplied to the ten foot scales, and so on up to the size of the globe... Yes you could change the weather. You could make it do something different from what it would otherwise have done. But if you did then you would never know what it would otherwise have done. It would be like giving an extra shuffle to an already well shuffled pack of cards. You know it will change your luck, but you don't know whether for better or worse.[3]

Chaotic dynamics mean that we will never be able to forecast the weather for more than a few days ahead.

Then in the early 1970s Swinney and Gollub started a series of experiments on turbulence in fluids. In 1977 Libchaber conducted experiments on turbulence in liquid helium. These and many other experiments proved the existence of strange attractors in turbulence. Turbulence in fluids and gases was shown to be a chaotic phenomenon. Chaos is present in nature. It is a fact, not just a mathematical phenomenon.

Throughout the 1970s and the 1980s the principles of chaos have been explored in one field after another and found to explain certain pathological conditions of the heart, the eye movements of schizophrenics, the spread of some diseases, the impact of some inoculation programmes against some diseases. The body's system of arteries and veins follows patterns determined by feedback rules with chaotic properties. The growth of insect populations has chaotic characteristics. The leaves of trees grow through a process of iterating deterministic rules contained in their spores; they are fractal and self-similar enough to allow us to distinguish one kind from another but no two of a kind are ever exactly the same. You can reproduce similar individuals, clearly belonging to one category, on a computer using the rules and iteration. Human cells divide in the same way following rules encoded in the DNA. The reason for no two snowflakes ever being the same can be explained using chaotic dynamics. The orbit of the moon Hyperion around Saturn follows a path which can be explained using the principles of chaos, as can the Great Red Spot of Jupiter. Water dripping from a tap has been shown to follow a chaotic time pattern, as does smoke spiralling from a cigarette.[4]

It is now clear that chaos is widely found in nature and provides a powerful insight into a great many phenomena that were little understood even a decade ago.

Chaos in economic systems

Mandelbrot, the father of fractal geometry was not an economist, but he was perhaps the first to indicate that chaos might be present in economic systems:

> ... economists ... shared certain articles of faith. One was a conviction that small, transient changes had nothing in common with large, long-term changes. Fast fluctuations come randomly. The small-scale ups and downs [of prices] in a day's transactions are just noise, unpredictable and uninteresting. Long-term changes however are a different species entirely ... determined by deep macroeconomic forces ... as it happened that dichotomy had no place in the picture of reality that Mandelbrot was developing. Instead of separating tiny changes from grand ones, his picture bound them together. He was looking for patterns not at one scale or another, but across every scale ... when Mandelbrot sifted the cotton-price data through IBM's computers he found the astonishing results he was seeking. The numbers that produced aberrations from the point of view of the normal distribution produced symmetry from the point of view of scaling. Each particular price change was random and unpredictable. But the sequence of changes was independent of scale: curves for daily price changes and monthly price changes matched perfectly. Incredibly, analysed Mandelbrot's way, the degree of variation had remained constant over a tumultuous sixty-year period that saw two world wars and a depression.[5]

So Mandelbrot demonstrated the existence of a constant degree of irregularity, a constant fractal dimension, in 60 years of cotton price data. And this is the scaling and self-similarity property of chaotic dynamics. In 1975 May and Beddington, studying biological cycles and chaotic dynamics in insect populations, suggested that chaos had implications for economics.

The 1980s have seen a few papers in economics journals which show that chaos could, at least in principle, arise in a number of economic systems. Economic theories of growth are an obvious starting point. The vast literature on economic growth models and business cycles always stopped at the point of identifying that the workings of the model itself could produce regular stable cycles. The fact that real economic systems do not ever follow the stable cycles predicted by the theory was ascribed to the existence of random shocks. The underlying pattern is stable, but it is continually perturbed by random events arising outside the model, such as changes in economic policies by governments.

Now, very simple economic growth models have been shown to be consistent with the idea of chaos in economics. One of the simplest economic growth models is the Malthusian one, in which the level of output determines the rate of growth of population, which in turn determines the size of the labour force, which in turn determines the level of output. This model produces both stable cycles and chaos.[6]

A rather more realistic model relates economic growth to savings and increases in the capital stock. If the propensity to save out of wages is lower than that out of profits, it can be shown that the behaviour of the capital stock over time can be described by a simple feedback rule. With the right parameter values, investment could behave chaotically.[7] Other studies have shown that optimal growth paths could behave in a chaotic manner.[8] Chaos has been shown to arise in simple ad hoc, macroeconomic models.[9]

Simple models analysing consumer behaviour over time have been used to develop both stable cycles and chaotic change. In one of these it is concluded that increasing wealth can cause complicated dynamics to arise.[10] Chaos has been shown to be a possibility in models of duopoly, in cobweb models of supply and demand, models of the oil market, models of productivity growth, the behaviour of the firm subject to borrowing constraints and in models of advertising expenditure.[11]

However in many of these studies rather extreme assumptions have to be made about the parameters of the feedback rule if chaotic behaviour is to be generated. So methods have been developed to test economic time series for the presence of chaos. The idea is to show whether a particular time series has been generated by chaotic dynamics with some noise or random shocks, as opposed to underlying stable behaviour with variations all coming from random shocks. There are also tests that try to distinguish between data generated by a deterministic system and data generated by a random system. There is evidence that deterministic systems generating chaos could apply to stock markets and foreign exchange markets.[12] But not all economists who have studied chaos are yet convinced that chaos applies to economic systems:

> All in all, the evidence for the existence of chaotic behaviour in real economic time series is far from compelling so far, though what there is does suggest the value of further research in that direction.[13]

However, it should be noted that all these attempts to find chaos in economic systems have so far been conducted within the framework of classical economic theory. The fundamentals of economics, the assump-

tions about rational economic man and market clearing leading to equilibrium are simply accepted. The questions being asked relate to whether
the structure of these laws is such that they could lead to chaos. The
challenge that chaos theory poses is far deeper than this – the question is
whether equilibrium models are appropriate at all. It may be that economic behaviour is better described by simple feedback rules where prices
are fixed by mark-ups on costs and are linked from one period to another,
while output decisions are taken independently in a manner related to
previous periods. This is a more realistic description of what actually
happens than the traditional market clearing, equilibrium model descriptions.[14] To explore for chaos it seems more appropriate to develop new
far-from-equilibrium economic theories. Chaos poses questions for the
very fundamentals of economic theory, not just for particular relationships and their structures. And these questions have yet to be addressed.

That chaos exists in nature's systems and explains many heretofore
unexplained phenomena in the physical sciences, that most of nature's
systems are far-from-equilibrium – is now well established. There is some
rather tentative evidence that these conclusions may also apply to economic systems. But work on this has only just begun at the simplest of
levels, using theoretical models that may well be flawed.

Intuitively chaos applies to business systems

The question of whether chaos provides insights into the functioning of
business organizations has received even less attention. Some of the
literature on decision-making,[15] some of the literature from social psychology and group dynamics,[16] is relevant here, but I have been able to
find only two publications in the English language that adopt a chaos
approach to management and organization.[17]

Intuitively, the patterns we observe in economic data, the behaviour
we see in companies, the way successful decisions are often made, all
point to the importance of the phenomenon of chaos in the practice of
business management. The failure to predict, or afterwards even adequately explain, major turning points in the economy, and the uncertain
impact of economic and business policies, provide further intuitive support. This book has sought to explain why it useful to think of a successful
business as a chaotic system.

Why scientific chaos is a revolution in the way we think

Scientific chaos theory is a revolution in the way we understand and
explain the functioning of nature's systems. It is a revolution in the

approach we adopt to controlling nature. It is a revolution in the scientific method itself. But social scientists, including those who have developed the explicit explanations of business behaviour to which managers pay attention, have all imported their approach to explaining from the classical natural sciences. It must therefore be a matter of great importance for managers, as well as for management and organization theorists, to explore what this revolution means for them. Consider why scientific chaos is a revolution.

Chaos destroys the machine view of the world

The whole frame of reference within which we develop explanations, the machine paradigm, has to be rejected. Chaos theory is a revolution because it has made it clear that classical science is a limited special case and the classical scientific method of enquiry has a limited application. It is now clear that most of nature's systems are far-from-equilibrium phenomena where the chaos and self-organization approaches have superior explanatory power. Far from working with the predetermined precision of a well-made machine, the natural world is one in which:

- small chance disturbances or fluctuations can be amplified by the laws of nature, so leading to unpredictable major changes in behavioural outcomes;
- inherently random, disorderly behaviour is used to break the symmetry of old forms of order;
- self-organization choice processes are employed at critical change points during periods of chaos to secure unique, inherently unpredictable transformations of whole systems; such transformations can take the form of new, complex patterns of order.

Innovation and creativity depend on ambiguity and chance

Chaos theory is a revolution because it tells us that phase transitions, whole system transformations, changes from one state to another are all inherently chaotic. Chaos and self-organization are the mechanisms nature uses to innovate; continuously to create. Unpredictability is a characteristic of innovation and creativity. Perfectly orderly machine-like systems, those close to equilibrium, cannot innovate. They are incapable of continuing creativity and they cannot change to produce that which is uniquely new. The essence of reality is not order but disorder and irregularity.

The long-term future is inherently unpredictable

In far-from-equilibrium states, where tiny, scarcely detectable disturbances can be amplified to change the total behaviour of a system within a relatively short time period, forecasting is clearly impossible. It would take infinite vigilance to detect all the disturbances affecting any given system; it would take infinite precision in the measurement of such disturbances to enable long-term prediction. Simulating the long-term behaviour of a system experiencing chaotic dynamics, generating a number of different scenarios, is a pointless exercise. When the dynamics are chaotic, the number of long-term outcomes is infinite, each one dependent upon tiny disturbances to the system as it moves through real time. Any manageable number of simulated scenarios is therefore unlikely to coincide, even approximately, with what actually happens.

But it takes time for tiny disturbances to be amplified through the system. It follows that short-term forecasting of the behaviour of chaotic systems is possible. And chaotic systems, while random at the detailed level, do have a global order. It is possible to identify that global order, to understand the dynamics in a macro, holistic sense and form judgements about its implications. Identifying what has been called the 'hidden' order does not however allow long-term forecasting or simulation. That 'hidden' order is the structure of the rule generating the behaviour; it is the sequence of behavioural patterns; it is the constant degree of irregularity in specific behaviour.

Finding this hidden order therefore allows us synthetically to generate individual patterns or events that belong to a particular category, but never exactly the same as any individual pattern or event that will occur in real time. So we can identify the rule that generates the fronds of a fern plant; we can create synthetic fern fronds that are quite clearly fern fronds; but each will differ individually from any other we produce and from those that nature itself generates. If we can identify the rules simulating chaotic behaviour on the stock markets, we can generate patterns in stock prices which have all the characteristics of those we observe, but we can never generate over the long-term, the patterns that will actually occur. But finding the hidden order will allow us to tell whether the system is currently in a chaotic phase or not.

Managing the outcome of change is impossible

The chaos view of the world is a revolution because it makes it quite clear that major changes, whole system transformations, real innovations cannot be 'managed' in terms of long-term specifics. The long-term outcome cannot be controlled because it is inherently unpredictable. If we cannot know what the long-term outcome of any intervention we make in the behaviour of the system will be, then we cannot control what happens in anything approaching a specific sense. All we can do is create the conditions within which fundamental change is a possibility. And these conditions are those of a system pushed far-from-equilibrium, one pushed away from what we normally understand to be order, regularity and stability. Control comes then to mean controlling the boundary conditions, control over process, simply because control over the outcome is impossible. Control comes to mean control over the process of discovering what is happening as we move through real time.

A chaos perspective therefore will give different insights into the process of decision-making, into the interpretation and use of the data we use to make decisions and into the use we make of decision-making techniques which depend upon the concept of probability.

Success as adaptation to the environment is too simplistic

The traditional scientific approach, including that adopted in the great majority of explanations of managing and organizing, relies heavily on the concept of systems adapting to their environment. So, biological species survive by adapting to a changing environment; they match their features and capabilities to the requirements of the environment. When the temperature drops substantially, successful species mutate in ways which will keep them warm; they develop thicker coats. In conditions of snow and ice they develop white coats as a camouflage protection. Business organizations survive by adapting to changes in their markets; they match their capabilities to the requirements of the customers; they implement strategies which secure fit with the environment.

But far-from-equilibrium there is no clear cut adaptation from a change in the environment to a change in the behaviour of the system to match it. It is a matter of chance which tiny disturbance the system will amplify into some major change. The outcome is a consequence of the self-organizing choices that the system makes at critical points during chaotic phases. Any system constitutes the environment of some other system, which in turn may constitute part of its environment. Therefore any one system may well generate small disturbances to other systems constituting its environment. As that first system moves chaotically and makes its unique choices at critical points it will affect other systems which will in turn affect it. The environment is not a given, it is a consequence of interactions between systems. It then becomes hard to say which system is adapting to which.

References

1   Lorenz, E. (1963), Deterministic Non Periodic Flow, *Journal of Atmospheric Science*, 20, pp. 130–41.

2   This is described in Gleick, J. (1988), *Chaos*, Heinemann, reprinted by permission of William Heinemann Ltd.

3   Gleick, J., op. cit., p. 21.

4   Gleick, J., op. cit., provides an account of the history of the development of chaos ideas and many examples of where and how it applies.

5   Gleick, J., op. cit., p. 85.

6   Day, R. H. (1982), The Emergence of Chaos from Classical Economic Growth, *Quarterly Journal of Economics*, pp. 406–414; Baumol, W. J., Quandt, R., (Jan–March 1985), Chaos Models and their Implications for Forecasting, *Eastern Economic Journal*, vol. XI, no. 1.

7   Baumol, W. J., Benhabib, J. (Winter 1989), Chaos: Significance, Mechanism and Economic Applications, *Journal of Economic Perspectives*, vol. 3, no. 1, pp. 77–105.

8   For a discussion on this see Kelsey, D. (1988), The Economics of Chaos or the Chaos of Economics, *Oxford Economic Papers*, 40, pp. 1–31.

9   Stutzer, M. (1980), Chaotic Dynamics and Bifurcation in a Macro Model, *Journal of Economic Dynamics and Control*, 2, pp. 353–376; Day, R. H., Schafer, W. J. (1983), *Keynesian Chaos*, Department of Economics, University of Southern California.

10 Benhabib, J., Day, R. H. (1981), Rational Choice and Erratic Behaviour, *Review of Economic Studies*, 48, pp. 459–572; Benhabib, J., Day, R. H. (1982), A Characterisation of Erratic Dynamics in the Overlapping Generations Model, *Journal of Economic Dynamics and Control*, 4, pp. 37–55.

11 Baumol, W. J., Benhabib, J., op. cit.

12 Shenkman, J., Le Baron, B. (1989), Nonlinear Dynamic and Stock Returns, *Journal of Business*, vol. 62, no. 3; Hsieh, D. (1989), Testing for Nonlinear Dependence in Daily Foreign Exchange Returns, *Journal of Business*, vol. 62, no. 3.

13 Baumol, W. J., Benhabib, J., op. cit., pp. 100–101.

14 Gerrard, B. (1989), *Theory of the Capitalist Economy, Towards a Post Classical Synthesis*, Basil Blackwell.

15 For example, March, J. G., Ohlsen, J. P. (1976), *Ambiguity and Choice in Organisations*, Bergen, Norway: Universitesforlaget.

16 Weick, K. (1979), *The Social Psychology of Organising*, Addison-Wesley.

17 Nonaka, I. (Spring 1988), Creating Organisational Order out of Chaos: Self Renewal in Japanese Firms, *California Management Review*; Gemmill, G., Smith, C. (1985), A Dissipative Structure Model of Organisational Transformation, *Human Relations*, vol. 38, no. 8.

Appendix B
The simple mathematics and exciting geometry of chaos

This appendix sets out some simple mathematics of chaos theory in order to explain key concepts that have been used in the chapters of this book. This mathematics is simple and a real understanding of what chaos means is enhanced by going through it.[1] The appendix has been written for those whose contact with mathematics lies in the distant past.

A mathematical equation is simply a metaphor for some piece of reality, for some aspect of behaviour. We make what we believe to be key abstractions of reality, key causal connections between one thing and another, and express them in symbolic, mathematical form. We are then able to analyse that symbolic abstraction to discover what insights it may yield about the workings of the real world. And the first key insight of chaos theory is that very simple non-linear feedback relationships can yield highly complex behaviour.

Simple relationships and decision rules can yield random behaviour

Proportional feedback rules

To keep matters as simple as possible suppose that the profit level (P) of a particular company in a time period (t) depends exactly upon its advertising outlay (X) in that period. Suppose further that there is a simple linear relationship between profit and advertising, in which profit increases in direct proportion to the amount spent on advertising according to some parameter (a). We can express this rather severe abstraction of reality as:

$P_t = aX_t$

Suppose also that the company always devotes a fixed proportion (b) of its profits in the previous period ($t-1$) to advertising. This can be written as:

$X_t = bP_{t-1}$

We can now substitute the second expression into the first to get:

$P_t = abP_{t-1}$

And if we define ab = c we can write the expression as:

$P_t = cP_{t-1}$

So we have a decision rule that says devote a fixed proportion of last period's profits to advertising, and we have a relationship between the organization and its environment by which a given level of advertising always results in a given level of profit. Life is then simple: profit in the last period determines profit in this and so on to the end of time, provided that neither the decision rule nor the relationship with the market changes. We can sit back and either watch the profits grow forever, or see them dwindle to nothing, or stay exactly the same. Figure B.1 demonstrates how this works. Each line depicts the equation for different values of c.

Take any starting point for last period's profits, say A. To find profit for the next period, project A up to the c<1 line at B. Project that on to the vertical axis to get profit for the next period at C. Now project C on to the 45° line at D (c = 1 here and therefore profit in this period always equals profit in the last along this line). The point D can be projected on to the horizontal axis at E so that we can repeat the procedure for the following period. When that process is repeated, going from E to F and then G we see that profit has fallen. If the whole procedure is repeated, starting from A again but this time projecting on to the c>1 line at H to get I, we find that profit grows. Along the c = 1 line profit just sticks at where it started.

Non-proportional feedback rules

But life is of course not that simple and we know that increased advertising has a diminishing impact on consumers and eventually some increase in advertising will bring in additional profit smaller than the outlay, so that total profit falls. To represent this more complex behaviour in mathematical terms we have to move away from linear equations – we have to introduce non-linearity into the equation to reflect the fact that profit is not related to advertising in some simple straight line, or proportional

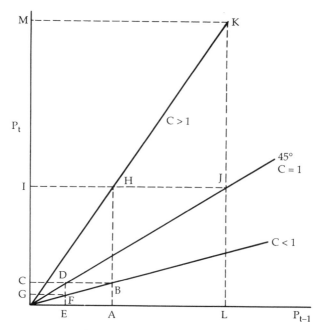

Figure B.1 *Linear feedback for profit*

fashion. We can represent the expected behaviour of profit over time, of first increasing and then decreasing under the impact of devoting a constant proportion to advertising, by using the following equation. This equation has many applications in various scientific areas and is known as the logistic difference equation:

$$P_t = cP_{t-1} \, (1 - P_{t-1})$$

And this can be represented graphically in Figure B.2, which also shows that the effect of increasing the parameter c is to raise the curve from the horizontal axis. The curve has the necessary property of showing profit as first increasing and then decreasing, with the increases and decreases being sharper as the the combined effect of allocating a higher proportion of profit to advertising and advertising having a bigger impact on profits, increases.

What we now have is a dynamic, non-linear feedback mechanism which will describe the time path of profits for any given relationship between profit and advertising and any constant proportion of profit devoted to advertising. In the case of the linear relationship it was quite clear what the path of profit over time would be. It either falls to zero, stays the same, or increases to infinity. And as you raise the value of the parameter c (bigger impact of advertising on profit and / or bigger proportion of profit devoted to advertising) past a critical point so the speed to infinity increases in a uniform way. There is always a perfectly predictable

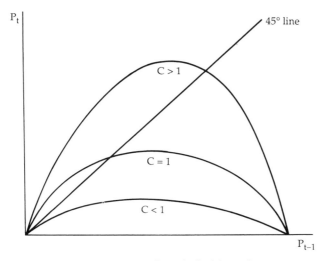

Figure B.2 *Non-linear feedback for profit*

time path and all time paths lead to equilibrium states – a constant profit level or explosive growth.

But what would we expect to be the time path of profit under the non-linear relationship? Surely what we would end up with, before long, is a state of equilibrium – a repetitive state in which the constantly continuing application of two fixed rules would yield a constant profit or continuing growth. Constant profit is certainly one possibility and is shown in Figure B.3.

To see how profit settles in a constant path, take any point on the horizontal axis in Figure B.3 to give a starting profit level, say A. Project this vertically to the curve to read off what profit will be achieved in the next period, labelled B in Figure B.3. To carry on we must transfer the profit level shown on the vertical axis back to the horizontal axis so that we can read off what the profit level will be for the period after that. We can do this by projecting B on to the 45° line since all points on this line are

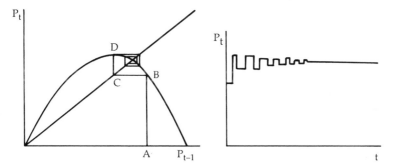

Figure B.3 *Stable time paths*

ones where the values on the horizontal and vertical axes are equal. This value C can now be projected vertically to find out what profit will be in the following period at D. Each iteration takes us step by step towards the point where the 45° line cuts the curve and that is the point where we reach profit stability.

And if we increase the parameter value c, that is raise the curve from the horizontal axis, a great deal more, we get an explosive cycle in which profit eventually shoots off to infinity – a growth equilibrium. In between these values of the parameter c, we get the regular cycles of standard economic theory – the hog price cycle or the cobweb theorem shown in Figure B.4. In all cases we have equilibrium, a clearly defined, predictable state of behaviour. Introducing a lag into the system, as we have done by having advertising depend on the last period's profits, introduces the possibility of a steady cycle. And that is as far as economic theory went.

The chaos theorists of the 1970s however looked at the whole matter in much more detail, exploring through thousands of iterations on a computer what would happen at numerous values of the parameter c. And this is what they found.

The effect of changing the parameters of the feedback rule

The change we are talking about here is that of tuning up the value of the parameter c. Select 2 to be the value of the c parameter and start the iterations with P_{t-1} at a profit level of £0.9m. If you make the calculations for a number of periods you will find that by period 5, profit is very close to £0.5m and by period 7 it reaches £0.5m to stay there for evermore. So, given the impact that advertising has on profit and given a constant proportion of profit ploughed back into advertising, together summarized by the number 2, profit starting anywhere between 0 and £1m will end up after a few iterations in a stable, steady state. We may say that the

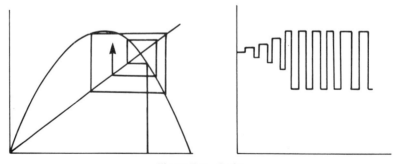

Figure B.4 *Cycles*

behaviour of this dynamic system with a parameter value of 2 is attracted to a stable point at 0.5; the system has a stable point attractor at this value of the parameter.

In fact the system has stable point attractors for any value of the parameter between 0 and 3. For all these values the system has equilibrium positions. If you increase the value of the parameter to any value above 4 the value of profit quickly shoots off to infinity. So for values of the parameter above 4 the final state of the system is attracted to infinity; for these values of the parameter it has an attractor to infinity. The system is unstable and explosive for all these values, but it is nevertheless a predictable equilibrium state.

What happens when the parameter is set at 3? The fixed point becomes marginally unstable in the sense that convergence to it is very slow; from any starting point it takes a greater number of iterations to reach stability. And stability now takes the form of regular cycles. So take the value 3.2 for c and you will find that profits fluctuate for a number of periods until by period 21 they have settled into a regular cycle of £0.799 in one period followed by £0.513 in the next. And this regular 2 period cycle continues for evermore. At a parameter value of 3.2 the behaviour of the system is attracted to a final state in which it has a stable 2 period cycle; it has a stable attractor of period 2. We still have equilibrium. But we have known all this for many decades now. What we did not know is what happens with the parameter values lying between 3.5 and 4.0.

At a value for c of 3.5 the period 2 attractor goes unstable and a period 4 cycle appears. So in one period profit reaches a value A, it then drops to B; it then rises part of the way to A to reach D; it then falls part of the way to B to reach C. Thereafter it goes back to A and repeats the whole 4 period cycle for ever. If you tune the parameter up to 3.56 the period doubles again and you get a period 8 cycle. By 3.567 the cycles are to period 16. Thereafter there are rapid period doublings until you reach a value for the parameter c of 3.58.

Before further exploring this behaviour as we tune up the value of c, consider the pattern so far described. It is shown in Figure B.5. Here the final values reached by profit are plotted (on the vertical axis) against the value of the parameter c (on the horizontal axis). So for each value of c between 0 and 3 we have a single stable point, a higher point for each value of the parameter shown by the rising curve from 0 to 3. At 3 we have two final values for profit: the peak and the trough of the cycle. The line splits into two, or bifurcates. And the peaks and troughs diverge as we go from 3 to 3.5. At 3.5 we get a further bifurcation to show two peaks and two troughs. They in turn bifurcate and soon at 3.58 there are infinitely many bifurcations. This diagram has been called a fig tree diagram, showing how, at successive values of the parameter, the trunk of final values splits into boughs, the boughs into branches, the branches into

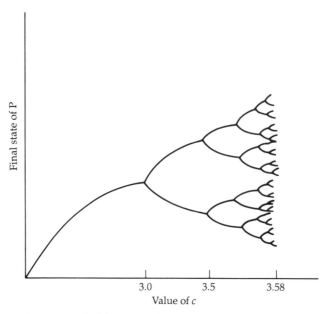

Figure B.5   *The bifurcation or fracturing of final states of behaviour*

twigs, the twigs into twiglets and so on. The behaviour of the system is far
more complicated than we could have imagined.

There are further surprises however. First there is the regularity of the
pattern we observe. Each set of cycles has a period exactly double that of
the previous set. A second point to notice is the property of self-similarity.
Look at the first bifurcation and you see that the top and bottom boughs
look similar. The top branch of the top bough looks similar to all the other
branches. The top twig looks similar to all the other twigs and so on right
to the edge of the diagram. As you proceed you see smaller and smaller
copies of the whole diagram, never exactly the same, but always similar.
And this property of self-similarity turns out to be very important.

Furthermore it is known that the copies of the whole diagram shrink at
a rate which approaches 4.6692016090 as you approach the parameter
value of 3.58. Or to put it another way, the ratio of the size of one branch
to the next one to sprout out of it reaches 4.6692016090 as the parameter
value of 3.58 is reached. It means that the further along the fig tree you go,
the closer to exact self-similarity you get. Even more surprising is that this
long number applies to any equation that can be graphed with a single
hump in it.

Chaos

Now we can return to where we left off in examining the effect of
changing the value of the parameter c. There are further surprises in

store. At the parameter value of 3.58 the behaviour of the system becomes random. There are no regular cycles; the values from each iteration shoot all over the place (within boundaries) and never return to any value they previously had. No matter how many thousands of iterations you try this remains true. And this is chaos. The final state of this dynamic system, at a parameter value of 3.58 is one of randomness and disorder. This chaotic state to which the system is attracted is known as a strange attractor. There is no way you could ever forecast what will happen to profit if the parameter value is 3.58. And that has nothing to do with environmental changes or random shocks. Nothing changes outside the equation, you follow the same constant rules as before and the parameter value sticks at 3.58, but the consequence is totally unpredictable disorder in the specific path of profit over time.

But this is not the end of the system's strange behaviour. Raise the value of the parameter to 3.835 and a cycle of period 3 suddenly appears. Increase the number very slightly and the cycle doubles to period 6. Increase it a little more and the period doubles again. So the periods double very rapidly until you are back into an area of chaos. Now try 3.739 and a cycle of period 5 appears. Increase it slightly and the period doubles again and so on until you are back into chaos. As you turn the value of the parameter up from 3.58 to 4, tiny windows of order keep appearing. And in each window there is a copy of the whole fig tree ranging from stability through to chaos again. The windows appear in a fixed order, the order in which the 3, 5 and all other cycle periods appear is fixed and known. And this fixed order applies to any mathematical function which can be graphed with one hump.

So the scaling phenomenon, the characteristic of self-similarity, continues at precise, tiny, predetermined intervals, always leading to chaos. And out of each new wave of chaos, patterns of stability emerge over smaller and smaller intervals. Figure B.6 illustrates these waves of chaos – black areas are chaos and the white stripes within chaos are the windows of order.

You now examine the first white stripe in the top part of Figure B.6. You do this by iterating for very small intervals of the parameter value which yields that white stripe. In effect, you 'blow up' the picture within the window of order. And you find that this magnified portion resembles the whole diagram. This is shown in Figure B.7.

You could repeat the blow up procedure for the first white stripe in Figure B.7. Once again there would be a picture which resembles the whole diagram. The structure is infinitely deep; there are pictures within pictures forever and they are always similar.

What we have, then, is a very simple non-linear feedback relationship; a simple behavioural and decision-making rule, which produces a highly complex pattern of results over time. Sometimes that behaviour is of the stable orderly type, equilibrium, which has always provided the underly-

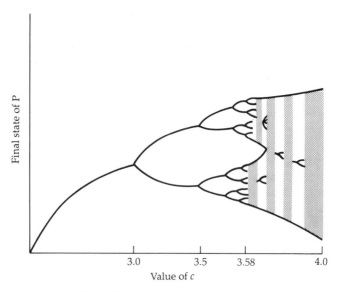

Figure B.6   *A picture of chaos and order*

ing focus of economic, management and organizational theories. That stable behaviour can either be a single equilibrium point or an identifiable, stable cyclical pattern. But over some range of the parameter values, relatively small in this case but not necessarily so for all behavioural rules, we find a highly complex pattern of results. And this pattern is non-equilibrium. It never settles into a clearly defined state. Here the system is far-from-equilibrium. At some values of the parameter the system is at or near to equilibrium, but at others it is far-from-equilibrium.

The pattern generated by the simple feedback loop contains phases that are random and disorderly in detail, but overall it has a precise sequence,

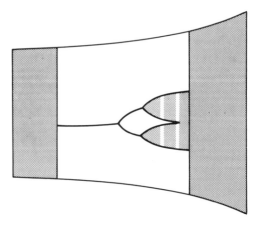

Figure B.7   *A window of order*

an underlying order described by the properties of scaling, or self-similarity. This property is described using the term 'fractal dimension', the extent to which the pattern fractures as we change the parameter values. In the region of chaos we cannot know what the outcome will be at any one point in time, but we can accurately describe the shape and characteristics of the total pattern of behaviour. The original rule contains within it a shape that is revealed by the process of iterative feedback; a process of scaling up or down that traces out the fixed, self-similar, scaling or fractal properties of the original rule. We cannot be precise about the outcome, at certain parameter values, but we can be precise about the overall shape – the sequence of behavioural patterns that are generated.

So chaos is not simply confusion or mindless disorder. It is far more intriguing than that. It is a complex intertwining of order and disorder that must ring an intuitive bell in the minds of business practitioners.

The impact of random shocks

So far we have considered the properties of this one simple rule as if it were isolated from everything else in the world – as if it were a completely closed system with no influences coming from outside it. In business, or in economics, we can of course never study closed systems. No matter how large and complicated we make our model of the economy or the firm, we will still be left with the impact of the weather, diseases, political events and so on. So in any rule, or set of rules, we will have to include a term that stands for influences outside the rule itself.

The simplest way to do this is to introduce an error term into the equation, a term that stands for the random disturbances or shocks that will move the result away from that which the rule on its own would have determined. The results will contain 'noise' and this noise can be simulated by including a random number term in the equation (e). We can then rewrite our original rule on profit behaviour as follows:

$$P_t = cP_{t-1} (1 - P_{t-1}) + e_t$$

Or we could say that the parameter itself is subject to random shocks and write the rule as follows:

$$P_t = (c + e_t) P_{t-1} (1 - P_{t-1})$$

It has been found that both of these systems behave in similar ways.[2] The system follows a mixture of the behaviours for values of the parameter c that are near to each other. The stable cycles that occur up to the borders of chaos are disturbed by the noise term, the peak and trough values falling within broad bands, rather than fixed points. If the noise term is large enough many of the cycles on the way to chaos will disappear altogether and the system will pass more rapidly into chaos. The period doubling sequence no longer occurs. The points of bifurcation are no longer clear, but become blurred. Within the chaotic region many of the windows of order disappear. Not surprisingly, the presence of noise in the rule makes chaotic behaviour much more common.

Tiny changes completely alter the behaviour of the system

By now, one of the most important points about the study of chaotic systems will have become obvious. Over certain ranges it requires only tiny changes to the value of the parameter to cause major changes in the pattern of behaviour. We only have to increase the parameter by a minute amount from 3.739 to go from a cycle of period 5 to one of period 10 and another minute change can plunge us back into chaos.

And it turns out that like scaling and self-similarity, this is a fundamental property of chaotic systems, one that has profound consequences. The property is known as sensitive dependence on initial conditions. If you wish to predict the time path of the results of the behavioural rule anywhere near the chaos region, you have to specify the starting value of the variable and the parameter to a infinite degree of precision. An error in the sixth, tenth or even the thousandth decimal place could eventually lead to a completely different time path. Since we cannot make measurements to such a high degree of precision, certainly not in the world of business, sensitive dependence on initial conditions means that forecasting in anything other than the very short term is totally impossible.

Furthermore, since different computer programs use different rounding procedures, it may be impossible to repeat a forecast or an experiment on different computers and get the same result. And this creates something of a conceptual difficulty, if not a highly practical one, for the scientific method that requires repeatable experiments and for simulation in business decision-making that has a similar requirement.

Summary

We have taken a plausible rule to describe the time path of profit under the influence of advertising expenditure. This rule, the logistic difference equation, can be applied in a large number of other areas, for example, population growth. And we find that this simple deterministic rule gives rise to very complicated behaviour, within a relatively small range of its possible parameter values. Adding noise, or random shocks, widens the range over which this complex behaviour occurs. The pattern of behaviour is summarized in Figure B.8.

A large number of other first-order difference equations (describing behaviour from one time interval to the next) have been explored and they give rise to the same kind of behaviour, not always within such

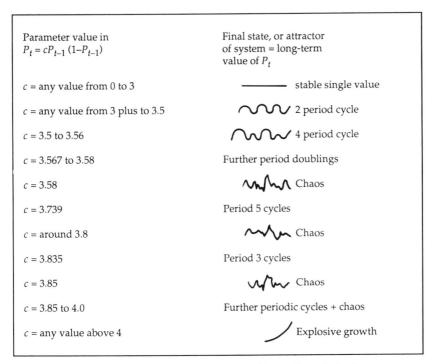

Parameter value in $P_t = cP_{t-1}(1-P_{t-1})$	Final state, or attractor of system = long-term value of P_t
c = any value from 0 to 3	——— stable single value
c = any value from 3 plus to 3.5	2 period cycle
c = 3.5 to 3.56	4 period cycle
c = 3.567 to 3.58	Further period doublings
c = 3.58	Chaos
c = 3.739	Period 5 cycles
c = around 3.8	Chaos
c = 3.835	Period 3 cycles
c = 3.85	Chaos
c = 3.85 to 4.0	Further periodic cycles + chaos
c = any value above 4	Explosive growth

Figure B.8 *The sequence of behaviours generated by non-linear feedback systems*

narrow ranges of the parameter values. Third-order differential equations (describing changes continuously over time) have also been explored and they give rise to the same kind of behaviour. So far, more complicated higher order equations, or large interconnected sets of such equations which might be required to explain some complex behaviour have not been explored, but they are surely likely to yield behaviour that is at least as complex.

The order within the disorder of chaos: fractal geometry

In reviewing the theory of chaos, the previous section was concerned with maps of attractors, the final states to which specified initial conditions of a parameter and a variable lead the system. Now we need to look at a map of the initial conditions themselves and the way in which they surround the attractors to which they are drawn. We have already seen how the simple logistic equation has a number of attractors and how the borders between one and another can be highly complicated. To explore this further, consider how a system chooses between one attractor and another.

You can think of each attractor as the bottom of a basin pushed into the middle of say a square piece of metal. If you place a marble, the initial condition of a parameter or a variable, in the basin of the attractor it will roll, be attracted to, the bottom of the basin. So a system with a number of attractors can be thought of as a number of basins joined together at their edges. The question of interest here is what happens if you perch the marble on the border of two of these basins. Which basin will it roll into?

This can be illustrated by considering the equation $x^4 - 1 = 0$. The problem here is to find the quadratic route of 1 and it cannot be solved analytically. The only way to solve it is through a process of iteration using a particular rule – the Newton Method. You have to select an initial value for x, make the calculation and feed the result back into the rule, repeating the iterations until a solution is reached. But there are four possible solutions or attractors. If you start the iteration with an initial condition which is close to the first of these solutions, the iteration process rapidly takes you to that solution. The further away you start from the solution the longer it takes to reach it. Eventually you must reach initial conditions close to those that would take you to the second solution or attractor. There has to be a border between the attractors and it would be reasonable to imagine that there is some clean line which divides the initial conditions leading to the first solution from those leading to the second. Nothing is further from the truth.

If you take any number and plug it into the iterative rule, it will lead you to one of the four solutions. If the first solution is the one you reach you could plot a red point for the number you started with. If the number leads to the second solution you plot it as a green point. If it leads to the third plot a yellow point, and if it leads to the fourth plot a blue point. Do this for many thousands of numbers and you will paint a picture of the set of initial conditions which leads to each of the four solutions, or attractors.

That picture would show solid areas of colour around each of the attractors – when you start near to one of the attractors, it leads to that solution. However, the borders between the attractors turn out to be quite astonishing. There is no clear cut separation between one set of initial conditions and any other at the border. What emerges is a highly complex border in which you find green areas, nowhere near the green attractor, tucked between red, yellow and blue areas – this is illustrated in Gleicks book *Chaos: Making a New Science*. So you can start with a number far away from solution one, far nearer to two other solutions and land up with solution one nevertheless. Along all the borders you find initial conditions for all the solutions. And there is a shape to the border, one with a property we have come across before – self-similarity. In the border you can see finer and finer detail, repeating the pattern in the larger sections of the border; the property of scaling or self-similarity. The edges are highly irregular, infinitely folding in and out on themselves, a property that is known as fractal. It turns out that systems in the same class all have the same degree of irregularity that can be precisely measured as a fractal dimension.

And there is also sensitive dependence on initial conditions. At the border, tiny differences in the initial condition will lead to completely different solutions or attractors. At the border you cannot predict what the solution will be. At the border of the initial conditions, the solution depends on chance. The border turns out to be a phenomenon of orderly disorder – deterministic chaos.

Consider one more example of the complex border between one attractor and another. Take the equation $Z_t = Z_{t-1}^2 + c$, where Z is a complex number (it is not necessary to explain what a complex number is) and c is a parameter. This too is a non-linear feedback mechanism.

Take any value for c and any starting value for Z and iterate in the usual way. If Z does not move off to infinity then it is part of what is known as the Mandelbrot set and you plot a black point. The point is part of a finite, bounded set of stable equilibrium points. If the point does move off rapidly to infinity you plot a white point. If you do this for thousands of points you will trace out a strange dumpy figure which has been called a gingerbread man. The important point is that there is a highly complex border between the set of black, bounded stable points and the set of white unbounded points. We have a non-linear feedback equation, which has only one attractor to a bounded set and another to infinity and the border between them is far from simple. This is shown in Figure B.9.

To see the complexity of the tendril-like border around the Mandelbrot set, you can magnify small portions of this border on a computer by taking smaller and smaller intervals between the initial conditions. So, take the area in the neck of the gingerbread man and magnify it on the computer. Then take part of the pattern in that magnification and magnify it further. Do the same thing again and again. Some of the results are shown in Figure B.10. The patterns contained in that border are extremely intricate and beautiful. That beauty is striking when colour graphics are used – the reader can see these in a book by H.-O. Peitgen and P. H. Richter, called the *Beauty of Fractals*, Springer-Verlag, 1986.

The properties we have come to expect are all present in this border around the Mandelbrot set. There is self-similarity – every so often little gingerbread men appear in the border, approximate replicas of the first one. The border is nowhere ever the same, but similar patterns do occur in particular regions. The border has scaling characteristics and it is highly fractal, curling in and out in itself, fracturing into similar patterns as it is magnified or repeated. And there is sensitive dependence on initial conditions – at the border, tiny changes in the initial conditions make all the difference to the patterns which emerge. Close to the border of the Mandelbrot set itself, we would have to be able to measure with exact precision to a very high number of decimal places to be able to predict what the consequences will be. And as we get closer and closer to the borders of the black Mandelbrot set itself, it takes longer and longer to determine whether a starting point in the border is part of the Mandelbrot

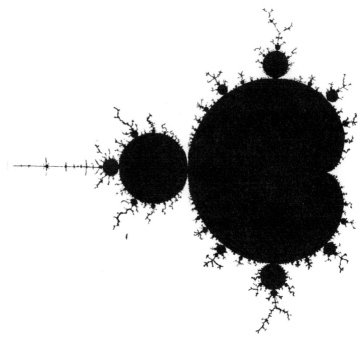

Figure B.9 *The Mandelbrot set*
Source: Penrose, Roger, The Emperor's New Mind, Oxford University Press, 1989

set or not. It seems that right at the border it takes infinitely longer to determine this.[3] Right at the border it appears to be impossible to predict the outcome. Because of this and because we cannot measure with infinite precision, the outcome of any single point close to the border depends on chance.

We have a deterministic system with two attractors, one to infinity and the other not, and we get random behaviour at the border because of sensitive dependence on initial conditions. But this sensitive dependence is closely tied to the fractal nature of the border, the twists and turns it makes, the way it is fractured as the rules are repeated. And it is the fractal dimension which provides the key to any pattern and order there is. Order and disorder are intricately tied together.

So this one rule has encoded within it an amazing complexity of behaviour, shapes in space and over time that are revealed by the process of iteration. A simple order leads to a complicated form of disorder, which nevertheless has a pattern to it, but the precise outcome depends on chance. A system of non-linear feedback rules that is operating with parameter or variable values along the borders between attractors is therefore inherently unpredictable in terms of detail. But such a system is highly creative. Using the feedback mechanism it can create patterns in space and time that are clearly part of the same generic group, but having no two members of the group the same.

Figure B.10   *The border around the Mandelbrot set*
Source: Penrose, Roger, The Emperor's New Mind, Oxford University Press, 1989

The Mandelbrot set describes much the same kind of overall pattern we saw for the logistic difference equations with which we started this exploration of chaos. There are two attractors, one to stability and the other to instability. And in both cases the borders between stability and instability are chaotic, or fractal.

The order within the disorder of chaos: self-similarity

Earlier in this appendix, we explored the final states to which the behaviour of any system driven by the first-order logistic equation is attracted at different parameter values. At low parameter values the behaviour of the system has a number of stable equilibrium attractors and at high values of the parameter it has unstable, explosive equilibrium attractors. No system can operate for long in an unstable, explosive state and so classical science concentrated on explaining stable equilibrium states. But it has now been discovered that the behaviour of this system is chaotic for parameter values that lie in the border between those yielding stable and unstable equilibrium states. Here there is the strange, chaotic or fractal attractor that is bounded instability. The specific path of behaviour is random, but that behaviour follows a fixed overall shape. If you turn to Figure B.6 above you will see that in the chaos region, the behaviour of the system always moves within fixed boundaries. Furthermore, as the value of the parameter is tuned up, the behaviour pattern fractures into approximate copies of the whole sequence of behaviours from stable equilibria through equilibrium cycles to chaos. There are patterns within patterns that are never exactly the same, but always similar. This is the property of self-similarity. It is called the scaling phenomena because as we examine the pattern on smaller and smaller scales it keeps repeating itself. The act of repeating the logistic equation over and over again traces out self-similar shapes that are encoded in the rule, and those branching shapes it traces out bear a resemblance to those we find in nature.

Another example of this property of self-similarity is given in Chapter 7. Figure 7.8 in that chapter depicts the strange attractor that the earth's weather system follows, called the butterfly or Lorenz attractor. Once again there are bounds within which the system always moves – some weather conditions are not allowed by the feedback rules currently governing the system. And within those bounds there is a distinctive overall shape to the patterns of weather that are produced. The weather system moves continuously, following the shape of the attractor, switching unpredictably from one lobe of the shape to the other. Because of this fixed overall shape, recognizable self-similar patterns of weather are repeated over and over again. But no two patterns are ever exactly the same.

Then, earlier in the discussion in this appendix we described the Mandelbrot set. Here the computer draws a picture of all the initial conditions which, when plugged into a simple feedback rule, lead to a stable equilibrium state or an unstable equilibrium state or the borders between the two. And the borders between the two equilibrium states are chaotic. Here the pattern fractures into self-similar shapes as we examine smaller and smaller differences in the initial conditions. Once again there are boundaries around the chaos region and within it behaviour is similar but never the same. And many of the shapes in that border bear an uncanny resemblance to those we find in nature.

It has also been discovered that all these chaotic, fractal or self-similar shapes have a property of constancy. Any given category of feedback rule generates chaotic patterns that have a constant fractal dimension. That is, the extent to which the specific pattern twists and turns is always constant; the degree of 'crinkliness' in the pattern is always the same. Self-similarity means that there is a regular degree of irregularity. So, as you examine a coastline in greater and greater detail, the extent to which it twists and turns into bays and peninsulas, into coves and promontories, will always be the same. The same point applies to clouds and trees and most other natural phenomena.

While we have always tried to explain the essence of behaviour in nature as regularity, we now come to see that essence as regular irregularity.

We can then define self-similarity in a number of ways. It means that shapes in space are always similar to each other even though they differ at the specific, individual level. As those shapes are increased or decreased in size they retain the self-similarity. If you break a bough off a tree it has a similar shape to the tree and to all the other boughs, but they are all different at a detailed level. Self-similarity means that patterns of movement over time are similar over different lengths of time, but they are never the same in specific terms. They have the appearance of cycles, there is something regular, but timing and amplitude are never exactly to same. In Appendix A the example of cotton price data was quoted and in Chapter 8 that of error transmission in electronic information flows was given. We have always thought that this similarity is true regularity generated by fixed laws upon which is superimposed random disturbances. The search has been to separate the two statistically so we can predict the underlying part. But with feedback systems the fixed law generates the whole path. Self similarity over time is what we mean when in one breath we say that history repeats itself and there is nothing new under the sun and then in the next breath say that nothing stays the same. Both are true but at different levels.

What we are talking about then, in terms of patterns over time and in space, is categories with certain characteristic general features but specific differences in the individual components of the category. The feedback rule traces out shapes that are qualitatively predictable at a general level but quantitatively unpredictable at a specific, individual level.

What this means for predictability is as follows:

- we can in principle identify the rules that generates the chaotic behaviour;

- we can predict when and where chaos will occur;
- we can establish the shape of the strange attractor and the quantitative boundaries within which behaviour will move;
- we can measure the fractal dimension or constant degree of variability of the behaviour;
- we can qualitatively describe the general category features of the behaviour, the patterns in space and over time that the system will follow at a general level;
- we can predict the short-term specific behaviour of the system;
- but we can never predict the specific patterns of behaviour over the long term.

So, self-similarity enables us to classify behaviours, to recognize them in qualitative terms, so accumulating experience. In organizational terms this means that we can build up experience of general categories of group dynamic, general patterns of how certain individuals behave, general patterns in sequences of choices and decisions, general patterns of relationships with the environment and general patterns of performance. When confronted by specific unpredictable situations we can draw upon this accumulation of similar patterns and situations we have experienced in the past to contribute, through analogy, to dealing with the specific situation we now face. Because of unpredictability at the specific level we cannot simply apply a general model or set of prescriptions, but we can create afresh a model to fit each unique case we face, drawing on self-similar experiences we have had before.

And chaos gives some further interesting insights into the way we have to think when we face unpredictability.

The Mandelbrot set: algorithms and undecidability

The Mandelbrot set is generated by a non-linear feedback relationship. We take a particular number and plug it into the relationship ($Z_t = Z_{t-1}^2 + c$) over and over again, so generating a sequence of numbers from the original one. We also apply a set of rules and procedures, an algorithm, to determine whether or not that starting number is part of the Mandelbrot set. It is part of the set if it is bounded in the sense that the feedback calculation (using the Z function above) comes to an end; the sequence of numbers definitely does not go on feeding back into the relationship forever; the sequence of numbers generated by the starting number is finite. Such a number is represented in the figure by a point coloured black (see Figure B.9). The important feature is that for all black points, the algorithm (the procedural steps we use to decide that the starting number, or point, is bounded) does stop; it does reach a conclusion that the number is indeed in the set. That algorithm, or decision-making process, does show conclusively that the series of numbers, calculated from the starting one, is finite.

The starting number is not part of the set if it is unbounded; that is, if the starting number yields a sequence that goes on feeding into the relationship (the Z function) forever, so generating a series that is infinite. Now if the algorithm that is deciding whether the starting number is bounded or not, reaches a conclusion that it is unbounded, after say five iterations, we colour the point representing that starting number red – such a point will be far away from the Mandelbrot set in the sense that it has a strong pull to infinity. If the algorithm takes, say, 10 steps to reach a conclusion that the starting number is unbounded, we colour it, say, green. This starting number will be nearer to the Mandelbrot set, in the sense that the pull to infinity is somewhat weaker than in the previous case. And so the algorithm proceeds, building up a contour map around the Mandelbrot set; the contours showing the speed with which numbers can be determined not to be part of the set. And as the numbers get closer to the set itself, as they approach the border between the set and all the numbers outside the set, it generally takes longer and longer, more and more iterations, before the algorithm can decide that the starting number is indeed outside the set.

So for some numbers, the algorithm decides rapidly that a starting number is unbounded, and for starting numbers very close to the set it usually takes much longer for the algorithm to make a decision. But this pattern as one approaches the border is not uniform. We may have one number close to the border where the algorithm takes a very long time to decide and another number only a minute fraction away from it, on which the algorithm can make a rapid decision – the property of sensitive dependence on initial conditions. Eventually we reach points very close to the border with the set where, it appears, the algorithm goes on calculating forever without reaching a conclusion that the starting number is outside the set. The algorithm cannot be sure whether the very next calculation will show the point to be inside or outside the set – it cannot make a decision; it does not stop. This has not been conclusively proved, but apparently no one is able to show that the conclusion is false.[4]

The algorithm cannot then be used to make a decision right at the border, in chaos. The question as to whether a point is inside or outside the set seems to be undecidable. There are other mathematical proofs that shows that in some circumstances algorithmic procedures definitely cannot be used to make a decision.

Undecidability

In 1920 and again in 1928, the mathematician Hilbert posed this question: is there a general algorithm for resolving, in principle, all mathematical questions belonging to some broad and well defined class? In other words, is there some general set of rules and procedures that could generate specific rules and procedures for solving any problem in a particular class of mathematical problems? If the answer to this question turned out to be affirmative, then we could identify the general algorithm, load it into a computer and that computer could then develop all new mathematical truths. An affirmative answer would be strong evidence that we think in algorithmic ways when we discover new mathematical truths. If the answer is no, then we must use some non-algorithmic thought processes when we discover at least some new mathematical truths.

Turing worked on an answer to this question and in the course of doing so developed the approach now used to write computer languages. Turing rephrased the Hilbert question in terms of the 'halting problem' for Turing machines (these are simply algorithms), essentially the same question we considered above in relation to the Mandelbrot set – is there a general algorithm that will conclude whether any particular algorithm in that class will stop or not? If there is no such general algorithm, then it would not be possible to generate all other algorithms in a particular class, using algorithmic methods.

> The question of whether or not a particular Turing machine stops is a perfectly well defined piece of mathematics... Thus, by showing that no algorithm exists for deciding the question of the stopping of Turing machines, Turing showed (as had Church, using his own rather different approach) that there can be no general algorithm for deciding mathematical questions. Hilbert's ... [problem] ... has no solution![5]

So there is a mathematical proof that there can be no general algorithm that works for all mathematical questions; that there is no general algorithm for deciding which particular algorithm to use in a specific case. The validity of an algorithm, the question of truth and meaning, must always be established by external means.

Even more generally, the mathematician Godel proved with his 'undecidability theorem', that any precise mathematical system of rules and procedures, provided that it is broad enough to contain descriptions of simple arithmetical propositions and provided it is free of contradiction, must contain some statements that are neither provable nor disprovable by the means allowed within the system. Truth is thus undecidable by the approved procedure. But the ability to prove this theorem means that the human mind is able to see whether a proposition is true or false, while an algorithmic procedure cannot. The human mind uses insights from outside a particular system to decide on truth and meaning, something an algorithm cannot do.

> Whatever (consistent) formal system is used for arithmetic, there are state-

ments that we can see are true but which do not get assigned the truth value
... by the formalists' proposed [algorithmic] procedure.[6]

The insight whereby we concluded that the Gödel proposition ... is actually
a true statement in arithmetic is an example of a general type of procedure
known to logicians as a reflection principle: thus, by 'reflecting' upon the
meaning of the axiom system and rules of procedure, and convincing oneself
that these indeed provide valid ways of arriving at mathematical truths, one
may be able to code this insight into further true mathematical statements
that were not deducible from those very axioms and rules... Reflection
principles provide the very antithesis of formalist reasoning. If one is careful,
they enable one to leap outside the rigid confinements of any formal system
to obtain new mathematical insights that did not seem to be available
before... The type of 'seeing' that is involved in a reflection principle
requires a mathematical insight that is not the result of the purely algorithmic
operations that could be coded into some mathematical formal system.[7]

For how are we to decide what axioms or rules of procedure to adopt in any
case when trying to set up a formal principle? Our guide in deciding on the
rules to adopt must always be our intuitive understanding of what is 'self-
evidently true', given the 'meanings' of the symbols of the system.[8]

... without Gödel's theorem it might have been possible to imagine that the
intuitive notions of 'self evidence' and 'meaning' could have been employed
just once and for all, merely to set up the formal system in the first place, and
thereafter dispensed with as part of clear mathematical argument for determining truth ... Gödel's theorem shows that this point of view is not really a
tenable one...[9]

It is these insights that cannot be systematised – and indeed must lie outside
any algorithmic action![10]

The Mandelbrot set: the boundary between an organisation and its environment

The Mandelbrot set may also provide an insight into the relationship
between an organization and its environment. Conventionally an organization is defined as a group of people with a common purpose. It is a
distinct entity separate from its environment. There is a clear boundary
separating it from its environment. The organizational task is one of
maintaining adaptive equilibrium with the environment. The need for
change arises outside the organization. That change is anticipated or
reacted to so as to adapt. The boundary line between an organization and
its environment is simple and therefore no attention is usually paid to it.

The organization may be regarded as a physical place, as a clearly
identifiable group of people, as a set of goals with systems, structures,
procedures, informal behaviours and cultures for achieving them, or as a
combination of all these things. The environment is then a physical place,

or a set of conditions, or a collection of individuals and other organizations, or some combination of these. There is a clear borderline between
the two.

However, the environment which is relevant to any organization, call it
A, is not really all physical places and groups of people around it. If there
is no potential action or perception from organization A, then whatever is
happening outside is irrelevant. Customers who have no conceivable
need for the product of a company, other companies who do not compete
with it, are no part of its environment. The only relevant environment is
customers and other companies who create the potential for action. The
environment of organization A is really that set of its own actions and
perceptions which are prompted or required by the environment, if
organization A is to survive and prosper. And that set of actions is
unbounded, to all intents and purposes infinite, because there are, potentially, so many actions and perceptions available for organization A to
take in order to relate to its environment.

But in addition to these actions, there is another set of organization A
actions that could either have nothing to do with the environment, or that
require the environment to respond. We can think of that set of actions as
organization A itself. An example of an action that requires the environment to adapt is pollution not prohibited by law. Another example is
advertising that prompts some change in perceptions of people outside
organization A. This second set of actions is bounded – there is a finite
number of organization A actions and perceptions that have nothing to
do with the environment or through which organization A has the power
to control, to force or persuade those other people and organizations who
are the environment, to adapt.

So, organization A itself is that set of its own actions and perceptions to
which the environment has to adapt and organization A's environment is
that set of its own actions and perceptions that it undertakes to adapt to its
environment. Together they equal the total of all possible actions and
perceptions of organization A, one set being bounded and the other set
being unbounded. All these actions are generated by non-linear feedback
loops of one kind or another. For example, organization A cuts its price
because one of its competitors does. Consequently, two other competitors slash their prices even further and A has to make yet another price
reduction. We have here an amplifying loop, a non-linear feedback mechanism, which is typical of the interaction between an organization and its
environment. We have here an initial event, or action, which sets off a
sequence of other actions, each one related to its predecessor in a non-
linear fashion.

Now relate this to the Mandelbrot set. To develop a picture of this set,
we take a complex number and use a non-linear feedback mechanism to
generate a sequence of numbers. Some of those sequences constitute a
bounded set and yet others fall into an unbounded set, the two sets

together accounting for all possibilities. In considering the interaction of an organization with its environments, we take an action and use a non-linear feedback mechanism to generate a sequence of actions, some of which are bounded (the organization) and some of which are not (the environment).

And in the case of the Mandelbrot set, the border between the bounded and the unbounded sets is amazingly complicated – fractal. As we get closer and closer to the boundary line between the bounded set of numbers and all others, it is probably impossible to determine whether an initial number is inside or outside the set; the procedure for deciding this question probably runs on and on forever without reaching a conclusion. And within the fractal border between the bounded and unbounded sets there is chaos with its self-similarity and sensitive dependence on initial conditions; a tiny difference in the starting point could make all the difference as to whether the point is bounded or not. Since we cannot measure with absolute precision, we cannot predict in advance whether a number will fall inside or outside the set when we are close to the border between the two.

Since, in action and perception terms, organization A is a bounded set and its environment is an unbounded set of its own actions, both generated by the organization's own non-linear feedback mechanisms, we must expect to find a highly complex, fractal border area between the behaviour of the organization and the behaviour of those in its environment. This is a consequence of the non-linear feedback interaction between the organization and its environment.

So for some particular action we can say quite definitely, in advance, that it is an adaptation of the organization to its environment. That particular action touches off a sequence of actions that in the end requires organization A to adapt. Some customer installs a total quality control system and requires that its supplier should meet a very low failure rate for the components it is supplying. That customer demands the right to inspect quality, on the supplier's site. To keep the business the supplier has to comply; it adapts to its environment. The sequence of actions it takes to comply is its environment.

For some other particular action we can say just as definitely, in advance, that it is an action which will require the environment to adapt to the organization. That particular action touches off a sequence of actions, but this time, in the end, it is some person or organization in the environment that adapts. In the above example, the company installing a total quality control system has compelled or persuaded its supplier to adapt. Here the supplying environment is doing the adapting.

In both of the above cases cause and effect runs in one direction; one action is consequent on another in a clear way. But in between, in the chaotic border area, where we are talking about interaction, there will be a large number of actions where we cannot be at all sure who is adapting to whom. The outcome of many actions in the border area will be inherently unpredictable. And since this border area is the area of complex interaction, as opposed to largely unidirectional action, it is where successful organizations will be most of the time. An example of this is the change from using CFCs to other forms of aerosol propulsion. Consumers are changing their buying habits and producers are changing products and production methods.

The point being made is this. Any organization's environment is quite simply a collection of people and organizations outside itself with whom its members deal in some way. The organizational actors do not simply do whatever those people and organizations outside it want. Passively waiting to be told what to do is not a recipe for success. Instead people within a successful organization persuade and negotiate with those outside, with suppliers, with customers, with government departments and with competitors. Sometimes people within the organization do what those outsiders want and sometimes they persuade the outsiders to do what they want. This amounts to interaction loops, feedback loops, which can be amplifying or damping. The attractors are complete adaptation on the one hand, doing what the environment wants, and complete isolation at the other, ignoring what the environment wants. Success is to be found in the most intense and sensitive interaction and in dynamic system terms that means as close as possible to the border between what insiders and outsiders want. And the properties of such borders in non-linear feedback systems are fractal, chaotic.

Once one accepts this chaos perspective, a number of important points follow. First, a successful organization is in a far-from-equilibrium state in relation to its environment. One equilibrium is complete fit or match of resources to the market. This is not creative interaction; it is passive and associated with minimal profit. Eventually such an organization will succumb to more imaginative rivals. The other equilibrium is isolation and this will suffer the same fate even more rapidly. The lack of response of tin can producers in the UK to the requirements of paint and lubricating oil manufacturers led to the loss of major markets. The natural tendency is for the organization to move to one or other of these equilibrium states, simply because it is so much easier than the constant interaction with customers and suppliers. Success, creative interaction, lies between them and is very difficult to maintain.

Second, the concept of a successful organization as some kind of organism adapting to its environment in an evolutionary manner ceases to have much meaning. Since it is so difficult to say who is adapting to whom in the border areas, it ceases to be meaningful to even ask the question. This calls the whole idea of contingency into question. Most theories of organization use the concept that the form an organization takes, its structures, systems, styles and so on, all depend upon the kind of environment it finds itself in. So, if it is in a stable environment it adapts by developing a mechanistic approach and if it is in a highly uncertain environment it develops an organic approach. But if the organization is usually operating in a fractal border area, sensitive to initial conditions, then two organizations in approximately the same environment will develop in substantially different ways. Just as snowflakes record the history of their passage to the ground, so too will organizations be the outcome of their passage through time and tiny difference in the experience of two organizations (they were founded by two different people) can be amplified so that they become substantially different.

Instead of equilibrium, evolutionary adaptation and contingent dependence on the environment, we need concepts of non-equilibrium and creative interaction; creative in the sense that the organization creates and is created by its environment.[11]

Two other points should also be made. The first relates to time. In order to see the chaotic nature of the border between the organization and its environment we have to look at long periods of time to allow all the interactions to unfold. The shorter the time period we consider, the fewer the number of interactions which are apparent. The shorter the time period, the closer we get to seeing unidirectional action, the more we see the border between the organization and its environment as a blurred and then a clear line. So when any organization is considering and acting in a short time period it is quite legitimate to do what current received theories prescribe, to act as if the organization and its environment are quite separate, to adapt to the requirements of the environment. But the longer the time frame, the less useful and in fact the more dangerous this approach becomes. This suggests that we have to reject those prescriptions of conventional strategic management that are about adapting to a given environment.

References

1   In the brief descriptions of chaos mathematics in this Appendix, I have drawn on the following two books: Gleick, J. (1987), *Chaos*, Heinemann; and Stewart, I. (1989), *Does God Play Dice? The Mathematics of Chaos*, Basil Blackwell.
2   Crutchfield, J. P., Farmer, J. D., Huberman, B. (1982), Fluctuations and Simple Chaotic Dynamics, *Physics Reports*, 92; also discussed in Kelsey, D. (1988), The Economics of Chaos or the Chaos of Economics, *Oxford Economic Papers*, 40.
3   Gleick, J., op. cit; Stewart, I., op. cit.
4   Penrose, R. (1989), *The Emperor's New Mind*, Oxford University Press, reprinted by permission of Oxford University Press.
5   Penrose, R., op. cit., p. 63.
6   Penrose, R., op. cit., p. 108.

7   Penrose, R., op. cit., p. 110.
8   Penrose, R., op. cit., p. 111.
9   Penrose, R., op. cit., p. 112.
10   Penrose, R., op. cit., p. 110.
11   Weick, K. (1979), *Organisational Psychology*, Addison-Wesley.

Appendix C
Order from chaos

This appendix describes how chaos is used by nature's systems.[1]

We saw in Appendix B that as the non-linear feedback system described by the logistic difference equation is forced further and further away from stable equilibrium, it passes through a number of change situations. The pattern or nature of change alters to states of stable 2 period cycles. They keep doubling to reach a state of random, chaotic change. As the system is pushed further from equilibrium it reaches a further state of stable 3 period cycles. They keep doubling, leading to yet more chaos. And so it goes, until the system breaks into a new orderly state which is an explosion to infinity. There is an orderly, structured sequence of change states which have fixed numerical properties, and that fixed sequence includes states of complete, unpredictable randomness.

More complex sets of differential equations, which are constrained by the environment within which they operate, constraints known as boundary conditions, show even more complex sequences of change states. One such set of equations describes a particular chemical reaction as the concentration of a control chemical is increased. This shows a sequence moving from equilibrium through periodic cycles, into chaos, then into mixed mode chaotic and periodic cycles and then into a more complex stable oscillation pattern.

This reaction is known as the Belousov–Zabotinski reaction. Here a particular chemical mixture starts off in a simple homogeneous state when it contains low levels of a catalytic agent, bromium. Visually it is a uniform colour. As the quantity of bromium rises, the behaviour of the chemical mixture changes. It passes through a state of chaos that can be seen as erratic swirls of colour in the chemical mixture. As the level of bromium rises further to a critical point, the chemical suddenly displays a new complex form of behaviour. This can be seen visually as alternations in the colour of the whole mixture – first it is blue and then it is red. The changes in colour are so precisely coordinated that this is called a chemical clock.

During this complex sequence of change states, the system in effect faces a series of choices as the control parameter (say the concentration of a particular chemical in a solution) is increased. That is, as the system is pushed further and further from equilibrium, it faces a series of choices between one pattern and another. Such a series of choices is depicted in Figure C.1.

Critical or singular points – bifurcation

So, as the concentration of say bromium in a particular mixture of chemicals is increased, the chemical reactions induced follow a stable, predictable, equilibrium path (A in Figure C.1.) until a bromium concentration equivalent to c_1 is reached. Here the system reaches a singular, critical or bifurcation point where it has, in effect, a choice between the stable path B, continuing along A which becomes chaotic (shown as a dotted line) along A^1, or path B^1 which is chaotic between the parameter values c_1 and c_2, but becomes stable at c_2. If the chaotic path A^1 is chosen and the system is pushed even further from equilibrium, it is faced with yet other choices, all chaotic at the critical parameter value c_4. If the system chooses the D path and it is driven even further from equilibrium, it reaches another point of choice at c_5 and one of these choices is a new stable, orderly state. The same thing happens at c_6 if the D^1 path is chosen.

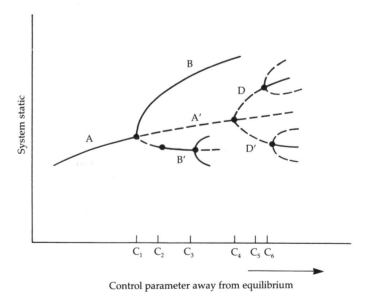

Figure C.1 Critical point choices

Symmetry breaking

What we observe is called symmetry breaking: an orderly configuration is broken and gives way to some other configuration which may or may not be orderly. And at each critical point the system passes through a random state, during which it, so to speak, makes up its mind where to go next.

This kind of pattern has been demonstrated for systems in physics, chemistry and biology. The pattern provides a comprehensive theory of change which explains how change states alter as any system moves, or is pushed, further and further away from equilibrium. It provides an understanding of the nature of change at, or near to equilibrium, as well as in conditions which are far-from-equilibrium. This distinction between change at/near to equilibrium and far-from-equilibrium turns out to be crucial.

Change at or near to equilibrium

At or near to equilibrium, linear (that is proportional) relationships exist between the variables in a system, or at least linearity provides a reliable approximation to the relationships. Feedback mechanisms are unimportant and the system can be treated as if it is closed, or isolated from its environment. Small changes in the environment, in the boundary conditions surrounding the system, have only small consequences for the state of the system. That is to say, perturbations, disturbances or fluctuations in the environment are quickly damped by the system and it returns to equilibrium or near to it. It takes a significant change to move the system from one equilibrium state to another state that is qualitatively different. At or near to equilibrium, systems behave in repetitive, predictable ways and the move from one equilibrium state to another is predictable. Such a move from one equilibrium state to another is called a phase transition. This is a qualitative change in behaviour to a new more complex state or order.

Phase transitions

A simple example of equilibrium phase transitions in physics is provided by the condensation of steam (one equilibrium state) to form water (another equilibrium state) and the freezing of water to form ice (yet another equilibrium state). At each stage a relatively featureless and simple state abruptly and spontaneously changes to another state which is relatively more structured, orderly and complex. What happens at the points of phase transition, just as the steam condenses, just as the water freezes to ice?

It is now known that such phase transitions are characterized by chaotic behaviour on the macroscale – as the temperature of water is increased it boils (a chaotic state) just before it becomes steam. What is more interesting, is that at the microscopic scale, the molecules suddenly organize themselves into a new pattern. Somehow the molecules 'communicate' and quite suddenly they all do the same thing – a phenomenon known as self-organization. Yes, Nobel prizewinners in chemistry, physics and biology are now talking about molecules which communicate and organize themselves!

This phenomenon of self-organization can be understood quite simply by considering the phase transitions displayed by a ferromagnet:

> For example, a ferromagnet at high temperature shows no permanent magnetization, but as the temperature is lowered a critical threshold is reached at which magnetization spontaneously appears. The ferromagnet consists of lots of microscopic magnets that are partially free to swivel. When the material is hot these magnets are juggled about chaotically and independently, so that on a macroscopic scale their magnetizations average each other out. As the material is cooled, the mutual interactions between the micromagnets try to align them. At the critical temperature the disruptive effect of the thermal agitation is suddenly overcome, and all the magnets cooperate by lining up in an ordered array . . . Their magnetizations now reinforce to produce a coherent large scale field.[2]

So what we find at or near to equilibrium are phase transitions, that is chaotic, fractal behaviour leading to self-organization and the making of a choice by the system which leads on to a different equilibrium state; a different organized, orderly structure. Chaos is intimately connected with the symmetry breaking that leads from one state to another. The outcome is a predictable, deterministic change in behaviour to a more complex state resulting from a significant change in a control variable or the environment. It is a movement from one equilibrium state through symmetry, order-breaking chaos to another static, frozen pattern of equilibrium.

Far-from-equilibrium

The situation is fundamentally different when the system moves or is pushed far-from-equilibrium. Here there is no linearity, there are no proportional relationships between the variables in the system, and linear approximations simply do not work. The far-from-equilibrium state is characterized by complex sequences of chaotic and regular patterns of behaviour generated by non-linear feedback mechanisms (autocatalysis and cross catalysis in chemistry) which can be positive or negative. Such systems cannot be treated as if they are closed or isolated from their environment. They are quite clearly open and are affected by changes, disturbances, 'noise' in those environments. They are affected by tiny fluctuations in their boundary conditions.

Fluctuations or disturbances

Systems far-from-equilibrium are sensitive to initial conditions. Tiny changes in the environment can be amplified by the system's feedback mechanisms and so dramatically change its behaviour. Small changes in boundary conditions can be amplified to produce qualitatively different behaviour. There may be abrupt transitions from chaos into some new complex order, or from such order into chaos.

> One such case is the laser. Near to thermodynamic equilibrium a hot solid or gas behaves like an ordinary lamp, with each atom emitting light randomly and independently. The resulting beam is an incoherent jumble of wave trains each a few metres long. It is possible to drive the system away from equilibrium by 'pumping', which is a means of giving energy to the atoms to put an excessive number of them into excited states. When this is done a critical threshold is reached at which the atoms suddenly organize themselves on a global scale and execute cooperative behaviour to a very high level of precision. Billions of atoms emit wavelets that are exactly in phase, producing a coherent wave train of light that stretches for thousands of miles.
>
> Another example of spontaneous self-organization in a system driven far from equilibrium is the so-called Bénard instability, which occurs when a horizontal layer of fluid is heated from below ... the warm liquid near the base is less dense and tries to rise. So long as the temperature difference between the top and the bottom of the liquid is small (near to equilibrium) the upthrust is resisted by viscosity. As the base temperature is raised, however, a threshold is crossed and the liquid becomes unstable; it suddenly starts to convect. Under carefully regulated conditions, the convecting liquid adopts a highly orderly and stable pattern of flow, organizing itself into distinctive rolls, or into cells with a hexagonal structure. Thus an initially homogeneous state gives way to a spatial pattern with distinctive long range order. Further heating may induce additional transitions such as the onset of chaos.'[3]

Unpredictable phase transitions

At each point of transition, systems far-from-equilibrium move through patterns of instability or chaos in which previous symmetry or order is broken, thus confronting the system with choices. The important point is that such phase transitions do not necessarily have predictable outcomes – the possibility is there in some cases for the system to make choices that produce new and unexpected behaviour. Chance may be involved in moving from one state to another and this is definitely not a possibility in near to equilibrium states, where the outcome is predictable.

Although the onset of these abrupt changes can sometime be understood on theoretical grounds, the detailed form of the new phase is essentially unpredictable. Observing convection cells, the physicist can explain, using traditional concepts, how the original homogeneous fluid became unstable. But he could not have predicted the detailed arrangement of the convection cells in advance. The experimenter has no control over, for example, whether a given blob of fluid will end up in a clockwise or anticlockwise rotating cell.[4]

Order out of chaos

So, some form of communication occurs at microscopic levels, leading to self-organization, through cooperation, from which the system spontaneously and abruptly emerges to a new macroscopic state. And that new state can be an unexpected, more complex form of behaviour. In this sense order can emerge from chaos. Indeed it is stronger than this. The period of chaos is a vital precursor to new unexpected, orderly behaviour. The result is the possibility of uniqueness and individuality, compared to the inevitable repetitiveness of equilibrium.

The system does not respond to all the disturbances or fluctuations presented by the environment. There is therefore some mechanism of selection at work; mechanisms which are not at all well understood. The response to the selected disturbance is amplified through the system by its feedback mechanisms, which are a form of communication system.

Dissipative structures

However it happens, the result of self-organization is often what is called a process or dissipative structure.[5] A dissipative structure is one which develops far-from-equilibrium; a new more complex form of behaviour. Its distinctive feature is that it requires continuous inputs of energy if it is to be sustained. So the ferromagnet is an equilibrium structure: at normal temperatures no input of energy from outside of it is required for the property of magnetism to persist. But the laser beam is a far-from-equilibrium phenomenon: the highly regular behaviour it exhibits will only persist while energy is pumped into the system to maintain the atoms at a critical level of excitement.

This kind of structure or state is called dissipative because it dissipates energy or information into its environment and that dissipated energy or information has to be continuously replaced. Dissipative structures embody more information, more energy, than those simpler structures which they succeed. Far-from-equilibrium systems may evolve to more complex stable states but this cannot be taken for granted. Such structures are preceded by phases of chaos, phases in which information, meaning, different perspectives are created. There is an element of chance and one possible outcome is a dissipative structure. And such structures are in a sense unstable in that they require the continuous input of energy to sustain them.

What we see therefore is that order can arise out of chaos, that chaos is a precondition for certain kinds of more complex states called dissipative structures. Far-from-equilibrium behaviour is characterized by the individual and the unique. And randomness and chance are essential to the generation of such behaviour. Systems operating far-from-equilibrium are able to create and innovate, while those near to equilibrium cannot. Systems that are far-from-equilibrium can continuously adjust to their environments – sensitive dependence on initial conditions and feedback mechanisms enable this. For such a possibility to exist near to equilibrium it would be necessary to introduce much more complex reaction schemes.

Self-organization in biological systems

What has been described applies clearly to far-from-equilibrium systems in physics and chemistry – small changes in boundary conditions can lead to abrupt, spontaneous changes in behaviour, occurring through self-organization without any global plan, many aspects of which are unpredictable and unstable. Aspects of such behaviour may be uncontrollable in detailed form. Any control which it is possible to exert is through manipulating the boundary conditions.

Biological systems, however, exhibit many differences from systems in physics and chemistry. For biological systems there is a global plan in the form of a genetic code (DNA) within the organism which determines the features of the system with great precision as it grows. And such systems are not highly sensitive to changes in their boundary conditions – tiny changes in temperature or nutrition do not dramatically alter the development of an embryo.

But the development of a biological cell does follow a path generated by the iteration of non-linear feedback mechanisms tracing out clearly recognizable features of the category to which it belongs. The mechanisms also trace out individual, unique characteristics so that no two individuals in a biological category are the same. This individuality may be due to sensitive dependence on certain border conditions, environmental disturbances, which the system selects and amplifies in a manner dependent on chance. The DNA or global plan may possess all the information required to develop the category features, but it is hard to imagine that it possesses enough information to develop billions of individuals. Once again deterministic necessity combines with chaos and chance to explain categories and individuals.

How do new biological forms emerge? Darwin's theory of evolution proposes a gradual process of random mutations. As environmental conditions change, individuals in a population adapt in small random ways. Some of these adaptations are successful and those individuals survive and pass on the mutation to the next generation. Unsuccessful mutants perish before they procreate. The survival of the fittest in a random process of mutation leads to more and more complex organisms.

But, there are several objections to a process that utilizes chance in this way. Purely random processes lead to increasing disorder and it is hard to imagine new, more complex, more ordered biological systems such as humans emerging from such a random process. There is also a problem with the idea that successful mutants are necessarily more complex. Single-cell organisms are more numerous than humans and have been around for billions of years. Complexity is not necessarily more success-ful. If the increasing complexity of biological systems cannot be explained by random selection of the fittest, how can it be explained?

A possible explanation is that some environmental conditions drive some biological categories far-from-equilibrium where they encounter critical bifurcation points, a state of chaos in which choices have to be made. The whole population may then spontaneously and abruptly move to a new more complex form through some process of self-organiz-ation. Or of course it may perish. The population is confronted with a choice at some critical point and the particular choice made is inherently unpredictable.

> ... the power behind evolutionary change, then, is the continual forcing of the biosphere away from its usual state of dynamic equilibrium, either by internal or external changes. These can be gradual, such as the slow build-up of oxygen in the atmosphere and the increase in the sun's luminosity, or sudden, as with the impact of an asteroid, or some other catastrophic event. Whatever the reason, if self-organization in biological evolution follows the same general principles as non-biological self-organization we would expect evolutionary change to occur in sudden jumps, after the fashion of the abrupt changes at critical points in physical and chemical systems. There is in fact some evidence that evolution has occurred in this way.'[6]

Collective behaviour

Not surprisingly, the concepts of chaos and self-organization have appli-cation to collective behaviour in the biological world. Social interaction in far-from-equilibrium conditions may be associated with self-organizing phenomena.

> ... ants were divided into two categories: One consisted of hard workers, the other of inactive or 'lazy' ants. One might over hastily trace such traits to genetic predisposition. Yet the study found that if the system were shattered

by separating the two groups from one another, each in turn developed its own subgroups of hardworkers and idlers.[7]

Or take another example, that of termites constructing a nest:

> The first stage in this activity, the construction of the base, has been shown by Grasse to be the result of what appears to be disordered behaviour among the termites. At this stage, they transport and drop lumps of earth in a random fashion, but in doing so they impregnate the lumps with a hormone that attracts other termites. The situation could be represented as follows: the initial 'fluctuation' would be the slightly larger concentration of lumps of earth, which inevitably occurs at one time or another at some points in the area. The amplification of this event is produced by the increased density of termites in the region, attracted by the slightly higher hormone concentration. As termites become more numerous in a region, the probability of their dropping lumps of earth there increases, leading in turn to a still higher concentration of the hormone. In this way 'pillars' are formed, separated by a distance related to the range over which the hormone spreads.[8]

In fact most of nature's systems are far-from-equilibrium. And it is this very fact that accounts for continuing creation and development. Because small disturbances can be selected and amplified through feedback we see the development of new more complex forms of behaviour, dissipative structures. Randomness and chance, the breaking of symmetries or old orders, and self-organization are all essential to this process.

References

1   This appendix summarizes the theories developed by the Nobel prize-winning scientist Illya Prigogine and draws on Prigogine, I., Stengers, I. (1984), *Order out of Chaos, Man's New Dialogue with Nature*, Bantam Books.
2   Davies, P. (1987), *The Cosmic Blueprint*, Heinemann, p. 81, reprinted by permission of William Heinemann Ltd.
3   Davies, P., op. cit., p. 82.
4   Davies, P., op. cit., p. 84.
5   Prigogine, I., Stengers, I., op. cit.
6   Davies, P., op. cit., p. 114.
7   Prigogine, I., Stengers, I., op. cit., p. xxiv.
8   Prigogine, I., Stengers, I., op. cit., pp. 186–87.

Appendix D
The language of chaos: a glossary of terms

Many of the terms used in discussing the applications and implications of scientific chaos in a business setting are not part of everyday business language. It would be very difficult to avoid using at least some of this unfamiliar terminology without also losing important aspects of the meaning of chaos theory. Unfamiliar terms are therefore used throughout the book and this appendix sets out what they mean and how they are translated into a business setting.

Algorithm   A set of step-by-step rules and procedures for calculating or reaching a conclusion.

Chaos   The term chaos is used in a specific sense where it is an inherently random pattern of behaviour generated by fixed inputs into deterministic (that is fixed) rules (relationships). The rules take the form of non-linear feedback loops. Although the specific path followed by the behaviour so generated is random and hence unpredictable in the long-term, it always has an underlying pattern to it, a 'hidden' pattern, a global pattern or rhythm. That pattern is self-similarity, that is a constant degree of variation, consistent variability, regular irregularity, or more precisely, a constant fractal dimension. Chaos is therefore order (a pattern) within disorder (random behaviour).

The term chaos is also used in a general sense to describe the body of chaos theory, the complete sequence of behaviours generated by feedback rules, the properties of those rules and that behaviour. It is also sometimes used in this book to describe the unstable, open and sensitive far-from-equilibrium state which precedes abrupt spontaneous choice.

In a business setting the term chaos is used here to describe random, inherently unpredictable sequences over time in the performance indicators of a business organization, in its interactions with people and organizations in its environments and in the decisions or choices yielding that performance and those interactions. It is also used to describe states of ambiguity, ambivalence, extreme uncertainty, confusion and conflict.

Chaotic dynamics Patterns over space or time which display the characteristics of chaos. In a business setting here the reference is to time.

Dissipative structure A complex state of orderly behaviour that requires continuous inputs of energy if it is to be sustained. It is therefore unstable and difficult to maintain.

In the business setting, a dissipative structure refers to consensus on and commitment to the implementation of an innovation, that is a new strategic direction or significant change in some aspect of the business. It requires continual inputs of attention, time and resource to sustain this state of consensus and commitment and cooperation. Such states are consequently short lived, periodic rather than continuous.

Equilibrium A state in which there is no tendency to move away from a given behaviour pattern. This may be a stable or an unstable state, but it is always orderly in the sense that the same behaviour pattern is always observed. Behaviour at equilibrium is repetitive and predictable, at least at some level.

Far-from-equilibrium A non-equilibrium state of the system, that is a state in which behaviour is easily changed to a qualitatively different form by small-chance disturbances. It implies instability, chaos, fractal behaviour.

Fractal The property of fracturing into self-similar patterns. Fractal dimension measures the constant degree of irregularity in a chaotic pattern.

Heuristic search A step-by-step set of rules and procedures which use trial and error, according to some criteria for success, to reach a conclusion.

Random Behaviour which is erratic and haphazard. A sequence of events in which no event occupies exactly the same position as it occupied before. Some describe chaotic behaviour as inherently random because it is unpredictable in specific terms. Others describe it as apparently random because it is generated by fixed laws and has the property of self-similarity.

Scaling This refers to the consequences of changing the parameters in a non-linear feedback mechanism, in effect examining the behaviour pattern in different time frames, at different magnifications in space. It refers to the patterns within patterns which are self-similarity.

Self-organization   A process in which the components of a system in effect spontaneously communicate with each other and abruptly cooperate in coordinated and concerted common behaviour.

In the business setting this means the spontaneous formation of interest groups and coalitions around specific issues, communication about those issues, cooperation and the formation of consensus on and commitment to a response to those issues. The term spontaneous communication arenas is used to describe the occasions on and the means through which this occurs, that is meetings and document exchanges.

Sensitivity to initial conditions   The amplifying property of non-linear feedback mechanisms which means that tiny changes can escalate to totally change long-term behaviour.

Self-similarity   The property of a chaotic pattern of behaviour such that inherently random sequences are always similar but never exactly the same, regular irregularity. This is measured as a constant degree of variation, or a constant fractal dimension.

In the business setting as used here self-similarity means that a sequence of performance indicators or decisions has a consistent degree of variability which actors in the organization can intuitively recognize. It means that performance and decisions move within recognizable bounds, that irregular interventions by other people in the organization are not a complete surprise. This does not mean that performance or decision sequences themselves are logical or consistent, only that the way they vary or jump around has some consistent pattern.

Symmetry breaking   A period of chaotic behaviour on the part of components of a system that has the effect of destroying existing states of behaviour, existing structures.

In the business setting this is a state of confusion and conflict around ambiguous issues during which existing perceptions and ways of doing things are questioned, old perceptions destroyed.

Index

Action, 43, 44–5, 48, 51, 116–17, 119
Advertising, relation to profit, 367–76
Algorithms, 46, 109, 110, 113, 116,
    121, 146, 205, 208, 210–12, 384–7,
    402
Analogy, 166–9
Attractors, 158, 161, 163–4, 240, 358,
    377–81
Authority, 124–5, 234–5, 241, 244,
    258–9

Behaviour, 34, 43, 47, 113, 119, 157,
    203–4, 244, 332; coherent, 55, 57;
    dysfunctional, 127, 142, 146, 147,
    330; group, 217–19; self-reinforcing,
    69
Belousov–Zabotinski reaction, 393
Bifurcation, 394, 400
Biological systems, 399–401; see also
    Darwinian theory
Brain, 207–9
Business organizations: adaptive
    equilibrium, 83–4; creativity, 84–7,
    288; control dynamics of, 181–2;
    dealing with uncertainty, 166–9;
    decision rules, 71–2, 76, 93, 95;
    distribution of authority, 258–9;
    entrepreneurial models, 105–7,
    115–23, 133–4, 145–6, 174, 328;
    exploration of open-ended issues,
    272–85; faulty understanding of, 5,
    293–7; feedback mechanisms in,
    66–72, 80–4, 97, 155–61, 175–80;
    forms of power, 232–7; implications
    of chaos for, 299–317, 339–43;
    importance of context, 246–7;
    inadequacy of long-term
    forecasting, 182–8; inadequate
    systems of power, 260–1; and

innovation, 171–4; and learning,
    55–7, 144–5, 214–29; need for
    variety of control forms, 61–3;
    performance irregularity, 78–9;
    political process, 123–8, 227,
    237–47, 254–67; potential futures,
    191–3; rational models, 106–14;
    relation with environment, 135–6;
    role of aspirations and ambitions,
    193–5; and short-term control, 189;
    tensions in, 97; types of culture,
    219–21; unpredictable choices,
    286–7, 309–10
Business success, 19, 315; conflicting
    explanations of, 3, 4; conventional
    views of, 295–8
Butterfly attractor, 164, 382

Cash inflow, 70
Cause and effect, 166–9
Chance, 51, 53, 55, 142–4, 229, 245,
    272, 303, 311, 353, 362, 401
Change, 2–3, 27; types of, 28–30,
    34–6, 41, 42, 48; unpredictability,
    38, 40; see also Open-ended change
Chaos: in business, 154–61, 239–46,
    361; and business dynamics, 181–2,
    189, 191, 196, 202; in economics,
    359–61; hidden pattern in, 162–5,
    169–71, 363; implications for
    thinking and learning, 205–16,
    223–4, 229, 299; and innovation,
    171–3, 177, 288, 354, 362; and
    managing change, 323–5;
    mathematics of, 366–91; nature of,
    153–4, 357–9, 393–401, 402; and
    non-linear feedback mechanisms,
    175–80; and political systems,
    239–46; in scientific revolution,